Our Faith in Evil

Our Faith in Evil

*Melodrama and the Effects
of Entertainment Violence*

GREGORY DESILET

McFarland & Company, Inc., Publishers
Jefferson, North Carolina, and London

Library of Congress Cataloguing-in-Publication Data

Desilet, Gregory E.
    Our faith in evil : melodrama and the effects of entertainment
violence / Gregory Desilet.
        p.   cm.
    Includes bibliographical references and index.

    ISBN 0-7864-2348-X (softcover : 50# alkaline paper)

    1. Violence in motion pictures.   2. Melodrama in motion
pictures.   I. Title.
    PN1995.9.V5D47   2006
    791.43'6552 — dc22   2005029555

British Library cataloguing data are available

On the cover: Snake and tree limb ©2005 Brand X Pictures; television set
©2005 Photodisc; television screen image ©2005 PhotoSpin

Manufactured in the United States of America

McFarland & Company, Inc., Publishers
  Box 611, Jefferson, North Carolina 28640
    www.mcfarlandpub.com

To my family,
whose support is much appreciated,
and to nonviolent competitive community

Acknowledgments

As a child of World War II survivors and a member of the boomer generation that grew up in the Vietnam War era of the 1960s and 1970s, it is difficult to say exactly how and when the meditation on violence that resulted in this book began for me. Over the past decades so many people have contributed in various ways to my thinking on issues of conflict, violence, and media representation that it is difficult to say who has not. Therefore, with regard to acknowledgments, the example of the thorough-minded Oscar recipient comes to mind who thanks "everyone, including the Academy." But the most crucial and influential contributors are, without question, the great teachers I have had the good fortune to know. These include especially Arnold Solkov, Bill Macomber, John Macksoud, Joyce Hocker, Wayne Brockriede, Phil Tompkins, and Craig Smith — each of whom has given me important pieces to the puzzle of human relations along the spectrum of competition, conflict, and violence. Craig Smith deserves a special thanks for recommending to me McFarland.

In relation to my thinking about violence in the context of this book, I must thank the late Jacques Derrida (1930–2004) for having exerted the strongest influence and for having served as a remarkable model. I began reading his work in the early 1980s but did not get to know him personally until the early 1990s during his visits to the University of California at Irvine. Of the many insights I gained from Derrida, one in particular stands out as provocative and deeply relevant as it links in an essential way to the heart of this book and its themes: "The determination of the self as one is violence." Merci, Jacques, et l'adieu. May this book, despite any limitations, serve his memory well and also the memory of those teachers mentioned above, some also deceased and some thankfully still with us.

Contents

PART II : ILLUSTRATING THE CASE

Preface

With its primary focus on entertainment violence, especially in film, this book confronts the claim that American culture is a "culture of violence"—a claim that is of interest and concern to a spectrum of readers ranging from the general public to the media specialist. Although a genuine attempt has been made to accommodate this broad range of readers, the experience of reading the book can be improved for readers of different backgrounds and interests by adopting different approaches. But before describing these approaches, it may be helpful to most readers to explain the general structure of the book and the particular approach it takes to the intersection of culture, violence, and film and fictional entertainment.

What began as an inquiry into the question of the attraction of violence in film quickly turned into other inquiries. Of these inquiries the one that presses for most attention centers on the question of whether fictional portrayals of violence have negative psychological and/or social effects. As will become clear in the introduction and the early chapters, in the pursuit of answers to these questions the notion of dramatic structure assumes a powerful role in regulating and making sense out of the buzzing confusion at the crossroads of culture, violence, and media. And, as the investigative narrative proceeds, the dramatic structure of melodrama, due to its prevalence, invites close scrutiny and eventually incurs heavy indictment. But however thorough this indictment might be in the context of dramatic arts, it inevitably and invariably confronts a powerful counter argument in its defense. That argument is the "reality" argument.

As a model of conflict, it is shortsighted to question melodramatic structure in art without also examining the merits of its applicability to

1

life in general. But if melodramatic form, defined for the moment as presenting conflict with a pole of radical and essential evil, is rightly applied — as has recently been argued to be the case — to the evil side of conflicts headed up by men like Saddam Hussein and Osama Bin Laden, then it may well be argued that melodramatic structure in film and other media is an appropriate structuring model for art and for life. As the indictment of melodrama progresses in the book, the reader will naturally ask the question: "But isn't melodramatic art simply a reflection of life?" In an important sense it is — as part of a long moral tradition. And that tradition is itself "art" — raising the question of the extent to which melodramatic structure is either a cultural reiteration or a reflection of nature. Thus, any examination of melodrama becomes immediately enmeshed in a critical examination of a significant plank of cultural tradition and the inherited ways of dramatizing life. The focus on violence in certain contexts of film and drama leads to a focus on melodramatic form, which leads to a focus on the particular notion of evil that has been handed down through many layers and levels of tradition. This accounts for the main title of the book: *Our Faith in Evil.*

As it turns out, then, the structure of the book follows a two-way street through the issue of violence: To what extent does entertainment violence affect life and culture and to what extent do life and culture affect entertainment violence? Although this two-way street operates throughout the book, Chapters 14, 15, and 16 move away from entertainment media and turn the focus of attention directly on broader social and cultural implications of the effects of the conjunction of melodrama and violence.

Returning to the suggestions for reading, three options are recommended in relation to particular purposes. Those interested primarily in the assessment of the effects of violent entertainment on consumers may want to "cut to the chase," read the introduction, and then skip to Chapter 8. The previous chapters are summarized at the beginning of this chapter and the following chapters through Chapter 13 present the substance of the arguments and conclusions regarding the effects of violent entertainment advocated herein. Those especially interested in film and those who prefer approaching the subject through concrete examples and illustrations may want to begin with the introduction, skip to Part II and sample some of the film reviews, and then, depending upon which views and conclusions provoke the most response, work backward into the chapters as a way of unveiling the theory grounding the reviews. Those who are curious and concerned about the appeal of violent entertainment, other aspects of the subject of entertainment violence and its relation to consumers, and its effects on the vitality of the broader cultural context may prefer to stay with the standard approach and start from the beginning and work toward the critical reviews in Part II.

With Chapters 14, 15, and 16, Part I culminates in a discussion of the effects of the consumption of fictional violence on the management of real-world conflict along with suggestions for a culturally adequate response to those effects. These three chapters should be included at the end of all three approaches since they provide a summarizing vision while at the same time thoroughly illustrating why it is important for every person to confront the issue of entertainment violence.

Introduction:
Ultraviolence and Beyond

Assessing the results of over one thousand studies on the effects of entertainment violence, the American Psychiatric Association (APA) asserts with conclusive finality: "The debate is over. Over the last three decades, the one overriding finding in research on the mass media is that exposure to media portrayals of violence increases aggressive and violent behavior" (APA, 2004).

Surveying the same research, University of Houston professor Jib Fowles and University of Toronto professor Jonathan Freedman independently arrive at a very different conclusion, emphatically paraphrased by Richard Rhodes of the American Booksellers Foundation for Free Expression: "There is no good evidence that taking pleasure from seeing mock violence leads to violent behavior, and there is some evidence ... that leads away. Bottom line: To become violent, people have to have experience with real violence. Period. No amount of imitation violence can provide that experience. Period" (Rhodes, 2004).

Obviously the debate is not over — at least for the American public. Between these equally vehement and certain conclusions the public is left in the middle with the task of deciding what to believe about the effects of entertainment violence.

Addressing the confusion surrounding the stalemate, the following chapters present the results of a critical inquiry into effects generated from the convergence of three overlapping contexts of social influence:

1. The media: violent entertainment, especially film and adapted and related literature

2. The consumer: the audience for violent entertainment — which includes nearly everyone

3. The culture: the broader backdrop of practices and attitudes within which violent entertainment is conceived, produced, and partaken

Because of the number and complexity of intersecting variables involved, such an inquiry is daunting to the point of seeming futile in relation to the goal of finding conclusive answers to questions concerning cycles of causes and effects. The complexity of the intersection of these variables is not made any clearer by the circumstance that cultural context plays a strong role in the creation of consumer appetites and consumer appetites, in turn, serve to recreate and reinforce cultural context. Nevertheless, in order to say anything pointedly to the issue of entertainment violence and its potential impact on consumers, it is necessary to take into consideration these converging spheres in a simultaneous juggling act — while attending to loose pins as well as possible. The result of such an inquiry may not prove decisive for many. But it is certain to provoke some and possibly persuade others while hopefully altering the balance of opinion through an improved understanding of those contexts in which violent entertainment may have beneficial effects as well as those contexts in which it may have unproductive or outright harmful effects. Before commencing a brief account of the contemporary state of the cultural debate on entertainment violence and the line of argument pursued, it will prove helpful in exposing the key issues involved to take a short excursion back in time for a review of a classic case history. To illustrate what is at stake, it is hard to improve on the questions, alarms, and quandaries presented in the controversy that followed the release of the film that introduced audiences to "ultraviolence."

Film and Violence, a Classic Case History

"THE PROBLEM WITH CANDY..."

On a foggy night less than a week into the new year of 1974, film director Stanley Kubrick and his entire family, using assumed names, boarded a ferry at Dun Laoghaire. They were making the trip from Ireland back to England days ahead of their planned return. This sudden cloak-and-dagger exit occurred shortly after resumption of shooting on the film *Barry Lyndon* (1975) following a Christmas break. Coming as a complete surprise to his production crew, Kubrick's departure brought an abrupt end to the work that had been scheduled. Within twenty-four hours, the entire crew, which had been active for several weeks near Dublin, closed operations and headed back to England to find a new location for the completion of filming. Shortly after his return, Kubrick consulted with executives at Warner Brothers, his studio partner and film distributor, and made the decision to withdraw his previous film, *A Clockwork Orange* (1971), from further distribution and viewing in the United Kingdom.

The extraordinary change in plans for production of *Barry Lyndon* and the subsequent withdrawal of *A Clockwork Orange* from its theatrical run were apparently triggered by a single incident. According to reports— officially denied by Kubrick — on the morning prior to his departure from Ireland a member of his staff had received a call from an officer of the Special Branch from Dublin Castle stating he had learned from a reliable source that Kubrick had been placed on the IRA's hit list (Baxter, 1997: 289).

Though no one seemed to know the specific details regarding the reasons for the IRA's death threat, speculation centered on two sources of aggravation — the staging of British "redcoats" in a field in Kilkenny for scenes in *Barry Lyndon* and the accumulated outrage over scenes of sex and violence depicted in *A Clockwork Orange*. These scenes had allegedly spawned an outbreak of copycat crimes in many urban areas where the film had been showing. The most recent of such crimes had occurred just across the Irish Sea in Lancashire only a little more than a month prior in November 1973. A gang of teenagers was reported to have been crowing "Singing in the Rain"— a favorite song of the film's anti-hero Alex— as they raped a 17-year-old girl (Parsons, 1993: 5).

According to Ken Adam, the interior set designer for *Barry Lyndon*, Kubrick dismissed the Kilkenny staging as the source of the IRA's ire and insisted that *A Clockwork Orange* was primarily to blame for the death threat. Apparently, similar though less credible threats— not from the IRA — had been received by Kubrick over the course of the last two years (Baxter, 1997: 290).

Kubrick's retreat from Ireland, however, was probably an action taken more with an eye for the well-being of his family than for his personal safety. Nevertheless, the withdrawal of the film was, for a man of his confidence and pride, an extraordinary about-face. But the film contained such wanton violence, presented from the cavalier point of view of the perpetrators, that it gave many consumers reason for pause and many others reason for outrage. Newspaper ads at the time of the film's release promoted it with a portrait of a slyly smirking Alex along with this caption: "Being the adventures of a young man whose principal interests are rape, ultraviolence and Beethoven"— to which could have been added "molestation, mugging, and murder."

Adapted from the book of the same name by Anthony Burgess, the film tells the story of a teenage hoodlum (Alex) of the future whose gratuitous criminal exploits, portrayed in graphic detail, are finally brought to a halt when government authorities arrest Alex and submit him to the "Ludovico treatment." A form of classical conditioning, this treatment reprograms Alex to become violently ill when he contemplates violent actions. Alex's attempt to commit suicide as an escape from his fate makes him the center of a public debate over the morality of the Ludovico treatment and launches a popular backlash that ultimately leads to the reversal of his programming and sets him free to roam the streets at liberty to commit crimes once again.

While Alex's unique "reform" by the authorities becomes a point of central focus in the story, his eventual release back into society at the end — free to return to his ultraviolent ways— brought to contentious conclusion a film that on the whole accomplished both less and more with audiences of the time than was intended by Kubrick.

Following its opening in December 1971, the film was constantly surrounded by controversy, criticism, and copycat crime. The British Board of Film Censors initially approved it for audiences over the age of 18, but several local authorities, incensed by its content, fought this rating and tried unsuccessfully to have it completely banned from public viewing. The Motion Picture Association of America initially gave the film an X rating for its sexual content and several newspapers from various major cities in the United States refused to run advertisements for it.

The reception among critics was remarkably divided. Vincent Canby of *The New York Times* enthusiastically proclaimed, "*A Clockwork Orange* is so beautiful to look at and to hear that it dazzles the senses and the mind even as it turns the old real red vino to ice." Rex Reed of *The New York Daily News* called Kubrick a "genius," claiming that the film was "a mind-blowing work of dazzling originality and brilliance ... one of the few perfect movies I have seen in my lifetime."

Other critics were very much of the opposite opinion. Andrew Sarris of *The Village Voice*, for example, warned that those who saw the film would "suffer the damnation of boredom" and that the film's soulless presentation of violence "manifests itself on the screen as a painless, bloodless, and ultimately pointless futuristic fantasy." Alluding to connections between social and cinematic violence, Sarris went on to add, "I am tired of the cult of violence. I am tired of people smashing other people and things in the name of freedom and self-expression."

Alex (Malcolm McDowell) at the wheel of the Durango 95 as he plays "hogs of the road" with his "droogs" in *A Clockwork Orange* (1971) (Photofest).

However, as the controversy over the film raged in the newspapers, critics unanimously defended it against censorship. Even Sarris argued against censorship, complaining that "movies have always made a splendidly superficial target for our lazier moralists." After the *Detroit News* made a public statement that it would not run advertisements for X-rated films (which then included *A Clockwork Orange*), even the media-shunning Kubrick submitted a letter to the editor in which he equated the paper's strident moralism and censorial stance to the attitude evident in the following rhetoric: "Works of art which ... need a set of instructions to justify their existence, and which find their way to neurotics receptive to such harmful rubbish, will no longer reach the public. Let us have no illusions: we have set out to rid the nation and our people of all those influences threatening its existence and character" (cited in LoBrutto, 1997: 362).

Kubrick then revealed these to be the words of Adolf Hitler in explanation of his censorship of a Munich art exhibition in 1937. At the close of his letter Kubrick cautioned, "High standards of moral behavior can only be achieved by the example of right-thinking people and society as a whole, and cannot be maintained by the coercive effect of the law. Or that of certain newspapers."

As public outcry over the film mounted, Anthony Burgess—the author of the novel—found himself increasingly pressed into the role of defending the film as the reclusive Kubrick withdrew from the public debate. Assaults of women attributed to the influence of the film generated even greater consternation and outrage in light of the irony emerging from Burgess's revelation that the book had grown out of his attempts to cope with the brutal assault on his wife by four American GI deserters near the end of World War II. Although robbery rather than rape appeared to be the motive, the severe beating his wife received for her resistance to the attack caused a miscarriage and health problems from which she never fully recovered.

Initially Burgess's reaction to the film was positive and he went on a publicity tour with Malcolm McDowell — the actor who played Alex. Over time, however, and adding to the irony stemming from the book's unusual inspiration and the film's unanticipated effects, Burgess's estimate of the merits of the film — as well as his own book — changed. Speaking about the writing of the book, Burgess remarked to Sheila Weller of *The Village Voice*, "I was very drunk when I wrote it. It was the only way I could cope with the violence [referring to the attack on his wife]. I can't stand violence.... I loathe it! And one feels so responsible putting an act of violence down on paper. If one can put an act of violence down on paper, you've created the act! You might as well have done it! I detest that damn book now" (Weller, 1972: 57).

Alex (Malcolm McDowell) and Dim (Warren Clark) prepare to rape Mrs. Alexander (Adrienne Corri) in *A Clockwork Orange* (1971) (Photofest).

In his autobiography, published in 1990, Burgess affirmed that his intentions in writing the book were consistent with the general message "that moral *choice* cannot exist without a moral polarity." But he acknowledged the book's effects—both on readers as well as himself: "I saw that the book might be dangerous because it presented good, or at least harmlessness, as remote and abstract, something for the adult future of my hero, while depicting violence in joyful dithyrambs.... I was sickened by my own excitement at setting it down, and I saw that Auden was right in saying that the novelist must be filthy with the filthy" (61). Regarding the film, Burgess had, at least by the time of the publication of his autobiography, come to the conclusion that Kubrick had dangerously altered the message of his book into what he believed to be a "terrible theme"—namely that "the violence of the individual [is] preferable to the violence of the state" (1991: 245).

So, as it turned out, Kubrick and Burgess shared the experience of having second thoughts. The aptness of the law of unintended consequences was doubtless not lost on a man of Burgess's literary acumen. His "text," inspired by violence and intended to be read as a statement against violence, is eclipsed by his obsessive detailing of the violent actions of the featured "hero" to the point where he must eventually recoil from what, to his horror, emerges as the dominant "subtext"—an unauthorized celebration of violence. This recoil is then mirrored and compounded by Kubrick's reversal of similar proportions in response to his adaptation of the book.

Kubrick's withdrawal of *A Clockwork Orange* from further viewing in the United Kingdom went largely unnoticed because it coincided with the waning stages of the film's theatrical run. Only several years after the fact, when the British National Film Theater sought to arrange a retrospective of Kubrick's work in 1979, did it become widely known, to the amazement of all, that Kubrick had banned the film.

Although he had never aggressively defended *A Clockwork Orange* from censorship in public appearances, Kubrick had published, as already mentioned, written defenses in the *Detroit News* and several other newspapers in the early part of 1972. In light of his written vehement condemnations of censorship, Kubrick's self-censorship of the film was astonishing and inexplicable. Despite the retrospective by the British National Film Theater in honor of his accumulated works, Kubrick refused to drop the ban and did not allow the film to be shown in 1979.

Confirming the fact that this decision was not merely a passing whim, Kubrick went out of his way to enforce the ban again in 1993 when he discovered that a bootleg copy of the film had been shown at the Scala Cinema in London. He unleashed lawyers from the Federation Against Copyright Theft who eventually charged the theater program manager and the projectionist with violations of the British 1988 copyright law. Adding to the general confusion, neither Kubrick nor Warner Brothers ever issued a public statement explaining why the ban had been initiated and why it continued to be enforced.

However, Kubrick's unremitting ban of the film in the United Kingdom coincided with continued reports of the film's role in copycat crimes in America where Kubrick had less control over distribution and the ban was not in effect. In June 1990 Michale Anderson of Pittsburgh, Pennsylvania, admitted wearing *A Clockwork Orange* T-shirt on the day he impaled 17-year-old Karen Hurwitz six times in the torso with a three-foot-long samurai sword. Anderson's attorney Jon Botula organized the defense strategy around the claim that Anderson was driven to commit the crime by habitual viewings of the Kubrick film. Botula showed the jury 50 minutes of the film as proof of its dangerously seductive portrayal of violence. Nevertheless, the jury convicted Anderson of the crime (LoBrutto, 1997: 370).

Just as Kubrick's initial defense of the film against censorship was sparse but vehement so also was his initial defense of the film's violent content, which he articulated in two rare interviews in 1972. In response to a question about the apparent celebration of violence in *A Clockwork Orange*, Kubrick told Andrew Bailey of *Rolling Stone Magazine*: "When you ask is it right for violence to be fun you must realize that people are used to challenging whether certain types of violence are fun. You see it when your western hero finally shoots all the villains. Heroic violence in the Hollywood sense is a great deal like the motivational researchers' problem in selling candy. The problem with candy is not to convince people that it's good ... but to free them from the guilt of eating it. We have seen so many times that the body of a film serves merely as an excuse for motivating a final blood-crazed slaughter by the hero of his enemies, and at the same time to relieve the audience's guilt of enjoying this mayhem" (1972: 22).

This account of cinematic violence corresponds to a cathartic theory of effects—a theory that emphasizes viewer competencies relating to the clear separation of fantasy and reality. Kubrick's endorsement of this view is further supported by comments made to Paul Zimmerman in a *Newsweek* interview: "From his own point of view, Alex is having a wonderful time, and I wanted his life to appear to us as it did to him, not restricted by the conventional pieties. You can't compare what Alex is doing to any kind of day-to-day reality. Watching a movie is like having a daydream. You can safely explore areas that are closed off to you in your daily life.

There are dreams in which you do all the terrible things your conscious mind prevents you from doing" (1972: 29).

Following the discovery of Kubrick's self-imposed ban of the film, some of his supporters wondered if he had ultimately come to conclusions that forced a radical revision of the views he expressed in 1972. Others speculated that the accumulation of criticism, controversy, and threats relating to the film had progressed too far and that Kubrick had finally had enough of it all.

Had Kubrick ultimately decided that *A Clockwork Orange* was too dangerous in its graphic violent content and its featured portrayal of a sadistic anti-hero? Was the line between fantasy and reality too easily crossed by too many members of an impressionable viewing audience? Does a film director owe more to the public than entertainment? Since Kubrick never spoke publicly in his later years to such questions, his answers were buried with him when he died in 1999.

In retrospect, *A Clockwork Orange* assumes the status of one of the most emotionally charged and hotly debated films of the twentieth century in relation to violent content and the question of the effects of that content on a viewing audience. Tony Parsons has with some justification claimed, "There are thousands of films more violent than *A Clockwork Orange*. But there is not one equal to its inflammatory power" (1993: 5). As the debate over the effects of the film progressed, it boiled down to an argument over the power of imitative effects on the one hand — evidenced in the copycat crimes credited to the film's "droogs" — and cathartic effects on the other hand — implied in Kubrick's early remarks in defense of the film's violence. In the same paragraph Parsons goes on to claim that *A Clockwork Orange* "remains just about the only example of art being a danger to society." Needless to say, Parsons's claim that *A Clockwork Orange* has unique status among films as a "danger to society" is a widely contested view.

The Culture and the Consumer

THE AMERICAN PSYCHE

The explicit scenes of rape and murder and the way in which they are depicted in *A Clockwork Orange* brought the debate over the effects of entertainment violence to a new focus and a new level of intensity. Along with other films such as *In Cold Blood* (1967), *Bonnie and Clyde* (1967), *The Wild Bunch* (1969), and *Straw Dogs* (1971), *A Clockwork Orange* appeared as a crown jewel in a countercultural cinematic trend—a trend showing violence committed by a system of authority (or what passes for authority) to be a worse evil than the violence of lawbreaking individuals.

This cinematic trend employs a particular modification of the standard Hollywood plot-vehicle for the depiction of violence—the melodrama of good versus evil and hero versus villain. In the usual Hollywood melodrama the hero is the featured protagonist. In the counter cultural and "noir"-influenced modifications the featured protagonist, the point-of-view character, is a person (or persons) embodying villainous or criminal traits or perhaps merely unexceptional traits. In this plot reversal the villain becomes the hero or anti-hero and villainous traits seem less reprovable and even appear oddly "heroic" in relation to the greater villainy of the system. This way of depicting violence seemed, to many critics, to grant a new license to the violence of an individual against a victim when the victim could be tied in some way to a corrupt system.

Although surely wide of their intended mark—both for Burgess and Kubrick—the book and the film *A Clockwork Orange* succeed in presenting violence in a way that maximizes the potential among viewers for minimizing traditional approbations and constraints against violence. In this respect *A Clockwork Orange* with its anti-hero Alex and its brand of "ultra-violence" (the expression used in film promotions and used by Alex in the film) and similarly structured films like those mentioned above serve as transition works between the classic horror genre of violent films and the more recent explosion of cinematic hyper-real violence.

In the 1980s the horror-turned-slasher film emerges as the standout genre for contributions to hyper-real depictions of violence featuring films such as *Halloween* (1978, with eight sequels), *Friday the 13th* (1980, with nine sequels), *Nightmare on Elm Street* (1984, with seven sequels), and *Hellraiser* (1987, with seven sequels).

Beginning in the 1990s, the hyper-real escalation of violence begins to become prominent in the popular action film genre featuring the work of directors such as Quentin Tarantino with *Reservoir Dogs* (1992), *Pulp Fiction* (1994), and *From Dusk 'Til Dawn* (1995); Robert Rodriguez with *El Mariachi* (1992), *Desperado* (1995), and *Once Upon A Time in Mexico* (2003); and the Wachowski brothers (and action film producer Joel Silver) with *The Matrix* (1999) and its two sequels.

Films of the hyper-real trend contain sequences of in-your-face graphic violence combined with extreme elevation of the tension between anti-heroes and increasingly insidious and corrupt systems (composed, of course, of corrupt individuals—or corrupt machines, cyborgs, androids, aliens, or, as in *The Matrix*, computer simulations). As the center of cinematic focus shifts from robust hero to morally compromised anti-hero, the focus on gore shifts from the depiction of the visage of a gruesome monster or killer to ever more explicit depictions of the bloody mutilation and death of victims. Films such as these have kept the debate over the effects of entertainment violence very much alive in public forums.

A *Clockwork Orange* combined within the same film two themes that have dominated contemporary domestic social and political concerns: violence in the "system" and violence in the "streets." In the growing wake of disillusionment from the assassinations of the 1960s through the Vietnam War and the Watergate break-in, the "system" takes a beating in American film more often than not. The themes of system violence and street violence emerge in the midst of and despite certain ironies—if not in American culture then certainly in American public discourse.

On the one hand, in the past century — a century of relentless worldwide bloodletting punctuated with horrendous crimes of genocidal violence — the United States stands out, at least by some accounts, as the leading nation denouncing, opposing, and sometimes thwarting the worst perpetrators of such violence. In the last half of the twentieth century the United States was repeatedly called on to play the role of peacekeeper in many areas of volatile conflict around the world.

On the other hand, however, the United States has for decades held the distinction, among nations of similar standards of living, of being the country where a person is most likely to be killed by violence, especially with guns. For many Americans, cinematic violence and its potential relation to violent crime or street violence remains an especially heated topic because of the perception of exceptional levels of violent crime — a perception fueled by high handgun crime statistics but also a perception routinely encouraged by selectively distorted, sensationalized, and needlessly repetitive news media coverage of such events.

The statistics have not been merely noteworthy; they have been stupefying. For example, in 1990 murders by handgun were recorded as follows for these countries: Australia — 10, Sweden — 13, United Kingdom — 22, Canada — 68, Japan — 87, United States— 10,567. Accounting for population differences does not help. Handgun murders in the United States were roughly 70 times greater per 100,000 persons than in Australia, the United Kingdom, and Japan.

When including all deaths by violent crime the differences narrow, but the United States is still by far the leader. Although the number of handgun murders declines 20 percent by the year 2000, this decrease follows the trend of a 20 percent across-the-board drop in violent crime —

a drop in part accounted for by the economic prosperity of the mid- and late 1990s. Since World War II the homicide rate, for example, matches the cycles of recession and the major peaks and valleys in the economic indicators. Analysts such as Franklin Zimring (1997) and Richard Rhodes dispute this connection, arguing that there is no evidence that "economic conditions ... impact homicide rates" (Rhodes, 2004: 2). Although it may not rise to the level of decisive evidence of connection, a significant correlation exists between low homicide rates and economic prosperity; until it can be adequately explained in other ways it must be taken into consideration when evaluating the causes for changes in crime statistics.

While violent crime in the United States may fluctuate according to the state of the economy, in doing so it remains at considerably higher volume than other countries of comparable economic circumstances. Adjusting for economic variables, the question remains relevant: Why is the United States a leader in violent gun crime while at the same time it plays the role of world peacekeeper and preaches liberty, human rights, and peaceful coexistence?

The discrepancy between expectation and fact implicit in this question evaporates in the opinion of those who argue that the United States is more realistically perceived not as a peacekeeper but as an aggressive practitioner of an ideologically (anti-socialist) and commercially (pro-capitalist) driven foreign policy backed by a strong militaristic philosophy that when circumstances warrant results in a decisive deployment of troops.

As a result of various forms of clandestine and overt gunboat diplomacy, the United States has been responsible, it is argued, for much human misery and numerous atrocities—especially in Southeast Asia and in Central and South America. One critic in particular, author and documentary filmmaker Michael Moore, has at the turn of the millennium become a nationally renowned and controversial lightning rod for drawing attention to the characterization of American policy and culture as overly aggressive, paranoid, and militaristic.

At one point in his commercially successful Academy Award–winning film entitled *Bowling for Columbine* (2002), Moore uses a montage of scenes chronicling post–World War II American military campaigns to suggest a cultural link between militarism and the social problem of gun violence. National gun violence and militaristically spearheaded foreign policy, Moore appears to be saying, are mutually reinforcing and rooted in similarly aggressive orientations.

But aside from this suggestive sequence, the link is unsubstantiated in the film by explicit explanation. Whatever validity this line of argument may have is largely lost in the absence of sufficient context. Moore's bashing of American military actions is essentially hit and run and is skewed in an especially egregious way in his portrayal of a Kosovo bombing run where the soundtrack carries the voice of an apparent newscaster reporting that "on the hit list were a local hospital and primary school" while bombs are shown dropping from an American warplane. In light of the highly questionable evidence for an intended "hit list" of this sort in the Kosovo conflict, this segment of Moore's work falls far short of candid critical commentary and detracts from a number of provocative questions raised in the film concerning issues of gun violence.

For example, Moore highlights the problem of gun violence in the United States by way of a comparison with Canada. Canada has a per-person gun ownership ratio similar to the United States but the death by gun ratio per person is not remotely comparable. Moore also brings to light the widespread paranoia and sense of vulnerability experienced within communities in the United States whereas in Canada people tend to feel less threatened. Moore illustrates this point by revealing the common Canadian practice of not locking doors when leaving a house or a car — which, of course, is no longer a common practice in most areas of the United States.

The remainder of the film continues to build on the claim that Americans live in a mental climate of intense paranoia. Politicians, corporations, and news media have discovered that fear motivates, sells, and captivates almost as well as sex. In an interview given at the Toronto Film Festival in 2002, Moore remarks that *Bowling for Columbine* is not ultimately about guns or gun control. Instead it is "a film about the American psyche and the American ethic — such as it is." Moore goes on to claim that America needs to change its ethic and that Americans need to aspire to be "more Canadian-like." He describes the Canadian ethic as rooted in the attitude "We are all in the same boat" and contrasts that with an American ethic summed up in the attitude "It's every man for himself."

INFLAMING THE DEBATE: "...CAN'T WAIT TIL I CAN KILL YOU PEOPLE..."

Concerning the theme of "every man for himself," Moore's film bears considerable relevance to a cardinal theme of recent cinema as mentioned above: the individual fighting his way through what is perceived to be a corrupt system or community. As indicated by Moore's title, his film is a contribution to the renewed search for solutions and explanations for gun violence that followed in the aftermath of the Columbine High School shootings of April 20, 1999, in Littleton, Colorado. The shooters involved saw themselves as two against the world, two against a hopelessly corrupt community that regarded them as nonentities.

The Columbine shootings left thirteen dead as two students, Eric Harris and Dylan Klebold, donned trenchcoats and smuggled several guns—including a Tech 9 semiautomatic 30-round assault weapon and two sawed-off shotguns—onto the school grounds where they opened fire at random on fellow students. Leaving a trail of terror behind them, they quickly progressed to the school cafeteria where, as some students scrambled for the exits, they killed others. Finally, more than 45 minutes after they had begun their attack, Harris and Klebold shot themselves as police surrounded the building.

Although the depths of the motives for their killings may never be fully plumbed, a message on Eric Harris's website gave reason to believe that the two had acquired a highly polarized sense of alienation and conflict that pitted themselves against the entire world. Speaking specifically of the people of Denver (of which Littleton is a suburb), Harris wrote, "I'm coming for EVERYONE soon ... with their rich snobby attitude thinkin they are all high and mighty.... God I can't wait til I can kill you people. Feel no remorse, no sense of shame. I don't care if I live or die in the shoot-out. All I want to do is kill and injure as many of you as I can" (cited in Gibbs and Roche, 1999: 46).

The Columbine shootings were for many the last straw in a series of teenage school shootings, beginning less than two years earlier: two students dead in a Mississippi high school; three dead and eight wounded in West Paducah, Kentucky; four killed — including one teacher — and 15 wounded in Jonesboro, Arkansas; and several students fired on and two parents killed in Springfield, Oregon. In the wake of this epidemic of school shootings the Columbine massacre came as a devastating blow and presented itself to many as indisputable proof that something was going very wrong in the hearts and minds of young people across the country.

As a result of the media coverage of the Columbine shootings it soon became well known that Harris and Klebold had immersed themselves in a constant barrage of violent first-person shooter video games such as *Doom* and *Quake*, as well as in films such as *The Basketball Diaries* (1995) and *The Matrix* (1999) — both featuring trenchcoat-clad gunmen. This news, combined with similar reports of exposure to violent media in the cases of the previous school shootings, launched a public outcry among victims, parents, and politicians for improved gun control legislation, restrictions on sales of violent video games to teenagers, and new approaches for controlling teenage exposure to violent films.

These outcries soon led to a backlash from the National Rifle Association and defenders of video games and entertainment media. For example, Joe Saltzman of *USA Today* wrote, "The reason the Colorado shootings became news around the world was the rarity, the unusual how-could-this-have-happened nature of the story.... Logic dictates that, if movies, television, video games, and the Internet are responsible for this kind of behavior, then why is it so unusual?" (cited in Torr, 2001: 15).

Responses such as this set the stage for a repetition of the continuing stalemate between a faction who believes that violent behavior is significantly promoted by a violent media culture and a faction who believes that violent behavior is the result of the psychopathology of a small minority who are, for a variety of reasons unrelated to media exposure, already predisposed to aggressive and violent behavior. Furthermore, this latter faction believes, consistent with Kubrick's statement cited above, that the popularity of violent media is a consequence of consumer tastes for violent entertainment that in the vast majority of cases produces a cathartic release of aggressive tendencies rather than the provocation of violent actions.

The Consumer and the Culture

CATHARSIS

The claim for the cathartic effects of violent media has many adherents. One of the more outspoken supporters of this theory, University of Houston Professor of Communication Jib Fowles, has drawn attention to the work of Carol and Peter Stearns in their book *Anger: The Struggle for Emotional Control in American History*. These authors, Fowles reports, claim that "the display of hostility is decreasingly tolerated in society.... An increasingly egalitarian [American] society has decreed — either through changing customs or changing laws — that living human beings of any sort are unfit targets for hostile impulses" (2002: 130).

The decreasing tolerance for emotional display and venting of anger has led, so the theory goes, to the creation of a climate in which young men in particular have insufficient avenues available for the acceptable and safe release of assorted testosterone-amplified frustrations and resentments. Entertainment media respond to this climate of constraints with violent games and programming that allow the cathartic release of aggressions through participation in a projected fantasy world that provides "safe" targets and symbols for violence. In other words, instead of bottling anger until it explodes in deadly violence, frustrated individuals can release anger periodically by identifying with characters in films who beat and/or kill victims designed specifically for such cathartic disposal.

James Torr, an author and editor on the subject of media violence, summarizes the cathartic formula found in violent films and its close connection to inclinations for clarity of moral choice and resolve: "One of the most appealing features of most violent films is their black-and-white morality: They provide an outlet for the average viewer's anxieties about the imperfect justice of the real world. Catharsis—the relieving of emotional tensions such as anger—is achieved when the protagonist destroys the villains. The cathartic effects of action films are a major part of their appeal" (2002: 128).

This formula, it is argued, has been endlessly repeated through a variety of action film subgenres and related genres such as cop films (*Dirty Harry* and the Joel Silver–produced *Die Hard* and *Lethal Weapon* series), muscle films (featuring Schwarzenegger and Stallone), spy films (*James Bond*, *La Femme Nikita*), sci-fi films (the *Robocop*, *Alien*, and *Terminator* series), westerns (classic American as well as "spaghetti" varieties), martial art films (featuring Bruce Lee, Chuck Norris, Steven Segal, and Jean-Claude van Damme), horror films (*The Exorcist*, *The Howling*, *The Shining*), and slasher films (*Halloween*, *Friday the 13th*, *Nightmare on Elm Street*).

MIMESIS

Critics of the catharsis theory steadfastly point out that numerous government and academic-sponsored studies over the past several decades have "consistently documented that *media violence contributes to the aggressive behavior* of many children, adolescents, and young adults, as well as *influencing people's perceptions and attitudes about violence*" (Torr, 2002: 106, emphasis added). Support for these conclusions rests substantially on two landmark studies: The Surgeon General's Scientific Advisory Committee report of 1972 and the National Institute of Mental Health (NIMH) Ten-Year Follow-Up report of 1982.

As James Torr recounts, the Surgeon General's report asserts that there is sufficient evidence to indicate "a causal relation between viewing violence [especially on television] ... and aggressive behavior" (2001: 13). This conclusion, however, is not without controversy. Professor of Communication Craig R. Smith, for example, cautions that the report speaks only of a "weak correlation between viewing violence and violent activity" and that the evidence does not warrant concluding that violent entertainment has a uniformly adverse effect. But the Surgeon General liberally "translated" the report's use of the phrase "weak correlation." He testified before Senator John Pastore's congressional committee that the report actually documents a "causal link" between viewing violence and aggressive/violent behavior and only appears to say otherwise because it window-dresses its conclusion in the "carefully phrased and qualified language acceptable to social scientists" (Smith, 2003).

Nevertheless, the NIMH follow-up report lent credibility, according to many analysts, to the Surgeon General's interpretation of the 1972 report. The NIMH report concluded further that heavy viewing of violence significantly increases the likelihood of the fear of being victimized by violence. Another study conducted in 1992 by the American Psychological Association's Task Force on Television Violence in Society added that not only does heavy viewing of violence increase aggressive behavior but it also promotes "increased acceptance of aggressive attitudes" (Torr, 2002: 108).

The combined results of these studies and similar ones have led to the identification of three primary potential effects resulting from the viewing of screen violence:

1. mimetic effects (increased imitation of aggressive and violent behavior)
2. victim or sensitizing effects (increased fear of becoming a victim of violence)
3. desensitization effects (increased acceptance of aggressive attitudes and behavior)

However, victim effects and desensitization effects can be understood as varieties of mimetic effects since both are rooted in forms of identification that precede and provide the basis for imitative effects. Victim effects, for example, derive from strong identification with portrayed victims and desensitization effects derive from acceptance of or identification with portrayed aggressive behavior. Which of these effects may become predominant for a particular person will depend, according to theory, on that person's psychological constitution and the nature of the violence being viewed.

Adherents of these studies claim that cathartic effects can be largely dismissed. As Sparks and Sparks conclude: "Despite its early popularity, the theory of symbolic catharsis suffered from various flaws in the studies that were presumably supportive. Most importantly, a number of other studies revealed that when angry individuals were exposed to media violence, their aggressive tendencies increased, in direct opposition to the theory's major prediction.... Current ... assessments of the theory conclude that the prediction of diminished aggression after exposure to media violence was simply mistaken" (2002: 122–123).

However, as emphatically as these conclusions have been asserted in the forum of public debate they have been equally emphatically rejected and criticized by the opposing faction. For example, despite the cited studies, University of Toronto psychology professor Jonathan Freedman claims, "There is no convincing, in fact, no substantial evidence that television [and film] violence affects aggression or crime" (cited in Torr, 2001: 15).

Professor Freedman came to this conclusion after reviewing over 200 studies relating to the impact of television and film violence on aggressive and violent behavior. Returning in kind the conclusion of the critics of catharsis, he found most of the studies to be crucially flawed in one way or another. Freedman's list of flaws included difficulties of relating "laboratory testing" to the real-life viewing experience, problems of the researcher's expectations influencing the subject's behavior (as well as the evaluation of that behavior), and the inconsistent findings and interpretations deriving from "field" or real-life studies.

Furthermore, many social scientists insist, contrary to the claims of the Surgeon General, that the studies on violence show correlation and not causality. In the words of one analyst: "Many dispute the idea that exposure to fictional violence *causes* people to become violent ... it may be that instead of people being made violent by entertainment, violent individuals may simply prefer violent entertainment" (Torr, 2001: 15).

This latter possibility stands on its head the argument that fictional violence begets real violence by foregrounding the possibility that an attraction to and fascination for violence *creates* the seemingly insatiable market for fictional violence — especially in a culture where, as some have argued, forms of aggressive behavior are increasingly repressed.

TONIC CATHARSIS: "IT'S THE JOY YOU'VE GOT TO TALK ABOUT ... THE JOY OF CRUELTY"

One of the most candid and outspoken expressions of the point of view that aggressive personalities seek violent entertainment comes from "thriller" novelist Andrew Klavan. Although by no means expected to be a neutral observer, Klavan's unapologetic defense of violent entertainment reflects an attitude very far removed from Auden's warning (repeated by Burgess) that the novelist, when writing of dark deeds such as rape and murder, must become "filthy with the filthy." According to Klavan, creating "bloodsoaked nightmares" of violent horror and terror is no easy thing, but "if you build it, they will come" (2002: 137). And Klavan has few, if any, qualms about building such nightmares.

Klavan's explanation for the attractions of violence initially follows the standard cathartic theory that suggests fictional violence provides a purge of bottled-up emotional tensions that become toxic if not released: "Whether it's Medea or Jason (from *Friday the 13th*), the character who commits acts of savage violence always has the appeal of a Caliban: that thing of darkness that must be acknowledged as our own.... Some emotions have to be repressed and repressed emotions return via the imagination in distorted and inflated forms: that's the law of benevolent hypocrisy, the law of civilized life" (138).

Remaining unhopeful and unenthusiastic regarding programs for "civilizing" the uncivilized impulses of aggression and violence, Klavan remarks, "It is an unstated underpinning of utopian thought ... that the repressed can be eliminated completely or denied or happily freed or remolded with the proper education. It can't. Forget about it" (138).

But Klavan is not content with equating the pleasures of violent entertainment entirely with the psychoanalytic couch and medicinal purges of the repressed. Having provided an account of the pleasures of violent entertainment consistent with a version of the cathartic theory, Klavan then takes the experience to another level, modifying the Aristotelian curative notion in favor of a more positive tonic release effect — a neo–Nietzschean Dionysian affirmation of danger and destruction.

The attraction of fictional violence goes beyond the curative function of controlled releases of toxic tensions to something more like the joyful exercising of natural predatory instincts and indulgence in electrifying thrills associated with threatening and being threatened, of hunting and being hunted. Violent entertainment does not want for an audience, Klavan explains, because of the irreducible fact of the "depth" and "power" this experience offers: "It's fun. Like sex: it's lots of fun.... This business of violent fiction as therapy — the modern-jargon version of Aristotle — it's a defense, isn't it, as if these stories needed a reason for being. In order to celebrate violent fiction — I mean, *celebrate* it — it's the joy you've got to talk about. The joy of cruelty, the thrill of terror, the adrenaline of the hunter, the heartbeat of the deer — all reproduced in the safe playground of art. A joy indeed" (138).

Klavan then adds the conclusion that the relationships between storytelling and the realm of the unconscious are so complex, overdetermined, interwoven, and multidirectional that it is impossible to discover clear indications of cause and effect. Similarly, it is not possible to understand the connections between violent portrayals and real-life violence and whether these effects are predominantly tonic (in the manner of Klavan's joyful arousal and excitement thesis), imitative, or cathartic. (See Appendix 1 for a discussion of the similarities and differences between these three effects.)

And so the debate continues, locked in stalemated and seemingly insoluble disagreement. But it is really not surprising that it should continue. It is a debate that has been contested in various guises at least since the time of Plato and probably since the beginning of storytelling. And it is not likely to be resolved by contemporary empirical research. In this regard Klavan is probably correct in asserting that clear indications of broad cause-and-effect connections between fictional depictions of violence and real acts of violence — especially in relation to a varied and general population — will always remain impossible to prove or demonstrate.

Although the proponents of empirical studies may argue that they are helpful, it remains clear that the evidence is not sufficiently compelling and free of interpretive latitude to carve out a consensus among the staunch defenders of each side of the debate. Therefore, a consensus by default ought to form around the conclusion that, due to the complexities of media presentation, ambiguities of context, differences of human perception, and lack of control of variables, the debate cannot be decided by empirical research methodologies. If so, where does this leave the debate?

Method and Thesis

As has become apparent in the controversy over mimesis and catharsis, much of the difficulty in assessing the effects of violent entertainment turns on the circumstance that works of narrative fiction — such as literature, drama, and film — require interpretation. They require the same kind of interpretation as do the spoken and written words through and around which such works are woven. In fact, anything examined for its significance assumes the properties of a signifier — and to that extent begins to function as a "text." As varieties of texts, entertainment media present the methodological problems of interpretation associated with modes of representation in general — and to that extent fall into the category of what is called rhetorical interpretation. Consequently, continuation and potential resolution, if there is to be one, of the debate concerning effects of entertainment violence must transpire within and through the arena of rhetorical interpretation, inquiry, and argument.

The problems surrounding rhetorical interpretation are in many ways closely related to the problems of imitation or mimesis that concerned Plato centuries ago. In his study of mimesis in *The Republic*, Plato famously draws attention to the sense in which art imitates life. But it is the sense in which life imitates art that more thoroughly preoccupies him. And here his concern centers not so much on the inevitable distortion that may take place in the course of the human imitation of the "text" of art as on the inevitable repetition of what is "read"—the imitation of the imitations.

In discussing tragic drama in particular, Plato reasons that in response to repeated viewings of the depiction of violent conflict the audience will be seduced—by the emotional outpourings of the characters—into similar emotional abandonment that will promote emotional hypersensitivity, suspension of rationality, and incapacity for action in the face of real violence and conflict. (See Appendix 1 for an extended analysis of the quarrel between Plato and Aristotle on the effects of tragic drama.)

Plato's concern about emotional hypersensitivity in response to depictions of violence contrasts sharply with the dominant contemporary concerns about the direct imitation of depicted violent actions and increased insensitivity to violence. A primary reason for this difference is presented in the discussion of differences between tragic drama and melodrama in the chapters that follow. For now, it is important to note only that emotions and actions are but two levels of potential imitation. Consistent with the "textual" nature of the media and the possibility for multiple levels of interpretation, the potential for imitation increases through other layers of significance.

Where particular kinds of emotions are consistently claimed to be reproduced through dramatic productions, it follows that it may be worthwhile to examine the extent to which such emotions may be induced by the consistent reproduction of particular kinds of situations. These situations correspond to structures of conflict. Examining them more closely exposes a deeply embedded and highly consistent layer of repetition that promotes a mode of imitation beyond and prior to emotion and action. This mode of imitation can be preliminarily described as a manner of "cognitive" or attitudinal orientation. Exposing this deeper and broader layer of potential influence and imitation conveyed through the structure of dramatic conflict brings a measure of compromise and resolution to the debate regarding the effects of viewing violent entertainment.

The chapters that follow show a way out of the current stalemate among views toward entertainment violence by progressively building a demonstration of the way in which each of the primary opposing theories of effects—mimetic and cathartic—has validity and relevance. Assumptions about conflict inherent in dramatic structure, especially assumptions regarding the nature of evil, exert crucial influence in determining whether portrayals of violence will *likely*, but not necessarily, have significantly harmful or beneficial effects.

Reworded, the general thesis is as follows: Effects of entertainment violence, whether primarily mimetic or cathartic in relation to aggression, are a function of a more fundamental imitation on the part of audiences—an imitation of attitudes toward conflict conveyed through dramatic structures within which notions of evil and depictions of violence are presented.

The path toward this formulation proceeds by way of pealing back multiple layers of significance surrounding relevant genres of violent entertainment. These progressive layers extend from the emotional, psychological, social, and historical to the religious, moral, mythical, and metaphysical. Adding to the complexity of the mix, these layers are also inextricably interwoven.

As something like the movement from a periphery to a center and from the physical to the metaphysical, the methodological tack resembles aspects of psychoanalytic, structuralist, and phenomenological methods. But the resemblance is somewhat misleading since the approach used, unlike those mentioned, is thoroughly neostructuralist in nature — exposing ways in which structure does not revolve around an ordering center but instead lies buried in conflict and contradiction. Further characteristics of this approach and its significance in contrast to more traditional alternatives will emerge as the discussion progresses in later chapters. For now, it can be said that the defining difference turns on the practical implications of a distinction between inclusionary and exclusionary analytical and evaluative operations. (See Appendix 2 for further discussion and comparison of methodological differences.)

The unfolding of layers of textual significance begins in Chapter 1 with an interrogation of a popular theory of the appeal of horror stories made famous in the work of James Twitchell, an award-winning author on the genre of horror and the horror film. The genre of horror is an especially good place to begin because the hero/monster of horror is the precursor to the violent anti-heroes of more contemporary ultraviolent films such as *A Clockwork Orange*. As popular entertainment, horror films also raise the question of consumer appeal perhaps more pointedly than other related genres—not only the appeal of portrayed violence but also the counterintuitive appeal of the experience of being horrorstricken.

Horror stories have something in common with all forms of drama. The late American literary and cultural critic Kenneth Burke, whose work is a major source of inspiration in these chapters, once observed, "You can't make a drama without the use of some situation marked by conflict"

(1966: 29). All conflict features confrontation between at least two parties. In its minimal dyadic form, conflict resembles the structure of oppositional relation, and, like varieties of oppositional structure, the quality of the possibilities and outcomes of the dynamic interaction of conflict is a function of the way in which the conflict is initially approached and structured.

The analysis in Chapter 1 of the horror genre progresses in succeeding chapters into a broader discussion of the historical roots of the meaning of evil and its relevance not only to the horror genre but also to the more encompassing genre of melodrama. Elements of melodramatic form are traced to the story of Adam and Eve and relevant associations with the theme of the origin of evil. Chapter 6 then introduces, by way of contrast to melodrama, the dramatic form made famous in Greek tragic drama, the roots of which are exposed and examined as they extend into an alternative myth of the origin of evil grounded in the stories from which much of Greek tragic drama derives.

Chapter 7 introduces alternative uses of Greek mythic tradition that overlap and contrast with the view presented in Chapter 6 while Chapter 8 brings to a focus and summarizes the cumulative lines of commentary and argument from the previous seven chapters.

Chapters 9 and 10 elaborate on the dramatic design of violence and the relation between violence and catharsis in melodrama. These themes lead to further discussion of the contrast between dramatic forms and a reevaluation of the debate over mimesis and catharsis in tragedy and melodrama as these forms relate to violent content — which herein may generally be taken to mean the portrayal of varieties of deadly conflict. Chapters 12 and 13 apply this reevaluation of the effects of violent content in dramatic media such as theater and film to entertainment media that figure prominently in the lives of younger audiences—fairy tales, comic books, and video games.

Chapters 14 and 15 move the discussion from the conflict and drama of entertainment media to a broader cultural level where previously derived conclusions regarding connections between violence and the structuring of conflict are tested against examples of real-life drama and conflict. Chapter 14 confronts the question: Does the structuring of conflict in melodrama, despite the potential drawbacks discussed in previous chapters concerning the radical polarization of conflicting parties, retain significant value for the accurate description of and effective predisposition toward real-life conflicts? In answering this question, this chapter addresses the problem of applying the distinction between tragic and melodramatic structures and their corresponding treatments of evil to real-world conflicts. For purposes of illustration it presents a comparison between the saga of evil in the character of Ahab in the fictional story of *Moby Dick* and the real-life drama that unfolded in the person of a modern iconic figure of evil—Adolf Hitler.

Chapter 15 begins by noting how dramatic structures and parallel conflict structures align in reinforcing ways with culturally popular traditions of moral structuring and evaluation. A critical analysis of melodrama and the relation between its conflict structure and its potential effects suggests the need for similar critical reflection on the same structure evident in the popular lineage of moral teachings and moral codes based on the dualism of good and evil. In the course of this analysis, a contradiction at the core of popular cultural teachings relating to moral choice and the structure of good and evil is exposed and examined. In terms of popular moral codes this contradiction appears in the tension between a morality of the golden rule and a morality of good and evil. It is argued that these structures contribute to various productive and unproductive responses to situations of competition and conflict throughout American culture and society.

The discussion in Chapter 15 then turns more directly to the problem of violence in American culture as it has been causally linked to sources of social tension such as competition, commercialization, instrumentalization, and individualism. Sections of the chapter under these titles variously illustrate how these tensions are destructively exacerbated when squeezed into the template of melodramatic structure while progressively demonstrating how this structure is a choice that derives more from cultural conditioning than from factors relating to instinctual promptings, situational constraints, or scarcity of resources.

The analysis returns finally to the problem, raised in the introduction, of high statistics on gun crime and violent crime in the United States and provides an explanation for why the difference in statistics between the United States and a country of equal economic and social development like Japan may conceal a sense in which the United States is ultimately better off despite its statistics. The chapter concludes by suggesting, nevertheless, what direction must be taken in the United States, based on the arguments and insights accumulated through all the previous chapters, to alter particular cultural factors that increase the potential for violent crime.

Continuing along the same vein, the final chapter summarizes conclusions that may be drawn from prominent connections between melodramatic form, the structuring of conflict, and moral and religious attitudes toward evil. It also provides a look forward toward what might help over the long term to redirect public attention, concern, and action regarding the feedback loops between cultural training, violent crime, destructive conflict patterns, and entertainment violence. Concluding comments offer suggestions concerning what will favorably improve the social climate for all forms of competition and conflict as well as the climate for the production and consumption of fictional entertainment.

Since the analysis of portrayed violence presented herein focuses primary attention on structural dynamics of the contexts in which violence is presented, film and literature that has been adapted to film are predominantly used for purposes of illustration because these media (as opposed to television productions) are the most widely available to those who may want to view or review particular examples in relation to the claims and arguments presented. In order to conserve focus and preserve the flow of argument, extensive analyses of films are reserved for Part II.

In Part II selected films are examined and reviewed in light of the preceding analysis of the relation between depicted violence and real violence in Part I. The films examined in Part II, due to their violent credentials and wide critical praise, serve as challenging yet instructive examples for illustrating aspects of theory developed in the preceding chapters.

PART I

ARGUING THE CASE

1

Fictional Horror

James Twitchell's *Dreadful Pleasures,* "an anatomy of modern horror," acknowledges that film has become the quintessential modern medium for consumers of horror — especially for the post–World War II generations. But in the attempt to understand the appeal of cinematic horror, Twitchell gives central attention to the roots of modern horror located in certain key texts of Romantic literature. These texts provide the basis for what in the hands of twentieth-century filmmakers becomes the archetypal pattern Twitchell summarily refers to as "the horror story."

At the time of its publication in 1985, Twitchell's book was well received and stood out from much of what had been previously written on the topic. After submitting the caveat that Twitchell was not a "fastidious stylist," one critic concluded that his detailed and insightful analysis "makes most other treatments of horror themes ... seem trivial" (Schoenbaum, 1986). Another admiring critic went so far as to say that the thorough synthesis Twitchell accomplishes would become "the starting point henceforth of all studies of modern horror" (MacDonald, 1986). As it turns out, however, this has not invariably proven to be the case. Twitchell's star has fallen somewhat in the wake of more recent postmodern critical appraisals. These critics regard his approach as a textbook example of a discredited or at least highly suspect methodology that deludes itself with unwarranted assumptions about the viability of genre distinctions and associated structural and psychological constants (for further discussion, see Appendix 2).

Nevertheless, Twitchell's views serve as a good starting point from which to explore and assess the possibilities for an incisive formulation of the horror theme in relation to consumers of horror. Without dismissing the relevance of contemporary differences that scramble and deform neat genre boundaries, the possibilities for such a formulation must not be abandoned too readily because, like fairy tales, there may be a sense in which the "same" stories retain a similarly compelling interest for each generation.

The Secret

By Twitchell's count three archetypal stories provide the thematic substance for the varieties of horror tales created during the last century and continue to provide inspiration in the contemporary era. These three are the Dracula, Frankenstein, and Jekyll/Hyde or Wolfman stories, which Twitchell generalizes into the vampire, the hulk-with-no-name, and the transformation or changeling myths. These classics introduce the characters that are the core of the "modern bestiary"— to which, according to Twitchell, the entire stock of post–World War II fright films owes a debt.

In fact, all such films, Twitchell argues, are variations on one of the three classic horror plots. For example, he finds the themes of blood pollution, possession, and curse in the Dracula story to have inspired cadaver, zombie, and devil incarnate films such as *The Mummy* (1932, 1999), *Night of the Living Dead* (1968, 1990), *The Exorcist* (1973), and *Alien* (1979); the theme of the mad scientist and his hulking creation or adopted charge spawns progeny such as *The Invisible Man* (1933), *King Kong* (1933, 1976), *The Phantom of the Opera* (1925, 1989), and *Hollow Man* (2000), along with an assortment of 1950s creature features; and the theme of the seemingly ordinary body that conceals a deadly fiend gives rise to films such as *Psycho* (1960), *Peeping Tom* (1960), *Altered States* (1980), *Friday the 13th* (1980), and assorted slasher films.

Not all of these variations succeed in conveying a strong element of horror. Genuine horror may be usefully separated from similar fright genres, Twitchell argues, by distinguishing between horror and terror. The genre of terror presents a highly concrete threat about which there is little doubt where it came from, what it wants, and where it will go next. An enraged grizzly bear or a hungry and aggressive shark may be sources of terror but not horror. Horror presents an element of the fantastic and the unknown. The engine of terror is a wild piece of nature whereas the engine of horror is *the monster*. The creature of the horror story is always mysterious in its origins, desires, and actions— and it is invariably linked with secretive and forbidden knowledge. A part of the horror creature remains opaque to the light of knowledge and preys on fears lurking in the shadow of uncertainty.

When discussing the attractions of the horror genre, Twitchell acknowledges modes of appeal mentioned in the introduction, including tonic, mimetic, and cathartic effects. However, these effects recede into the background, according to Twitchell, against the cognitive and social pleasures consistent with exposure to the "secret" and initiation into the "club" of new awareness. As a disturbance within the sphere of knowledge, the monster brings to the horror story a seductive fascination associated with

A medieval image of the monstrous emerges from stone (gargoyle from Baddesley Clinton Church, Warwickshire, U.K.) (© Paul Gambling).

the fears and pleasures surrounding an ominous secret and the desire to be let in on the secret.

But what remains hidden and forbidden does not rise to the level of a profound existential mystery that would be relevant to any age group. The nature of this forbidden knowledge is easily anticipated by older audiences. The first layer of the secret of horror art, Twitchell explains, concerns puberty, sexual awareness, and the code of sexuality — the socially prescribed do's and don'ts of mating behavior.

According to Twitchell, knowledge of sexually prescribed do's and don'ts instructs "the soon-to-be-reproductive audience exactly how to avoid making horrible mistakes — namely monsters" (1985: 65–66). The horror story transcends ordinary terror through its representation of the more extreme kind of terror aroused by the anomaly of the monster. The monster, as an aberration and violation of nature, is itself the product of a mysterious (pro)creative act gone wrong and it threatens the protagonists by co-opting, redirecting, or destroying the protagonists' procreative life energy.

The Deeper Secret

So, in general, the secret in the horror story is the power of reproductive sexuality and the knowledge thereof. But Twitchell believes that it is even more than that. In the three classic horror films, the unique quality of horror, the appeal of horror, and the cultural significance of horror lie in a more closely kept secret concealed just under the surface of sexual allusions. Probing deeper, Twitchell uncovers what he believes to be the core of the secret.

> At first glance horror sagas perversely seem to do more than articulate the anxieties of puberty; they seem to excite it. They appear to do more than acknowledge sexual frustration; they almost encourage it. If these horror monsters are from the id, it is only because the superego feels the necessity of letting them out to air, and then presumably sends them back only after they have taught us something necessary. But what have they taught us?... What is it that we sexually want to do that we must repress, subvert, sublimate — anything rather than express for too long?... I think it is incest [1985: 92–93].

For many who have grown up with extensive exposure to these particular horror classics Twitchell's claim that they are fundamentally about incest may appear to be more fantastic than the monsters they project. Certainly if a poll were taken to see how many would guess incest to be at the crux of these horror tales, not a great number, if any, would hit on that response. Granting as much, the results of such a poll, however, would perhaps only show that incest is not a blatantly obvious theme in these tales and that it must therefore be the case, if Twitchell is correct, that horror stories function in a way similar to dreams—conveying their message more subconsciously than consciously. In fact, at one point Twitchell suggests that the depths of horror are seemingly "accessible only through psychoanalysis" (1985: 20).

It will not be possible here to examine all the evidence, arguments, and details that Twitchell advances to support his claim but the tenuous and subtle nature of his rationale can be grasped from key examples he cites from each of the three horror storyboards.

In the case of the Dracula story Twitchell notes that the vampire, as a "specific older man," and the "young virgin" of the story represent either a father-daughter — or a "blood" relationship — and that the bite on the neck is a symbol of sexual intercourse. In the Frankenstein story, the monster, as the surrogate "son," eventually attacks a woman who is clearly the surrogate "sister" of the monster's creator. In the Jekyll and Hyde story (the film version), Mr. Hyde — reacting in frustration at the postponement of Dr. Jekyll's wedding — eventually attacks a "displaced" version of Jekyll's fiancée — a "woman of the streets" — presumably because Jekyll is prohibited from premarital sex by the prevailing social codes.

In each case evidence of an incestuous theme requires granting considerable interpretive latitude. Twitchell admits that in some cases the Hollywood versions of these stories are not as clear in their implications of incest as the texts from which they derive — although in the Jekyll/Hyde story he points out that the reverse is the case. Nevertheless, he argues that "if we want to understand the horror myth, we need to follow the path, not ... the footprint[s]" (1985: 83). In this analogy the footprints correspond to particular versions (texts, films, etc.) and the path refers to the histories of these mythic types and their role in the cultural tradition.

The Riddle Within the Secret

In making the case for the broad and lasting cultural significance of these myths for a particular age group, Twitchell also acknowledges, "The fact of the matter is that most of us, most of the time, simply have no interest in committing incest" (1985: 95). Having, to his credit, made this admission, Twitchell leaves himself in the position of needing to explain why incest is given such prominence in his theory and why the incest taboo is culturally significant.

In support of his case, Twitchell cites studies showing that the incest taboo is not instinctive or grounded in genetic code. Instead, research has demonstrated that the incest prohibition is culturally rooted and socially learned. Accepting these conclusions, Twitchell explains, expands the understanding of the origin of the social ban against incest from concerns centered primarily in the nuclear family and the Oedipus complex to concerns relating to kinship groups wider than the immediate family, such as clans and tribes.

Following this reasoning, it becomes clear that the point of the incest taboo is not primarily to prevent sexual unions between blood relatives. Instead it is designed to discourage members of a given group or clan from mating with members of the same group or clan. In other words, the social prohibition against incest conceals and serves a more fundamental prohibition — what sociologists and anthropologists call an endogamic taboo.

Twitchell cites psychological and anthropological support for this theory from the work of Freud in *Totem and Taboo* (1913/1950) and Robin Fox in *The Red Lamp of Incest* (1980). Elaborating on Freud's thesis in *Totem and Taboo*, Fox speculates about the machinations of a theoretically postulated "primal horde" at the beginnings of human civilization. Incest becomes a social and cultural taboo that must be imposed from one generation to the next, Fox argues, because it serves as an impediment to sexual rivalry and violence among the blood relatives of the older and younger men and thereby preserves cohesiveness crucial for the survival of the clan and its members. It also strengthens the clan by expanding its influence and membership beyond its own tightly knit relations. Incest becomes a taboo, therefore, not because it leads to genetically compromised progeny but because it prevents the group from fracturing into destructive chaos in situations of limited mating options.

In sum, Twitchell essentially argues that in the case of the horror story an implicit prohibition against incest becomes a riveting symbol for the more general prohibition of mating too narrowly within "the clan." This conclusion reinforces his view of the cultural significance of the horror myths whereby the classic Dracula, Frankenstein, and Wolfman (or Jekyll/Hyde) stories (and stories based on similar themes) convey the "prescriptive codes of modern Western sexual behavior." They begin to have their appeal to both sexes during the sexually latent period between ages five and twelve and at puberty eventually become extensive "rites of initiation" as well as "memory banks of social and sexual possibilities both for the individual and the group" (1985: 104).

However, as is evident in this last citation, Twitchell ultimately stretches the theme of incest and its social prohibition to include *any* sexual involvements that are for one reason or another socially forbidden (such as premarital sex). As a result, the symbolism of the stories becomes so vaguely informative that the usefulness of incest as an interpretive key begins to dissipate.

The Monster

Because the subconscious clues of the film experience of horror remain murky, Twitchell appeals to the monsters themselves and their haunting strangeness as the clearest evidence of the profound nature of what is at stake: "the one thing [monsters] clearly do is show consequences of socially inappropriate sexual action" (1985: 99). Plainly, monsters are extraordinary consequences of something, but, contrary to Twitchell's insistence, it is *not* clear that it need be a sexual act with a blood relative. In fact, it is certainly not clear that monsters need be the implied consequence of any form of inappropriate or socially prohibited sexual union.

Even if Twitchell were correct in his claims that particular incidents in the classic stories are depictions of incest, it is not certain that incest is the functional meaning or theme of these incidents. The late American literary critic Kenneth Burke, for example, cautions against readily interpreting as a symbolization of incestuous desire those passages in modern literature that plausibly suggest incest:

> Sometimes it may well be just that. But until such an interpretation is forced upon us by many other aspects of the plot's imagery, we might do well to watch for a totally different possibility: that symbolic incest is often but a roundabout mode of self-engrossment, a narcissistic independence, quite likely at the decadent end of individualism, where the poet is but expressing in sexual imagery a pattern of thought that we might call simply "communion with the self" [1973, 42].

This "communion with the self" suggests a line of interpretation more compatible with Twitchell's analysis in the early part of his book where he focuses more generally on the mysterious nature of the monster and the response it arouses. As he has carefully noted, the monster in these stories gives rise not merely to terror but to the darker and uncannier sensation of horror.

But if the secret of the horror story does not reside specifically in the theme of incest and the prohibitions surrounding this forbiddven motive, what, then, remains sufficiently dark and powerful in sexuality to arouse horror? And what is it, more precisely, about sexuality that it should be crucially invoked and covertly implicated through a monster?

2

The Troubling, Doubling Self

In her study of the appeal of horror in *The Naked and the Undead*, Cynthia Freeland makes an observation that exposes the interpretive tensions between the theme of incest and a variety of the theme of self-engrossment mentioned by Burke. Discussing Mary Shelley's *Frankenstein*, Freeland remarks, "The monster's crimes accumulate, and he is finally shown as the Gothic male who threatens the heroine. This threat takes on a specifically erotic form; he will rape or steal the hero's human partner, Elizabeth, on their wedding night. The Creature thus functions as a sort of evil twin of the male scientist, an externalization of this figure's evil agency — suggesting that this human man, too, might pose a threat to his fiancée" (2000: 35).

Interpreting the monster as a version of Dr. Frankenstein himself, rather than, for example, a surrogate son, moves the symbolism of the story toward a more complicated view of the relationship between the monster and its creator. To the extent male audience sympathies align with the doctor, the story leads, on the basis of that identification, to the appalling discovery that the monster is oneself. As terror arises in response to an assault from the outside, horror arises in response to a threat that has found a way of getting inside. The difference in quality results from the fact that in the case of horror there is no place to run or hide.

The Doppelgänger

The fear of being or becoming a monster animates the Wolfman and Jekyll/Hyde stories in ways even more explicit than the Frankenstein story because in these cases monster and hero reside in the same body. And the Dracula character also presents a deceptive visage concealing a dark secret — a man of substance (owning a castle estate) with a title (a Count) on the one hand, and a blood-sucking fiend on the other. All three classic stories play on the theme of a normal — perhaps even exceptional — ego alongside an alter ego of a monstrous nature. Twitchell identifies this division into two selves of radically contrasting natures as the Doppelgänger theme.

Translated as "double-goer," the German word Doppelgänger refers to the twin counterpart of a person whose body and psyche manifest a dual nature. The conflict between the hero and the monster symbolizes an internal conflict. The dominance of this internal conflict in the horror story supports Burke's intuition about the possibility of a theme of self-engrossment operating through symbolism that superficially appears to imply incest. Although Twitchell mentions the Doppelgänger theme as a significant element of horror art, he does not explore the way in which it may be used to ground an alternative to his incest interpretation of the horror symbolism.

In the case of the Frankenstein story Twitchell interprets the relationship of the doctor/monster to Elizabeth as confirming the theme of incest because Elizabeth, having been raised with the doctor since childhood, functions as the symbolic equivalent of a sister and also because the doctor has a dream in which Elizabeth transforms into the image of his mother. There is, therefore, the possibility that Elizabeth functions as a doubly incestuous mother/sister persona in relation to the doctor and his Doppelgänger.

However, in keeping with Burke's previously mentioned precaution, a "totally different possibility" suggests itself. The Doppelgänger device may be seen to represent a narcissistic theme more than an incestuous one. In this connection the double — in its capacity as evil alter ego and expendable substitute — serves as an expression of the doctor's fear of loss of control and self-identity, the fear of the bubble of well-ordered self-containment bursting on the barb of an unanticipated intrusion. By this reading, the alternating and ambivalent actions of approach/withdrawal and attraction/repulsion toward Elizabeth by the doctor/monster do not spring from attempts to dissociate from the shame of a sexual taboo but rather from fear and anger triggered by aroused needs and desires relating to love and sexual attraction in general.

A classic example of the Doppelgänger: Jekyll (Richard Mansfield) and the shadow of Hyde (double-exposure photograph by Henry Van der Weyde for Mansfield's performance in *The Strange Case of Dr. Jekyll and Mr. Hyde* opening in London in 1887) (from the book *Richard Mansfield: The Man and the Actor* by Paul Wilstach, 1909. New York: Charles Scribner's Sons).

Reflecting a deep emotional and motivational division within the self, the hero/monster conflict is the central tension driving the horror story. Consequently, it may be theorized, along psychological lines, that the appeal of these stories consists significantly — although not exclusively — in the reflections they mirror of the divided selves of the consumers of such stories. But if such is the case, why and in what ways may consumers be counted on to present themselves in relevant states of dividedness? And how and to what extent is this dividedness related to narcissistic motives?

First Crisis

The 21 year old may still be regarded as "green," but that official age of responsibility does not arrive without forced passage through formidable crises. The journey to adulthood is never an easy one. The late adolescent psyche has confronted and continues to confront, with varying degrees of success, the stresses of at least two major divisive tensions. Ironically, these inner conflicts are triggered by emotional currents associated with varieties of bonded relationship wherein the merely "other" becomes a "significant other."

The first bond in life emerges, of course, in the emotional attachment between parent and child. This bond also becomes the source of the first major inner conflict — the initial division of the self into conflicting selves.

Sigmund Freud labels complications associated with this first conflict as the Oedipus complex. Among psychological theories it is one of the first and perhaps the most famous to come to mind. However, in the previous chapter, the relevance of the theme of incest, the crux of the oedipal complex, was found to be questionable in providing a basis for understanding the importance of the horror story for adolescents. More significantly, the substance of Freud's theory in providing a general psychological account of the tensions in the nuclear family has been challenged by a simpler and more compelling account. This more recent explanation offered by literary critic and philosopher René Girard (1996) has rightly gained prominent attention.

Although Freud explains the Oedipus complex as originating in dawning sexual motivations directed toward the parent of the opposite sex, Girard finds that the tensions for which it appears to provide an account need *not* be understood as fundamentally rooted in incestuous or even sexual motives. Instead, he proposes a theory that shifts the motivational ground to the process of imitation or mimesis.

According to Girard, at a very early age children begin to imitate those closest to them, those on whom they depend and whom they admire. Initially these models are same-sex parents but later they may also include older brothers or sisters and other blood relatives. As this mimesis becomes increasingly thorough, children come to desire the same things desired by those they imitate. This naturally creates the possibility for competition over an object of desire — thereby providing the basis for conflict in feelings toward the person imitated.

Girard's theory of mimesis explains the oedipal conflict in nonsexual terms by showing that imitation of the father, rather than elemental and repressed sexual desire, accounts for the son's interest in the mother while also explaining how that imitation, by inducing rivalry, also leads to conflicted feelings and motivations toward the father.

This inner conflict not only initiates in but is also further amplified through imitation. Since children most readily imitate those they depend on, dependency and imitation are mutually reinforcing as they become bound up in emotional ties of love and trust. But any emotional bond grounded in imitation and dependency will also be divided — in the sense of being ambivalent and conflicted.

Conflict arises as dependency brings with it a sense of vulnerability and risk. A child loves and trusts a parent as a result of the parent's providing for the child's needs. But occasions inevitably arise where the child perceives the parent to be failing or refusing to fulfill needs or desires. On these occasions dependency often leads to feelings of resentment, anger, and distrust. Under certain circumstances of disappointment or parental inattention, dependency may also fuel fears of rejection and abandonment. Through imitation, admiration grows. But precisely through that imitation a dependency builds that will invariably lead to degrees of doubt, separation, and conflict. This sense of conflict is especially keen in relationships of appreciably imbalanced dependency — as is the case in the parent/ child relationship — where one side is not as codependent as the other.

Girard's theory of mimetic desire, therefore, accounts for the existence of ambivalent feelings for both parents. In young children these feelings often result in strong fantasy images of contrasting personas for each parent — the "good" and "bad" mother and the "good" and "bad" father. As this conflict is also internalized, the division results in a sense of the "good" self and the "bad" self. The mimetic theory, consistent with much psychoanalytic theory, reveals an inextricable link between relational conflict and inner conflict.

This self-alienation and the division of the parents into opposing personas stem not merely from children's attempts to understand why their needs and desires are not always met by the parents but more fundamentally from the experience of vulnerability in dependency. However, as will be examined more thoroughly in Chapter 11, these tensions of early childhood are more relevant to the themes of fairy tales than to those of horror stories.

The sense of subordination and insufficient power in dependency necessarily creates conflict with parents through a growing restlessness and desire for freedom from dependency that becomes increasingly intense in the transition to the teenage years.

Second Crisis

The first inner conflict or "mimetic crisis" is soon followed by another also rooted in an experience of bonded relationship. Although the imagery Twitchell cites to support his assertions about the relevance of incest to the horror story may be overinterpreted, it nevertheless provides reason to suspect that something significant having to do with the trauma of coming-of-age sexually moves on and beneath the surface of these stories.

The second crisis surfaces with reproductive sexual function at puberty, bringing with it another inevitable split in the psyche. This crisis of identity comes prominently into play when taking the first steps into sexually charged friendships. Similar to the mimetic crisis, the sexual crisis emerges from the circumstance of dependency — the fact that sexual libido desires and requires a partner for fulfillment. This inner conflict need not be driven entirely by a particular emotional involvement. It may also arise more generally from competing dual images of adequate and inadequate selves as reflected in perceived or imagined responses of acceptance or rejection by those of the opposite sex.

The more a sexually charged relationship develops, the more varieties of dependence grow. As the level of attachment increases it feeds a sense of loss of control that often leads to degrees of anxious vulnerability as each partner asks with growing concern: "What if he/she is less attracted or loses interest?"

The stronger the degree of attraction and involvement in relationship, the greater the vulnerability. Increasing vulnerability raises the anxiety concerning potential obstacles to anticipated fulfillment, especially the worst possible obstacle — rejection. The person of growing admiration and desire becomes equally a source of growing concern and loss of control triggering emotions of distrust, withdrawal, and even resentment simultaneous with feelings of fascination and attraction.

The budding autonomy teenagers begin to achieve by working through childhood separation anxieties and gaining a sense of self independent of parents and family is thrown into turmoil by the revelation of new needs and desires that can only be met by a member of the opposite sex. This assault on the narcissistic bubble of self-containment, while having its rewards and attractions, is understandably not met with complete delight. The most shocking part of this external assault on the ego as autocratic center of appropriation and control turns out to be that it is also an assault from the inside. The unfolding bodily and emotional transformations of sexual maturation involuntarily cede power to an alien entity emerging within as well as to seductive strangers from without. This new loss of self-control will at the very least be experienced as unsettling, and for some it is even horrifying.

Predictably, then, teenagers desire and dream most of all to be perceived (and to perceive themselves) as capable, powerful, and in control. In short, they desire the persona of an adult (or what they idealize the control of adult existence to be like)— someone who is secure in an identity and an area of knowledge, expertise, and accomplishment. Over and against this ideal lurks the awareness of the reality of vulnerability and conflicting feelings. Into this murky milieu of the identity crisis steps the Doppelgänger, the "monster" of the horror story.

Granting the conflicts underlying the adolescent identity crisis, it is not hard to imagine the reception the split identity of the horror story protagonist will have among those coming of age. It is also not hard to imagine the complexities and entanglements of plot that can be spun around the contradictory feelings, identity doublings, and emotional intrigues that will inevitably surface from such a cauldron of potential personal and relational conflicts.

The horror story conflict between the hero and the monster reflects an internal conflict within the divided self of the hero, which is itself a function of the tension between the hero and the heroine. The tension between the hero and the heroine dramatizes the great fears associated with adolescent sexuality — separation from or rejection by the beloved on the one hand and loss of autonomy on the other. These fears are embodied in and given expression through the Doppelgänger.

On one level of interpretation, the heroine's abhorrence of the monster betrays the hero's secret fear, indeed horror, that the heroine will find him and his sexual advances unwanted, even, God forbid, repulsive and monstrous. As the embodiment of qualities deserving of rejection, the monster is to be vilified. In its capacity as vilified pollution, the monster, as the hero's double, may also be seen to work as a foil in order to drive the heroine into the protecting arms and adoring control of the hero.

Scandalously, however, the monster will not stay strictly confined to the category of the entirely loathsome. It may also deftly elicit a measure of surreptitious admiration from male consumers of the horror story for the revenge in the form of terror it wreaks on the heroine for her intrusive threat to his autonomy as a result of his growing dependency on her for the fulfillment of his needs.

Alternatively, the heroine, and the female members of the audience identifying with her, inwardly fears she will find herself in the position of being preyed on by a monster instead of courted by a hero. The monster as the hero's double represents, then, any undesirable traits and qualities that would lead the heroine to reject him.

On yet another level of interpretation, however, the monster may be paradoxically seductive to a heroine as an avatar of virile, inflamed, and passionate obsession with her — even to the extreme of wanting to possess and destroy her. As those of the Romantic period of literature were well aware, a love/hate, love/death embrace such as this cannot be faulted for incompleteness or reservations.

In their brevity, these lines of interpretation are intended to be only suggestive of some of the motivational complexities that may revolve around the impulses associated with early sexuality. The emergence of sexuality reinforces the adolescent sense of an already divided self and raises doubts about the nature and quality of this new aspect, this new addition to the self. The hero and the monster correspond to the tensions surrounding judgments of acceptance and rejection — tensions rooted in the hero's fear of unworthiness and the heroine's fear of being deceived or making herself vulnerable to the desires of the monstrous.

I Love You, I'll Kill You

Responses to flirtation and sexual advances from members of the opposite sex have an enormous impact on the way in which doubts and fears will be met. These emotions and self-assessments are in many cases amplified by responses from friends and peers. These responses often carry sufficient weight to shape self-image and can thereby potentially escalate the intensity of the adolescent identity crisis.

Sexual tensions, which are especially intense in adolescence because they are new and unpredictable, can ignite male/female conflict with anger and resentment of a profoundly disturbing nature when attraction is experienced as a kind of aggression. This circumstance can work either way between the sexes, but it seems to occur more often and more unmanageably among men.

The action of female beauty on male senses can often resemble the order of causality Aristotle describes as the "unmoved mover." A woman may unwittingly perpetrate a kind of random violence on a man who finds himself attracted to her quite beyond any volition on his part. This love-struck condition, even when completely unnoticed by the woman (and especially when completely unnoticed), can be experienced, depending on the man, as a casually cruel assault.

The male who finds himself, for whatever psychologically twisted reasons, incapable of adequately coping with incidents of random attraction may, over time, build sufficient frustration and resentment to motivate acts of physical violence, torture, and even murder against "randomly" selected females (who must nevertheless fit a certain profile). To the perpetrator this may appear as one victim of random assault and torture dealing out random payback to the appropriate class of perpetrators of another form of random assault and torture. Needless to say, this thinking belongs to an order of "logic" characteristic of the serial killer or slasher in whose psyche sex and violence, pleasure and pain, torture, and murder are all perversely and perhaps hopelessly scrambled.

The serial killer and the slasher, like the monster of the horror story, represent extreme instances of the phenomenon of psychic division and "rejection" that results in the Doppelgänger. As Twitchell has noted, the horror story — especially the transformation monster story — is the precursor to the more contemporary slasher film, which serves as one popular brand of retellings of classic horror for more recent generations. Serial killer sagas, slasher films, and horror stories all present a stark clarity and polarity of conflict that panders and appeals to the exaggerated states of inner conflict and heightened identity crisis especially relevant to young audiences.

Like the horror story — only to more pronounced effect — slasher films make great use of the stylistic device of triggering extreme swings of emotional arousal effects between pleasure and pain, lust and fear. For many viewers the plunging thrill and visceral shock induced by such intense and radically polarized stimulations constitutes— much like a roller coaster ride — a primary attraction of slasher films. These emotional swings are often accomplished through the technique of slyly substituting the monster or slasher for the lover in a scene of anticipated amorous exchange with the "heroine" or current victim. From the point of view of the audience an increasing tension builds through the "emotional play" generated from scenes that raise the question: lover or murderer, sex or violence?

This technique of suspense and shock resonates so effectively with young audiences that it has become the basis for the entire plot in more sophisticated thrillers such as *Body Heat* (1981), *Fatal Attraction* (1987), and *Basic Instinct* (1992). The horror subgenre of the slasher film, along with the intense double identity and gender issues it raises, is explored in greater detail in Chapter 19.

The message in the horror story and its variations contains a thinly veiled sexual subtext, but in order to appeal to the extent box office receipts have indicated, this message cannot be too concealed or too complicated. In fact, it must be obvious—just beneath the surface. Twitchell's thesis about the centrality of incest in accounting for the consistent appeal of the horror story for each generation is an intuition that is on the right track (with the focus on adolescent sexuality) but is still wide of the mark. The monsters of the horror story fall unconvincingly short of posing as misfit progeny resulting from a sex act with an incestuous partner. If there is a "forbidden" sexual act alluded to in the horror story, it is not incest but rather the implied (or in some cases explicit) rape by the monster of the heroine.

More important, instead of merely admonishing against the dangers of a particular type of sexual activity, the horror story confronts the adolescent initiation into sexuality in a broader and deeper way. It efficiently exacerbates and exploits fears associated with the changes of puberty. These fears revolve around insecurities and anxieties arising from feelings of loss of control and identity conflict associated with the tension of acceptance and rejection, attraction and repulsion that is particularly intense in sexually charged adolescent involvements. These tensions and their accompanying emotional swings and plunges are then amplified to maximum levels in the theater by the extreme characterization of the monster — a creature who is an uncanny departure from nature and a threatening anomaly in the comprehensible order of being.

But insofar as the seemingly limitless appeal of the monster lies in resisting comprehension, more always remains to be comprehended so long as the monster beckons. And the monster may still beckon. As Jonathan Lake Crane has complained of Twitchell's analysis: Is the horror story nothing more than "mythic" Clearasil® for salving the anxieties of youth? (1994:27). Surely an experience as disturbing and uncanny as horror engages something more profound than teenage sexual angst. It must be possible and perhaps necessary to go deeper. Something continues to lurk in the shadows of its portrait that requires putting the question once again to the monster: Who are you?

3

Inside the Doppelgänger

If the horror story submits a narrative featuring a characterization that mimes the newly awakened sexually innocent, insecure, and conflicted self and offers a way to respond to the anxieties that a divided self-image presents, it does so also in large measure through the theme of death and death-dealing inherent in the monster's symbolism. While the linkage of sexuality with themes of violence and death may be necessary to explain horror, is it sufficient? In revealing alienating and predatory faces of sexuality, alterity, and mortality, the monster shows that it has borrowed more than one mask from the ancient gallery. But these masks of fear, division, and conflict are all linked to yet another layer of horror behind a mask that is equally ancient and more potent.

Husk of a Human

Features behind this further layer of the mask of horror can be glimpsed in the light of a more detailed examination of a representative type of the monster. Who, or what, for example, is Dracula? While most know that Dracula is the kind of monster called a vampire, that answer evokes the question: What is a vampire? And while the answer may seem obvious enough to those familiar with vampire stories, it is nevertheless entangled in strands of tradition that merit a closer look.

As Cynthia Freeland has observed, the vampire legend has proven to be "a gold mine of endlessly varied imaginative possibilities" for the pleasures of storytelling and fantasy (2000: 125). But as Freeland admits, certain noteworthy themes persist in popular retellings. The vampire legend has a long and complex cultural history—and a considerable amount of that history worked itself into the text of Bram Stoker's famous novel. Tracing the changing elements of the legend over time brings into view the deep structure that necessarily informed Stoker in his creative vision of the Dracula figure that has now become the classic portrait of the vampire.

The word "vampire" derives from the Magyar dialects of Hungary and the central and southwestern section of Romania traversed by the Transylvanian Alps—the mountains that give their name to the historic province in central Romania that Count Dracula called home. The legend of the vampire migrated to Romania and Eastern Europe from Asia Minor where it is believed to have originated in northern Turkey in pre–Christian times from Persian witch tales featuring the power to reanimate the dead.

The pre–Christian legend ascribes notorious characteristics to the vampire that distinguish it from other creatures. It is a supernatural, nocturnal, and death-dealing spirit whose violence dispenses a death beyond corporeal destruction. By sucking blood from the living it not only takes possession of the body but also claims or destroys the spirit of the victim, and it thereby propagates itself by creating another vampire. Being essentially a spirit, it cannot be overcome and eliminated by conventional methods. The body invaded by the spirit must be beheaded or burned in accordance with the magic of particular ritualistic words and actions. Garlic and the berries of a rare bush are the only means of protection against vampire attack.

While the vampire in ancient legend has qualities distinguishing it from other terrors, it nevertheless conforms to a long and broad tradition of belief in harmful supernatural agencies—a belief common to most, if not all, cultural groups. In the decades following the initial wave of Christian influence, the tradition of the vampire continues to thrive through changes that bring it into conformity with Christian belief.

At the time of early Christian influence, methods for opposing the vampire begin to resemble Christian rituals and the Christian symbolism of the sacred. The vampire's primary enemy becomes the parish priest and the old weapons of protection are replaced by holy water, images of the cross, and other Church icons. The preferred method of vampire slaying changes from decapitation or burning to driving a wooden stake, as a symbol of the cross, through the heart. More significant, the vampire begins to acquire the most salient features of Christianity's primary symbol for the anti–Christ. On this point Twitchell's account is admirably on the mark. He rightly points out that not only is the vampire now more popular than the devil but that the competition is somewhat illusory because "the vampire really *is* the devil. The vampire is simply the husk of a human that has been commandeered by the spirit of Satan.... The human form is simply the soma, the undead hulk, carrying around the demon and letting it pass through society undetected" (106).

As Twitchell goes on to note, the resemblance between Satan and the vampire extends beyond their identification, indeed unification, in the Christian theology of the spirit of evil. They also converge in the means by which they are graphically represented: the vampire, like Satan, has hairy palms, projects an eerie glow from catlike eyes, and displays other menacing animal-like deformities such as a reptilian tongue, marsupial fingernails, and extended canine teeth. Like Satan, the vampire can — from a certain perspective — appear as a somewhat beguiling creature until caught in a revealing sweep of light that exposes one or more of his (or her) less charming physical attributes. But the similarities do not stop here. They extend to yet another level of Christian theology.

The Transubstantiation of Evil

Twitchell notes that the Roman Catholic Church found in the vampire mythology another fortuitous pattern that proved useful in the difficult task of explaining one of its most fundamental yet mysterious and, in many cases (to the dismay of Church leaders), less credulous rituals—the sacrament of the Eucharist. In this ritual, through a process called "transubstantiation," a wafer of unleavened bread is transformed into the body of Christ and wine is transformed into his blood. The vampire myth presents a kind of transubstantiation — but with a different moral polarity. Twitchell explains, "In the Middle Ages the Church fathers found their congregation understandably hesitant about accepting that the wafer and the wine were the actual, let alone the metaphoric, body and blood of Christ. How better could the transubstantiation be explained than on the more primitive level, the level the folk already knew and believed in — namely, the vampire transformation. For just as the devil/ vampire drank the blood and then captured the spirit of a sinner, so too could the penitent drink the blood, eat the body, and possess the divinity of Christ" (1985: 108).

Grafting onto the tree of the vampire tradition, while helping the Church clarify its transubstantiation doctrine, also helped to further establish its particular understanding of evil. As Twitchell remarks: "What the medieval church found in the vampire legend was not just an apt mytholo-

Max Schreck displays classic vampire traits in F.W. Murnau's *Nosferatu* (1922) (Photofest).

gem for evil, but an elaborate allegory for the transubstantiation of evil" (1985: 108). But the elaborate allegory of the vampire and the transubstantiation of evil are founded on a common primitive belief. The idea of appropriating another living creature's spirit by partaking of its flesh derives from the most ancient traditions of hunter-gatherer and cannibalistic tribes.

The principle of transubstantiation implicit in the vampire transformation was also applied to the circumstances of the great plague of the seventieth century as virtually the only available and viable way of making sense out of the otherwise baffling symptoms and inexplicable spread of the disease. The bubonic plague was widely believed to be spread by vampires who infected their prey by stealth in the night — seizing the spirits of victims and leaving behind only the husk of a body to finally waste away and die. These dead bodies would rise again at night, having themselves become vampires, to roam the neighborhoods in search of more victims.

Twitchell explains that this belief accounts for why plague-stricken corpses were burned. When completely destroyed, the bodies could not be assimilated by vampire cults to further the demonic assault on towns and villages. It was only fortuitously coincidental, as became apparent to later generations, that the burning of bodies did in fact help control the progression of the plague — which was caused by a bacterium initially spread from rodents to humans by way of fleas.

For the majority of those during the seventieth century, the plague was understandable only in terms of the demonology of the times — which alone could explain how it was possible for a healthy body to suddenly become ill and atrophy to death. The source of the trouble was understood to come from outside the body and enter into it and to be spiritual in nature since there appeared to be no purely visible path by which it could be observed to have traveled.

Conclusions reached in the previous chapter suggest that the horror in the horror story is, in good part, a consequence of the discovery that the "monster" is, in a sense, oneself. But, as it turns out, this identification of the monster within is misleading. The example of the vampire story reveals that the conflicted self — as presented through the narrative details of action and character — is more a product of invasion than division.

The "Fall" into Living Hell

The mysterious transformation brought about through sexual maturation also lends itself to the notion of alien agency and confirms the explanation for varieties of illness, whether physical or spiritual, as the result of a malign invasive intrusion. The perfect and innocent prepubescent body suddenly experiences visible changes in the direction of "animality"— the deepening of the voice (for males), the appearance of hair in strange places, the gaining of weight — all coinciding with a set of completely new motives. Given the nature of the sudden emergence of the pubertal metamorphosis and associated alteration of desires, it is not surprising that sexuality becomes aligned, in some cultural communities, with a "fall from innocence" and with the notion of an alien force that enters and takes possession of the body. This modeling of the divided self suggests that the strange new side of the self may be portrayed in the remarkably eerie and potent image of the monster because that side is understood to have questionable desires of its own that radically threaten the budding autonomy and balance of the prepubertal self.

If applied to the divided self of the conflicted adolescent, the vampire story imposes a clear and persuasive orientation on the inner conflict. As previously discussed, the tension of acceptance and rejection leads to the creation of dual self-images. Those traits and qualities imagined to be a part of the self accounting for radical rejection are not conceptualized — in the symbolism of traditional vampire mythology — in ways that permit them to be merely shoved aside or repressed into the background. The logic set in motion by the creation of a *monster* calls for an appropriate resolution — a resolution that, in remaining consistent with the nature and severity of the threat, requires nothing less than complete destruction.

The monster, finally, is not simply a being with a deformed and ugly visage — for that would inspire ultimately only sympathy or revulsion. The monster is an unstable merger — part human, part something else — and a walking contradiction, an amalgam of life and death, form and formlessness, potency and decay. As an impossibility, shaded in darkness, the monster is, in a word, horror. And horror, while closely allied with death and death-dealing, is more than death. The monster is death with the taint of hell, the contamination of an entirely malevolent "other," a contradiction marked by evil.

Victim of Fate

The invasion of the body by a malevolent, intangible spiritual agency or force, the "transubstantiation of evil" as Twitchell describes it, conforms to the imagery and mythology belonging to the tradition of the notion of evil. The significance of the overlapping symbolism between the vampire and the devil lies in the common understanding of evil implicit in and projected through each of these demonic lineages — an understanding of evil that, like the vampire myth, is nearly universal among world cultures. As Paul Wells, British professor of cultural studies at Teesside University, explains, "The prevailing archetype of the monster is the Devil, the symbolic embodiment of evil that is a constituent element in monist religions and which appears in various forms in myths from across the globe" (2000: 8).

However, as Freeland has noted, the image of Dracula as a specter of unremitting evil does not wholly apply to him nor does it wholly apply to all the monsters in the stock of vampire lore. Many films in the vampire subgenre, according to Freeland, "offer complex and nuanced visions of the fine shadings in between good and evil" (2000: 124) wherein vampires are portrayed in ways that appear sufficiently human to solicit human sympathies. Lake Crane has also noticed that the Dracula of the 1931 film, contemplating the curse of his immortality and an endless future of death-dealing, projects an enormous weight of gloom when he says, "To die. To really be dead. That must be glorious." In fact, Lake Crane argues that all the monsters of '30s and '40s cinema carry out their deadly tasks in "profound misery" (1994: 73). These creatures may do evil things, but unlike Satan they seem to take no pleasure in them. Consequently, they are capable of arousing a measure of sympathy from audiences who recognize an element of fate in their characterizations.

Granting that the monster — as the dark double of the self — is not in every case an unqualified stand-in for Satan, however, does not let the monster off the hook when it comes to resolving the dramatic conflict. The monster is almost always destroyed and in its destruction there is ultimately a sense of resolution and celebration. But why should this be the case if the monster is not wholly — that is to say, essentially — evil? The answer to this question presses the inquiry into even deeper — and older — layers of the horror story.

4

The Origin of Evil

Oddly enough, the tradition from which the horror story draws its structure, its basic stock of characters, and its conception of evil rests on a story in which the monster is not slain. But similar to horror narratives, it is a story that reenacts how evil comes into the world. In Western tradition, however, this story does not stand alone in providing an account of the grand entrance of evil. Much like the conflicted self, the entire tradition of the West is also fundamentally conflicted — divided between competing accounts of its origin and identity in relation to evil.

In his work entitled *The Symbolism of Evil*, Paul Ricoeur discusses with great care the tension that develops between different branches of the early Western tradition. One side of this tradition maintains a clear distinction between the divine and the diabolical and provides for separate origins of good and evil. Another side of the tradition maintains that the differences that come to be called good and evil have their origin in equally divine sources.

The roots of this tension extend, on the one side, along the path of the story of Adam in Genesis and, on the other side, along the path of the poetic and mythic roots of Greek tragic drama. At this point the line of analysis and the inquiry into the significance and appeal of the horror story converge around the question: What are the origins of evil and what is the social and cultural importance of such origins as conveyed through traditions of storytelling?

"...A Part of Ourselves ... We Do Not Recognize"

In his discussion of Genesis, Ricoeur deliberately refers to the story of Adam and Eve as the "Adamic myth." Since all of the characters in the myth seem to play significant roles, the special emphasis Ricoeur places on Adam requires explanation. It will be useful for illustrating the relevance of the Adamic myth in the context of the analysis of the horror story to first approach the story of Adam and Eve as drama instead of mythic or religious text.

In terms of dramatic structure, the Adamic myth presents itself as a prototype of melodramatic form. For purposes of an initial orientation, melodrama may be defined as a drama featuring conflict between good and evil through the persons of a hero and a villain along with crucial complications provided by a damsel in distress. Often the story begins with the meeting, mutual admiration, and idyllic relationship between the hero and the female protagonist or heroine. The heroine is then approached by the villain and soon thereafter finds herself in danger. The hero then confronts and overcomes the villain and thereby rescues the heroine.

The Adamic melodrama, however, has a catastrophic outcome rather than a timely rescue. Adam and Eve find themselves, by the grace of God, in a garden paradise where they want for nothing. All that is asked of them by God is that they not eat of the fruit of a particular tree. A Serpent who lives in the garden refers to this tree as the tree of knowledge and tells Eve that by eating the fruit of this tree "your eyes will be opened and you will be like God, knowing good and evil" (Genesis 3:5). Persuaded by Eve, Adam eats with her the fruit of the tree. As punishment for breaking his prohibition, God expels Adam and Eve from the garden, thereby consigning them to a world in which they do indeed know evil — the evils of suffering, sickness, sin, and death. This brief summary of the basic structure of the story provides a superficial glance at the dynamics between the main characters. Beneath the surface lie many layers — all relevant to the melodrama of the horror story.

The combined symbolism between the characters of man, woman, and Serpent in conjunction with a "forbidden knowledge" strongly suggests a deeper subtext. Ricoeur begins the excavation of this subtext by inquiring into the significance of the Serpent. In one sense the Serpent dramatizes a crucial aspect of the experience of temptation — namely the experience of the source of temptation as external. Temptation initially appears as a seduction from the outside, as an appeal to the heart. Granting as much, to sin is the same as to yield. Ricoeur concludes that "the serpent, then, would be a part of ourselves which we do not recognize; he would be the seduction of ourselves by ourselves, projected into the seductive object" (1969: 256).

Living happily in the Garden of Eden, Adam and Eve symbolize the time of sexual innocence of prepubescent children. But even for innocent children there is a faint hint of sexuality giving rise to blindly groping questions that receive evasive answers from elders such as "wait until you are older." These questions, hints, and evasions cultivate a growing sense of "forbidden knowledge." The entrance of the Serpent corresponds to the increasing desire for the forbidden knowledge — which is, of course, the knowledge of procreation. And the ability to create life is indeed knowledge "like that of God." But close on the heels of the knowledge of procreation and life necessarily follows the knowledge of death and the difficulties and suffering associated with mortality.

More explicitly, the Serpent, as the "part of ourselves which we do not recognize" represents the emergence of the desires and physical transformations associated with reproductive sexuality. The promptings of sexual desire correspond to the "seduction of ourselves by ourselves" and the power of seduction is projected onto the external agent — the Serpent. This projection accounts for Ricoeur's use of the term "quasi-externality" to convey the sense of the ambiguous origin of temptation as external while in fact also being internal — an ambiguity for which, as will be seen, the Adamic myth is specifically constructed to offer a resolution.

Insofar as the Garden of Eden may correspond to a childlike state of blissful sexual ignorance, the expulsion from the Garden that follows the eating of the forbidden fruit and its attendant knowledge brings with it a "graduation" into the carnal world of postreproductive sexuality and the many hazards of sin, sickness, suffering, and death. This dark view of sexuality as a symbol for marking the beginning of a "fall from grace" or "descent" has a strong lineage in the religious traditions of Western culture, in some cases to the point where sexuality itself seems to have become the villain (as, for example, in the late period of St. Augustine's writings; cf. Elaine Pagels, 1988: 130–150).

The Mystery of "Yielding" and the Origin of Evil

In his analysis of the Adamic myth, however, Ricoeur does not make sexual temptation the fundamental theme. The sexual subtext of the myth, according to Ricoeur, may be better understood as itself symbolic of the experience of "yielding" in a broader sense. In the tradition of courtship ritual, for example, not only must the hero exhibit the strength of self-

Adam, Eve, and the Serpent (Hans Holbein's Dance of Death series, 1538) (from the book *Hans Holbein the Younger, His Old Testament Illustrations, Dance of Death, and Other Woodcuts* compiled by Arthur Mayger Hind. 1912. New York: Fredk. A Stokes Company Publishers).

control by not yielding too easily to the seductive power of the heroine and sexuality, but he must also show control and mastery in other tests and trials of strength and character. The fact of yielding on any given test provides grounds for rejection. These tests are imposed not only by the heroine but also by the heroine's father and tribal elders—represented in the Adamic myth by God.

Adam's failure in this test reveals that his weaker self—symbolized by his Doppelgänger in the form of the Serpent—has become dominant and consequently he must be rejected. Since the Serpent must be understood as the projection of Adam's "unworthy" or "weaker" self, Adam, not Eve, becomes the focus of blame.

Understood as a courtship ritual in which Adam has failed, the Adamic myth raises the question: Why are *both* Adam and Eve rejected by being expelled from the Garden of Eden? The answer to this question exposes a deeper and more fundamental layer of meaning in the myth. The expulsion of both Adam and Eve can be explained by the fact that the Adamic myth, as Ricoeur rightly stresses, is a myth of the *origin of evil* in the world and not essentially a myth of awakening sexuality and courtship tensions. The courtship structure—no doubt because of its strong association with the idea of loss of innocence—is used as an allegorical tool for assisting in conveying a sense of the nature of evil and how the entrance of evil into the world can be understood.

In the midst of God's perfect creation of the world of which the Garden of Eden is a part, the Serpent exists as something alien—an invasive intrusion that is not an essential part of a wholly good creation, as is made clear in the first part of Genesis (see especially 1:31). By contrast, because he is a part of the initial perfection of creation, Adam's "weakness" in yielding must be understood as a result of a subsequent incursion from the outside and not the consequence of a flaw originating at his point of creation. Adam is essentially contaminated through the Serpent's guile. In this sense he serves as a catalyst for evil or a door through which evil—already present and latent in the form of the Serpent—enters and becomes powerful in the world of human experience.

As the mythic symbol of the point of entrance of evil into the world of human action and experience, Adam's failure befalls not just him but everyone. Eve's expulsion from the Garden along with Adam is consistent with the universality of evil's entrance into *the world*. Neither the world nor its creatures is any longer free of imperfection.

Adam, along with Eve, is held accountable by God and, in this sense, it may well be asked how it is possible (1) for a Serpent, representing an intrusion of imperfection and evil, to exist amidst God's perfect creation

Adam and Eve driven from the Garden of Eden (Hans Holbein's Dance of Death series, 1538) (from the book *Hans Holbein the Younger, His Old Testament Illustrations, Dance of Death, and Other Woodcuts* compiled by Arthur Mayger Hind. 1912. New York: Fredk. A Stokes Company Publishers).

in the Garden of Eden and (2) for a perfect creature of God's creation such as Adam to be sufficiently imperfect or weak as to yield to the temptation of the Serpent. The implicit sexual symbolism of the Adamic myth inherent in the Serpent's approach to Adam through the use of Eve emphasizes an inner weakness of character in yielding to temptation as opposed to an alternative symbolism that might have emphasized the necessity of yielding as a warrior in battle overpowered by superior numbers or a stronger adversary. This contradiction between Adam's perfection as part of God's creation and his imperfection in yielding to temptation is essentially an unresolved scandal in Genesis that is superficially resolved by holding Adam accountable.

That Adam is corrupted and in some profound sense accountable, and along with him the entire human race in perpetuity, becomes a cornerstone of Christian dogma codified in St. Augustine's notion of "original sin." This dogma plays an important role in European culture and in American culture through the Puritan Christian tradition. In his comprehensive account of the "mythology of the American frontier," Richard Slotkin, for example, notes that "the heart of Puritan religion was its concept of conversion, in which the man born in sin first discovers the truth of his sinful nature and seeks to purge himself.... Each man ... inherits the dregs of Adam's original sin with his blood, and his corrupted nature must be purged and renewed before he can be saved. The quest for salvation is thus in large measure a ritual exorcism of the evil that is organically inherent in human nature" (1973: 148).

The manner of entrance of evil into the world portrayed in the Adamic myth helps to explain the complexity of the monster in the horror story as well as the responses of the audience toward the monster. The Serpent is not Satan and therefore not evil itself. Instead it is the agent of evil, the husk of a life form appropriated by evil and made to do its bidding. Similarly, the monster in the horror story is the husk of a life form — usually human — retaining some vestiges of humanity but essentially compromised and colonized by evil. And just as the Serpent serves as a door through which evil enters the world by way of the action of a yielding human agent (who is also a "door"), so the monster in the horror story serves as the humanly activated agency through which the evil that already lies latent in the world emerges and begins to take control.

Consequently, in the hands of some horror storytellers the monster may be portrayed in ways that elicit sympathy for a being that retains a semblance of the human and in the hands of other storytellers the monster may appear as being almost entirely appropriated by evil. In either case the logic of evil dictates the same fate for the monster. It matters not whether the monster "deserves" what it gets. Its fate is one with the evil that it bears.

Although it requires crossing genres from the horror melodrama to the Western melodrama, a riveting illustration of this point surfaces in the cryptic words of William Munny as he finishes off the "monstrous" Little Bill in Clint Eastwood's *Unforgiven*: "Deserve's got nothin' to do with it." This sentiment is consistent with the logic of a mythos that places the emphasis ultimately on the fact or reality of corruption and the necessity for identifying and eliminating it above any exacting consideration for where it came from, how it came about, or what its reasons may be.

The Separate Origins of Good and Evil

As a myth of the origin of evil, the Adamic myth expresses something new in mythic cultural history by describing the origin of evil as separate from an earlier and more fundamental origin of the good. According to Ricoeur, the Adamic myth represents an extreme attempt to mark off a radical and irruptive origin of evil as entirely separate from the more primordial origin of the good. Thereby good and evil are kept essentially and radically apart both conceptually and spiritually. This separation inaugurates a profoundly mysterious and value-weighted cosmological orientation involving a monotheistic belief in a God of goodness immersed in a radically polarized and dualistic universe of good and evil.

This attempt at separation presents certain logical and philosophical problems about which Ricoeur remarks that "whatever the strictly philosophical difficulties of this attempt may be, the distinction between radical and primordial is essential to the anthropological character of the Adamic myth; it is that which makes man a *beginning* of evil in the bosom of creation which has already had its absolute *beginning* in the creative act of God" (1969: 233).

The text of Genesis assumes that evil cannot originate with God and must therefore somehow originate with Adam, the first human. Ricoeur, then, labels the story of Genesis the Adamic myth or the "anthropological" myth because it accounts for the release of evil into the world as a consequence of its having first entered into an ancient and originary member of the human race. Although St. Augustine famously proclaims, "There is no possible source of evil except good," he explains this evil as initiated by God as punishment for Adam's disobedience — which, of course, begs the question of how to explain the origin of the evil of Adam's disobedience (cf., Pagels, 1988: 134–136).

As a myth of the origin of evil, the most significant news in the Adamic myth is that evil is not equiprimordial or simultaneous in origin with the good. Evil breaks into a perfectly good world after the event of creation. Ricoeur notes further that although the Adamic myth functions as a cosmological myth because it tells the origin of evil in the natural world, it is not such a myth in a strictly cosmological sense insofar as the Serpent, the agent of Satan and evil, already exists in the Garden of Eden before Adam's sin. The origin of the agent behind the Serpent and thereby the ultimate cosmological origin of evil is never made clear — other than that it does not originate with the good of creation.

As previously mentioned, the courtship ritual with its sexual allusions and tensions is used in the Adamic myth as primarily a pedagogical tool for helping to explain the origin of evil in the world. The myth resolves the problem of the origin of evil by allegorically revealing that evil originates from a place other than the godhead. As Ricoeur indicates, the philosophical difficulties of this view are not resolved. This portrayal of the origin of evil, however, creates a relationship with the good that establishes certain constraints by which the nature and quality of evil must be understood in order to remain consistent with the facts of the mysterious origin, or silence about origin, provided for it in Genesis and the Adamic myth.

What comes into play with the emergence of evil bears crucially on what is at stake in the horror of the horror story. The relationship between the monster and evil requires pressing beyond the origin of evil to yet another layer of significance and a deeper question: What lies at the heart of evil? What is evil?

5

The Nature of Evil

In a cosmological landscape of a perfect and whole creation, described in Genesis, the presence of evil can be accounted for only by way of a limited number of options. These options must be consistent with the fact that, at some point in time after the event of creation, evil burst in on all that was good. Evil burst in on a creation that, as perfection, lacked nothing. As a late arrival on the cosmic scene of creation and offering no clear address of origin, evil is the ultimate outsider — the alien of all aliens. As a result, what is called "evil," as an agency from the outside, can contribute nothing constructive to the work of creation.

Defilement in Hebraic Tradition

In *The Symbolism of Evil*, Ricoeur details the extent to which both Hellenic and Hebraic traditions make extensive use of one particular metaphor well suited to convey the essence of the outsider for which there is no place and no need. This metaphor draws meaning in contrast to notions of the "good," the "pure," and the "whole" by way of its oppositional role. In a word, that operation is *defilement*.

Ricoeur finds the notion of defilement to be crucially operative in the major philosophical and religious traditions of the West. In particular, he shows how defilement lies at the root of understandings of sin and guilt in Judeo-Christian symbolism and mythology. These understandings, of course, play a significant role in moral teachings. In addition to the Ten Commandments, God gave to Moses the Law of the Burnt Offerings (Leviticus, i) as a means of cleansing the defilement of sin and as an atone-

Moses Receiving God's Law of the Burnt Offerings (Hans Holbein's Images of the Old Testament, 1538) (from the book *Hans Holbein the Younger, His Old Testament Illustrations, Dance of Death, and Other Woodcuts* compiled by Arthur Mayger Hind. 1912. New York: Fredk. A Stokes Company Publishers).

ment for guilt. Ricoeur's discussion of the network of connections between defilement and guilt illustrates the way in which the defilement of intrusive demonic agency informs themes of sin, sinner, and sickness and thereby underscores the common metaphorical ground shared by widely held understandings of spiritual disease and physical disease.

The metaphor of defilement linking understandings of spiritual and physical disease helps to explain the ease with which demonic possession was adopted, as mentioned in the previous chapter, as an explanation for outbreaks of the plague. Ricoeur begins his discussion of the links between sin and disease by noting part of a previous discussion where he acknowledges the trace of a negative sense of sin. In the negative sense, sin is a "breaking away"—a turning away from what has already been joined together, as in breaking a promise or a pact. This negative sense appears to be in conflict with the positive agency of defilement as a "breaking in" in the form of an encroachment on an existing order. However, this contrast turns out to be too simple as Ricoeur argues that "here again, it was easy to recognize a survival of the system of defilement and of the theme of '*possession*' that belongs to that system.... What assures the continuity from one type to the other is the consciousness of alteration, of alienation, which is common to the two types" (1969: 86).

The continuity between the types of sin Ricoeur discusses centers on the theme of "possession" or alteration by alienation — an alienation achieved through the appropriative power of a wholly alien other. An implicit awareness or consciousness of this possession and alienation belongs, according to Ricoeur, to all his previously catalogued types of sin. He then identifies the quality of the substance of this consciousness as "maleficent." In the sacred texts of both the East and West this maleficent substance or alien consciousness is "dramatized in the shape of demons or evil gods" or "quasi-personal forces of a demonic character" that through the action of sin "literally take up their abode in the sinner" (86).

This alienation parallels the "transubstantiation in reverse" mentioned in Chapter 3 whereby instead of the entrance of a higher deity into the body through partaking, for example, of the body and blood of Christ, a demonic force enters and "takes up abode" in the body — a body first made weak and vulnerable through prior smaller entrances of defilement in the form of sins.

This treatment of sin leads Ricoeur to obvious metaphorical connections and parallels between the physical and the spiritual and between sickness and guilt. Here the confusion between sin and sickness supports not only a type of dualism between the soul and the body but also "the dualism of a moral agent, author of moral evil, and a course of events that brings sickness, suffering, and death ... and invasion by an evil demon" (86–87). The theme of dualism brings the discussion back to Adam in the Garden of Eden where, as "moral agent," Adam becomes the "author of moral evil" but must nevertheless be clearly distinguished from the source and agency of the evil that passes into him by "invasion." This dualism between invasive contamination and moral agent structures not only the drama of the myth of creation but also the drama of salvation enacted in churches and theaters through many centuries of Western tradition.

In Judeo-Christian theology the dominant concept of evil conforms to the positive sense of defilement as an active, corrupting agency. This agency of defilement is personified in the being of Satan as the eternally opposing archenemy of Christ and God and all that is good. According to its traditional Hebrew meaning as "one who opposes" in the sense of "plotting against" for the purpose of doing harm, the word "Satan" evokes the positive sense of evil as an actively destructive agency.

Defilement in Hellenic Tradition

While the conjunction of corruption and evil in the theme of defilement clearly permeates biblical texts, it is also evident, Ricoeur argues, in texts from the Greek side of the Western tradition. Choosing to give primary attention to the traces of defilement in the cosmology implicit in the stories recounted by Hesiod and in the Orphic mythology, Ricoeur mentions only in passing a particular theme of defilement expressed in Plato's dialogues, most notably in *The Republic*. However, this thread of the tradition is significant for its contribution in the direction of a more philosophically, as opposed to mythologically, styled treatment.

For example, in Book X of *The Republic* Plato asserts, "That which destroys and corrupts in every case is the evil, that which preserves and benefits is the good." He goes on to point out that everything has its special evil, its particular variant of corrupting agency: "for the eyes ophthalmia, for the entire body disease, for grain mildew, rotting for wood, rust for bronze and iron, and, as I say, for practically everything its congenital evil" (608e–609a).

Furthermore, the corrupting agency has the power, through its incursions, to transform the host into a corrupting and finally corrupted agency: "when one of these evils comes to anything does it not make the thing to which it attaches itself bad, and finally disintegrate and destroy it?" (609a).

Consistent with his analysis of evil as essentially a corruption, Plato argues in Book II of *The Republic* that insofar as a supreme deity such as God is conceived to be good then such a God cannot also be the *source* of evil, harm, or corruption since the good, by definition, cannot be a corrupting agency. Plato concludes: "For the good we must assume no other cause than God, but the cause of evil we must look for in other things and not in God" (379c).

This argument reveals one of the reasons why Plato opposes philosophy to poetry (which during his time, of course, drew significantly on mythology). The poets make contrary and apparently illogical assertions when they say such things as the following, which Plato attributes to Homer: "Zeus is dispenser alike of good and evil to mortals" (379e). Plato proceeds to explain that by including "dispenser ... of evil" among Zeus's powers Homer does not merely mean to be saying that Zeus is the "chastiser of the wicked." Rather, Homer intends that Zeus be understood as a "dispenser of evil" in the broadest sense, as the source of all harm and destruction even to those who do not deserve such calamities or beyond what may be deserved.

It is clear from Plato's analysis in *The Republic* that the notion of evil and the notion of a supreme deity as wholly and essentially good do not belong together — and they certainly do not share the same origin. Laws of logic preclude that that which is wholly and essentially good can also be the source of the opposite of what is good.

In light of Platonic texts concerning the origin and nature of the good, it is difficult to say whether a monotheistic concept of God as pure goodness gives the decisive impetus to the dominance of the contrasting notion of evil as defilement or whether an older notion of defilement serves as fertile ground for the creation and dominance of the contrasting monotheistic concept of God. Nevertheless, both the Bible and the texts of Plato support the notion that a monotheistic concept of God as pure and essential goodness requires a notion of evil as an invasive and inessential contaminant. This resolution of the problem of evil results in an ambiguous and confusing metaphysical posture in which a monotheistic concept of God requires a corresponding notion of radically antagonistic cosmological dualism.

Altogether, the biblical and Platonic traditions of the origin of evil may be seen as consistently pointing toward one informing and controlling metaphor through which the nature and "logic" of evil is understood — namely defilement. And from this understanding the tensions and conflicts of awakening sexuality and courtship are also often fundamentally organized and understood. In the case of the Adamic myth, for example, the story superimposes the moral structure of good and evil over the human conflict structures — imparting a highly polarized and value-weighted orientation to every instance of conflict (whether inner or outer).

From Genesis to Melodrama

The tradition from the Adamic myth to the horror story and contemporary melodrama is a tradition that presents a solution to the problem of evil in the world that is also the model for the solution to the troubles of "yielding," "rejection," "unworthiness," "failure," and "sin" arising through conflict. The nature of evil in weakness and in every other manifestation is understood to be an intrusive agency of contamination in an otherwise perfect environment. And the path to purification is found in reversing the dramatic course of events in the Adamic myth.

Strictly speaking, Adam is a failure: a hero who instead of rescuing the damsel, Eve, from the dangers lurking in the malevolent intentions of the villain — the Serpent — succumbs to the Serpent's designs and thereby brings misery and mortality on himself, Eve, and his progeny. This unhappy ending sets up the need for "sequels" that will restore hope and harmony to the human saga by offering a means of redemption to future heroes, the surrogates of Adam.

Although the Adamic myth does not portray Adam entering into direct conflict with the Serpent, the necessity for such conflict among Adam's surrogates, as a "casting away of the Serpent," becomes a major theme in future variations and reenactments of the myth as religious, moral, and courtship traditions demand a better performance from the Adam character. These reenactments can be understood as melodramatic variations of a quasi-courtship ritual where the Adam character is portrayed as successful, as entering into direct opposition with the Serpent — ultimately expelling or destroying the Serpent as the archetypal pollution.

Lord of the Rings, for example, is a popular contemporary retelling of themes surrounding the Adamic myth. The viperish Gollum, the Serpent — who is merely the tool of a corrupting and malignant evil — persistently tempts Frodo Baggins, the Adam character. The power of an evil ring must be destroyed — a goal that can be accomplished only through the destruction of the ring. Like the apple in the Garden of Eden, the ring serves as a material symbol of the temptations of evil in worldly attractions. For further discussion of *Lord of the Rings*, see Chapter 21.

Abjection: Death as Ultimate Reality

Ricoeur's assessment of the significance of the metaphor of defilement at work in the deepest layers of Western symbolism and myth receives thorough corroboration in Julia Kristeva's *Powers of Horror*. However, Kristeva does not discuss an alternative to the metaphor of defilement grounded in tragic myth and drama and included in Ricoeur's analysis — which is discussed in the next chapter. Nevertheless, it will be useful to briefly characterize Kristeva's work on horror and its similarities and differences with the current thread of argument because her views provide an exceptional way of introducing the missing alternative.

Kristeva's understanding of horror is consistent with psychoanalytical themes already discussed and is similarly rooted in the imperatives of narcissism — the need to protect an imagined whole and healthy identity from the incursions of alien otherness. Consistent with postmodern conclusions about the deceptiveness of boundaries between subject and object, Kristeva argues that attempts to protect the ego/subject from contamination are rooted in forms of denial. By way of the Doppelgänger device, the ego unconsciously attempts to preserve its integrity by separating itself

Portrait of abjection, the Coat of Arms of Death (Hans Holbein's Dance of Death series, 1538) (from the book *Hans Holbein the Younger, His Old Testament Illustrations, Dance of Death, and Other Woodcuts* compiled by Arthur Mayger Hind. 1912. New York: Fredk. A Stokes Company Publishers).

from influences and effects its views to be both entirely other and entirely threatening and disintegrating. The body attempts to conceal from itself the fact that as soon as it comes into being it is engaged in a struggle with forces of decay—a struggle that it will eventually lose. In this sense the ego, the subject, the body—as bounded forms—are never securely bounded at all but are instead regions of strife in a shifting give and take between life and death.

For Kristeva the forces of negation depicted in the horror genre (whether text or film) represent more than merely a disturbance that might be explained as lack or absence but are in fact the work of decay, of a positively active agency of destruction she refers to as the "abject." Her notion of the abject fits well with Ricoeur's account of defilement and its role as the predominant meaning in the tradition of evil. Comprising everything signaling the radical negation of life, the abject — as Kristeva recounts it — includes images and signs of death from the corpse to all forms of decomposition ranging from mutilation, putrefaction, and excrement to spilled blood, bile, and every other loathsome graphic evidence of sickness, rot, and defilement. From the point of view of Kristeva's dark vision, Twitchell's notion of horror as grounded in unruly sexual desires appears breezily lighthearted.

Kristeva's vision coincides perfectly with the dark tradition of evil as radical negation, as the corrupting alien intrusion of defilement into the good of a harmonious whole. As already suggested, this structure of radical antagonistic polarity is readily superimposed over the fractures and conflict structures emerging with the challenges confronted by the maturing ego— especially with regard to the demands of sexual development and attraction. When superimposed over these conflict structures, this radical partitioning exposes the darker truth around which life precariously quivers— the horror that life is a creeping death or, more precisely, a living hell.

In the view proposed by Kristeva, life is presented as a "whole" that, ideally, could flourish alone and without the intrusion of death. Life and death are locked in the antagonistic relation of mutual negation — in which, because life never achieves "immortality," death is the ultimate reality. In Kristeva's view, therefore, horror offers the supreme fascination by stripping away every vestige of, every hiding place for, every indulgence in, innocence. This immersion in negation and destruction is shocking, exhilarating, and ironically empowering in its stark confrontation with the "truth" of existence.

However, Kristeva's understanding of the structure of oppositional tension does not necessarily present the truth of existence or the truth of the agon between life and death. Although her excavation of the theme of horror is broadly consistent with Ricoeur's analysis of evil as defilement, Kristeva's analysis is too narrowly conclusive in its privileging of the reality and finality of death over life. An irony inheres in her postmodern analysis of horror insofar as its critique of dualities is not sufficiently postmodern. While acknowledging in her explanation of horror a superficial motif of postmodernism — namely that the boundaries between dualities such as life and death and subject and object interpenetrate and are therefore not rigid and secure — as provided in classical schemes — Kristeva ultimately fails to adhere to the most crucial postmodern theme regarding dualism: that the tension between opposites does *not* at bottom consist of radical and essential antagonism.

Life and death may more justifiably be viewed as locked in an inseparable exchange of essential reliance and relation even while remaining essentially different and separate from each other. To understand this view it is only necessary to imagine what life would be like on earth if such processes as death and decay did not make way for the continuing entrance of new life. When seen as essential to life, death cannot be understood as exclusively and essentially defiling or corrupting of life. In Kristeva's view, death and decay are portrayed as forms of defilement and corruption of life and in this capacity serve as metaphors for evil in a dualism that is effectively one of radical antagonism.

This speculation about the structure of oppositional relation bears relevance to the discussion of horror by introducing the possibility of imposing an alternative structure on the oppositions and conflicts dramatized in the horror story. The emergence of an alternative oppositional or conflict structure exposes the potential for an alternative relational tension and raises the question: What choices are being offered in the dramatic design of the horror story, why are they being made, and what are the consequences? But the nature and quality of these choices cannot be fully weighed and appreciated apart from the presentation in more concrete detail of the contrast that has so far only been hinted at and abstractly drawn at the beginning of the discussion of the origin of evil in Chapter 4. After presenting this contrast it will then be possible to draw together the analysis and arrive at conclusions about the potential effects of depictions of violence in relation to the horror story and melodramatic form in general.

6

Tragic Myth and
the Origin of Evil

The structure of tragic drama made famous by the Greek tragedians presents an alternative orientation to opposing sides in a conflict and to oppositional relation in general that in itself does not originate with the Greeks nor does it end with the Greeks. This structure is as ancient as the antagonistic conflict structure of good and evil that is fundamental to melodrama. Tragedy offers an orientation toward conflict in sharp contrast to melodrama and through this contrast it becomes possible to understand more clearly the nature of the effects that can be achieved through each structure and the significance of these effects in relation to the depiction of violence.

In his landmark work *Tragedy and Melodrama*, Professor of English Robert Heilman claims that these two dramatic styles are significant not merely as art forms but more important as also "versions of experience." Heilman asserts, "Tragedy is a specific form of experience that needs to be differentiated from all other catastrophic disturbances of life." In Heilman's view, the essence of tragic experience centers on a *divided* character. More specifically, "There is a pulling apart within the personality, a disturbance, though not a pathological one, of integration" (1968: 7). The nature of this nonpathological disturbance of integration comes to a head in the tension between " 'conflicting 'values' with 'authentic claims': here indeed is a primary source of 'genuine tragic tension' " (9). In other words, a tragic confrontation involves conflict in which values or factions rightly claim a fundamental measure of legitimacy or inclusion.

In melodrama, by contrast, Heilman argues that the main protagonist is essentially "whole." He notes that "this key word implies neither greatness nor moral perfection, but rather an absence of the basic inner conflict that, if it is present, must inevitably claim ... primary attention." As a consequence, the hero in melodrama is "not troubled by motives that would distract him from the outer struggle in which he is engaged." By way of summarizing the differences between these two forms, then, Heilman concludes, "In tragedy the conflict is within man; in melodrama, it is between men, or between men and things" (79).

Heilman's view of melodrama seems, at first glance, to be the reverse of what has been proposed thus far. His description of tragic drama, with the emphasis on inner division, appears to coincide with the divided self and the Doppelgänger motif argued to be central to the horror story, which is a subgenre of melodrama. A closer look at the structure of tragic drama, however, reveals that this discrepancy results from what is merely a superficial similarity between tragic drama and the horror story.

The significance of the differences between the horror story — as an instance of melodrama — and tragic drama can be more fully appreciated against the background of explanation and analysis provided by one of the first and most compelling commentators on tragedy: Aristotle. Aristotle's analysis of tragic drama in his *Poetics* is important to review because of the way in which it weaves together the *structure* of tragedy with the *effects* of tragedy on an audience. While concluding the presentation of themes relating to the myths of the origin of evil, this chapter and following chapters explore in growing detail the relationship between structure and effects along with differences of structure and effects between tragic drama and melodrama.

The Plot: Changes in Fortune

Aristotle explains tragic drama as most significantly an imitation not of persons but of action and life — that is, it is a particular combination or convergence of incidents and actions. Consequently, according to Aristotle's analysis, "the action in it, i.e., its plot ... is the end and purpose of the tragedy; and the end is everywhere the chief thing" (1450a). This statement must be read keeping in mind Aristotle's definition of tragedy where he notes that tragic drama is not just any combination of actions and incidents but is specifically the "imitation of an action" with "incidents arousing pity and fear."

Of the two Greek words *eleos* and *phobos*, loosely translated as "pity" and "fear," "pity" is the most misleading translation. No adequate English equivalent exists but Walter Kaufmann's choice of the archaic word "ruth" at least avoids the overly sentimental tone of "pity" and thereby improves the chances of imparting the tone of the Greek *eleos*. This tone corresponds, approximately, to the sharing of another's profound grief arising from misfortunes uncannily disproportionate to actions, intentions, and circumstances. Tragic *phobos* is also not adequately translated as "fear." *Phobos* used in connection with tragic drama is closer to a strong sense of "heedful awe" arising from an especially powerful insight into the dangerous complexity of life made evident through the unfolding of the tragic plot. In the commentary and translations that follow, the word "ruth" is consistently substituted for the word "pity" when used in reference to emotions aroused by tragic drama. Similarly, in these same contexts the word "awe" is substituted for the word "fear."

Because Aristotle equates action in the drama with the plot, the plot becomes "the chief thing" insofar as the arousal of ruth and awe depend on its construction — as does the overall quality of the drama. Whatever rewarding effects may be generated, whatever artistic currency and value a tragic drama may have, derive directly from the nature and quality of the plot. Accepting as much, Aristotle's examination and critique of plot structure deserves central attention in understanding the unique merits distinguishing tragic drama from other genres.

In the course of defining the plot structure peculiar to tragic drama, Aristotle turns his attention first to those forms of plot that must be avoided. These include the circumstance whereby a good man passes from good fortune to bad and also that whereby a bad man passes from bad fortune to good. The test for ruling out these choices turns on their inability to arouse the relevant emotions. These structures are clearly unable, Aristotle argues, to inspire awe or ruth. The first instance may arouse an emotion close to the English word "pity" but does not arouse ruth and both instances are more likely experienced, Aristotle says, as "simply odious" (1452b).

A third kind of plot wherein an extremely bad man is seen falling from good fortune to bad is also not appropriate to tragic drama for similar reasons. Aristotle concludes that the action in tragic drama must center on a specific type of reversal of fortune for a character through whom the audience may see themselves.

> pity [ruth] is occasioned by undeserved misfortune, and fear [awe] by that of one like ourselves.... The perfect plot, accordingly, must have a ... change in the subject's fortunes ... from good to bad; and the cause of it must lie not in any depravity, but in some great fault on his part; the man himself being either such as we have described, or better, not worse, than that [1453a].

Aristotle elaborates further, adding that the central protagonist must be an "intermediate" kind of person not "preeminently virtuous" but endowed with character of sufficient strength and nobility to win a measure of admiration and identification on the part of the audience. A reversal of fortune in the life of this person, precipitated by a "great fault," arouses the desired emotional response in the audience and thereby constitutes "the perfect plot."

Here it is important to emphasize that Aristotle's use of the expression "great fault" should not be understood as a kind of "sin of commission" or a failure as a result of weakness of character. Instead the "fault" must be understood as a given. Every human being is born with a fault or faults insofar as everyone falls short of omniscience, omnipotence, and godlike perfection. In this sense to be human means to fall short, to have faults of one sort or another. The hero in a tragic drama may have many human faults but, for purposes of the drama, will have at least one fault that may at first appear predominantly as a strength but that nevertheless becomes especially defining and prominent in the course of events leading to catastrophe.

At this point a question may well arise about the aim and purpose of tragic drama: Why is it so important that the audience be moved to feel ruth for the chief protagonist or protagonists? Why prefer moving an audience to feel ruth for the hero instead of constructing a drama whereby the audience is moved to *rejoice* with the hero? The beginning of an answer to this question lies in the particular orientation and varied sensibility the Greeks had toward conflict, especially forms of violent conflict.

The Tragic Vision and Its Version of Conflict

Thus far in his description of the perfect plot, Aristotle has not yet made reference to the structure of the conflict that governs the action leading to the tragic events. Clearly the tragic plot must have a tragic deed and, in Aristotle's words, the tragic deed is "murder or the like." A slaying or an action just short of a slaying is, of course, the consequence of an extreme conflict. The tragic hero's fall from good fortune to bad fortune transpires, therefore, through violent or near violent conflict and such conflict becomes a further defining feature of the tragic plot.

Aristotle describes the structure of the conflict framing the deadly violence in the following passage where he begins by noting that there are necessarily three general categories or possibilities. Making reference to the tragic deed, he excludes two of the three possibilities: "Now when enemy does it on enemy, there is nothing to move us to pity [ruth] either in his doing or in his meditating the deed, except so far as the actual pain of the sufferer is concerned; and the same is true when the parties are indifferent to one another" (1453b).

These exclusions leave but one possibility and that is the type of conflict of greatest interest to the tragic poets. "Whenever the tragic deed, however, is done among friends—when murder or the like is done or meditated by brother on brother, by son on father, by mother on son, or son on mother — these are the situations the poet should seek after." (1453b).

Aristotle identifies conflict between "friends"—of which conflict among family members is the most intense variety — as the situation tragic poets seek out because such conflicts arouse the greatest response of ruth and awe. These situations therefore represent the essential and defining structure of conflict that lies at the core of all tragic drama.

Because, as Aristotle has previously indicated, "pity [ruth] is occasioned by undeserved misfortune" (better translated as "disproportionate misfortune" since it is not entirely undeserved) and awe is occasioned when such misfortune befalls someone "like ourselves," the interest in creating tragic drama — in arousing ruth and awe — is a consequence of the interest in the kind of conflict that produces a palpable sense of disproportionate misfortune to those like ourselves.

The possibility that such misfortune can befall those like ourselves was, for the Greeks, a profoundly disturbing but seemingly unavoidable revelation concerning an essential quality of life — the way in which "the world" often appears fundamentally indifferent and even inhospitable to human existence. In this respect Greek tragic drama, from the point of view of the Greeks of the time, imitates life insofar as it is an expression of the tragic vision of life.

This tragic vision colors the entire spectrum of life for the Greeks but emerges most poignantly and prominently in conflicts between "friends." Misfortune resulting from such conflict — usually involving someone's death or near death — arises not by way of an alien evil but from where it is least expected: the friend or blood relation. The fidelities of relation and the distancing emotions generated by the conflict pull in opposite directions. The relational bond symbolizes the elements of complexity in all conflict as it severely complicates the featured conflict in a way that minimizes tendencies toward radical moral polarization into good and evil sides.

In tragic drama the sources of conflict and violence are carefully depicted in ways that ensure these sources will not be understood as alien. Conflict *within* the tragic hero mirrors the complexity of the relational or external conflict the hero confronts. The flaw in the tragic hero that contributes to his or her downfall is not an acquired flaw or a result of an encounter with some form of contamination. Instead, the flaw is an essential part of being and character without which the hero would no longer be uniquely human. The extent to which a dose of the celebrated Greek affliction of "divine madness" may be seen to exacerbate such a flaw serves only to underscore the symmetry between the conflicted spheres of the human and the divine. As will be expanded on below, neither of these spheres is clearly split by radically antagonistic sources of good and evil.

Similarly, the persons with whom the hero enters into conflict are selected and depicted in a way that will effectively eliminate the tendency to view them as entirely alien. By entering into conflict with friends or blood relatives, the hero has taken on adversaries who are as much from the hero's inner circle of familiar and bonded relation as would be possible. The choices on the part of the poet in the construction of plot, character, and conflict are deliberately designed to deepen the complexity of the conflict, in both its internal and external aspects, and work against tendencies, evident in melodramatic structure, toward radical emotional and moral polarization.

The difficulty in applying value-weighted radical polarization to the conflict holds true for the audience as well as for the tragically fated characters. In the conflict between friends, audience members are unable to easily side with one or the other and are thereby brought to identify in some measure with both sides. This nonpartisan identification with both sides of the conflict on the part of the audience corresponds to what analysts refer to as the "dramatic irony" of tragic drama. Initial identification with the tragic hero evolves into the broader compass of dramatic irony as the audience understands that the hero is not entirely right and does not grasp the situation completely.

This type of conflict serves the ends of the poet through arousal of the emotional effects of awe and ruth that function to emphasize the tragic insight into life — which is itself embodied in the conflict. In other words, the plot, as Aristotle initially states, is the end. But the core of the plot is the conflict and the conflict illustrates a truth about life. And this "truth" about life suggests an attitude toward conflict that recommends appreciation for its complex and sometimes inscrutable nature.

At this point, however, a qualification may be introduced concerning Aristotle's listing of the "enemy on enemy" kind of conflict as inappropriate for tragic drama. The Greek appreciation for the complexity of conflict in general is reflected in the fascination for conflicts that consist of a clash between two powerful wills that at the inception of the conflict each have a kind of legitimacy. In the course of the conflict this mutual legitimacy spirals into deadly confrontation through peculiarities of circumstance and partial blindness induced by human flaws. The Greeks understood this kind of conflict to be especially but not exclusively exemplified in conflicts among family, friends, and lovers or former lovers—as in the case of the love triangle complications played out in Homer's epic poem on the Trojan War. They also understood the sense in which *all* conflict, even conflict between deadly enemies, is characterized by complexity and scrutable and inscrutable measures of injustice.

As an example of conflict between enemies, *The Persians* is one of Aeschylus's most famous and controversial tragedies because it is based on the historical event of the second war between Persia and Greece and features the Persians and their king Xerxes in the role of the "tragic heroes." Considering the fact that this war was fought on Greek land and sea and inflicted enormous carnage and suffering on Greek citizens, Aeschylus would seem to have sufficient motivation to portray the conflict in starkly melodramatic terms.

By choosing instead to elicit ruth and awe by promoting identification with the Persians and the catastrophic loss that befalls mighty Xerxes and his overwhelming land and naval forces, Aeschylus exposes the extent to which fate defies odds and plays no favorites among the privileged and the strong in dealing hard lessons and humbling ruin. And while the tyrant Xerxes may be thought deserving of his suffering, Aeschylus does not press this point in his dramatic design but instead powerfully evokes the question: What catastrophe of birth and rearing brings a man to regal heights while also preparing the way for his and his kingdom's utter ruin? How and why is such a thing possible? By encouraging identification with the Persian side, Aeschylus presents a perspective among the victors rarely encountered in the annals of history and thereby immortalizes the breadth and complexity of the orientation toward conflict implicit in the Greek tragic vision of life.

As Above, So Below

The tragedy in tragic drama resides in the perception of the measure of injustice in what befalls the characters. No one seems to get what they deserve as inequities abound on all sides—especially in the case of the tragic hero. Insofar as the audience is led to comprehend a measure of merit on each side of the conflict, alignment quandaries develop, which the tragic poets often dramatize by revealing the support and additional motivation provided by sympathetic gods. In the case of Aeschylus's *The Persians* the Persian people are not without their gods in the heavens.

Although it may be argued that the point at which conflict turns to violence in tragic drama is reached through what the ancient Greeks may have understood as the influence of a god and the visitation of a destructive "divine madness" on the conflicting parties, the *daimon* of such madness corresponds to a significantly different structure of godhead than the *demon* associated with possession by a spirit of evil. Within the Greek pantheon, none of the Greek gods or daimons are understood to be essentially or exclusively evil. In this respect the Greek heavens bear out the famous saying "as above, so below" and also the inverse "as below, so above."

The last play of Aeschylus's *Oresteia* trilogy, the *Eumenides*, also illustrates the point. Apollo (the god of truth) comes to the aid of Orestes (the slayer of his stepfather, Aegisthus, and his mother, Clytemnestra) while the Erinyes (godlike enforcers of retributive justice) press the case for the ghost of Clytemnestra (slayer of her husband and Orestes' father, Agamemnon). The human conflict is broadened and deepened by way of the symmetrical conflict taking place in the heavenly sphere. In the words of the noted authority on tragic drama, H. D. F. Kitto, "a civil war in heaven" exists between the younger Olympian gods represented by Apollo and the

Orestes slaying Aegisthus, with Clytemnestra threatening (left) and Electra warning (right); image from a Greek vase (from the picture book *Bilderhefte aus dem Griechischen und Romischen Altertum. Sagenkreis des Trojanischen Krieges. A Baumeister. 1889. Munchen: Druck und Verlag von R. Oldenbourg*).

Elder Deities represented by the Erinyes. This civil war extends all the way through the Greek heavens and is embodied in the person of Zeus about whom the chorus in the *Eumenides* says in reference to the conflict (a rephrasing of Homer's expression): "through Zeus, who is the cause of all things" (90).

Given the conflict dividing heaven and earth, Zeus, as "the cause of all things," becomes a symbol of a divided cosmos within which injustice seems inevitable. But this injustice does not arise through the polarized conflict of good against evil. The conflict between Orestes and Clytemnestra, between son and mother, reflects competing claims for justice that are each grounded in legitimate but simplistic desires for justice. Even though the Erinyes, as Kitto acknowledges, are depicted in the drama in ways that "may well remind us of Satan and his hellish crew," their fearsome appearance is clearly intended to indicate not malevolent motives but the unyielding demand for retributive justice in recompense for Orestes' crime of matricide — which was itself motivated by retributive justice.

The bitter conflict that extends from humans to the divine stage and back again with its competing claims appears to be, in its destructive power, a cause for lasting despair and resignation and a confirmation of the futility of life in the face of a cosmic design sufficiently inhospitable to permit gross injustice. But the divine and the human have motivational resources that exceed the call for one type of justice: retributive justice. In consideration of these resources the complexity of the conflict increases once again. In the *Eumenides* these resources are represented by Athena and the human members of the "jury" designated to serve in a crucial evaluative capacity to weigh the claims of the two sides of the conflict.

The trial in the *Eumenides*, with its explicit appeal to reason as intervention in the case of conflict, has lent support to the contention that Aeschylus created drama that was *not* essentially tragic. Walter Kaufmann explains that Aeschylus "alone had the sublime confidence that by rightly employing their reason men could avoid catastrophes. His world view was, by modern standards, anti-tragic, and yet he created tragedy" (1968: 193).

However, contrary to Kaufmann's claim, Aeschylus's view is not anti-tragic. The trial in the *Eumenides*, for example, does not serve to undermine the tragic vision of life — the view that the world is at bottom indifferent, inhospitable, or confounding to human aspirations. Rather, it serves to advance the modest claim that human effort and reason can potentially mitigate the ravages of bitter conflicts that *inevitably* arise in human community. The split vote among the eleven jurors and Athena reinforces the notion that there is no clear resolution to be hoped for by way of a sympathetic tipping of the tension of retributive forces in favor of communal well-being. Whatever hospitality the world may offer must come through fragile and contingent human intervention — spiritually inspired (symbolized by Athena) and humanly implemented and enforced (symbolized by the jury).

Keeping with the symmetry of earth and heaven, the same struggle continues to play out among the gods. But this struggle is not fundamentally a war of good against evil but rather a shifting competition between forces brought into conflict through the interaction of multiple wills and desires — all of which have contexts of legitimacy of assertion and expression.

Returning again to Ricoeur's work and the mystery of the origin of evil, Ricoeur argues that the tragic vision of life expressed in the dramas of the tragic poets contains an implicit theme he describes as corresponding to the theology of the "wicked god." The misfortune that occurs, for example, in *The Persians* and the *Eumenides* all transpires through the will of Zeus. Speaking of the work of Aeschylus in particular, Ricoeur states that "with the figure of Zeus the movement tending to incorporate the diffused satanism of the ... [fates] into the undivided unity of the divine and the satanic reaches its highest pitch. All the lines of tragic theology converge upon this figure of the wicked Zeus, which is already adumbrated in *The Persians*" (1969: 218).

In a similar vein, George Steiner, in his study of tragic drama entitled *The Death of Tragedy*, refers to "the vengeful spite and injustice of the gods" as evidenced in the fateful and often fatal disasters befalling the heroes in tragic drama. Steiner goes so far as to declare that the human estrangement evidenced in tragic dramas emerges from a hostile world "resulting from a malignancy and daemonic negation in the very fabric of things (the enmity of the gods)" (1980: xi).

The notion of the "vengeful" or "wicked" god, however, is potentially misleading in relation to tragic drama. The godhead in which, as Ricoeur states, the divine and the satanic are an "undivided unity" is a godhead in which what is traditionally referred to as good and evil are *equiprimordial* — of simultaneous and equal origin. In such a case the traditional distinction between good and evil must collapse as neither can be seen as essentially polluting of a prior "whole" since both are of equal status in their simultaneous origin.

In another passage Ricoeur is clearer in his description of this situation when he notes that this ambiguous god appears in many contexts and that it "tends toward the tragic when such a polarization [of demonic and divine] does *not* occur and when the *same* divine power appears *both* as a source of good counsel *and* as a power to lead man astray. Thus the nondistinction between the divine and the diabolical is *the implicit theme of the tragic theology and anthropology*" (1969: 213–214, emphasis added).

Such a theology of nondistinction in origin between the divine and the diabolical implies an altogether different tension between what is called good and evil. The hierarchical dualism of what was thought to be evil befalling a prior and original goodness is displaced in the "wicked" god myth by an "evil" or "wickedness" that is of equal origin — indeed the same origin — with goodness. The hierarchy is thereby thrown into confusion, for if "evil" is also of divine origin, then the status of evil as a corrupting intrusion must be rethought. Myths of origin that reflect this equiprimordiality present binary differences as *synagonistic* (different, but mutually inclusive) rather than *antagonistic* (different, but mutually exclusive) oppositions.

The myth of the wicked god ultimately presents the godhead as a duality comprised at the origin of qualities that are essentially different (such as male and female) but that are not hierarchically arranged and radically opposed as in the case of good and evil. In this cosmology, good and evil reflect contingent judgments, not primary qualities. The original difference — through the extremes and constraints of particular contexts — gives rise to the potential for good or evil effects.

From the Greek perspective, for example, success (and the ambition that leads to it) is not in itself an evil but in certain contexts of power and adulation it can exert an evil influence and lead to an instance of what the ancient Greeks called *hybris*. And hybris can contribute to a lack or an excess or a form of blindness that then plays into the hands of misfortune and further evil.

In this context of contingency deriving from the "wicked god" cosmology — or what has just been proposed as an instance of a divided godhead cosmology — the word "evil" and its associated metaphor of defilement can be reinterpreted in a moderate sense that must be distinguished from the more radical sense derived from the cosmology of the godhead of whole and original goodness. In the moderate sense that which corrupts is an agency in itself neutral or benign that, when lacking entirely, accumulating to excess, or occurring in the wrong place, becomes harmful. In the radical sense, on the other hand, that which corrupts is an agency wholly alien and thereby essentially and actively destructive, having no proper place anywhere.

The divided godhead cosmology and its approach to understanding the contingent opposition between good and evil leads to a worldview that postulates that there is no primordially essential evil force or agency operative in the world. Misfortune, injustice, cruelty, and catastrophe result from a contingent contextual convergence of factors that individually and separately have no basis in a supernatural, nonhuman, or alien essence of evil (in the sense of defilement).

At this point it should be added that such a worldview does not provide the basis for assuming that persons need not be held accountable for actions. Instead it provides a basis for understanding that, while an element of blindness is inescapable in human thought and action, insight regarding the reality and the dangers of that potential for blindness is also readily evident and available to every person. And while awareness of the possibility of blindness may not prevent catastrophe, the extent to which the capacity for blindness has been appreciated and factored into a person's actions must figure prominently in assessing culpable contribution to ensuing catastrophes. The other side of the Greek preoccupation with hybris lies in the implied necessity for multiple forms of strength in humility. Chapter 14 explores further the extent to which it may be reasonable or advisable to adopt in a practical sense the view implied in the tragic myth of origin and the tragic vision, or "version" as Heilman suggests, of life experience.

Tragic Vision versus Despair

A further point should also be made concerning the "tragic vision" of conflict. It would be a significant misunderstanding of tragic drama to regard the vantage of its bearing on life and conflict as consistent with a pessimistic outlook on life. The idea that the world is arranged in ways not essentially hospitable to human existence need not mean that fates and fortunes must inevitably go badly or that fortunes are thoroughly arbitrary and that there is therefore no point in trying to make a good life. An ever-present potential for error, pain, and disaster along with the inevitability of conflict are not sufficient conditions in themselves to always guarantee iniquity or catastrophe. In a passage that must be quoted at length, Walter Kaufmann is eloquent as well as accurate in explaining that tragic vision is consistent with strong optimism.

> [T]ragedy is generally more optimistic than comedy. It is profound despair that leads most of the generation born during and after World War II to feel that tragedy is dated; they prefer comedy, whether black or not. Tragedy is inspired by a faith that can weather the plague, whether in Sophoclean Athens or in Elizabethan London, but not Auschwitz. It is compatible with the great victories of Marathon and Salamis that marked the threshold of the Aeschylean age, and with the triumph over

the Armada that inaugurated Shakespeare's era. It is not concordant with
Dresden, Hiroshima, and Nagasaki. Tragedy depends on sympathy, ruth,
and involvement. It has little appeal for a generation that, like Ivan Kara-
mazov, would gladly return the ticket to God, if there were [for him] a
god. Neither in Athens nor in our time has tragedy perished of optimism: its sickness unto death was and is despair [1968: 194].

In Kaufmann's view, tragedy arguably requires more forbearance and
presupposes more optimism on the part of an audience than do certain
types of comedy such as black comedy, Juvenalian satire, and burlesque.
These varieties of humor impose radical moral and evaluative polarizations similar to the dualism of good and evil, identifying "pollution" by
way of derisive and alienating forms of humiliation, caricature, ridicule,
and sarcasm. In addition to the ascendancy of this type of comedy among
the post–World War II generations, it must be added that there is also an
equal if not greater preference for melodrama — and especially for modern and postmodern "noir" melodrama along with the more contemporary era of horror films discussed in Chapter 19.

Kaufmann's comment that tragedy depends on "sympathy, ruth, and
involvement" provides a point of return to Aristotle. Aristotle's claim that
tragedy is best framed in the conflict between friends is consistent with
eliciting maximum emotional involvement on the part of an audience for
both sides of the conflict. The Greek capacity for extending this involvement and sympathy even to the conflict between enemies is evident not
only in Aeschylus's *The Persians* but also in Homer's account of the Trojan War.

The unusual capacity among the Greeks for involvement in the perspective of the other side of a conflict is compatible with and perhaps
reflected in a famous saying that dates to classical Greece: "Every stranger
conceals a god." The Olympic games founded by the Greeks exemplify this
spirit in the related attitude of respect for the opponent in the sporting
competition as part of the spectacle of entertainment — an attitude, however, that admittedly was not always evident, if written accounts can be
believed, among the competitors in the ancient games. This attitude
became less and less evident as the violence in competition escalated, culminating in the melodramatically staged Roman gladiatorial contests.

7

Alternative Applications
of Greek Mythic Tradition

The discussion from Chapter 1 to this point has led to the marking off of a significant difference in attitudes toward conflict between the genres of tragedy and melodrama — a difference that is rooted deeply enough in dual strands of tradition to trace all the way to cosmological myths of origin. Although this difference in attitudes toward conflict is illustrated through myths belonging to Greek and Judeo-Christian cultural traditions, the difference does not describe an essential difference between Greek and Judeo-Christian cultures. Both of these cultural traditions remain open to a variety of interpretations through a variety of mythic stories and these traditions also exist alongside other powerful cultural influences. Nevertheless, there is considerable agreement among cultural analysts and critics about the mode of structuring conflict that habitually dominates Western cultures. Additional views on this way of structuring conflict reveal some of the differences of opinion about its origin as well as differences about appropriate responses to it. These differences prepare the way for a broader understanding of the conclusions arrived at in Chapters 8 through 11.

The "Werewolf Complex"

The French scholar Denis Duclos, for example, finds the dominant structure in Northern countries to be one of radical polarization of good and evil, but he traces the roots of this cultural trend to the influence of the Nordic warrior-myth tradition. However, he readily admits the presence of overlapping and reinforcing traditions: "The Nordic myth of the mad warrior, which ... contributed to a large extent to forming the base of crime culture in America, is never very far removed from similar myths in classical culture" (1998: 206).

Placing the emphasis on Nordic myth, Duclos draws the vectors of tension between competing myths along different lines. In *The Werewolf Complex: America's Fascination with Violence* he develops a contrast between the Nordic and Greek (or Greco-Roman) mythic traditions in a way that resembles, though not entirely, the contrast between the Adamic and tragic myths of origin presented by Ricoeur.

In the Nordic tradition the myth of Odin serves as "the paradigm for all binary legends" and it models a precarious ongoing struggle between radical extremes of good and evil. Duclos argues that the Nordic tradition reflects and fosters a view of the self as a schizophrenic cauldron of equally potent, irreducible, but incompatible antagonistic opposites.

On the other hand, the Greco-Roman tradition presents, according to Duclos, a stable hierarchical order in the model of Olympus where "Zeus (day) is the sovereign ruling over Hades (nonday, night)" (130). This tradition features nostalgia for a lost wholeness that can be retrieved, albeit at considerable cost, through a ritual exemplified in a part of the Greek mythic folklore. This path requires a confrontation with and a turning away from the madness of the "islands of magic and death" and the rediscovery of "the road home" that leads the "mad warrior" and his warring psyche back to the stability of "wholeness." The "islands of

Lon Chaney with his version of the "werewolf complex" in *The Wolf Man* (1941).

magic and death" and "the road home" are images taken from the Homeric tales of brave Ulysses, which Duclos uses as a paradigm instance of Greek mythic tradition, informing his proposed resolution to the unhealthy Nordic mythic influence.

Duclos's use of the "werewolf complex" refers to the radical binary tension portrayed in the Nordic myths between nature and culture — between an uncivilized "beast within" (a notion that Duclos finds to be ultimately based on a dominant cultural belief in the essential corruptness or corruptibility of human nature) and the repressive stability of a systematically imposed social order. This radical nature/culture dichotomy is played out in the Nordic myths of Odin and Loki and ends ultimately in an apocalyptic exposure and collapse of the "ephemeral order" of the gods— a violent conflict repeated endlessly, Duclos argues, in the personal lives and social orders of Northern cultures. The tendency toward this oscillation between extremes ending in destruction is evidenced, Duclos continues, in the prevalence of and fascination with serial killers in Northern countries (especially America) and the consistent popularity of horror and thriller stories (Stephen King, in particular). The themes of crime and order operating in the film *A Clockwork Orange* are also relevant to the Nordic mythic themes of a wild and corrupt human nature pitted against a repressive social and cultural order.

The "Frankenstein Complex"

In its general thematic organization, Duclos's distinction between the "mad warrior" of the werewolf complex and the "domesticated warrior," symbolized in the Greek story of Ulysses and his return to the homeland, is also consistent with the lines drawn by Janice Hocker Rushing and Thomas S. Frentz in *Projecting the Shadow: The Cyborg Hero in American Film*. In this work they acknowledge important contributions to their views in references made to Richard Slotkin's analysis of dominant mythic themes from colonial and postcolonial American culture. For Rushing and Frentz, Duclos's domesticated warrior is a spiritual warrior and the participant in a sacred hunt that leads to the realization of a whole Self. This warrior contrasts with a technological or cyborg mad warrior who engages in a profane hunt that leads to increasingly more profound fragmentation and self-division with destructive consequences.

Where Duclos emphasizes the dark connection with nature and the myth of savage, animalistic evil in featuring the "werewolf complex," Rushing and Frentz identify the dark connection with modern technological culture by featuring the "Frankenstein complex." They borrow this image, of course, from Mary Shelley's novel, which they note is based, according to Shelley, on the Greek myth of Prometheus. For Rushing and Frentz, then, the story of Prometheus serves as the paradigm from Greek mythology. But instead of providing an example to emulate, as the tale of Ulysses does for Duclos, this story presents, they argue, the dystopian model of antagonistic dualism (within self, between self and nature, and between self and community) that Duclos finds in the Nordic myth of Odin. And instead of finding the more utopian model of spiritual whole-ness and harmony with nature and society in Greek mythology, Rushing and Frentz find this wholeness best exemplified in Native American cul-ture and mythology. However, they also rely on the theory and descrip-tive terminology of psychologist Carl Jung for expressions of this wholeness.

Like Duclos, Rushing and Frentz find the escalated postmodern immersion in automation and information technology to be a primary contribution to the destructive fragmentation of individuals and societies. Consequently, they have strong reservations about the kinds of effects created by the "postmodern condition" and the social, political, and philosophical outlook advocated by pro-ponents of a postmodern cultural orientation. In explaining their view, Rushing and Frentz highlight the way in which the growing sophis-tication of technology increases the separation of implements of the hunt from the hand of the hunter. In the evolution of weaponry—from the spear and the bow and arrow to computerized robotic probes—technologi-cal tools take on a life of their own in which, according to Rushing and Frentz, they begin to turn on their makers.

Boris Karloff as the monster in *Frankenstein* (1931).

Duclos also expresses his reservations with technology

by arguing that technological culture dangerously advances the evils of the myth of savage natural energy through a "transformation of human nature into a cybernetic machine." For Duclos, technology adds an automating and mechanizing power to the underlying mythos of an inherently corrupting evil existing in nature. This transformation becomes evident, Duclos argues, in the shift from the cultural popularity of the werewolf to the serial killer — the latter being nothing more than the werewolf transformed by mechanized and commodified culture into an affectless, coldly calculating, murdering machine.

In their comments about technology, Duclos along with Rushing and Frentz tend to characterize it as predominantly destructive in its effects. In Rushing and Frentz's view, technology contributes crucially to a hierarchically arranged nature/culture split where — insofar as technology may be viewed as a product of culture — nature is essentially privileged over the potentially corrupting influence of culture. In Duclos's view, where culture is privileged over nature, the effects of technology serve merely to magnify the prevailing mythos of the already corrupt and evil essence of human nature. In Chapter 15, this devaluation of the technological is challenged when it is argued to be an unnecessary and thereby unjustifiable structuring of the tension between nature and culture.

Returning to the differences in their applications of mythology, Duclos and Rushing and Frentz part company, then, in their use of Greek mythology. Whereas Duclos finds in the Greco-Roman myth of Ulysses a model for integration and wholeness in self and community, Rushing and Frentz find in the Greek myth of Promethean revolt a model for radically antagonistic dualism in self and community. Duclos finds wholeness modeled more in the healing properties of a culture that draws on an alternative mythology, a more "ancient purification ritual" that, like the journey of Ulysses, creates a reverse path for the mad warrior to return from the darkness and corruption of Hades back to the light of civilization. Rushing and Frentz find wholeness modeled more in the healing properties of a shamanistic-inspired spiritual progression characterized as offering, at its most profound level, the fundamental unity of "transconscious" being. The transconscious level provides the ground for "an awareness of the essential wholeness of the self and of the oneness of the universe" (1995: 37).

Although Duclos explicitly rejects the archetype theory of psychology and its associated theme of a transpersonal collective unconscious and Rushing and Frentz appeal to the collective unconscious in the course of presenting their notion of "transconsciousness," these theorists converge in their opinions regarding the powerful cultural influence that particular myths acquire. This influence derives from "the solidity of certain myths" through time combined with an ability to continue producing "blindly affirmed" reenactments (Duclos, 1998: 207).

The Ideal of "Wholeness"

While analysts such as Ricoeur, Duclos, and Rushing and Frentz disagree about which mythic tradition — Judeo-Christian, Nordic, and Greek respectively — dominates the contemporary Western cultural milieu and which tradition may provide the source of corrective models, there is complete agreement regarding the underlying problem that must be addressed: namely, the radically antagonistic models of cosmos, society and self.

Duclos and Rushing and Frentz believe it necessary for individual and social health to resolve this radical division in favor of processes that lead to unification and wholeness. As a sense of unification and wholeness takes root in the individual psyche of the majority of the members of a community, the likelihood of conditions for cooperative and nonviolent society improves. They adequately diagnose the primary ills of postmodern society but in their general disparagement of (Rushing and Frentz) or disengagement with (Duclos) postmodern views they misjudge the benefits inherent in the postmodern critique of these ills and consequently propose a path of resolution that risks compounding the problem through further misunderstanding.

Metaphors of wholeness, integration, and unity, while not entirely misleading, contain an implicit privileging of sameness that tends to elide and conceal the productive, generative role of division and difference. The misleading connotations of metaphors of wholeness can be improved on by employing metaphors of engaged division, such as "tension," "oscillation," and "interaction." This will at the same time help to remove from oppositional pairs the unnecessarily imposed associations of stark, rigid, and absolute moral hierarchy. In the postmodern view, which will be presented more thoroughly in the next chapter, division is as fundamental as wholeness. The problem lies not in division but in the way in which division is organized and understood.

Pursuit of the ideal of wholeness amounts to a reactionary retreat that goes against the grain of worthwhile recuperations of difference apparent in certain (not all) postmodern positions. According to the best expressions of postmodern theory, difference and division and the conflicts to which these separations inevitably give rise present not merely a fundamental challenge in life but are essential for the possibility of life. As one contemporary philosopher, Leszek Kolakowski, argues, "Life, at least in the sense we are able to conceive, involves differentiation and tension" (1988: 40). Without irreducible division there is no life, and, consequently, division is a necessary and omnipresent state of affairs psychically, socially, and cosmologically.

Because this schism of universal breadth is traditionally understood as deeply rooted and profoundly problematic, it has been labeled by Kolakowski as the "metaphysical horror"—an expression addressed in greater detail in the next chapter. Kolakowski's use of "horror" in this context evokes the traditional sense of dismay at the fundamental division and contradiction that persists at the basement level of explorations into the question of "being" and that has, over the ages, resisted every philosophical attempt at resolution.

The irreducible division yet essential relation between male and female is only one example of the way in which nature affirms and is essentially grounded in an ecology that ultimately favors neither wholeness nor division. Yet this difference and the conflict and competition that arise from it need not be configured in the manner corresponding to the radically polarized and hierarchical dualism of good and evil—the dualism that is, at least according to the analysts discussed, repeated in the Nordic and Greek myths cited above.

Nevertheless, as has been argued, an important part of the Greek mythic tradition provides the inspiration for the Greek tragic poets and their tragic vision of life. This tragic vision, as Ricoeur demonstrates, draws on a cosmology of the origin of evil very different from the cosmology provided in the Adamic myth. This alternative myth of origin offers a way of configuring conflict that preserves irreducible division without antagonistic dualism.

This difference in the configuration of conflict is explored further in the next three chapters, which focus on the contrasts between tragic and melodramatic structures in relation to violence while placing the quandary of the "metaphysical horror" at the fulcrum point of these two differing "worlds of violence."

8

Metaphysical Horror

By way of recapitulation, the argument thus far has progressed approximately along the following route:

• Twitchell's thesis that the horror story is about incest was found to be tantalizing — with its focus on adolescent sexuality — but ultimately too narrow and limited in scope to account for the broad appeal of the classic horror genre.

• Instead, it was proposed that the dual aspects of the protagonist — evidenced in the Doppelgänger theme — appeal successfully to the adolescent audience in particular as a reflection of the intense experience of internal division and confusion resulting from pubertal changes and anxieties relating to acceptance and rejection by members of the opposite sex.

• This "internal division" was then found to be explicitly thematized in the horror story as a division brought about by the external incursion of an entirely alien agency that, once having penetrated the whole and autonomous self, continues its assault from the "inside."

• The theme of sexuality then appears as but a metaphor for advancing the characterization of evil as alien agency; as demonic, satanic and coextensive with the power of death both bodily and spiritually; as active and wholly destructive in relation to life and the "good." As such, evil must be understood to have an origin independent of the "good" and its moment of creation.

• Being of an origin independent of creation, evil necessarily acquires the properties of a "pollution," as a defilement of an original and autonomous whole.

- The notion of evil as defilement dominates the moral code and the moral structure of tradition, including the tradition of melodrama, and serves as a template for conflict including especially the internal divisions arising from sexual anxieties.
- As a way of drawing into perspective the theme of evil and its role in melodramatic conflict, an alternative way of understanding the presence of evil in the world was proposed through the example of tragic drama and the tragic myth of the origin of evil.
- This different way of understanding the operation of evil in the world was argued to be consistent not only with the tragic vision but also with the potential for structuring an alternative orientation toward conflict.

Turning to a recapitulation of levels of analysis, the inquiry into the potential effects of entertainment violence begins at the level of fictional narrative with the horror story — a form of melodrama where the plot revolves around an extraordinary creature. Horror is manifestly apparent in the monster and the monster emerges as monstrous by way of its mode of existence as a being of antagonistically divided substance — a walking contradiction, something that cannot and should not be. This division at the core of the being of the creature is an embarrassment, a monstrosity that cries out for a "logic" through which the division can be understood. This necessity to understand becomes the mother of invention, giving birth to an agency that combines with *what is* to transform it into what *should not be*. This agency is, of course, the ultimate antagonist — evil.

Through its dramatic action and relational involvements, the superficial text of the horror narrative suggests another level or subtext of motivations relating to internal or psychological phenomena. The embarrassment of divided substance, shifted to the region of psychic conflict, produces a layer of analysis or "logic" structured around mimetic and narcissistic motivational imperatives.

This psychological subtext, however, moves on a more subterranean level of tensions emerging through symptoms of evil manifested in the monster. This additional layer of interpretation coincides with a cosmological "logic" relating to the question of the origin of evil. The dramatization of concerns that may be traced to the question of the origin of evil also necessarily gravitates toward the question "What is evil?" — the structure of questioning peculiar to a mode of philosophical investigation. In other words, the horror story carries within its plot structure deeply embedded philosophical questions and answers.

Slipping into the Metaphysical

The economy of exchange between layers of interpretation relating to traditional stories has been described and detailed by the mythologist Joseph Campbell. Campbell provides an interpretive map for working out the relationships between the logic of the psychological realm, its trace in storytelling and myth, and the philosophical layer, which is closely related to the cosmological layer. Campbell notes that "heaven, hell, the mythological age ... and all the ... habitations of the gods, are interpreted by psychoanalysis as symbols of the unconscious. The key to the modern system of psychological interpretation therefore is this ... the unconscious = the metaphysical realm" (1973: 259).

As an experience of unwhole and unholy division gives birth to the narrative of the monster, the "double-goer" of the horror story, it mirrors tensions that obstinately assert and reassert themselves at three deepening levels of horror:

1. the psychic horror of schizophrenic division
2. the cosmological horror of the mystery of the origin of evil
3. the "metaphysical horror" of divided substance — the oppositional tension encountered at the heart of every inquiry into the being of what is.

As previously noted, the phrase "metaphysical horror" is borrowed from Leszek Kolakowski's text of the same name — although the use herein stretches his use of the term. Kolakowski describes the *horror metaphysicus* as the remarkably stubborn philosophical quandary that invariably recurs when attempts to resolve the division in the essence of what is (Being) with the postulation of an Absolute (the One) produce what philosophically reduces to an Absolute indistinguishable from Nothing (non–Being). The tension between the Absolute and Nothing reproduces, in a highly abstract way, the original (and apparently irreducible) division (cf., Kolakowski, 1988: 36–51).

Those struggling to make sense of this metaphysical quandary may find some relief in confronting it at a more familiar, though perhaps no less disturbing, level. To grasp the metaphysical horror viscerally requires only a brief return to an instance, any instance, of the fictional monster. The "zombie" of voodoo legend, for example, presents an impasse that illustrates the salient trait that is in one way or another true of all the classic monsters. The zombie is a walking contradiction. Neither alive nor dead, it moves as if alive but responds as if dead — seemingly devoid of all human sensibility. As such, it is an undecidable superimposition of what would traditionally be understood as mutually exclusive or canceling categories. The zombie cannot be put to death because it has already passed through death. It cannot be brought back to life because it has already passed through life. It is stuck in between. Consequently, the zombie must be dealt with, at the experiential level, in necromantic or magical ways (cf. Collins, 1996: 22–23). At the philosophical level, an analogous contradiction is often dealt with through various dialectical and metaphysical acrobatics and sleights of hand.

But as divided substance, the zombie is not just any type of undecidable or oppositional tension. In films such as *Night of the Living Dead* (1968), the zombie presents a particular structure in which life and death are locked in an extraordinary display of antagonistic and destructive opposition. Death is aligned with evil and is radically antagonistic as a source of absolute corruption of the good that is life. This structure parallels the structure offered in Kristeva's analysis of horror, which purports to be a reflection of the real and ongoing horror of the relentless and ever-present negative incursions of death and decay in living bodies.

Zombies on the prowl in *Night of the Living Dead* (1968).

It would be difficult to find a more apt and concise rendering of the metaphysical structure underlying this notion of the zombie than the account provided by the French philosopher Jacques Derrida. Derrida identifies this structure as the dominant metaphysical approach evident in the Western tradition, but it is also equally dominant in Eastern traditions—a topic addressed in Chapter 15. This structure presents an original and sacred center of being that is safe, secure, whole, autonomous, and self-identically pure on which befalls an ugly accident, an intrusion, a complication, an illness, a deterioration that is essentially corrupting (cf., Derrida: 1988, 93).

This model of pollution repeats itself throughout the core oppositions in the tradition reproducing an inherent, lasting, and fixed hierarchy of priority and value among the elemental components of every opposition such that good comes before and above evil, pure above the impure, life above death, positive above negative, pleasure above pain, truth above falsity, and even male above female — all in such a way that the higher element in the hierarchy can be imagined as ideally standing alone and unmolested by its accidental and oppositional twin.

Antagonism and Synagonism

If dualism cannot be avoided, the question then becomes how best to frame the nature and quality of the conflict that appears to take place at the various levels of the psychological, the cosmological, and the metaphysical — while admitting all the available evidence. As suggested in the discussion of Kristeva's view, the metaphysical horror of divided substance can be understood in an alternative way. This alternative metaphysical view covers similar ground, but in this case the oppositions are not imagined to stand in a lasting and fixed hierarchical arrangement of priority and value. The elemental components are rather understood to be of such a nature that neither side of the opposition can stand alone and yet neither can be identified with or merged into the other. Derrida imagines this oppositional tension as presenting an irreducible component of *undecidability*: an inability to establish a temporally lasting or evaluatively decisive separation of the two components in any instance of their interaction.

In comparing these two metaphysical systems, it becomes clear that the alternative system does not contain an evaluative category corresponding to the category of radical exclusion — as is the case with the devalued "bottom" term in the traditional system. Both of these systems can account for conflict, violence, and strife but, of the two, only the alternative system is not necessarily and essentially violent because it is grounded in the essential dependency of the relation. The traditional system, on the other hand, is grounded in the essential autonomy of the higher element. This imagined fundamental autonomy inaugurates a "logic" through which whatever is designated as corresponding to the "bottom" may be regarded as eminently and ultimately worthy of elimination.

Both of these divided kingdoms of worldly substance project forms of metaphysical dualism. For purposes of convenience of reference in the remaining discussion these divisions will be given labels. In keeping with its privileging of an originary whole violated by a subsequent negating intrusion, the traditional system will be described as monistic antagonism. The alternative system will be described as holistic synagonism, consistent with an essential division extending all the way to the moment of origin — the moment that also reflects and symbolizes abiding essential relation.

Derrida's postmodern critique of dualism includes especially the displacement of oppositional ant-agonism into syn-agonism, a regime of exchange whereby oppositional tension consists of essential relation as well as essential difference. This latter relation is syn-agonistic in the sense of exchange where neither side of the opposition can ever be reduced to the other (essential difference) and where neither side can occur without the other (essential relation).

Returning to the example of the monster, applying the metaphysics of holistic synagonism to the case of the zombie requires a reinterpretation of its divided substance. As a walking model of conflict, the zombie is classically presented as an instance of the metaphysics of antagonism between life and death. But this antagonism need be understood as neither sufficient nor necessary with respect to its implications for real life. Other models are possible for configuring the same tensions of divided substance between life and death. In the parallel world of this alternative way of structuring tensions, another type of model exists, another interpretation of the zombie — a zombie in which the division is modeled on the inclusionary principle inherent in synagonistic conflict. But in this instance the zombie will cease to be a zombie in the traditional sense. It will cease to be a classic monster and will instead become the image of another way of understanding nature and the dance of life and death. Of course it would then draw around itself an entirely different dramatic structure — one that need not be any the less attractive to Hollywood.

Substitution of Violence for Conflict in Melodrama

With this understanding of the metaphysical logic corresponding to oppositional structures, it becomes possible to see more clearly Heilman's distinction between the different approaches to conflict in melodrama and tragic drama. In a significant sense, the metaphysics underlying melodrama does not provide the ground for producing an experience of genuine conflict for the protagonist (or the audience). Conflict, as an experience of genuine doubt and division, must present alternatives of competing value, necessity, or attraction; it must produce an experience of undecidability.

With regard to the alternatives presented in melodrama, the issue is already clear and decided and therefore conflict does not gain traction. The dramatic action turns on carrying out the decision in the manner of a mopping-up operation, which explains why melodrama is inherently predictable often to the point of monotony. It is not about conflict; it is about housecleaning. The only questions at issue are: When will the protagonist discover the source of the pollution, which cleaning agent will be used, and how long will it take? The mopping-up operation emerges as the central action in melodrama and because it involves violence — necessary for the riddance of the pollution — violence becomes the culminating focus of the drama.

In tragic drama, on the other hand, the protagonist is confronted with situations or alternatives that create a dilemma of choice, a clash of interests, imperatives, desires, or obligations, producing the genuine conflict of undecidability. Sometimes the protagonist creates or magnifies this dilemma through the blindness of personal choices or actions (as in the case of Oedipus in *Oedipus the King*) and sometimes the dilemma arrives at the doorstep of the protagonist through inextricable involvement in the actions of others (as in the case of Orestes in *The Choephori*). The question at issue in tragic drama is how the protagonist will deal with, decide, or live with the dilemma, the conflict, with which he or she is confronted. Consequently, in tragic drama the dilemma becomes the dramatic focus and any violence attending the response to the dilemma serves only to magnify the extent of the tragic predicament into which the protagonist has been drawn. In tragic drama, while violence may bring a conclusion to conflict it does not bring complete resolution or provide an occasion for relief or rejoicing.

The genealogical origin of tragic drama in the metaphysics of holistic synagonism does not result in nonviolent drama. Both monistic antagonism and holistic synagonism are metaphysics of violence, but in the case of holistic synagonism, while the potential for violence is theorized as irreducible, violence is not inevitable. The polluting evil implied in antagonism, however, makes deadly violence not only necessary and inevitable but also obligatory wherever genuine evil has been identified.

The problem of attempting to identify genuine evil in real life is addressed in Chapter 14. The question of the role and effects of violence in relation to tragic drama is taken up in Chapter 11. In the next chapter the focus turns toward a summary of conclusions regarding melodrama, its effects in relation to violence, and a reintroduction of key counterarguments regarding effects that require further evaluation in light of the conclusions offered.

9

Violence and Melodrama

Recalling the chronicle of an escalating sense of a divided self progressing from childhood, culminating in adolescence with sexual maturity, and continuing in similar but also different ways into adulthood, the
model of the divided self seems useful and perhaps inescapable. Internal
tensions may intensify beyond internal conflict to erupt into symptoms
of extreme identity crisis. And this inner crisis will be reflected in various
ways in relational crisis. The dynamic tension between inner and outer
conflict is reciprocal in the sense that inner conflict is both a reflection of
and is reflected in outer or relational conflict.

Considering the potential for drama in a broad sense, the sources of
division and conflict comprise not only the conflict of sexually charged
relationships but also every form of alienation. This alienation may derive
from conflicted relations within, through, and between groups, clubs,
teams, work environments, neighborhoods, communities, military corps,
as well as natural environments and even products (such as the alienation
of worker from wares resulting from assembly-line production). Different
genres of drama will present these conflicts through differing structures.

Melodramatic form is the expression of the logic of a metaphysical
formula. This formula reflects and repeats the deeply rooted structure of
the metaphysical tradition of monistic antagonism. This tradition includes
philosophical, religious, social, psychological, ethical/moral, biological,
and medical layers that all evidence extensive use of the radical dualism
of good and evil and the metaphor of evil as defilement. Being rooted in
tradition at the metaphysical level, melodramatic form, despite transformations through variations in structure and changes in source of conflict,
is not a form from which it is easy to escape — either dramatically or meta-

physically. As a template of partisan division and identification of evil, melodrama may be applied to any form of aggravated conflict.

Melodramatic Design and Effects

Specifically, melodrama presents a structure of conflict conforming to the following twofold design:

1. Presentation of conflict as a radical antagonism between value-weighted poles of good (or relative good) and evil (or extreme evil).

2. Depiction of evil as a pollution of sufficient virulence to produce a strong desire for or even require violent destruction as a means of resolution of the conflict.

When combined with a violent resolution repeated endlessly through film and other media and reinforced by the concept of evil dominantly operative in the moral tradition, this radically polarized orientation toward conflict and toward an adversary results in a strong conditioning effect on audiences to apply a similar attitude to real conflict and to feel that it is natural to do so.

Although the evidence for copycat crime, discussed in the introduction, resulting from the film *A Clockwork Orange* suggests that direct imitation is an effect that should never be entirely discounted, melodramatic entertainment does not promote significant numbers of incidents of violence through forms of direct imitation of portrayed behavior. Instead, through constant repetitive exposure to films with melodramatic structure, the "message" communicated through the melodramatic plot assumes the power of a medium and amounts to a strong "massaging" (to borrow a McLuhan usage) of the viewers' attitudes and orientations toward acceptance and application of a highly polarized template for conflict management. This includes the approach to self-conflict as well as relational or other-directed conflict. The twofold design noted above aligns with a twofold effect.

1. In concert with the potent tradition of a culturally endorsed moral polarity of good and evil, melodrama reinforces in consumers a radically divided and partisan model of conflict in which adversaries are systematically devalued.

2. Through its presentation of conflict, melodrama predisposes consumers to anticipate, accept, and use violence as an appropriate response to identified partisans in intense real-life conflict.

This twofold effect is promoted (in the sense of "conditioned" as well as "advertised") and likely induced (but not necessarily "caused") by repeated viewing of entertainment conforming to melodramatic structure. This effect is essentially a cognitive imprinting effect and must be included as a species of imitation effects. Imitation effects, identified in the introduction, include direct imitation of aggressive and violent behavior, sensitization effects, and desensitization effects. Of these three, the desensitization effect offers the closest parallel to the twofold effect itemized above in that it has been described as corresponding to tolerance and/or approval of aggressive attitudes.

The American Psychological Association study, for example, conducted in 1992, and mentioned in the introduction, concluded that heavy viewing of violence promoted "increased acceptance of aggressive attitudes and behaviors."

However, the words "desensitization" and "acceptance" are too passive to accurately describe the imprinting effect associated with melodrama. This effect is more actively promotional and programmatic of a particular way of structuring conflict rather than desensitizing toward violent behavior in general. And, unlike the APA study, the claims made herein specifically name melodrama — and only melodrama — as a form of dramatic entertainment promoting violence. In this respect the APA is too general in its conclusions and thereby the study is potentially more harmful than helpful in the understanding it generates. Furthermore, the claims made herein differ from the APA study in that they are grounded in an extensive analysis that offers an explanation for why melodramatic structure in particular has strong audience appeal while also promoting potentially destructive orientations.

Counterarguments

Despite the fact that all violent entertainment is *not* herein indicted, even these qualified conclusions are not likely to be well received by the supporters of violent entertainment. Consequently, as a way of further clarifying and defending these conclusions, the most significant counterarguments will be addressed here and in the following two chapters.

Those who oppose any notion that fictional entertainment can exert a broad and potent influence toward aggressive, violent, and dehumanizing behavior in real life generally take one of two approaches: they emphasize either the weaknesses of proposed imitation effects or the strengths of cathartic effects.

For example, on the one hand it is claimed that fiction and reality are different and their realms of effects must not be confused. Fiction is a realm of fantasy that promotes predominantly harmless play of the imagination rather than imitative behavior in the real world. As noted in the introduction, Stanley Kubrick expresses this view — a view that concedes reality is a "world of grays" against which the black-and-white morality of melodrama brings emotional cathartic relief through vicarious participation in simplifications of judgment and action. Borrowing Kubrick's candy metaphor, when aiming for cathartic effects, the trick is to get the audience to dismiss the guilt and enjoy the taste — in this case the vicarious tasting of violence.

On the other hand, it is claimed that fiction and reality may indeed be different but melodramatic structure is not one of the points of difference. Cathartic fantasy release may occur through destruction of fictional villains but the representation of good and evil is not part of the fiction. This view asserts that although the world may appear to be very complex, beneath the complexity lurks the profound truth of an ongoing war between good and evil. Melodrama cuts through the layers of complexity, dramatizes this truth in ways not normally experienced in real life, and thereby reflects and affirms the relevance of the moral perspective for the audience.

Both of these arguments rely in part on claims for the beneficial effects of catharsis. These cathartic claims for melodrama, thoroughly detailed in the next chapter, are rebutted in Chapter 11. The argument about the relevance of melodramatic structure to real life is addressed in Chapter 14.

Regarding the argument for the clear separation of fiction and reality, the response to this must begin by noting the law of circularity inherent in the process whereby art imitates life and life imitates art. Attempts to deny or minimize the power of the effects of this circularity are dangerously delusional. In addition to the following comments this theme is also addressed in Appendix 1.

Fiction's powerful potential for influence on real life is so unavoidably evident that when attempting to argue against it, even a strongly opinionated debater such as Andrew Klavan — the novelist of thrillers—cannot avoid contradicting himself within the space of a few lines. In his 1994 article in defense of violence in fiction published in the *Boston Review*, Klavan claims, "Fiction cannot make of people what life has not." But two paragraphs later he asserts, "Stories are the basic building blocks of spiritual maturity" (140). This last claim escapes him like a Freudian slip. In the case of melodrama, the structure and resolution of the portrayed conflict, as essential components of the story, unquestionably constitute a large part of what Klavan refers to as building blocks. As such, these particular blocks must indeed figure crucially, as Klavan claims, in building "spiritual maturity." Certainly, then, melodramatic stories— no differently than other stories— help to "make of people what life has not" and they do so in a way that may well be brought into question.

The film critic Jake Horsley, who has written extensively on the subject of violent films in his book *The Blood Poets*, makes a similar admission, but in a less accidental and much more candid way: "It may be that, although no one mistakes movies for reality, a lot of people, maybe the majority, adopt many of their ideas about and responses *to* reality *from* the movies" (1999b: 152). Of these "ideas" gained from movies, those about the structure of conflict and moral order are among the most deeply entrenched and most often repeated. Horsley's opinions are explored further in Part II where several films that have become classics in the genre of violent entertainment are examined and evaluated.

Most cultural commentators minimally grant that "fiction and reality do interact" and Klavan also acknowledges as much. However, he then adds what he believes to be a decisive blow: "But we don't know how, not at all" (136). While the link between fiction and reality is not causal and therefore not precisely predictable, it is nevertheless reliable in many respects, as any Madison Avenue executive will confirm. Images exert powerful influence and they do so by way of a simple principle already much discussed: mimesis. This principle is in fact the mainstay of all graphic and screen advertising. The representation of conflict in melodrama does not appear as a subtle nuance that is likely to be missed by the receptive and imitative instincts of a viewing audience. The process of mimesis relevant to melodrama is addressed further in Chapter 11 along with the reconsideration of catharsis.

The argument that images do in fact exert a powerful imitative influence also encounters the further rebuttal, expressed by Joe Saltzman and cited in the introduction, that if images of violence are so powerful why are there not more acts of violence taking place?

The obvious first answer is that the United States does in fact have more than its share of violence. A second and less obvious answer, discussed in more detail in Chapter 15, is that the influence of violent entertainment may not manifest itself primarily in violent *actions* but rather in devaluing and dehumanizing *attitudes* toward others— especially in situations of conflict. These attitudes may then promote forms of destructive, abusive, or defrauding relational behavior that are covertly violent and therefore never appear at the level of national statistics but that are evident locally — for example in schools, community relations, and in the workplace.

A third answer resides in the likelihood that the vast majority of Americans, *despite* a constant barrage of images of violence, succeed in managing aggressive impulses. Who can say how much easier such management would be for the majority — as well as the minority who commit violent crimes— if the media and cultural environment were sending and reinforcing a predominantly different message?

The thought of a different message suggests a fourth answer — an alternative to melodramatic structure through which powerful depictions of violence may occur but to arguably different cathartic effect. The presence of this dramatic structure in popular culture is not nearly as pervasive as melodramatic structure but it does exert influence in the current cultural environment and that influence may contribute to attitudes that reduce or retard the recourse to violence. This alternative is, of course, tragic drama and related forms. One such related form is discussed in Chapter 14. Some post–World War II examples of tragic drama include films such as *Red River* (1948), *The Bridge on the River Kwai* (1957), *Women in Love* (1970), *Days of Heaven* (1978), *Blade Runner* (1982), *Merry Christmas, Mr. Lawrence* (1983), and *Troy* (2004). Chapter 17 offers a detailed analysis of *Red River* as an example of a classic contemporary, as opposed to ancient Greek, form of tragic drama.

In the next chapter, catharsis in classic melodrama is examined in detail and several variations of melodramatic form are introduced and briefly defined. Following the discussion of catharsis in melodrama, Chapter 11 shifts the focus to catharsis in tragic drama and the conclusions derived launch a critical reappraisal of Chapter 10's presentation of catharsis in melodrama.

10

Catharsis and Melodrama

Although devised in response to the identity crises of childhood and early adolescence, the model of the divided self never outgrows its usefulness. It remains relevant beyond adolescence in a broader existential sense relating to more complex tensions between identity and control, relation and dependency. Those emerging from adolescent identity crises continue to grapple with issues of a divided self through an evolving process of self-discovery — a process that ideally will be more journey and less crisis.

The popular view of classic catharsis relevant to melodramatic form coincides with the psychological model provided in the theory of the "shadow" self as explained in the work of Carl Jung (1964) and Erich Neumann (1973). The evolving self repeatedly rediscovers that it is not in complete control, that it cannot see to the bottom of itself, that it cannot know itself and its motivational sources in a grasp of intuitive insight. The self continually confronts itself as a "shadow," as an abyss— extending ultimately beyond reach. Social, cultural, and personal circumstances may widen this abyss.

Scapegoating

In the years following adolescence, the mystery of self-division may in some cases continue to be experienced as exceptionally troubling, disturbing, or threatening. Under these circumstances the confusion and the anxiety may be regarded as unacceptable, the self may enter (or reenter) into war with itself, and unwanted aspects of the self may be targeted for sacrificial negation by the projection of those unwanted aspects onto symbolic victims. It is not surprising that this "war" may be structured according to the familiar pattern presented in the moral tradition and reiterated in melodramatic form.

This form of projection, when applied to real or symbolic victims, accounts for the process of classic scapegoating whereby a "goat" is chosen to serve as agency for the "sins" or unwanted aspects of the self or a community. The potent threat of the polluting agent or agency requires that cleansing be accomplished through thorough sacrifice or destruction. In being adequate and thorough, the countermeasures must take into consideration, as in the case of the vampire, the particular virulence of the villain and adopt the necessary means, often in a ritualized manner, to ensure absolute destruction. This labor of destruction may become a devotional obsession to the point that it imitates the protocols of religious rituals of purification.

The ritual of purification conforms to the commonly expressed views about classic melodramatic catharsis. In the good/evil value-weighted moral structure of melodrama, emotions of apprehension and anxiety for the threatened "damsel in distress" are aroused along with moral outrage and anger against the villain.

Through a successful violent resolution of the conflict by the hero, the viewers' vicariously aroused emotions of anxiety and anger, along with any similar lingering emotions derived from real-life conflicts, are, according to the cathartic theory, expelled as the evil of the villain is purged from the portrayed community.

The cathartic effects of melodrama for members of a viewing audience are then twofold: both personal (emotional) and relational (civic). By way of identification with the hero, the elimination of the villain produces emotional catharsis— as anxieties and anger relating to the portrayed conflict are purged —and also a corresponding relational or civic catharsis, as a perceived menace and evil (which may be a projection of the double or shadow self) is dispatched from the community.

Amplifying Emotional Arousal

Through the design of the melodramatic plot, the audience is led to identify exclusively with the hero. This partisan moral alignment creates an attitude of great tolerance for extreme violence when that violence is directed toward the villain. Not only are viewers willing to witness acts of violence that ordinarily might be experienced as distasteful or repulsive, often the melodramatic plot, through conscious design, contains provocations and twists and turns of action that foment the audience to the point of impatience to see violence done to the villain.

Generally speaking, the villain in a classic melodramatic plot, if given any redeeming qualities at all (as, for example, a handsome appearance), is given such qualities only for the purpose of showing the beguiling or deceitful nature of evil (e.g., the "Adonis" villains in *Rocky II* [1976] and *Rocky IV* [1979]). The emotional response to the villain on the part of the hero and the heroine (including the mirroring response of the audience) can also be amplified by portraying the villain as doubly repulsive. He may be presented as ugly in appearance as well as in his actions, making him a case of sufficient corruption and pollution that all restraints of conscience concerning the use of violence in his disposal are lifted (e.g., the villains in *Mad Max* [1979] and *The Road Warrior* [1981]). In such cases what may begin as indignation toward the villain and his actions turns into a festival of contempt and vengeance as the villain meets an orchestration of richly anticipated and well-deserved doom (e.g., the villains in the Sergio Leone "spaghetti" Westerns).

"Angel Eyes" (Lee Van Cleef), the "designed for disposal" villain in Sergio Leone's *The Good, the Bad, and the Ugly* (1966).

The more thoroughly the villain is portrayed as a pollution, the more the righteous censure associated with the use of violence is removed. The growing portrait of pollution invites, or in many cases propels, the audience toward progressively greater states of emotional arousal combined with a sense of exceptional freedom to enjoy the violence heaped on the villain. The demise of the villain works as a kind of "justifiable homicide"— a resolution that in its structure has been likened by many film analysts to the sexual act and its corresponding climax (cf., Black, 1991: 121).

Continuing with the sexual theme, while the melodramatic plot serves to release viewers from inhibitions that might otherwise obstruct enjoying the displayed use of violence, it also serves, perhaps in a more subtle way, to release male viewers from another set of inhibitions. Speaking of the particulars of this form of release, Kenneth Burke suggests that classic melodramatic form may be understood as unapologetic dramatization of an archetypal male fantasy. Burke sees the fantasy of the "gallant coming to the aid of the Damsel in Distress" as a "mild and pleasant instance of pity as a subterfuge" whereby "the lady, who would otherwise be aloof, is imagined as being placed in a situation that would justify the gentleman's advances. Without the assistance of her 'pitiful' condition, he would be in the position of 'forcing' his attentions upon her" (1961a: 113).

This "subterfuge" also constitutes, for the hero, a fortuitous instance of the "double bind" where the distress of the lady properly *requires* a gentleman to come to her assistance when he may also *want* to come to her assistance. This damsel-in-distress wrinkle in the melodramatic plot creates an intensification of the sexual elements of the story by adding fuel to natural inclinations.

Given such inclinations, it is not difficult to imagine male members of the audience overtly or covertly desiring that the heroine find herself pitifully helpless in a threatening situation precisely so that it will be necessary for the hero to come to her aid. Here again, Burke makes a revealing comment: "Since the arousing of pity requires the imitation of suffering, there are the deviations whereby the ambiguous relation between love and pity becomes rather an ambiguous relation between the erotic and cruelty" (1961a: 114).

With these possible motivations working just beneath the surface of the plot, the villain's cruelty toward or calculating manipulation of the heroine acquires a new significance. In consideration of the hero's attraction to the heroine and the moral weighting given the hero in melodramatic form, the villain is ideally portrayed as little more than a person of abject depravity whose cruelty serves to draw together the hero and the heroine just as his demise serves symbolically as the jettisoning of the hero's (and identifying audience members') shadowy and unattractive aspects.

In this light, the Doppelgänger of the horror story appears doubly convenient—as the cruelty that magnifies the damsel's helplessness also expedites the hero's advances. Herein lies one explanation for the use within melodramatic structure of scenes alternating romantic and sexual content with scenes of violent content—played to great effect in the *Indiana Jones* series, for example, as well as in many comic book plots adapted to film.

In summary, the classic melodramatic plot and its horror story subspecies depict characters of a heroic nature on the one hand and those of an arch-villainous and eminently disposable nature on the other. Such characters correspond to a radically polarized good/evil structure of conflict, the partisan nature of which arouses highly polarized emotional responses that achieve corresponding measures of cathartic release from tensions rooted in both personal (inner) and relational (outer) conflicts.

This description of classic melodramatic catharsis, however, does not necessarily account for responses that may take place in the audience when the melodramatic plot departs from classic structure. Some of these variations include, for example, psycho(melo)drama—where a villainous character assumes the position of featured protagonist—as in *Psycho* (1960) and *Raging Bull* (1980); reverse melodrama—where the exploits of a villainous character are featured and that character triumphs in the end, as in *A Clockwork Orange* (1971); reverse point-of-view melodrama—where most of the story follows the actions of a villainous character whose nefarious designs are ultimately foiled—as in *The Jackal* (1997); noir melodrama—where "hard-boiled," morally compromised characters are featured and appear quasi-heroic in comparison to the extreme villainy of other characters—as in *Bonnie and Clyde* (1967) and *Pulp Fiction* (1994); and multi-melodrama—which offers more than one variety of melodramatic form such as the combination of the classic plot with the reverse plot in *The Silence of the Lambs* (1991).

These variations in structure achieve entertainment effects by introducing elements of shock and surprise through playing with the audience's expectations. However, despite appearing to break the mold, these variations remain well within the melodramatic fractal landscape by generating creative variations of the exposure and thorough depiction of instances of extreme evil. Examples of most of these forms, along with more detailed discussion of their effects, are presented in Part II.

11

Catharsis Reconsidered

Thus far, the cathartic theory of effects in relation to melodrama appears to make perfect sense. Emotions are aroused and expended along with the disposal of an identified source of communal pollution. Melodrama thereby appears to promote emotional hygiene and civic restoration by providing a collectively cleansing emotional, cognitive, and moral experience. But this resolution of the difficulty relating to effects is not entirely convincing. The best way to illustrate the continued problem is to take a particularly clear and pronounced case of emotional arousal and treat it as a paradigmatic instance of emotional arousal in general.

In a sexually explicit film, for example, the depiction of seductive behavior and sexual acts arouses sexually charged emotions. But the stimulation of sexual desire does not in itself produce or guarantee a catharsis of aroused emotions. Although a peak of aroused sexual interest may subside somewhat when the viewing of a sexually explicit film ceases, an increased level of sexual interest will likely remain with the viewer until engaging in a sexual act dissipates it. In other words, viewing a sexually explicit film does not in itself purge sexually aroused interest and emotion. Instead, it will more likely lead to sexual acts. Pornographic films, for example, are often used for the purpose of initiating sexual acts.

It may fairly be argued, then, that films arousing a significant degree of sexual interest may not, in themselves, produce anything like a catharsis of such aroused emotions—even though characters may be depicted achieving the catharsis of sexual climax. The arousal of sexual emotion may be understood, then, as separate in significant measure from the form of catharsis corresponding to that emotion. In fact "emotional catharsis"

115

may be misleading in the sense that catharsis cannot effectively occur without an accompanying or culminating physical expression.

Using the sexual case as the emotional paradigm, a similar argument may be made concerning the presentation of violent acts in films. Viewing violent conflict may accomplish primarily only an arousal of emotions ranging from fear, anger, hatred, contempt, pity, and the like. Which emotion or emotions are aroused in a particular viewer will depend on the emotional alignments formed in relation to the character or characters with whom the viewer identifies. And although the level of aroused emotion may diminish by the end of the film, it may well be the case that cathartic effects are superficial, minimal, or even illusory.

Even when the character or characters with whom the viewer identifies may experience a resolution of conflicts, that may not produce, as in the case of the sexually explicit film, a significant catharsis for the viewer. Any sensation of catharsis of fear, for example, that may be experienced merely through viewing drama may function as only a pale and weak semblance of the cathartic release involved in a physical response of, for example, fight or flight in the face of fear. A full cathartic experience in relation to emotions such as fear or anger may require a form of physical response similar to what would naturally occur in response to real situations in which fear, anger, horror, and related emotions are predominantly aroused.

Weak and Strong Cathartic Effects

Granting the relevance of the sexual model of arousal and catharsis when applied to potent emotions in general, two different, but not incompatible, ways of understanding catharsis in response to viewing drama emerge. The first theory proposes that the sensation of catharsis is a function of the process of merely viewing a film whereby energy is expended through aroused emotions resulting in a relative sense of depletion. For purposes of reference this process will be called the weak cathartic effect.

The second theory proposes that emotions are aroused but no significant cathartic effect occurs until there is a sufficiently overt physical action accompanying and in effect concluding the emotional response. In the case of fear, for example, this might entail screaming or a fight or flight response. In the case of sexual arousal, a significant catharsis of emotion would require engaging in a sexual act. In the case of anger, effective catharsis might consist of acts of physical release like shouting and animated gesturing or more aggressive acts like screaming, pounding, striking out, and fighting. In the case of pity or ruth, the full cathartic physical response is tears. And in the case of burlesque and humor, the cathartic response is laughter. For purposes of reference this overt physical cathartic process will be called the strong cathartic effect.

This distinction between differing orders of completion and sensation in the cycling between emotion and catharsis has important implications in relation to different dramatic structures. Dramatic entertainment arousing primarily emotions such as anger, fear, and sexual desire will likely produce only weak cathartic effects because the confined conditions of theater viewing constrain the relevant overt physical responses necessary for an effective catharsis of these emotions.

This understanding of weak cathartic effects lends support to Plato's concerns, mentioned in the introduction (and detailed in Appendix 1), about mimesis and drama. Viewing forms of drama that result in the predominance of imitative arousal effects largely undissipated by catharsis predispose viewers to further expression of emotion by lowering the threshold for arousal. Since Plato apparently did not subscribe to any version of cathartic effects, this may have been part of his reasoning when claiming that the mimetic art of dramatic representation will serve only to encourage emotional arousal and thereby promote a hypersensitivity that will prove to be unproductive in real-life situations that require emotional control and clear thinking.

The relevance of mimetic theory to forms of entertainment arousing principally emotions of anger and outrage provides explanation and support for those studies indicating that viewing violent conflict and violent acts leads to ensuing imitative responses. The residual arousal effects lead to greater susceptibility to future arousal combined with the need to bring lingering emotions to full cathartic release through some form of physical action.

If such is the case, however, the mimetic model will not be sufficient to account for what takes place in those instances where cathartic effects are genuinely predominant. Since the overt physical reactions of tears and laughter can be adequately expressed in spectator viewing circumstances, dramas that successfully elicit such responses can achieve strong cathartic effects. Aristotle, as noted in Chapter 6, has argued that tragic drama can be sufficiently intense to arouse ruth to the point of cathartic reaction in tears. A strong cathartic effect in association with arousal of the emotion of ruth supports the view that the portrayal of violent conflict in tragic drama may follow a pattern of response very different from dramas that produce weak cathartic effects.

Burke's "Charitable" Interpretation of Dramatic Victimage

A pattern of response associated with strong cathartic effects can be better illustrated by elaborating further on Aristotle's notion of catharsis. Since Kenneth Burke has done so in a relevant and provocative way, his findings, once again, serve to chart the way. Burke acknowledges that Aristotle's definition of tragedy asserts that tragic drama achieves its ends "through pity [ruth] and fear [awe], bringing about the catharsis of such emotions," but he introduces a significant addition to the understanding of this clause.

Noting that the explanation for what Aristotle means by this clause may have been contained in a section of the *Poetics* that has been lost, Burke argues that the only clues guiding contemporary interpretation derive from the passages where Aristotle speaks of musical catharsis in the *Politics*. Working from these clues, Burke suggests, "Those paragraphs in the *Politics* at least give reason to infer that the treatment [of catharsis] in the *Poetics* was not essentially different, and that the kind of 'purge' produced by tragedy may have been specifically considered from the 'civic' point of view (as a species of political purge)" (1959: 337).

In the discussion that follows this remark, Burke explores the various avenues of exchange between emotional catharsis and political or civic catharsis whereby the catharsis of tensions in the body politic can be conveyed by imagery of bodily purgation just as the catharsis of tensions in the physical body can be expressed by imagery drawn from related processes in the body politic or even the "world's body."

In working out the analogical relationships between these two realms, Burke suggests that bodily disease may be used by dramatists to indicate the presence of an internal conflict that has its analogue in the body politic in one form or another of civic conflict. For Burke, conflict, whether in the physical body or the body politic, reflects the presence of an excess or imbalance. Civic or relational catharsis is the process whereby this tension is purged, "dis-ease" is restored to "ease" or peace, and the divisive conflict is resolved. Burke speculates that Aristotle may have believed that emotional tensions (ruth and awe) aroused by the dramatic conflict lead to a cathartic resolution in the audience paralleling and complementing a similar catharsis of civic tensions through the portrayal of the tragic outcome of the conflict.

However, with respect to tragic drama, it is not immediately apparent in what sense the word "resolution" is relevant when the outcome is manifestly tragic. In addressing this point, Burke's analysis becomes especially interesting. In relation to the "civic" slant that he brings to the interpretation of Aristotle's famous clause, Burke is forced to ask a crucial question: "Whereas religion so often lays great stress upon the curative role of love (and psychoanalysis does the same regarding sex), why does the *Poetics* fail to treat of such a motive, specifically mentioning only the curative effect of pity [ruth] and fear [awe]?" (1959: 359).

Following the implications of the analogy between the physical body and the body politic, Burke seeks a consistency between the emotional catharsis and the civic catharsis. If a civic catharsis entails bridging of relational divisions, the emotion or motive of love might be expected to appear at some level of the dramatic design. But Burke reports that this expectation is not supported by any mention in the *Poetics* of the topic of "love" or any of its erotic or agapetic variants.

Burke then fastens on the following solution: "Fear [awe] prepares for pity [ruth]. And pity [ruth] is a surrogate for love" (1959: 359). This solution also adds to an understanding of the quality of fear aroused in tragic drama.

Through the arousal of *fear for* a protagonist with whom the audience identifies, a measure of ruth is also aroused, which is (ideally) itself physically consummated or purged by being brought to the point of tears. The arousal and consummation of this ruth creates a bond between the audience and the protagonist that dissolves, overcomes, or "forgives" any alienating feelings the audience may have toward the protagonist as a consequence of actions stemming from a fatal flaw. This is the sense in which ruth serves as a surrogate for love.

However, the full relevance of this analysis in regard to the body politic and civic catharsis does not become apparent until Burke adds another element, which he supplies almost as an afterthought: "Insofar as pity [ruth] is employed to arouse our moral indignation, it is not wholly cathartic" (1959: 360–361).

Burke uses an example specifically from Greek tragic drama to illustrate his point. Drawing from Sophocles' *Antigone*— in which the conflict between two brothers leads to a deadly confrontation between Creon, King of Thebes, and Antigone, sister of the two brothers— Burke remarks: "Tragedy can also become partisan by not going beyond such [emotion] as arouses moral indignation. For instance, had Sophocles' Creon not retracted, the audience would have felt pity only for Antigone, and that pity would have made them gloat vindictively at Creon's 'well deserved' misfortunes" (1959: 362).

As previously noted, the word "ruth" is substituted for the word "pity" when used in reference to an emotion aroused in the context of tragic drama. The emotion that arouses moral indignation is closer to the English word "pity" and is partisan and not wholly cathartic because it does not achieve a broad suspension of divisive emotional currents within the community. In this sense pity may be distinguished from ruth. In other words, the pity aroused along with moral indignation and outrage inhibits full civic and emotional catharsis by creating alignment with only one protagonist, one faction, one side of the civic or relational conflict.

Greek tragic drama, on the other hand, for which Sophocles' *Antigone* is but one example, is deliberately designed, Burke suggests, to produce what he calls nonpartisan catharsis. Burke's attempt to locate an analogue for emotional catharsis in the body politic leads him to conclude, "Perfect catharsis would arise from a sense of universal love. Insofar as such a condition is not attained, the next best thing is a sense of radical pity [ruth] that lies on the slope of tearful release. Fear is not directly cathartic; but it is cathartic indirectly, insofar as it sets up the conditions for the feeling of pity [ruth]" (1959: 360).

With this analysis, Burke has clearly shown how the emotional catharsis previously discussed in the "strong" form may be seen to merge with and contribute to the process of nonpartisan catharsis in relation to the conflict within a "body politic" (whether as family, community, city, or nation). The ruth aroused in tragic drama is an especially powerful emotion because it is aroused for *both* sides of the conflict. The breadth of this emotional catharsis facilitates the civic catharsis of the lessening of divisive tensions in the body politic and heightens appreciation for the complexity of conflict.

Burke demonstrates that within the context of tragic drama his understanding of Aristotle allows "for a 'charitable' interpretation of dramatic catharsis by victimage. That is, it ... explain[s] how such a principle could arise outside the motive usually stressed by psychoanalysts: the 'projection' of one's own ills upon a scapegoat" (1959: 361). Catharsis derived from the depiction of violent conflict in tragic drama does not promote the polarized, "scapegoating" principle characteristic of melodrama and in fact serves to lessen the alienation and division that foster violence and the perpetuation of cycles of violence.

According to Aristotle, the emotion of anger will dominate the emotions of ruth and awe when aroused in the same context. When partisan emotions are aroused, as in the case of melodrama, anger and outrage will take control and dominate the mix of emotional responses. Rather than being a primary emotional effect, then, the arousal of ruth — or, as it turns out in melodrama — the arousal of pity is of limited scope and partisan effect in a story that ultimately unfolds in a way that arouses predominantly outrage and anger. And, as previously argued, anger aroused through dramatic conflict can achieve only weak cathartic effects in the context of a theatrical viewing.

Briefly summarizing, in those cases where a dramatist seeks cathartic effects through melodrama, the portrayal of victimage will stimulate and transport an audience little further than a state of aroused indignation, aggressive emotions, and arrested and partial forms of catharsis through partisan identification. On the other hand, where a dramatist seeks to achieve cathartic effects through tragic drama, the portrayed victimage will transport an audience beyond arousal of emotions to full emotional and civic (relational) catharsis through meaningful identification with both sides (or all sides) of a conflict.

Plato and Aristotle Realigned

Recalling what has been roughly sketched of the tension between the views of Plato and Aristotle, it may now be said that Plato's theory of mimesis and Aristotle's theory of catharsis are both accurate when considered in the appropriate contexts.

Aristotle's theory of catharsis is accurate specifically in the context of tragic drama. Ruth and *fear for* (awe in response to the fate of the protagonists) are the primary emotions aroused and catharsis must be understood as the process of bringing these emotions to completion in an intense action of physical release or expression. In tragic drama this action can occur in the physical release of tears. The Greeks were inclined to view tragic dramas that failed to produce such a reaction as not of the highest quality. This full emotional cathartic reaction is of a piece with — and could not be achieved without — the civic catharsis accomplished through the nonpartisan extension of the emotional response to both sides of the conflict. In the *Poetics* Aristotle does not adequately explain the part of the theory relating to civic catharsis, although, as Kenneth Burke has indicated, this theory is suggested in a related passage in the *Politics* and may have been fully explained in a lost part of the *Poetics*.

Although when discussing his theory of mimesis Plato had in mind the tragic poets including Homer, it turns out that mimetic effects are more relevant to melodrama than tragic drama. As has been argued, melodrama arouses primarily emotions of anger, indignation, outrage, and *fear of* (a threatening agent). Because of the nature of the response needed, these emotions cannot be brought to the point of an intense action of physical expression in the context of the theater. Consequently, while arousal effects

Plato (left) and Aristotle (right); Roman marble copies of Greek busts (from the picture book *Bilderhefte aus dem Griechischen und Romischen Altertum*. Griechische Bildnisse und Sitten. A. Baumeister. 1889. Munchen: Druck und Verlag von R. Oldenbourg).

may be strong, cathartic effects are weak and temporary and, as in the case of the emotional effects aroused in sexually explicit films, lead to the desire for further arousal in order to bring about an effective catharsis. These arousal effects combine with the partisan portrayal of conflict to induce the replication of that pattern of conflict in real experience in order to bring to cathartic completion the emotions aroused. If these emotions are not brought to such completion, they will be repressed and will build toward such time as they can be effectively expressed. This circumstance creates greater sensitivity to situations that may cause the arousal of such emotions. Such hypersensitivity is consistent with Plato's theory of mimesis where (in the absence of catharsis) susceptibility to repeated stimulation is predicted.

As a result of the predominance of mimetic effects, real-life tensions or conflicts that members of the audience may bring with them into the theater are ultimately more likely to be reinforced and amplified rather than reduced by the model of conflict presented in melodrama.

Of the many who have written on the subject of entertainment violence, Sissela Bok (1998) is alone in having explicitly commented on the significant difference in cathartic effects achieved by portrayals of violence in tragic drama versus other forms of drama. Speaking of Aristotle's view of catharsis in tragic drama, Bok notes that "there clearly are films and television programs and works of art that arouse both fear and pity in ways that can have transformative effects on viewers— as much in our day as in past periods" (42). Bok recognizes that the catharsis that initiates or constitutes these "transformative effects" is "precisely not at issue in much entertainment violence." She goes on to argue that the bulk of entertainment violence (which herein is grouped under the category of melodrama) is of little of no value in achieving emotionally or psychologically potent cathartic effects. The cathartic effect of tragic drama, however, is potent because it "permits a schooling of the emotions and a deepening of one's understanding of human nature and of the paradoxes relating to the role of violence in human life" (42). This appreciation of the paradoxes relating to the role of violence arises from the breadth and depth of identifications with the characters involved in the "tragic situation." Unfortunately, Bok does not extend this insight into tragic drama in the direction of an explicit analysis and thorough critique of melodramatic structure.

Violence as Sport, Sport as Violence

It has been argued that in conflict presented in such a way that the audience sees reason to identify with both sides, the victimage and violence resulting from the conflict may be adequately understood as tragic. In conflicts presented for purposes of ensuring the enlisting of clearly partisan identifications, the victimage and demise of villains is not likely to be understood as in any sense tragic — and is in fact most often experienced by the audience, as a result of dramatic design, as cause for celebration.

It has been argued further that melodramatic entertainment cannot bring about an effective recreational or therapeutic catharsis of associated emotions such as anger, resentment, and fear (of). Therapeutically significant catharsis of these emotions requires the kind of intense physical response that can only be expressed in aggressive activity — preferably (from the point of view of communal accord) the controlled aggressive activity of sporting contests, martial arts instruction, self-defense training, model-mugging classes, emotional expression workshops, and similar activities.

However, a potential danger exists even here when the model of conflict portrayed in melodrama is transferred to these activities. In this case a sporting activity, for example, rather than providing an outlet for aggressive emotions, becomes itself charged with the highly polarized construct of good and evil — transforming it in essence from competition into scapegoating, from sport into the spirit of violence regardless of whether or not physical violence occurs. In such cases the model of conflict as confrontation featuring catharsis as culmination or release of emotional, physical, and relational tension becomes confused and combined with the model of conflict as purification featuring catharsis as the sacrifice or cleansing of a social and moral pollution — a distinction that even Burke is not always sufficiently careful to make in his discussions of catharsis.

Violence presented in any context whereby it can be experienced as something to celebrate and as something about which little or no concern need be raised, no loss acknowledged, serves not only to cheapen human life but also to degrade the quality of human community. To present violence in such contexts trivializes it and renders it a commonplace similar to beating an opponent in a sporting contest. Whether sport is amplified to violence or violence is reduced to sport, the net effect amounts to human loss and waste, both collectively and individually.

The careless misappropriation of the sporting analogy in relation to current trends in melodramatic film was prominently brought to national attention in the pages of *The New Republic* by Gregg Easterbrook (1999a). Easterbrook condemns what he argues to be a trend in the decade of the '90s toward the depiction of violence as recreational sport — citing as flagrant examples such films as *Natural Born Killers* (1994), *Pulp Fiction* (1994), *Seven* (1995), *The Basketball Diaries* (1995), and *Scream* (1996). In these films characters are shown committing acts of egregious and largely unprovoked violence with attitudes of casual spontaneity or engaged amusement that would more readily be associated with playful teasing or a game of Trivial Pursuit.

The makers of such films, at least in some cases, claim nevertheless that these portrayals of wanton victimage do no more than merely reflect current extremes of violence evident in the real world and to that extent present themselves as varieties of "docudrama." This "reality defense," however, overlooks the crucial importance of the context and dramatic structure through which the violence is, by the conscious filmmaker's design, presented. In the cases in question, the violence is framed within crudely drawn varieties of melodramatic plot and is obsessively featured and focused on in ways analogous to the kind of attention devoted to sex in pornographic films. The remaining chapters address additional aspects of this "reality defense" — especially as it relates to younger audiences.

Chapters 13 and 15 also discuss further the potentially destructive inter-action of melodrama and sport.

Amending Conclusions of the AAP

In July of 2000 five prominent medical organizations, led by the American Academy of Pediatrics, convened for a Congressional Public Health Summit in Washington, D.C., and submitted a summary of their findings regarding media and violence entitled the *Joint Statement on the Impact of Entertainment Violence on Children*. This summary concludes that consistent exposure of children to entertainment violence "lead[s] to emotional desensitization towards violence in real life," "feeds a percep-tion that the world is a violent and mean place," and "increases fear of becoming a victim of violence, with a resultant increase in self-protective behaviors and a mistrust of others." Such exposure also substantially increases the likelihood of viewing violence as "an effective way of settling conflicts" (AAP, 2000).

The preceding analysis suggests that this conclusion is too broad and ought to be amended to read in the following way:

> When presented in the context of melodramatic structure, entertain-ment violence contributes significantly to existing culturally instilled and reinforced tendencies to view the world as organized into good and evil factions and to readily impose that polarized structure as a template for orienting to and managing intense frustrations and conflicts; the con-vergence of these media and cultural trainings inevitably results in increased tendencies toward destructive devaluations of others as well as greater tolerance, acceptance, and even endorsement of deadly violence as a means of conflict resolution.

By omitting specific reference to children this rephrasing also broadens the scope to assert that exposure to melodramatic violence may be counter-productive for everyone — not just children.

Nevertheless children are a primary concern. This rephrasing also invites a reevaluation of children's literature and entertainment. Melo-dramatic form is clearly evident, for example, in many versions of fairy tales and classic children's stories that include significant violence. In addi-tion to the issue of whether melodramatic violence in fairy tales is dan-gerous to children, the comparison of melodrama and fairy tales raises the question of whether it can be the case that the combination of violence and melodramatic form used in stories and found to be acceptable and even beneficial for children over many generations of retellings can pose a significant danger when combined in stories for adolescents and adults. In this sense the phenomenon of melodramatic form and violence in fairy tales either significantly undermines the case for the hazards of melodrama in adult media or it requires thorough reappraisal of melodramatic violence in the context of children's media. The next chapter conducts this reappraisal of melodramatic violence using fairy tales as the illustrative medium.

12

Melodrama and Fairy Tales

> Our character is formed by the stories we learn to live in.
> — *William Kittredge*

Thus far, many of the prominent spokespersons who do not agree with the conclusion that violent entertainment (in whatever form) exerts a largely divisive and inflammatory influence on consumers have been either mentioned or discussed. Especially interesting to consider in this context are those who have focused attention on entertainment for young audiences and who have lauded the benign or beneficial effects of portrayed violence. Whatever may be argued to be the effects of violence in entertainment, the young are the most vulnerable. Media directed toward them deserve primary attention and close scrutiny. In this and the next chapter, the arguments of prominent advocates for the benefits of depictions of violence in the genre of fairy tales and the formats of comic books and video games are rehearsed and evaluated.

In her introduction to a collection of Grimm's fairy tales, Maria Tatar credits folklorist and cultural critic Carol Clover for pointing out that "the plots of both folk tales and horror films ... are driven by a stock cast of characters, one that often frames the central conflict in terms so emphatically polarized that we appear to be in a clear cut world of good versus evil" (1997: 10). Long before they enter the darkened theater to view the horror film, most teenagers have been prepared for the type of plot and the kinds of characters horror films present through the much more concise and dreamlike narratives of fairy tales.

In his pioneering study entitled *The Uses of Enchantment* (1976), child psychologist Bruno Bettelheim makes a compelling case for the importance of fairy tales in child development, especially in helping children

overcome the disappointments, dilemmas, anxieties, rivalries, insecurities, and dependencies of these early years. Bettelheim confirms the opinions of Clover and Tatar regarding the plot structure of the fairy tale and
he offers an explanation for that structure worth examining in the context
of the preceding analysis of melodrama.

> The figures in fairy tales are not ambivalent — not good and bad at the
> same time, as we all are in reality. But since polarization dominates the
> child's mind, it also dominates fairy tales. A person is either good or bad,
> nothing in between.... The juxtaposition of opposite characters is not for
> the purpose of stressing right behavior, as would be true of cautionary
> tales.... Presenting the polarities of character permits the child to com-
> prehend easily the difference between the two, which he could not do as
> readily were the figures drawn more true to life, with all the complexi-
> ties that characterize real people. Ambiguities must wait until a relatively
> firm personality has been established on the basis of positive identifica-
> tions. Then the child has a basis for understanding that there are great
> differences between people, and that therefore one has to make choices
> about who one wants to be. This basic decision, on which all later per-
> sonality development will build, is facilitated by the polarization of the
> fairy tale [9].

Fairy tales, then, reflect and confirm polarized moral weightings of good
and bad that already dominate a child's organization of the world.
Although drawing from a traditional psychoanalytic rationale, Bettelheim
describes doublings of the childhood self — as well as corresponding doublings in the perceptions of siblings and parents—consistent with the doubling effects predicted by the mimetic theory of admiration, dependency,
and rivalry presented in Chapter 2.

   In its earliest form, by Bettelheim's account, this doubling results
from conflicts between impulses and internalized parental expectations.
The doubling of siblings and parents results from behaviors on their part
perceived by the child to be punitive, unloving, and hateful and thereby
in contradiction to other behaviors the child experiences as caring and
nurturing. Finding these contradictions difficult to comprehend, the child
resolves the problem by imagining that where there was one there are now
two— a good and bad self, a good and bad version of each sibling, and good
and bad versions of each parent.

   Despite these observations, Bettelheim stresses that fairy tales are not
fundamentally morality plays: "A child's choices are based, not so much
on right versus wrong, as on who arouses his sympathy and who his antipa-
thy.... The child identifies with the good hero not because of his goodness,
but because the hero's condition makes a deep positive appeal to him. The

question for the child is not: 'Do I want to be good?' but 'Who do I want to be like?'" (9–10).

A child is drawn into the fairy tale by seeing that he or she is like one of the heroic characters because of the situation or predicament that character faces. Then the story shows the child how that character faced the predicament and resolved it to the point of a happy conclusion — thereby extending the initial identification into a projected future with the response: "This is who I want to be like."

Fundamentally, fairy tales portray situations and emotions that may be troubling a child and model ways to address and resolve the problems and conflicts associated with them. As Bettelheim says, "the child must make choices about who one wants to be" and the hero provides the model for the child to imitate with respect to judgments and actions. And this is as it should be — at least insofar as fairy tales are, as Bettelheim claims, helpful developmental aids in the growth of children.

Although fairy tales resemble the melodramatic structure of moral polarization, the potential danger in fairy tales, as in the case of melodrama in general, arises not primarily from the unreal polarization presented in its world of moral clarity but rather from the radicalization of that polarization consistent with the recourse to violent resolutions.

However, Bettelheim defends the portrayal of violence in fairy tales as a resolution to their dramatized conflicts and does so by offering three arguments or justifications for the use of violence: the guilt argument, the fantasy release argument (a version of the cathartic theory), and the justice argument. These arguments can be understood and illustrated through three popular and exemplary fairy tales.

Cinderella

The Cinderella story, Bettelheim notes, is fundamentally a story of the agonies of sibling rivalry and is interwoven with many subtle symbols and lines of interpretation relating to the pressures of competition for parental love. Consequently, the central conflict takes place between Cinderella and her stepsisters. At the end of the Brothers Grimm version of the story, the two stepsisters are punished for their wickedness toward Cinderella by having their eyes pecked out by avenging doves. Even though it is the birds that carry out this punishment and not Cinderella, it is clear in the context of the story that the birds represent Cinderella's wishes. Bettelheim addresses the issue of this violent ending in the following way:

> Another aspect which holds large appeal for the child is the vileness of
> the stepmother and stepsisters. Whatever the shortcomings of a child
> may be in his own eyes, these pale into insignificance when compared to
> the stepsisters' and stepmother's falsehood and nastiness. Further, what
> these stepsisters do to Cinderella justifies whatever nasty thoughts one
> may have about one's siblings: they are so vile that anything one may
> wish would happen to them is more than justified. Compared to their
> behavior, Cinderella is indeed innocent. So the child, on hearing her
> story, feels he need not feel guilty about his angry thoughts [240].

According to Bettelheim, the fairy tale relieves the feelings of guilt a child
may have as a result of having wished violence, even death, upon a sibling. In another context, Bettelheim states the argument in a slightly
different way when he claims that "learning that others have the same or
similar fantasies makes us feel that we are a part of humanity, and allays
our fear that having such destructive ideas has put us beyond the common
pale" (122).

Given Bettelheim's own premises about the nature of fairy tales, this
is an extraordinarily weak justification for the portrayal of violence. While
fairy tales are projections and externalizations of emotions and conflicts,
they also serve as models for how a child may overcome these feelings and
situations. And while it is also true that children should not be made to
feel guilty for the emotions they are experiencing, such as jealousy, it is
not appropriate or necessary to affirm all of the ways in which they may
imagine acting out those emotions.

Inclusion of the kind of grotesque violence carried out by the doves
at the end of the story risks lending legitimacy to such violent wishes from
the child's point of view. And it is difficult to understand how Bettelheim
can guarantee that the violence depicted will function primarily, as he suggests, to alleviate guilt rather than serving to legitimize such violence as
appropriate and acceptable in the eyes of the child.

Furthermore, Bettelheim's point that the story has been devised in
such a way as to present characters who are "so vile that anything one may
wish would happen to them is more than justified" raises many red flags,
not the least of which is: What kind of general attitude and response does
this *promote* (never mind reflect) on the part of children in relation to
their real-life conflicts?

To the extent that it is true, as Bettelheim suggests, that children's
minds are oriented along the lines of fairly simple moral polarities (and
this may not be as true as Bettelheim believes), that polarization, when
portrayed in fairy tales, need not be combined with grotesque or deadly
violence.

Contrary to what Bettelheim claims, failing to affirm a child's vengeful thoughts by, for example, excluding portrayals of violent draconian justice need not necessarily aggravate guilt feelings about the vengeful thoughts. Instead the child can be shown that justice is served in other ways. The cruel and unusual punishment given the stepsisters is not even consistent with the general theme of resourcefulness established in the story whereby Cinderella, with the aid of the sympathetic birds, consistently outsmarts and outmaneuvers her stepmother and stepsisters. The stepsisters are frustrated in all their plans, bested by Cinderella in their pursuit of the prince, and punished by their own hand when they cripple themselves by amputating parts of their feet in the attempt to fit into the golden slipper. Amplifying these facts at the conclusion by dwelling on the well-deserved misery of the stepsisters rather than adding the attack of the birds would adequately serve the purposes of the story.

Maria Tatar has, in fact, noted that in the first edition of the story published by the Brothers Grimm the stepsisters were not blinded at the end. Only in the second edition, through the editing of Wilhelm Grimm, did the bloody attack of the doves get added — apparently, according to Tatar, as a result of a trend in disciplinary norms, current to the times, to show wicked behavior reaping brutal punishment. The violent ending to the Cinderella story was tacked on as a contemporary embellishment and is certainly not central to the story's general structure and import.

Given these facts, Bettelheim's protestations against bowdlerizations of the "traditional" stories in an effort to remove extreme violence seem unwarranted. Before they were codified in written forms, fairy tales passed through countless changes in accordance with the cultural trends and perceived needs of the times. In this sense there is no "sacred text" in relation to fairy tales. Extreme violence is not an element of all fairy tales and it is certainly fair to question the need for it in those stories where it does appear.

Hansel and Gretel

In the Hansel and Gretel tale the act of pushing the wicked witch into the oven near the end of the story presents another instance of violence that Bettelheim attempts to justify in a slightly different way. He rightly criticizes attempts to outlaw traditional fairy stories because they present various monsters, ogres, giants, and witches who may, it is argued, frighten children. Speaking in a way that points out the parallels between the horror story and fairy tales, Bettelheim claims that this concern about the presence of monsters in fairy tales misses the point by missing what a child is most concerned with: "the monster he feels himself to be, and which also persecutes him" (120). By depriving the child of fairy stories these monsters are kept buried in the child's unconscious instead of being freed into a fantasy world that presents an opportunity to come to terms with them.

This understanding is fair enough as far as it goes, but Bettelheim then concludes that without such fantasies children will not come to understand and confront their monsters. In the absence of such stories, Bettelheim argues, a "child remains helpless with his worst anxieties—much more so than if he had been told fairy tales which give these anxieties form and body and also show ways to overcome these monsters. If our fear of being devoured takes the tangible form of a witch, it can be gotten rid of by burning her in the oven!" (120).

Regardless of what the witch may be understood to symbolize in the story (Bettelheim suggests that she is an "image of the threatening mother" who would suspend continued nurturing — a personification of regressive dependence), the act of dealing with her by burning her in the oven would seem to be a needlessly excessive and provocative symbol for "overcoming" whatever she symbolizes. It is also inconsistent with the theme of the story — which, like Cinderella, centers on the resourcefulness of Hansel and Gretel in outsmarting those who are designing against them (in this case their parents as well as the witch). In this story it would have been very easy to have shown Hansel and Gretel tricking the witch into taking Hansel's place in the pen and caging her there rather than tricking her into the oven — where she burns to death. What purpose does destroying the witch serve in relation to the larger context of the story?

Bettelheim's response is that an alternative conclusion that does not involve the destruction of the witch would violate the child's sense of justice. This sense of justice requires that the hero or heroes be rewarded and that the evil person meet an appropriate fate. This fate, Bettelheim argues, will meet the child's tests of appropriateness when what the evildoer wishes to have done to the hero matches in severity what is inflicted on the evildoer.

This balanced economy of threat and retribution is also important in relation to what is needed for the proper resolution of the story. Bettelheim explains that true consolation for the hero "requires that the right order of the world is restored; this means punishment of the evildoer, tantamount to the elimination of evil from the hero's world — and then nothing stands any longer in the way of the hero's living happily ever after" (144).

Seeing her chance, Gretel prepares to push the Witch into the oven (drawing by Arthur Rackham) (from the book *Fairy Tales of the Brothers Grimm* by Jacob and Wilhelm Grimm. Trans. Mrs. Edgar Lucas. 1911. London: Constable).

This consolation symbolizes emergence into a developmental state of "higher integration"—an integration Bettelheim makes contingent upon the elimination of evil. Referring to Hansel and Gretel, Bettelheim states, "These children achieve their higher humanity as soon as the witch is burned to death" (146).

Standing alone, this last citation is a startling eye-opener. With this remark Bettelheim dramatically expands his central thesis that fairy tales revolve around the theme of self-worth and empowerment by revealing the means to this goal to be through the destruction of the threatening agent. Bettelheim is not oblivious to the possibility that to many consumers this view of the child's need for justice may seem extreme. He offers a justification for children's demands for violent or deadly retributive justice by appeal to the illustrative example of another well-known fairy tale.

Little Red Riding Hood

Of the many fairy tales, "Little Red Riding Hood" must be grouped among those with the closest parallels to the horror story. In his book on the horror story, Twitchell in fact treats this fairy tale as a paradigmatic precursor to the horror story. Both Twitchell and Bettelheim favor a Freudian-influenced interpretation of this story and identify its central conflict as oedipal in nature. As Bettelheim expresses it, the wolf represents "an externalization of the dangers of overwhelming oedipal feelings" (178). These feelings correspond to a more general tension in the story between desires to seek pleasure and the demands of reality that require sacrifice, discipline, and obedience to parents' admonitions and other prohibitions.

Bettelheim interprets the action at the end of the story—where Little Red Riding Hood kills the wolf by placing stones in his belly—as necessary because she must be the one who plans and carries out the wolf's demise: "If she is to be safe in the future, she must be able to do away with the seducer, be rid of him. If the father-hunter did this for her, [she] could never feel that she had really overcome her weakness, because she had not rid herself of it" (178).

Bettelheim proceeds to explain further that the violent ending is justified because children's anxieties about failing to "overcome" whatever monster is depicted in the story are extreme anxieties associated with being completely rejected, abandoned, and "utterly destroyed." Consequently, only a story in which the hero or heroine is threatened with destruction will be sufficiently adequate and correct from the point of view of children and the dire consequences they associate with failure.

Accordingly, this threat of destruction—often depicted as being eaten—must be balanced by the destruction of the evil threat in order for children to feel secure and triumphant. Bringing the story to a successful conclusion for the hero or heroine will have little significance for children if their fears and anxieties are not adequately resolved. Bettelheim claims that in the fairy tale this resolution must be symbolized by "the destruction of the evildoer. Without that, the hero's finally achieving his rightful place would not be complete, because if evil continued to exist, it would remain a permanent threat" (141).

Here, surprisingly, Bettelheim does not question the psychological consequences of imprinting involved in prompting a child to resolve anxieties by identifying the source of those anxieties as "evil" and by utterly destroying that evil. As a Holocaust survivor, Bettelheim should know better than anyone the potential costs involved in promoting this way of "organizing" ideal fictional worlds—where the ideal can all too readily be made real.

The metaphor of the kill, when used in fairy tales as a metaphor for the negation or rejection of offending desires and behaviors in the self and in others, is *overkill*. It implies and therefore *risks* more than is necessary for the purposes of the story.

In the context of "Little Red Riding Hood," the metaphor of the kill conveys, albeit unconsciously through (by Bettelheim's account) its oedipal symbolism, Little Red Riding Hood's need to rid herself of desire for conjugal attachment and exclusive possession of the father. But it is unclear how the child is supposed to know that it is not sexual feelings in general that must be targeted for riddance. How does a child sort out clearly, consciously or unconsciously, various prohibitions the wolf may symbolize?

Bettelheim himself illustrates this ambiguity in what the wolf symbolizes when he says that the story of Little Red Riding Hood "externalizes the inner processes of the pubertal child: the wolf is the externalization of the badness the child feels when he goes contrary to the admonitions of his parents and permits himself to tempt, or to be tempted, sexually" (177). The issue has now shifted to include not just the temptation of sexual or quasi-sexual feelings for a parent but also the temptation of sexuality in general. Bettelheim then proceeds to explain that the story is in fact designed to instruct children to rid themselves of sexual feelings in general—since children of the age in question are not yet ready for the encounter with sexuality.

The symbol of the wolf, like the symbol of the monster, represents the danger—and the attraction—of powerful emotions. Response to that danger is not modeled well by the metaphor of the kill—especially when it is not entirely clear, because of the ambiguous symbolism of the story, *what* is being killed. Therefore, it is better, when powerful natural emotions are in question, to use metaphors less extreme and less likely to be misunderstood or misapplied in a needlessly destructive way.

Although it may be important for the purposes of the story that Little Red Riding Hood be portrayed as an active agent in overcoming the wolf, that end need not be accomplished by having her kill the wolf. This is especially true insofar as temptations or "weaknesses" the wolf symbolizes are natural and will remain, to some degree, a part of the little girl's nature and thereby a part of her "future."

As in other fairy tales, such as the Arabian Nights' tale "The Fisherman and the Jinny," the Brothers Grimm's "Genie in the Bottle," or the British folk tale "Jack and His Bargains," the monster or threatening creatures can be confronted and overcome through resourcefulness and self-

Little Red Riding Hood meets the wolf (drawing by Arthur Rackham) (from the book *Fairy Tales of the Brothers Grimm* by Jacob and Wilhelm Grimm. Trans. Mrs. Edgar Lucas. 1911. London: Constable).

mastery. This approach teaches a child how to accept his or her emotions and desires along with the understanding that they are not always appropriate and must be modified and controlled for various reasons in various contexts. In the case of "Little Red Riding Hood," this could easily be accomplished by showing the girl — after being set free from the wolf — placing stones in his belly to make him sick and to chase him away rather than to kill him.

Such a modification of the story need not be understood as motivated by hypersensitivity to violence. Rather, it should be understood as preference for the symbolism of a metaphor other than death, a more inclusive metaphor. A metaphor of punishment, for example, does not needlessly risk arousing multiple forms of extreme rejection and destruction and instead orients children toward becoming more accepting and balanced but nevertheless appropriately wary and wily toward their own natures as well as the world.

In being shown how to tame, outwit, or outmaneuver rather than eliminate evil, a child will be better served with respect to personal emotions and desires as well as conflicts and relationships with others. Moreover, the child will not be as much at risk of acquiring the dangerous and illusory idea of weakness as a part of a projected self that must be excised and destroyed. And in being shown that overcoming is possible, a child will be given a more viable sense of security in developing an abiding personal strength in the ability to manage emotions and challenges that remain in one form or another "permanent threats" throughout life.

Fairy Tale and Myth

In his discussion of fairy tales Bettelheim makes an important genre distinction between fairy tale and myth. For Bettelheim, myth is pessimistic while the fairy tale is optimistic. Both forms present symbolic depictions of internal conflicts. After discussing the story of Oedipus, as an exemplary myth, and the trail of unhappiness among Oedipus's ancestors from Tantalus to Pelops to Laius, Bettelheim summarizes his comparison of myth and the fairy tale by claiming that "in myth there is only insurmountable difficulty and defeat; in the fairy tale there is equal peril, but it is successfully overcome. Not death and destruction, but higher integration — as symbolized by victory over the enemy or competitor, and by happiness— is the hero's reward at the end of the fairy tale" (199). The successful outcome and the move to a higher level of personal integration model what children desire for themselves. In this sense fairy tales combine beneficial amusement with mentoring.

Before examining Bettelheim's comparison of myth and fairy tales, it should be emphasized that for many fairy tales he is not entirely accurate in stating that "higher integration" is symbolized by "victory" over the enemy. It would be more accurate to say that in many cases integration is symbolized specifically by victory as the "slaying" or "destruction" of an enemy — which is followed by celebration and the "happily ever after" ending. Insofar as fairy tales following this structure closely resemble melo-drama, Bettelheim's contrast between myth and the fairy tale can be extended to apply equally to the contrast between myth and melodrama.

And because Bettelheim's description of myth as involving "difficulty and defeat" resembles an aspect of tragic drama and because his selected example of the Oedipus myth serves as the basis for several Greek tragedies, his contrast between the fairy tale and myth may be viewed, for the pur-poses of the present inquiry, as analogous to the contrast between melo-drama and tragic drama. Therefore, in extolling the benefits of the fairy tale over myth Bettelheim argues a case parallel in form but contrary to the position that has been argued herein. In Bettelheim's view it would appear that melodramatic form presents a context in which deadly conflict is much more likely than tragic drama to produce positive effects on con-sumers.

Nevertheless, his contrast between the fairy tale and myth prompts a good question: Does not the developmental path to "higher integration" symbolically portrayed in the triumph of a hero through the destruction of an enemy outweigh the potential for harm conveyed through the images of violent resolution?

The late mythologist Joseph Campbell provides an analysis of myth that serves well as a platform from which to sort out this question and the issues raised by Bettelheim's contrast between the fairy tale and myth. Campbell's view of myth runs in the opposite direction of Bettelheim's view. While Campbell acknowledges that certain myths emphasize tragic failings, he argues, "It is the business of mythology proper, *and the fairy tale*, to reveal the specific dangers and techniques of the dark interior way from tragedy to comedy" (1973: 29, emphasis added).

Equating rather than contrasting the functions of myth and the fairy tale, Campbell claims that both conform, broadly speaking, to the struc-ture of comedy. In Campbell's usage "comedy" refers to the "wild and careless, inexhaustible joy of life invincible." In other words, comedy depicts a "down-going" that is followed by an "up-coming" resulting in the triumph of a happy ending. This arc of the hero's path in mythic adven-ture appears in Campbell's formula of the mythic progression as "separa-tion, initiation, return" that he describes in the following famous passage:

> A hero ventures forth from the world of common day into a region of supernatural wonder: fabulous forces are there encountered and a deci-sive victory is won: the hero comes back from this mysterious adventure with the power to bestow boons on his fellow man [1973: 30].

This hero who ventures forth is the "hero with a thousand faces"—and a thousand stories. And in most of the myths that Campbell surveys, the "decisive victory" over "fabulous forces" does not involve destruction of these forces but rather a variety of overcoming through modes of enduring, outwitting, deflecting, transforming, or appropriating the threat. Only in the warrior myths, such as represented by the stories of Theseus, Perseus, and Herakles, does the formula of separation, initiation, and return include confrontations with evil and pollution of sufficient virulence to require destruction on the way to the happy conclusion.

Thus, Campbell's examination of myth suggests that it is a form that is broader than melodrama while also different from tragic drama. Myth includes story forms that show heroic triumph but that do not contain the radical polarization and violence of melodrama. For lack of a better term, these stories may simply be called dramas. But, insofar as myth involves passage through the "dangers and techniques of the dark interior way from tragedy to comedy," it may be significantly distinguished from tragic drama primarily by way of more consistently reliable happy endings. In which case Bettelheim's broad association of myth and tragedy appears, by way of Campbell's analysis, to be questionable.

Similarly, in light of Campbell's close association of fairy tale and myth, Bettelheim's separation of the two seems questionable if not largely mistaken. In being clearly different from and broader than melodramatic form, Campbell's formula for myth does not *require* the use of the metaphor of the kill as the path to resolution of conflict and to a happy ending.

Where slayings occur in tragic drama and associated myth, the violence of the kill is the path to the complication of conflict and tragic consequences. In tragic drama, violence is portrayed in a context that exposes its tragic quality and thereby launches the tragic hero toward what may more justifiably be called a "higher integration"—or a closer approximation to what has been called herein a *synagonistic* tensing of internal and external conflict.

In many ways the Oedipus myth provides the most compelling illustration of the argument against liberal use of the metaphor of the kill to tutor ways in which to bring "boons" to the hero and his community. Even after being warned that he would kill his father, Oedipus nevertheless plunges into the act without realizing what he is doing.

In this regard, it may be asked: What separates a hero such as Theseus from Oedipus? What ensures Theseus, or anyone, against Oedipus's fate? Suppose Theseus discovers after slaying the minotaur that the minotaur is his father? Or, to take a more contemporary example, what if, in

Theseus slays the Minotaur, with Ariadne (left) and King Minos (right); image from a Greek vase (from the picture book *Bilderhefte aus dem Griechischen und Romischen Altertum*. Herakles und Andere Mythen. A. Baumeister. 1889. Munchen: Druck und Verlag von R. Oldenbourg).

the case of *Stars Wars Episode V: The Empire Strikes Back* (1980) Luke discovers that the minotaur in his life — Darth Vader — is his father? Or what if Little Red Riding Hood discovers that the wolf is...? Bettelheim has suggested as much already.

The tragedy of the Oedipus story illustrates not so much that it is hard to know whom one's father is as that no foolproof protection from unsuspected blindness exists. The irreducible possibility of various forms of blindness—symbolized in the Oedipus myth by Oedipus's failure to know his father—ought to give pause to anyone who, although reasonably certain of his or her father's identity, is inclined to use the sword at the crossroads. But, as is explained in Chapters 14 and 15, this need not be an argument for pacifism. It is most fundamentally an allegorical illustration of the terrible complexity and responsibility of the human condition.

This view toward the use of violence should not be taken to suggest, in the case of fairy tales, that the simplified and polarized nature of the conflict in these stories should be amended into something more complex. It suggests only that in many fairy tales the metaphor of the kill is used too loosely and freely and the resulting violence is consequently minimized and trivialized. In order to reduce as much as possible the chances for confusion and misunderstanding, the metaphor of the kill ought to be used in contexts that adequately convey the meaning of violence and its consequences— especially where young consumers are the primary audience. In other words, deadly violence ought to be taken as a matter of sufficient seriousness that it should be used as a metaphor for something other than what it is *only sparingly* and in carefully selected contexts. This rule applies especially, as will be discussed more fully in the next three chapters, in cultures and social contexts where the opportunities for conflict are greatly heightened.

13

Comic Books
and Video Games

The genres of the fairy tale and the horror story are also close genealogical relatives of comic book plots featuring endless varieties of "superheroes." The comic book superhero is a transformation of the Doppelgänger. The dual identity of the hero/monster in the horror story converts in the comic book into the dual identity of the hero/superhero. In the comic book the supervillain assumes the function of the monster and becomes the superhero's archenemy. Compared to the horror story, this innovation in the melodramatic plot softens the focus on conflict within the hero while centering attention on the radical external conflict between the superhero and the supervillain. Nevertheless, the theme of internal conflict continues between the two personas of the hero and the superhero.

Similar to the horror story, the hero of the comic book plot is a representative, although not necessarily luminous, member of the community who does not, at least initially, stand out — especially in the eyes of the featured woman. The monster and the superhero, however, get the attention of the woman in a heartbeat. The hero/superhero doubling, for example, may present, on the superficial ego side, an ordinary and perhaps somewhat bungling and insecure figure — as in the case of Clark Kent or Peter Parker — and, on the serious alter-ego side, the extraordinary, awe-inspiring, superheroes of Superman and Spiderman. Or the pair may present a stuffed-shirt business tycoon such as Bruce Wayne or a milquetoast gentleman such as Lamont Cranston as the counterpoles to amazing and fearsome (especially to criminals) superheroes such as Batman and

Primary superhero types: Spiderman, Superman, Batman, and the Shadow (author's collage).

the Shadow. In each case the monstrous and evil half of the horror story double-goer is replaced in the comic book by a superhuman power, sometimes animal-like (as is often the case in the monster of the horror story), but always representing a prodigious extension of the power for good.

The Case for Empowerment

The classic superhero alter-egos show that a seemingly transparent, predictable, and unassuming person may have a hidden and exceptional dimension that is a secret to all but a privy and select few. This device enhances self-image among comic book fans, as they are encouraged to imagine themselves as also possessing a persona of exceptional quality that goes undetected by almost everyone. In this sense the dual identity of the hero works as a device to empower the consumer whereas in the horror story it initially works to introduce shock and fear while also eventually serving to effect a sense of empowerment through the destruction of the monster.

In his popular book on the effects of media violence entitled *Killing Monsters: Why Children Need Fantasy, Super Heroes, and Make-Believe Violence* (2002), Gerard Jones confirms Bettelheim's findings about fairy tales and the sense of empowerment they provide and extends that claim to comic books and video games. Children and adolescents want to feel secure, confident, and capable. Jones believes that children are served in beneficial ways by violent entertainment because it can help them to act out — through imaginative fantasy and physical play — anger and aggressive impulses.

In making a case for this view, Jones sides with proponents of the cathartic theory of effects but offers a slightly more sophisticated version. He acknowledges the research studies that have lent support to those who have reasoned that "if children play more aggressively after watching aggressive images, then surely the images are stimulating their aggression rather than aiding its release" (39).

In rebuttal to this view, however, Jones argues that this need not mean that catharsis is not occurring because watching television and playing afterwards are not separate processes. Jones points out that "catharsis requires the emotions to be stimulated before they can be released. Just *watching* a video usually won't bring about a release of tension or anger, but many times I've seen a roomful of kids get wound up over a *Pokémon* scene and then jump off the couch and reenact it physically until they're tired and relaxed" (39–40).

Citing Penny Holland's studies at British preschools, Jones explains that she found that kids who were allowed to play with toy guns became more aggressive in the short term but notably more relaxed later in the day. In light of such provocative studies, Jones suggestively asks: "If mock-aggressive play is good for children, and if these experiments demonstrate that entertainment violence inspires children to engage in mock-aggressive play, could it be that the experiments actually demonstrate that entertainment violence is *good*?" (40).

Thus far, Jones's reasoning corroborates the argument advanced in the section on catharsis that viewing violent entertainment does not in itself accomplish a catharsis of aggressive emotions but instead produces an arousal that may end in genuine catharsis only when it leads to a form of active physical expression. Unlike many analysts writing on the topic,

Jones at least acknowledges that it is unlikely the viewing of violent (melo-dramatic) entertainment is genuinely cathartic in itself. Although lucid on this point, Jones then overlooks the larger issue: What *kind* of mock-aggression is a child being encouraged to act out?

Which Empowerment?

Up to a point, Jones is accurate in his summary of the situation with regard to children and teenagers and their needs: "For young people to develop selves that serve them well in life, they need modeling, mentor-ing, guidance, communication, and limitations. But they also need to fan-tasize, and play, and lose themselves in stories. That's how they reorganize the world into forms they can manipulate. That's how they explore and take some control over their own thoughts and emotions. That's how they kill their monsters" (60).

But do they need to *kill* their monsters? Must a child's confidence, assertiveness, or release of bottled energy be purchased at the price of play-acted slayings of those who have been offered up to the imagination as debased, unworthy, and expendable pollutants in the world? Instead of being encouraged and shown how to kill their monsters, young people need to be shown that "monsters"—whether as projections of a part of themselves or as genuine threats in the world around them — are more productively confronted by an attitude that does not readily assume they are suitable for the knife.

Even though "slaying" may be thought to serve in these forms of fictional entertainment as a metaphor for the negation of some unwanted trait or imagined external threat, it is a metaphor that nevertheless frames the negation in a structure of radical exclusion. In the formative years this structure of radical exclusion is easily appropriated as the model for under-standing all intense conflict. It also provides a foundation for cruel and devaluing forms of behavior toward those who end up on the other side of any competition or conflict.

The presentation of an imaginary world exhibiting simple moral polarities is, as Bettelheim has suggested in the case of fairy tales, appro-priate for children as they learn to make basic discriminations. But, as Bettelheim also points out, as a child transitions into adolescence and adulthood, the imaginary world of simple polarities becomes less and less adequate as a model for comprehending and coping with the real world. However, even in the developmental stage of childhood, the radically exclusive antagonism of good and evil presented in a conflict resolved by death or destruction appears unnecessarily extreme and needlessly violent for the purposes of entertainment, play, catharsis, or moral instruction.

The ability to discriminate between right and wrong and good and bad is an ability that must be taught to all young people in a variety of ways and contexts. But the model of moral choice offered in the discriminations between right and wrong and good and bad must be distinguished from the more extreme discrimination evident in the contrast between good and evil. The difference lies in the fact that evil, as has been argued in the previous chapters, functions through the weight of traditional imprinting as a label of sufficiently extreme negation to not only warrant but require destruction.

Jones is no doubt correct to point out the benefits of the interrelation of play and entertainment when he explains that play " 'explodes' tensions through emotional arousal and make-believe aggression ... [and] provides correctives, happy endings, that help children to believe that what frightens them can be overcome. It helps them navigate their concerns through structures and rules that they can learn and predict and so feel they've mastered" (101). For Jones, entertainment fits into this process when young people construct fantasies around what they view and then work those fantasies into their social lives or into video games.

But here again the question must be asked: What are the particular "structures and rules" being mastered? When children engage in play after viewing violent entertainment of a melodramatic nature, the play may indeed provide beneficial recreation and release of emotions but it will also conceal attitudes toward conflict and toward make-believe adversaries — attitudes derived directly from the viewing — that can only serve to predispose them to radical modes of devaluation of others in the course of managing real conflict.

Although most children learn to distinguish well between fantasy and reality, the constant repetition of deadly resolutions of imaginary conflicts works in a highly effective way — not unlike repetitive media advertisements (which are notoriously influential on young people) — to structure and condition attitudes toward real conflict and toward the real world.

Real-World Education

In defending his catharsis thesis Jones also makes the same mistake Bettelheim makes by arguing that the extremes of violence evident (or believed to be evident) in the real world must be equaled by extremes of violence portrayed in fictional entertainment. Jones insists, for example, that "children crave fantasy violence for many reasons, but one reason they so often crave it raw, loud, and angry is that they need it to be strong enough to match and master their anxiety and anger. Entertainment violence has become far more intense and explicitly gory over the past forty years because the reality with which we confront young people has become so much more intensely and explicitly violent" (101). James Twitchell advances a similar argument in *Preposterous Violence: Fables of Aggression in Modern Culture* (1989) where he claims that repetitive viewings of extreme and outrageous depictions of violence have a ritual socializing function for adolescents driven by extreme anxieties about themselves and their world.

Here Jones and Twitchell, like many others, do not pause to consider the possibility that the increasing intensity in violence in both the entertainment world and the real world may be aided and accelerated by competitive commercial interests in an unholy alliance with fundamental attitudes toward moral order and conflict management embedded in cultural tradition — attitudes that are then only further aided and accelerated by being constantly mirrored and reiterated in various media.

Jones develops his argument further by explaining that "what television news programs are willing to show, what parents are willing to discuss within earshot of their children, gives young people thoughts and images to grapple with that demand fantasy images just as potent" (101). But the fundamental problem has little to do with the *potency* of images — either real or fantasy.

Children do not need *more potent* images of violence to cope with a violent reality. They need instead images of violence presented in a structure and a context that will help them confront and express their feelings in ways that do not exacerbate them to the point of destructive extremes of devaluation and dehumanization of themselves or others. Melodrama cannot provide such a structure. It can only provide weak and temporary forms of catharsis of anxieties and aggressions while feeding further the same cycles of emotions and the potential for their violent expression.

During the 1970s the television program *Kung Fu* provided weekly illustrations of the attitude and the behavior corresponding to an aggressive response to deadly threats without a primary recourse to deadly violence. This program did not sanitize violence but confronted it directly with many scenes of explicit violence. But, Caine, the main protagonist (played by David Carradine), had a perspective toward violence that modeled the advantages of retaining respect for the other even in the midst of violent conflict. This program was as popular — if not more popular — than many of the traditionally melodramatic Westerns of the same or previous television era. *Kung Fu* proved that if audiences, especially young audiences, were given something other than the simplistic conflict and violence of traditional melodrama, the response to it would match the popularity of melodrama.

Modeling intentions and actions displaying competitive but nonlethal and nonmaiming forms of aggression will accomplish the same purposes of empowerment without the downside ramifications of modeling deadly violence.

There can be no question that kids are drawn to violence — just as they are drawn to sex. Sex and violence tap into the most elemental and powerful emotions because they are associated with the two

David Carradine as Caine, a Shaolin monk in the Old West, in the 1970s television series *Kung-Fu.*

most essentially defining and profoundly mysterious aspects of life: procreation and death. Sex and violence have entertainment value because, as a function of their unsurpassed import for life, they have shock value. Purveyors of entertainment as well as advertisers find them reliable and useful bait for grabbing attention.

Media is big business and there are many hours and days to fill with entertainment and television programming. Considering the need to keep personnel in film and television production companies busy and the enormous blocks of time to fill on network and cable television, it is not surprising that program creators rely on stock formulas and mechanisms for gaining attention. When adding to this demand the enormous additional opportunities in foreign entertainment markets along with the corresponding need for programs that reduce translation difficulties by emphasizing visual storytelling appeal, the time constraints and financial enticements of quick formulaic solutions for programming become even greater. Sex and violence come to the rescue.

The same is true of news media, especially with regard to violence. In today's media world the popular saying "If it bleeds, it leads" is no exaggeration. Even though the statistics support the contention that the United States is a more violent society than other nations with a comparable standard of living, news media attention can augment these facts to create extreme impressions. The focus by news media on violence and the inflated sense of a violent environment it elicits has led some to speculate, along with Jones, that "if young people grew up in a society less preoccupied [in the news] with violence and horror, they might crave less entertainment gore. They might be better off, too" (103).

Here Jones reiterates again the idea that exposure through news media to a violent world — however exaggerated that might be — sets up a potential coping need against which "it's unreasonable to ask [children and adolescents] to be satisfied with make-believe that is more sanitized than their reality. Taking away the entertainment that enables them to grapple with reality won't make their reality better but may only leave them more defenseless against it" (103).

But the increasing intensity of entertainment gore may have little to do with keeping pace with real-world violence. A likely alternative explanation, discussed in detail in Chapter 19, presents itself in the view that escalation of entertainment gore is a function of an ill-considered attempt to keep pace with competition in the marketplace rather than a function of the coping needs of consumers. New extremes of graphic violence and more shocking plot turns may well be driven by responses to recent innovations by competitor film and television producers and the need to find something new that will offer a difference that can be exploited to promote the current investment project. As discussed in the early chapters of this book, young audiences are attracted to horror and entertainment violence in the course of dealing with growth and identity crises and this vulnerability is overexploited in the depths to which the entertainment business will stoop in the depiction of violence to maintain or gain competitive edge and increase revenue streams.

Nevertheless, the idea that entertainment violence does no harm or has beneficial effects meets with reactions strongly divided between those who wholeheartedly agree and those who vehemently disagree. The possibility that both sides can be right, depending on the structure and context within which the violence is presented, explains, at least in part, why both sides can feel so justified in their positions.

However, the belief that depicted violence can be beneficial in its effects when presented in certain contexts such as tragic drama and related forms does not alleviate the concern that a great many young people choose melodramatic violence as a source of entertainment. Having been exposed to the easily assimilated but polarized fantasy world of fairy tale ogres and comic book villains, teenagers find the attractions of melodramatic films familiar, compelling, and entertaining. But this need not be taken as proof that melodramatic fictions offering deadly violent resolutions are harmless.

Video Games and the Real World

The development of video game technology over the last two or three decades has added another source of entertainment, often violent in nature, that many, including Jones, argue is potentially more beneficial in its effects than other forms of violent entertainment. The potential for greater benefit derives from the fact that video games offer a dimension of participation, interaction, and physical response that is absent in spectator media. This added dimension of engagement, it is argued, makes it possible for video games to achieve greater or more complete cathartic effects.

It is also argued that while many, if not most, video games center on various themes of warlike violence the games nevertheless have little to do with violence. The simulated modes of fighting are instead ways to practice game skills involving reaction times, accuracy of aim, and strategy.

In light of the preceding analysis, however, it should be obvious that these beliefs about video games are extraordinarily misguided. The structure of violent video games revolves around the presentation of a "target" in response to which the prime imperative is to destroy the target with as little thought between perception and pulling the trigger as possible. The target is usually an "enemy" (soldier, criminal, spy, or gangster) or an evil monster (ghoul, beast, or alien). This structure entirely conforms to melodramatic design and the element of "participation" is predominantly visual and cognitive and minimally emotional. As with melodrama, the potential for catharsis in relation to any emotions aroused is superficial and highly transitory at best.

The structure of video games also facilitates the predisposition toward extreme devaluation of an adversary who, in its destruction, offers no sense of human verisimilitude. Some defenders of violence in video games find this fact to be a positive quality that serves to mitigate the harmful effects of the participation in violence. For example, one commentator, whose views reflect those shared by many video game enthusiasts, blithely notes that there is no suffering in video games and that "the pain is never shown and the victim can be completely run over and then pop back up without harm. The characters ... are not given a substantial personality and they lack real life motivations and emotions. They remind more of toys than

One among many selections of video games with violent themes at a shopping mall arcade.

of living creatures" (Ioannidis, 2003). A disturbing complacency resides in this view in the astounding ease with which it assumes that the influence in video games is all unidirectional and that substituting humanlike "toys" for real humans in video games need not give rise to any troubling concerns in the reverse direction regarding conditioning effects whereby humans may be reduced to mere toys or targets in the heat of real-life conflict.

Perhaps intuitively sensing the oversight in his disconnect between the cognitive imprinting of video training with humanlike toys and conflict management in the real world, this same commentator goes on to make an extraordinary concession: "I don't mean that simulated violence is a good or even acceptable subject for games or films."

However, this surprising concession immediately precedes another astonishing disconnect: "but this [simulated violence] is a completely different matter having to do with the poverty of original ideas and inadequacy of dominant value systems characteristic of our society and not with the mechanisms behind insensitive or violent behavior." As argued herein, the "dominant value system" underlying melodrama and promoting a particular structuring of conflict evident in video games must be included as a primary contributor to the "mechanisms behind insensitive or violent behavior."

This disconnect, however, does not diminish the correctness of the additional point about the "poverty of original ideas." Video game manufacturers could easily devise games that would achieve the purposes of testing reflexes, hand and eye coordination, accuracy, and modes of strategy without resorting to formats and scenarios that involve the depiction of killing opponents. However, simulations of the slaying of adversaries should not be censored. Parental warnings and age controls, on the other hand, are more appropriate and ought to be required, as is now the case in most areas of the United States. Censorship only raises the value of violent game simulations as attractions to young gamers. But violent games can nevertheless be discouraged and boycotted in homes and malls and reserved for military use where the context of the action can be prepared for in ways that adequately take pains to minimize the potential for dehumanization effects. Ensuring that the military provides such context and preparation in relation to combat training introduces an additional area of cultural concern.

At this point it becomes especially evident that the analysis of the effects of portrayed violence on an audience broadens into larger social issues relating to attitudes and moral codes dealing with conflict, competition, violence, and war. The question of the propagation of attitudes toward conflict in fictional entertainment cannot be separated from the broader social context and cannot be adequately addressed without a more direct confrontation with a question that has been looming in the background of the entire discussion thus far: Is there such a thing as "evil" in the world? And if so, what could be more right than to target it for elimination?

14

Real Horror

It would seem natural to suppose that the conflict structure presented in melodrama derives from and has corresponding examples in real life. But if the assessments of some observers of public opinion are to be believed, this assumption is, in current times, no longer an automatic assumption. For example, popular television commentators Bill O'Reilly and Sean Hannity have on occasion found it necessary to assert, in the face of what they perceive to be widespread belief to the contrary, that there is in fact evil in the world. And in making such assertions O'Reilly and Hannity do not merely intend to point out the fact that people do terrible things to each other. They intend primarily to draw attention to the presence and the workings of something analogous to a natural force, a corrupting agency of evil in the world, consistent with the notion of evil as defilement. In the twentieth century, this view was strongly evident in social, political, military, and religious confrontations.

Real World as Melodrama

The identification of evil in the world, articulated in expressions of real-life imperatives, was a commonplace in the mass media and political rhetoric of many countries of the twentieth century — including prominently fascist nations but also including democracies such as Britain and the United States. In his book *Faces of the Enemy* (1986), Sam Keen documents the many ways in which both the Allies and the Axis powers of World War II used images and metaphors of evil, corruption, and defilement to depict the essential nature of their enemy nations. According to

Keen, Winston Churchill and Franklin Roosevelt made use of the words "evil" and "evildoers" during World War II in reference to the fascist threat of the Axis powers.

At the outset of the cold war, Harry Truman used the phrase "evil spirit" to describe the Soviet threat. During his presidency, Richard Nixon continued this tone in no uncertain terms: "It may seem melodramatic to say that the United States and Russia represent Good and Evil. But if we think of it that way, it helps to clarify our perspective on the world struggle" (cited in Keen, 1986: 31). The terminology of evil again rose to prominence in the late era of the cold war when Ronald Reagan, echoing the rhetoric of previous presidents as well as the rhetoric of popular culture in the *Star Wars* films, described the Soviet Union as "the evil empire" (Ivie, 1984).

In labeling the war against terrorism as a war against an "axis of evil," George W. Bush attempted to invoke and extend the spirit and attitudinal resolve implicit in the rhetoric of evil employed through the entire period of World War II and the cold war. In an extensive study of Bush's public addresses following the events of September 11, 2001, rhetorical scholar Denise Bostdorff argues that his statements clearly promote analogies between the conflict of World War II and the current crisis. Bostdorff notes that in the months following 9/11, Bush's speeches repeatedly "urged the younger generations of Americans to uphold the faith of their 'elders,' the World War II generation, and encouraged all Americans to recommit themselves to the nation by supporting the war on terrorism" (2003: 294).

In a speech before the Joint Session of Congress on September 20, 2001, Bush specifically compared Al Qaeda terrorists to the Nazi and Soviet regimes, finding the terrorists— in their radical vision and fanaticism — to be "the heirs of all the murderous ideologies of the 20th century ... follow[ing] in the path of fascism and Nazism and totalitarianism" (cited in Bostdorff, 304). Having pressed this analogy on several occasions, Bush then fused the rhetoric of World War II with the rhetoric of the cold war in his State of the Union speech when he identified the terrorists and their rogue government allies as an "axis of evil." Confronted with a threat of this nature, Bush concluded that the nation must remain consistent with the resolve of previous generations and that Americans must rise "to answer these attacks and rid the world of evil" (cited in Bostdorff, 2003: 304). Princeton University Professor of Ethics Peter Singer, in *The President of Good and Evil* (2004), continues further in the direction of Bostdorff's analysis and provides thorough documentation of Bush's reliance on the rhetoric of good and evil.

Bush's leadership in choice of rhetoric set the tone for the flood of public discourse that poured forth from many commentators and pundits in the months following the events of 2001. David Frum and Richard Perle, for example, authored a book entitled *An End to Evil: How to Win the War on Terror* (2003) and Rachel Ehrenfeld published *Funding Evil: How Terror is Financed* (2003). Television commentator Sean Hannity's acceptance and continuation of Bush's rhetoric is evident in broadcast comments such as, "There are evil people plotting our demise and we need to destroy them" (Fox Network, July 25, 2003), as well as in his latest book *Deliver Us from Evil: Defeating Terrorism, Despotism, and Liberalism* (2004) where he paints a cosmic battlefield and speaks of evil as a force personified with quasi-human intentionality: "Evil exists. It is real, and it means to harm us" (2). Hannity's views, although among the most strident, are nevertheless consistent with many renowned expressions in the mass media of the belief in the fact of evil in the world and the kind of polarized judgment and action it requires.

Considering these statements in light of the interrogation thus far conducted of the structure of good and evil in melodrama raises an inevitable question — a question posed by Hannity in the book just cited: "How could anyone witness the horrors of that day [9/11], or the mass graves discovered in Iraq after the fall of Saddam Hussein, and dismiss the idea of evil?" (2). Phrased in language keeping with the themes addressed herein: Are there, all theory aside, instances of radical evil in real life with corresponding villains? Are there "evil people" who are clearly pollutants deserving of the label of evil and thereby thoroughly worthy of destruction?

If the answer to such questions is yes, it would seem that melodrama does nothing more than portray a type of radical evil consistent with a type of radical conflict that must be acknowledged and dealt with in real life. If such is the case, it may be fairly argued that there is a necessity for the melodramatic structuring of conflict that cannot and should not be overlooked or repressed for the sake of a perhaps overly "genteel" and romantically idealized approach to conflict.

Chasing White Whales

The question of the applicability of melodramatic structure to real life can perhaps be best approached through the illustrative rigors of a test case. When the question of evil is raised in the context of the twentieth century, Adolf Hitler emerges as perhaps the greatest figure of evil, playing the role of a real-life villain in a melodrama of world historical proportions.

Hitler's suitability for such a role has not been overlooked by Hollywood. Many entirely fictional screenplays—such as *The Boys of Brazil* (1978) and *Raiders of the Lost Ark* (1981), to name two—have made use of Hitler and the Nazi regime to fill the requirements for the role of the villain in melodramatic plots.

But viewing Hitler as an evil of world historical proportions conceals an unsettling irony. Hitler becomes a figure of great evil precisely by way of attempting—with a thoroughgoing sense of righteousness—to rid Europe, if not the world, of what he perceived to be a great evil. Consistent with the tradition of understanding evil as defilement, his program to restore and preserve the purity of the Aryan race centered on identifying the Jews as evil and as an essential contamination.

In his 1938 review of Hitler's *Mein Kampf*, Kenneth Burke describes how, in the case of Hitler, evil ought to be identified and confronted.

> It may well be that people, in their human frailty, require an enemy as well as a goal. Very well: Hitlerism itself has provided us with such an enemy—and the clear example of its operation is guaranty that we have, in him and all he stands for, no purely fictitious "devil-function" made to look like a world menace by rhetorical blandishments, but a reality whose ominousness is clarified by the record of its conduct to date. In selecting his brand of doctrine as our "scapegoat," and in tracking down its equivalents ... we shall be at the very center of accuracy [1973: 219].

Here Burke points out that a "purely fictitious 'devil-function' [can be] made to look like a world menace by rhetorical blandishments," as was the case with the Jews as the target of Hitler's rhetoric. Burke claims that the *correct* "scapegoat" should be the policies and practices of *scapegoating*— evident in "Hitlerism." With this recommendation he turns the principle of exclusion inherent in scapegoating on itself, fighting fire with fire and making the practice of scapegoating itself the scapegoat.

The war against what Hitler viewed as the "Jewish problem" became itself the great evil; it not only fueled World War II but also culminated in the Holocaust. The process of scapegoating, as a mistaken projection of evil on a victim, appears in a very real sense to be itself the evil that needs to be identified and confronted.

Insofar as scapegoating, as previously suggested, may be seen as structurally consistent with the melodramatic form of hero versus villain and good versus evil, the redirection of scapegoating back upon itself—when considered in the context of dramatic structure—suggests a corresponding alteration of dramatic form. A well-known story from the realm of classic fiction can serve to illustrate the point.

Herman Melville's *Moby Dick* presents a good example — perhaps the greatest in American fiction — of the tension of redirection of scapegoating and its effects on melodramatic structure. Along the melodramatic line of interpretation, the story of Ahab and the white whale would seem to follow, in superficial respects at least, the structure of the horror story. The whale is the monster, Ahab is the hero, and the relational role normally filled by a woman is in this case performed by the loyal yet conflicted crew of the *Pequod*.

The whale, as the monster, is also Ahab's Doppelgänger. As the mysterious and threatening creature lurking below the waters of the horizon, the whale reflects the shadow side of Ahab beneath the horizon of his self-awareness. His obsession with killing the whale leaves no doubt about his understanding of it as evil and, by extension, his unconscious understanding of the shadow side of himself as worthy of expulsion and destruction.

In the case of *Moby Dick* doubts surface early and continue to grow concerning who or what is in fact evil. If Ahab is to be believed, the whale is the great evil. But as the story unfolds, early uneasiness grows into serious doubt about whether Ahab's judgment can be trusted. By the end of the story the alignment of good and evil has turned full circle with the realization that Ahab himself may well be the source of evil.

Given a melodramatic reading, the whale appears as the symbol and embodiment of evil, a demonic will bent solely on destruction and against whom Ahab's heroic dying efforts are finally successful. But the tale, as Melville tells it, finally elicits a viewpoint from which the whale appears as the unfortunate victim of Ahab's misguided and fanatical persecution.

What functions as evil in *Moby Dick* may be more the *idea* of evil, the notion of evil as defilement operative in Ahab's worldview, which includes his self-understanding. This idea of evil and its scapegoating effects may well be what Melville wants to single out for exceptional attention.

The hero/villain reversal in *Moby Dick* is not a simple role reversal within melodramatic form. It is instead a radical reversal of reader orientation that succeeds in altering melodramatic structure by placing the structure itself in question. As the scapegoater is transformed through the "strength" of his conviction into the scapegoat, the mechanism of scapegoating — grounded in the notion of alien agency and radical and essential pollution — is exposed itself as a kind of villain.

Ahab believes that he, among a select few, can identify genuine evil and destroy it — and he sees this evil in the whale. Or, if preferred, he sees this evil in himself and projects it on the whale as something that must be eradicated. Conviction, drive, and passionate belief are — it would seem — traits corresponding to great strength of character. But this strength of character, similar to the fatal flaw in the character of a Greek tragic hero, contributes crucially to Ahab's undoing.

The white whale stands out among whales because of its unusual color and size. The whale functions for Ahab as something "monstrous" because it seems not to belong. Its size and color make it appear disturbingly different as a violation of nature having no place and belonging nowhere. His previous encounter with Moby Dick—in which the whale takes his leg—confirms for him that it is malevolent. These exceptional traits lend themselves to Ahab's belief that the whale is a form of pollution. And, consistent with a psychological reading of the story, they confirm the whale as an appropriate symbol for the way in which Ahab regards the shadow side of himself.

With further similarity to tragic drama, Ahab's single-minded devotion to his vision of evil leads to his own complete destruction as well as the demise of all but one of the crew. Because he is, to the best of his obsessive understanding, seeking to do good by destroying evil, Ahab's violent fate has an ironic quality. Nevertheless, it becomes clear how his fate is an outcome consistent with his way of seeing.

As an interpretive model, the fictional drama of *Moby Dick* can illuminate the real-life drama of Adolf Hitler. Assuming, for the sake of comparison, that Hitler is analogous to Ahab in *Moby Dick*, the Jews, as the subjects of Hitler's persecution, are analogous to the white whale. As with Ahab, Hitler's intense preoccupation with the themes of purity and the riddance of impurity function as his fundamental guide, the ground of his sacred core of belief, his "strength of character." His extraordinarily thorough adherence to this guiding belief is revealed through the course of events, to be his great weakness, his crucial flaw, his *hamartia*.

Hitler. Third Reich stamp image, issue of 1941.

Like Ahab, Hitler is a man who believes he is on the path of righteousness in his ability to identify and oppose evil. Like Ahab, he believes he is doing

Ahab (drawing by Raymond Bishop) (from the book *Moby Dick or, The Whale* by Herman Melville. 1939. New York: Albert and Charles Boni, Inc.).

good. In Chapter 2 of *Mein Kampf*, for example, Hitler writes, "I am convinced that I am acting as the agent of our Creator. By fighting off the Jews, I am doing the Lord's work." But while Ahab's persecution of the white whale may be grotesquely disturbing, Hitler's radical persecution of fellow human beings is horrifying in the extremes of its program of purification by deadly violence. Hitler and Ahab differ significantly in their choice of scapegoat, but the underlying belief that drives their violent actions is precisely the same. It is rooted in the tradition of understanding evil as a pollution that can only be cleansed through its destruction. It is worth noting in this context that the classic and starkly drawn melodrama, *King Kong* (1933), was one of Hitler's favorite films. (See Chapter 25 for a discussion of the "creature feature" form of melodrama.)

But in the case of *Moby Dick*, the structure of melodrama undergoes a reflexive redirection. It shifts from being good versus evil and the identification and elimination of destructive alien agency to being a confrontation with a human being engaged in scapegoating as a consequence of blind adherence to a particular logic of evil.

As a result of the redirection, the drama is no longer classic melodrama. The stakes have changed and the conflict has become more like the conflict of tragic drama, bringing forth a broadly encompassing ruth and awe rather than fear followed by celebration in the destruction of evil. Although tragic ruth in response to victims of violence is appreciably different from ruth in response to the blindness of the perpetrators of violence, ruth nevertheless extends to both sides of the conflict.

The "Evil" in Evil

In reflexive melodrama, the attitude of the audience toward a dark or villainlike protagonist (for example, Ahab) fundamentally changes through deepening character revelations. Similar to tragic drama, the troubled protagonist appears as a complex human being who has adopted, through a form of partial blindness, a ruinous set of instructions for operating in the world. Instead of being presented with a character aligned with evil and designed for destruction, the audience encounters a character who appears mistaken in orientation in a way that becomes tragically destructive.

This way of structuring dramatic conflict, when applied to real life, suggests a broadening of orientation toward conflict. The great problem with the notion of evil as defilement lies not merely in the possibility that it *can be* misapplied but rather in the reality that it is *always* misapplied.

As already suggested in the context of the discussion of tragic drama, the logic of evil as a way of structuring conflict can be displaced by another approach to conflict and by a less potentially destructive way of looking at evil. In this alternative way of looking at what is usually regarded as evil, evil is essentially a misperception of the nature, the functional relation, and the ecology of beings. Nothing is essentially a pollution and nothing is fundamentally worthy of elimination from the order of being. In this sense there is no "evil."

The notion of a force of evil or evil as absolute impurity has been thoroughly examined and debunked by ethical theorists such as Michael Shermer in *The Science of Good and Evil* (2004). Consistent with the preceding analysis, Shermer concludes that as a noun and an active agency *"there is no such thing as evil"* (68; emphasis in the original).

It could be argued that the new role for the word "evil" becomes the old *concept* of evil. The notion of evil as pollution, as that which is in its essence worthy of elimination, is the *real* evil because it is precisely through the introduction of this notion that the possibility of *finding* something to be inessential to the whole emerges. This concept of evil introduces the justification for the radical sacrificial negation of beings. Without this justification, it would be much more difficult, if not impossible, to kill with a sense of the productiveness of the act. And certainly it would not be possible to kill with any sense of celebration. Hitler became an "evil" of enormous proportions not through personal actions alone but through nationwide susceptibility to the dangers of scapegoating, conditioned by the prevalence and acceptance of a way of thinking about evil rooted deeply in Western culture.

In the passage cited above, Burke suggests a way to oppose this evil. He urges combating the "evil" of the traditional concept of evil with a "fighting fire with fire" approach when he maintains that the way to oppose Hitler and Hitlerism is to make the scapegoater the scapegoat. But there is little profit and no ultimate success in attacking an instance of scapegoating by *repeating* the logic of scapegoating. In its pure desperation, such a tactic can yield only expedient short-term gains while only reinforcing the structure and exacerbating difficulties in the long term.

In one sense, targeting Hitler's brand of doctrine as the "scapegoat" would seem to be "the very center of accuracy" as Burke claims. But the process of identifying scapegoating as the "evil" and turning it back upon itself proves to be an inadequate measure. It perpetuates the destructive dangers inherent in the radically dualistic logic of pollution on which scapegoating rests. Through its tacit, albeit ironic, acceptance of the logic of scapegoating and the principle of radical exclusion implicit in the idea of the scapegoat as, in its essence, worthy of elimination, this redirection of scapegoating only repeats in yet another way the same principle of victimage.

The idea of evil as radical pollution falters on the reality that everything that exists functions, through one context or another, as pollution in relation to something else. In this respect, everything is a contingent pollution. The traditional idea of evil takes the concept of pollution out of all contingent context and places it in the universal context of essential and absolute pollution in relation to a perceived "whole"—whether viewed as community, nation, or world. Through this radical idealization, the concept of pollution, which is not essentially a destructive concept in itself, assumes enormous destructive power by inaugurating a "pollutant" that has no context, no role, no functional place anywhere.

In *Moby Dick*, Ahab adheres to this radical idea of evil that functions by way of pushing a concept, such as "pollution," to the extreme whereby it serves to designate "that which has no place, no context in the world"— a concept that then gives license to the belief that the white whale does not belong, that it has no place.

But the idea of something as absolutely out of all worldly context fundamentally breaks down against the necessity that whatever has made its appearance in the world must in some way "belong" or must be essentially "natural"—otherwise it could not have come into being.

In the melodramatic plot the dramatist purposefully designs a character to be perceived as essentially disposable. In real life there are likely no such characters and the advantages of structuring conflict in a way that creates such characters may be far less than is usually assumed. Granting the "human frailty" of which Burke speaks— evident in the ease with which humans find enemies and the ease with which enemies are turned into devils and "pollutants"— a moratorium on the logic of evil as defilement and the attendant possibilities for scapegoating is at the very least worth considering.

The opposition to Hitler in World War II need not be understood melodramatically as an instance of the purging of a world-class contaminant. Scapegoating tyrants like Hitler can be opposed — even militaristically — through an inclusive attitude that preserves the essential humanity of an adversary even in the midst of violent conflict. Such an attitude can play an important role in war by preventing self-destructive doses of hatred and needless escalations of collateral destruction and civilian genocide that have been all too evident in human history. In this connection Sam Keen, in his book *Faces of the Enemy*, captures something of the requisite attitude for taking up arms: "And when we must fight, it must not be as holy warriors but as deeply repentant men and women who are caught in the tragic conflicts of a history that we have not yet had the vision, the will, or the courage to change" (1986: 181).

In the case of Hitler this attitude ensures that, despite all appearances, he is understood first and foremost as a human being, a person with *human* qualities, motivations, and limitations—no matter how uncomfortable it may be to share that category with him. Any approach that categorizes persons of his type as evil, in a way consistent with the tradition of evil as defilement, strips them of essential humanity. Such radical devaluation serves only to justify a sacrificial immolation, dissolution, and cleansing from memory rather than lending support to the effort to comprehend the events, influences, and ideas that converged to make the *type* of human being exemplified in Hitler possible.

The need for preservation rather than eradication of Hitlerism in human memory can be understood by way of a medical analogy. Should, for example, the smallpox virus—by all measures an inordinately destructive "pollution"—be included alongside a human population? Its complete eradication would seem to be a good thing. But here it must be remembered that the destructive effects of this virus were brought under control not by eradication but by immunization through inoculation. Immunization makes it possible to live with exposure to the virus—which in light of the recent predicament resulting from its possible use as a biological weapon—seems preferable to the artificially "safe" condition created by attempts at complete eradication. These attempts leave populations ultimately vulnerable to the possibility, which can never be ruled out, of the future reemergence of the virus or a similar strain.

In the same manner the destructive effects of Hitlerism can be brought under control in human communities by "immunization"—by presentation and re-presentation of the relevant history in contexts that adequately comprehend, address, and expose its dangers. With respect to the problem of the notion of evil as defilement and its potential manifestation in varieties of scapegoating, the real-life story of Hitler and the fictional story of Moby Dick serve as instances of immunizing media.

Certainly Hitler was not immunized against the dangers of scapegoating. But acknowledging a connection between the influence of the tradition of the idea of evil and Hitler's actions need not be taken as a rationale for absolving him of culpability. It is not possible to know the depths of his motivations and what actions he would have been capable of in other contexts (both social and spiritual/cultural). Without the influence of this tradition and the role of the concepts of pollution and defilement in his understanding of evil, Hitler's actions may have been significantly different.

Possibly the dictates of his personality and the quality of his judgments would have led him to other extremes, but perhaps of a less destructive nature. While not absolving Hitler of anything, this analysis exposes the dangers associated with an orientation that is potentially seriously destructive in its practical effects and applications.

Radically exclusionary agendas prescribed through varieties of metaphysical orientation herein described as monistic antagonism and consistent with melodramatic structure have had ample opportunity through their dominant sway over the past millennia to give sufficient evidence of their destructive effects on global community. These exclusionary campaigns have operated within societies, developing ever-increasing technological inventiveness in the means of waging competition, conflict, and war. But while deadly conflict may be the most urgent social and international concern stemming from forms of exclusionary metaphysics, it should not be the only concern. Some of the less overtly violent effects of melodramatic structure operative in American community are examined in the next chapter along with additional conclusions regarding the reciprocal relations between violence and culture.

15

The Melodramatization
of American Culture

Conflicting Moral Codes

The analysis in the preceding chapters has revealed two very different types of drama whose structures are essentially defined by orienting the audience in two contrasting ways toward the dramatic conflict. These two orientations toward conflict, exemplified in melodrama and tragic drama, are rooted in attitudes that reflect a deep division within the spiritual and philosophical traditions of Western culture: traditions embedded in Hebraic and Hellenic literature and ritual. This division runs not so much *between* the Hebraic and Hellenic but *within* each of these branches. In this regard, tension between these two cultural sources is more adequately understood as a tension within each source. And this internal tension is not unique to Western or European-influenced culture. In addition to examining the influence of attitudes about conflict, this chapter explores two related themes along two lines of argument that claim (1) different cultures are generally not different, contrary to popular assumptions, in harboring a deep division between melodramatic and tragic orientations to conflict (specifically this similarity is, in addition to the Hebraic/Hellenic similarity already mentioned, briefly outlined in relation to other cultural tensions influencing the American mix: Indian and White and East and West); and (2) within a given culture obfuscating confusions may arise from various attempts to locate the root causes of genocidal, compulsive, and serial forms of homicidal violence more in environmental or instinctual sources of tension instead of culturally induced attitudes toward structuring and managing conflict.

In American culture the contrast between orientations to conflict parallels a similar contrast between different teachings relating to moral codes handed down through tradition. This contrast may in fact run deeply enough to be regarded as posing a motivational contradiction.

On the one hand, the traditions embody, in a variety of expressions, what has come to be called "the golden rule"—which, in essence, extends to others a value commensurate with the value placed on oneself. This attitude of essential respect for the "other" is reflected in the core religions through teachings such as "love thy neighbor" and "do unto others as you would have others do unto you." The golden rule, as a moral imperative, promotes, under the symbolism of the heading of "neighbor," an inviolable respect that rests on the recognition and affirmation of the essential inclusion of the "other" in the order of being. In its broadest conception, it teaches a regard for the "other" not only as other persons but also as the "other" of difference reflected in all manner of beings. The golden rule also serves as the cornerstone for liberal constitutional democracies founded on the principles of equal rights and equal protection under the law. Respect for the "neighbor" includes even, and especially, those who may, in the order or disorder of things, become categorized as the "enemy." However, as suggested in Chapter 14, regard for others, even as enemies, need not be confused with a principle of passivity or acquiescence in response to aggression and brutality.

On the other hand, both the Hebraic and Hellenic traditions—as has been discussed—contain within their presuppositional ground, the dualistic screening and separation of "the world" into radically oppositional codings. These traditions teach that the world is essentially divided between antagonistic forces of good and evil. Positing this fundamental conflict, they also teach the value of conscience in the ability to distinguish and choose between good and evil as these are manifested in relational (external) and motivational (internal) conflicts. The logic of the oppositional structure of good and evil brings with it the possibility for the "other" to become evil or corrupt through being possessed, controlled, or colonized by evil. A world in which it is possible for the "other" to become evil or to be an embodiment of evil is a world in which occasions must arise when it becomes acceptable, even necessary, to suspend the golden rule. A neighbor is not one to be "loved" when found to be the incarnate presence of evil. Real-life conflict has an uncanny way of eventually bringing into direct confrontation the war against evil and the golden rule.

Contradiction between moral codes and between orientations to conflict in American cultures, both indigenous and emigrant, is well documented in the work of Richard Slotkin (1973). In his comparison of the myths and rituals of Native American Indians and European colonists (predominantly of Puritan background), Slotkin initially notes that in broad themes there appears to be a strong contrast *between* these traditions. In characterizing this contrast Slotkin relates that "to the Indian the wilderness was a god, whether its face at the moment was good or evil ... all the gods and the earth itself were referred to as members of one's own immediate family, as close blood relations. For the Puritan the problem of religion was to winnow the wheat from the chaff, the good from the evil, and to preserve the former and extirpate the latter" (51).

This characterization of Indian and Puritan spiritual orientations presents a contrast analogous to that between tragic and melodramatic ways of structuring conflict. But just as has been argued to be the case with Hellenic and Hebraic traditions, Slotkin finds that this contrast must be more carefully understood as one that runs powerfully *within* both the Indian and Puritan traditions. Slotkin even argues that "in point of fact, the Puritan and Indian responses to the life of the wilderness were, at bottom, strikingly similar" (55).

The sense in which a contradiction inheres within the social and moral imperatives of the Judeo-Christian heritage — of which the Puritan tradition is one example — has already been described. Concerning the Indian tradition, Slotkin locates the contrast in the different attitudes and behaviors displayed by the "warrior/hunter" and the "shaman"— both of which have analogues in the white emigrant cultures. Both the warrior and the shaman mediate between the tribe and the larger social and natural environment. The warrior exercises control in an active, aggressive, and often violent style, usually in a manner that relies on exclusionary and sacrificial modes of categorizing competing tribes and obstructive elements of nature. The shaman exercises control in a neutral, receptive, and catalytic style that is broadly inclusive and affirmative of forces within the totality of the social and natural world.

Since, as Slotkin notes, "in order for the tribe to grow and expand its power and food-gathering territory, it had to extend its borders and win its peace by military or quasi-military conquest," the way of the warrior often dominated Indian cultures. Among many possible instances Slotkin cites the particularly prominent examples of the Iroquois and Aztec — two cultures whose social and spiritual organizations, featuring the warrior model, resembled European cultures (55). Considered broadly, Indian and European cultures do not differ significantly with respect to susceptibility to imperialistic ambitions.

But care must be taken in understanding territorial ambition. This ambition, whether European or Native American, readily presents itself as a likely impetus in the search for the root causes of deadly human violence — perhaps contributing more importantly than modes of structuring conflict.

For example, the work of Konrad Lorenz, popularized by Robert Ardrey (1966), offers a persuasive argument for the existence of an aggressive instinct among animals and humans that is closely tied to marking and defending territorial boundaries. But Ardrey is careful in his summary of Lorenz's work to note that Lorenz's demonstrations of an aggressive instinct must not be confused with those views that make a case for the existence of an *instinct to kill* that is separate from predatory instincts toward other species for the purpose of providing food. Whether in humans or animals, Lorenz does not believe that the instinct for aggressive behavior between members of the same species translates into an instinct to kill.

In fact, the instinct for aggression in relation to territorial and mating imperatives seems to include a directive that constrains behavior short of killing. Ardrey's summary of Lorenz makes two important points: "The Lorenz approach to human aggression is, first, that we must recognize that it is healthy, that it is necessary, that it is innate, that it is ineradicable ... [and] that to deny innateness of human aggression is to approach its possible control from an inevitably impossible quarter." Ardrey then notes that nature provides a model that contains an answer to the problem of aggression: "second, that the solution to the human problem is to be sought in the direction of imitation of nature, in other words by the enlargement of all those less-than-lethal competitions, ritualizations and displays, whether between individuals or groups, which absorb our hostile energies and turn them to ends either harmless or constructive" (302).

For Lorenz, instinctual aggression is a positive motivational resource in that it helps to strengthen and preserve members of a species from natural threats and, consequently, is not properly understood as merely a response to the frustration of needs. In the animal kingdom, according to Lorenz, "nature ritualizes and inhibits actual fighting so that the individual may benefit by aggression's values while the species is saved from aggression's toll" (302).

An inclination within a species to kill members of its own kind, even as a result of territorial disputes, is clearly counterproductive. Lorenz's belief that the "solution to the human problem [of violence] is to be sought in the direction of imitation of nature" implies that humans ought to accept about themselves what is clearly the case with the animal: that aggression to the point of killing members of the same species is not a "natural" gift. Nevertheless, the inclination to kill within its own ranks is evident within the human species on a scale found in no other species. If nature is the guide, the human proclivity for intraspecies lethal violence appears to be a form of learned behavior or adaptation. In the context of this understanding of aggression, moral codes and orientations toward conflict, as cultural choices, move to central focus in accounting for intraspecies violence.

The oppositional logic of essential exclusion belonging to the moral structure of good and evil and the oppositional logic of essential inclusion corresponding to the self/other moral structure of the golden rule are socially and culturally formed. Neither of these oppositional logics is inherent in the species nor is one or the other of these orientations characteristically developed and expressed universally within a given culture.

Since the structure of oppositional relation that may dominate the moral fabric of a given culture is readily superimposed over all the oppositions encountered in the conflicts and life choices made by each member of that culture, it is only prudent that this structure be carefully considered and examined. Social cohesion and individual prosperity require that this structure promote as productive an orientation to choice and conflict as possible.

The contradiction between the golden rule and the moral structure of good and evil becomes evident and pragmatically operative when people are confronted by any form of conflict. The exhortation to love the other collides with the necessity for opposing and eliminating evil. This collision produces contrasting and often mutually exclusive imperatives that compete for dominance in characterizing all forms of conflict.

One source of conflict given much attention thus far, especially in the early chapters, has been the adolescent identity crisis. As argued in Chapter 1, the horror story constitutes one important example of a form of cultural training in regard to the structuring of conflict. The popularity of the horror story derives from its appeal to adolescents as they struggle with the inner conflict or identity crisis triggered by the onset of sexual maturity. The continuing appeal of variations of melodramatic form for young audiences aging from 20 to 35 suggests the possibility of the pressure of an identity crisis that continues beyond the adolescent years. Writing on the Hollywood action film genre, Mark Gallagher confirms the existence of such a crisis when he remarks, "The contemporary action film ... uses various formal and narrative strategies to respond to cultural crises about masculinity and male social roles." He goes on to claim, "For men in contemporary capitalist society, a society that provides a social and economic structure that severely limits and codifies the bourgeois male's ability to establish his identity through physical activity, action films provide fantasies of heroic omnipotence and of escape from, or transcendence of, cultural pressures" (1999: 199).

Gallagher's claim that men are detrimentally constrained by cultural imperatives and codes in their ability to establish identity through "physical activity" dovetails with the findings, noted in the introduction, of Carol and Peter Stearns regarding the "increasingly egalitarian society" that stifles male physical expressions of anger and hostility. In Gallagher's judgment many contemporary action films build up the male superhero image to such absurd extremes of prowess and potency through relentless sequences of gore and destruction that the effect becomes comprehensible only as the male "action" equivalent of what has been labeled female "emotional hysteria." Gallagher cites as an example the film *True Lies* (1994). Later examples such as *Terminator 3* (2003) and *Once Upon a Time in Mexico* (2004) indicate no abatement of this trend. If this "hysteria" trend in the action film genre does in fact play to and reflect the existence of a culturally broad male identity crisis, it suggests that the crisis is significant.

These assessments of the current cultural climate are consistent with the emergence of processes similar to the following vicious circle:

• Certain changes or challenges in the social or psychic environment motivate anxieties.
• These anxieties are then pandered to and superficially assuaged through the melodramatic presentation and resolution of conflict in various media.
• This melodramatic modeling of conflict presents and reinforces attitudes consistent with morally polarized orientations toward the perceived sources of tension in the cultural environment.
• A feedback loop forms that further exaggerates and escalates the perception of the sources of tension as threatening and destructive in the manner of unremitting evils.

This process constitutes what may be called the "melodramatization" of cultural tensions. The argument presented in Chapter 14 that there is never sufficient cause nor productive reason to apply the melodramatic template to real-life conflict must nevertheless confront the reality that there is an abundance of motivation for doing so—motivation rooted in all the themes previously discussed relating to the history and tradition of evil and the reinforcement of this tradition in the abiding appeal and abundant supply of melodramatic entertainment.

In keeping with the principle of mimetic circularity—whereby art imitates life and life imitates art—varieties of melodrama in American film both reflect and promote an attitude toward conflict that competes with the alternative tragic view in every manifestation of conflict and competition — with the effect that America presents two faces to itself and to the world.

Of these two faces, one that lends itself to nonviolent competition and mediation and another that lends itself, however unintentionally, to greater polarization and violence, the latter clearly dominates American cinema and culture. But real violence in American society, while attracting the most media attention, does not constitute the greater part of the problem relating to concerns surrounding social conflict and violence. America's statistics on violence reflect only the tip of the iceberg of a larger mass of abusive and destructive behaviors incited or aggravated by the melodramatic structuring of conflict.

At this point it will help to illustrate these claims by addressing two questions: What are some additional cultural factors or tensions in this postmodern era — in addition to the proposed crisis in the male social role and male identity — that contribute to the potential for conflict? And what is the evidence for the current dominance and acceleration of the melodramatization of these tensions in society?

As will become apparent in the following analysis, these questions raise issues that are closely related to the question posed at the outset. In the introduction it was noted that the United States holds the distinction, among developed nations, of being the country where a person is most likely (by far) to be killed by violence, especially gun violence.

The usual suspects— poverty, unemployment, and lack of opportunity —cannot be cited as crucially operative factors in accounting for the violence statistics because countries of similar standards of living and economic circumstances do not have similar statistics on violent crime. Of all the nations in the world, the United States is among the most affluent and among the most promising in offering opportunity for success. But if — as many politicians have argued — it is the "best" country in which to live, why are so many of its citizens committing acts of violence?

Many cultural critics of the postmodern era have argued, as evident in Gallagher's views cited above, that the American "culture of violence" is rooted in the peculiarities of the American "solution" to the fundamental collective need for social, political, and economic organization. These criticisms emphasize one aspect or another of "late capitalist society" of which the American solution is argued to be the most prominent or, as some would have it, egregious exemplar. The general argument and identification of tensions goes something like this:

• The relentlessly competitive engine of late free-market capitalism runs with unbridled efficiency in the American economy more than in any other national economy. The predatory factor inherent in competitive practices is further fueled by rampant commodification and commercialization promoted through the virtual world of American media images. Pervasive and omnipresent advertising relentlessly drives desire and increases the temptation among those of every level of means to live a lifestyle well beyond the reach of their available income.

• Commercialism accelerated through the virtual world of advertising media fuels a circularity of influence between the virtual and the real. The pervasiveness and seductiveness of the virtual eventually fosters an orientation of sufficient fascination to induce a reversal, whereby the virtual world of media images becomes a hyper-reality that dominates and in some cases supplants the value and authenticity of the real.

• Coordination between corporate business and media enterprises fuels a political system in which money and media attention shape and control the hyper-reality that favors increasingly predatory practices among special interests at the expense of popular interests.

• Furthermore, the marriage of modern and postmodern technologies— computers and robotics and varieties of electronic automation and mechanization — produces a growing tsunami of instrumentalization that leads to loss of jobs, "dehumanization" of the workplace, and an encroaching sense of valuelessness for many in the job market.

• Finally, the combined American economic and political structure favors an extraordinary emphasis on individual freedoms, including the freedom to exploit and, of course, be exploited. The extremes to which these freedoms have been developed, encouraged, and protected have led to the questionable sacrifice of community relations and basic law and order.

By way of this account of American postmodern ills, the primary sources of cultural tension can be identified as competition, commercialization, instrumentalization, and individualization. Often taking the form of exceptional emphasis on wealth, image, technology, and autonomy these areas of tension undoubtedly produce increased opportunities for conflict. But increased opportunity for conflict is not in itself sufficient to account for a "culture of violence." Adding to those opportunities a culturally induced pattern of managing conflict in a way that promotes routine devaluation of the opposition, however, goes a long way toward accounting for not only a "culture of violence" but also a culture of cutthroat and ruthless competition. The following sections offer representative anecdotes illustrating in specific detail not only how this process is taking place but also how melodramatization is a function of cultural training and choice of attitude more than a strategically viable or necessary response to sources of social tension.

Competition and Commercialization

In the cultural stew of American late capitalist society, competition is the name of the game, especially in corporate commerce, sports, and politics: a triumvirate of interests that becomes more inseparably welded together with every passing year. An example drawn from the arena of corporate business merits attention first because it offers an extraordinarily clear instance of key features of melodramatization in practice as well as the contrasting orientation toward conflict that divides the American cultural landscape. The fact that the roots of this story extend back to 1921 illustrates that the division in American culture is not new while, nevertheless, certain facts of the story belonging to the current era present evidence of ongoing contributions to a newly resurgent contemporary phenomenon.

CORPORATE COMMERCE: A CASE HISTORY

The leadership and practices of the McWane Corporation of Birmingham, Alabama, founded in 1921, present an instructive case history. The story of this corporation was made famous by a January 2003 *Frontline* presentation entitled "A Dangerous Business." The importance of this story in relation to the broader climate of American business practices was also prominently brought to public attention in Phillip K. Tompkins's January 2003 keynote address to the Rocky Mountain Communication Association. Tompkins's address was entitled "The Crisis of American Organizations and Institutions: Speaking Truth to Power." Much of its content is now included as a chapter in his recently published book on the crash of the shuttle Columbia entitled *Apollo, Challenger, Columbia: The Decline of the Space Program* (2005). The Columbia shuttle disaster, by Tompkins's analysis, further illustrates the dominant trends at work in American business and institutions while confirming salient features of the *Frontline* story.

After nearly a year of investigative journalism (through the combined efforts of the Public Broadcasting System, *The New York Times*, and the Canadian Broadcasting Company), the McWane Corporation emerged as one of the most dangerous companies to work for in America. McWane produces sewer pipes with manufacturing plants located in several states and in Canada. During the period of time its operations were researched, from 1995 to 2002, it was discovered that McWane had more safety violations in its facilities than the *combined totals* of all of its major competitors.

These safety violations did not occur without consequences. Within the seven-year period of investigation, the journalists learned that significant and sometimes traumatic injuries of various kinds had been incurred by numerous workers ranging from severe burns, amputations, and broken bones, including one case of a broken back. Still more alarming, they were shocked to discover that nine workers were killed as a direct result of violations of federal safety standards. Some of these cases were referred to OSHA — the Occupational Safety and Health Administration — and eventually to the Justice Department. Of the nine deaths during the period studied, only one came under the review of the Justice Department and was settled with a misdemeanor plea on the part of McWane. In addition to over 400 safety violations there were also over 450 environmental violations. There were also numerous instances in which McWane had been cited or sued for emissions violations.

Upon first reaction it might be assumed that the McWane Corporation suffers from an extraordinary lack of management and proper supervision. However, as the investigative journalists learned, the opposite turns out to be the case. McWane's safety and environmental violations are a direct result of a well-thought and tightly regulated business strategy. With respect to general operations, this approach translates into the practice of "corporate raiding"— buying failing and outdated facilities for pennies on the dollar and then cutting operational expenses to the bone to maximize advantage in relation to the competition. With this strategy McWane gains the public reputation of "rescuing" faltering corporations but does so at the expense of workers' safety and the environment.

Furthermore, as an integral part of its management philosophy, McWane included in the calculation of its operating expenses an estimate for legal fees and fines associated with its routine and deliberate violations of safety and environmental regulations. The corporation had concluded that it was less expensive, and thus more competitively advantageous, to incur these expenses than to operate within the rules.

According to the *Frontline* presentation McWane top management refused all requests for interviews but did submit a written response in defense of its practices, which included the following: "We're fighting for survival, competing against foreign manufacturers who have little or no regard for the safety of their workers or ... the environment" (15).

At this point the *Frontline* exposé ascends from the noteworthy to the exceptional as it proceeds to make an extraordinary comparison. One of McWane's competitors goes by the name of the American Cast Iron Pipe Company (ACIPCO). This company has been in business longer than McWane, has a long record of commercial success, is consistently rated as one of America's best employers, and has worker productivity ratings much higher than the McWane ratings. Oddly enough this company was also founded in Birmingham, Alabama. Its founding owner was John Eagan. Upon his death in 1924, Eagan willed his foundry to his workers.

In the years following his death, ACIPCO continued to implement Eagan's business philosophy built on the golden rule and, as a consequence, its management priorities and practices contrast sharply with those of McWane. At ACIPCO facilities production is always second to safety and, unlike the practice at McWane facilities, supervisors have the authority and are obligated to shut down production lines when there is a safety risk. Needless to say, these practices have resulted in an extraordinary track record of minimal accidents and injuries and work-related health problems.

However, the instructive and peculiar nature of the contrasts and similarities between these two corporations goes even deeper. In explaining this deeper connection it is hard to improve on the words of the *Frontline* narrator: "There was one notable dissent when John Eagan announced that he was going to operate his foundry on the Golden Rule. The president of the company quit. His name: J. R. McWane. He crossed town to start his own pipe company and a dynasty based on a profoundly different vision. That was more than 80 years ago. In a new millennium the McWane foundries thrive, still faithful to his austere philosophy, now called disciplined management practices" (cited in Tompkins, 2005: 209). The contrast in personalities between these two men is as fascinating as the contrast in business philosophies is instructive.

McWane Corporation's "disciplined management practices" are a direct result of a corporate attitude that reflects an extreme subordination of the golden rule to a radically value polarized, exclusionary, and antagonistic evaluative principle. But an explanation is offered for this subordination. From the point of view of McWane management, the nature of commercial competition is characterized — like Hobbes's state of nature — as a circumstance in which "survival" is ultimately at stake. The competition is the *enemy* and consequently the rules must be tossed out the window in the effort to confront what is essentially viewed as "warfare."

This attitude reflects a relation between the corporation and its competitors whereby competition is reduced to a conflict in which the "com-

petitor" is devalued to the point that it becomes, as a matter of practical
consideration, what falls outside the category of an agency that need be
accorded basic respect. In this climate of mere survival, the spirit of competition is stripped down to a "win at all costs" mentality. As a further consequence of this mentality, those who work for McWane are subordinated
to the value of production to the point that they are functionally regarded
as of less value than the company's costly instruments and machines.

A small degree of plausibility might be accorded the explanation that
the McWane Corporation offers for its business practices if the situation
were as desperate as their comment about foreign manufacturers suggests.
The side-by-side comparison of the McWane and ACIPCO corporations
and their different management philosophies conducted through precisely
the same economic circumstances illustrates that such philosophies toward
commercial competition are more a *choice* in keeping with the attitudes
and priorities of management than they are a strict *consequence* of the constraints of the business environment or the nature of competition itself.

The story of these two corporations illustrates two paths to what may
hesitantly be called "corporate success." It also illustrates that the melodramatization of competition practiced by the McWane Corporation is
not a path that is necessitated by desperate competitive circumstances.
Rather, it is a choice that derives directly from the way in which the corporate leadership defines the nature of the conflict in which they perceive
the corporation to be engaged. In essence, the leadership of McWane
decided that its competition was of such a nature that it should be beaten
by any means necessary. This resulted in applying the same reasoning to
its own workers to the extreme that they become adversaries and even enemies in relation to the corporate goals.

The marriage of competition and commerce that results in the radical devaluation of competitors as well as workers is an aberration made
possible only by the adoption of polarizing attitudes that undermine and
circumvent the rules that separate competition from warfare. In light of
the comparison with ACIPCO, the practices of the McWane Corporation
can be likened to a runaway train. Such examples, the critics of capitalism may be quick to point out, show that its dangers in relation to meeting the economic needs of a society may lie not so much in its failure as
in its "success." But "successful" capitalism need not necessarily resemble
a runaway train in its effects on social and economic prosperity — as the
history of ACIPCO demonstrates. Nevertheless, as the economic engine
picks up speed, the cultural tensions of competition can be accelerated by
other factors that increase the potential for losing control.

Raising the Bar

The extraordinary acceleration in communication and information dissemination made possible through the invention and proliferation of radio, television, computer, satellite, microchip, cable, laser, fiber-optic, internet, and cell phone technologies has in many respects inaugurated a new age: a postmodern age of political, economic, and social community. It has transformed the once insurmountably vast world into what Marshall McLuhan called the "global village." However, the age of enlightenment, science, and industrialization often referred to as "modernity" has not, as a consequence of the new information age, receded into the background. The modern wave of endless products and services made possible by mechanization and industrialization has been accelerated rather than supplanted by postmodern information technology. Information technology has sparked an increase — with a vengeance — of commercialization and its attendant consumerism.

Not only has the program content of various entertainment and information media been bracketed on every side by advertising but the programs themselves— whether music, television shows, or motion pictures— have become extended advertisements as cars, jackets, soft drinks, shoes, phones, sunglasses, watches, houses, and sundry items ad infinitum are highlighted and implicitly (or explicitly) endorsed by their inclusion in program sounds and images. As advertising over radio, television, and now even at movie theaters has adopted the style, in mini-slices, of the action drama or the sitcom, so also songs, shows, and movies have become extended ads by way of their ability to frame and spotlight what is (or will soon become) culturally popular products.

As film critic Jake Horsley warns, "Hollywood movies have become every bit as much a science as an art, and probably have a closer affinity to advertising than we would care to admit.... Advertisements are gauged and designed according to their observed *effects*; movies are becoming a similar kind of commodity ... and perhaps every bit as insidious (and even nefarious) an influence upon — and invasion of — our psyches" (1999b: 150). Through endlessly inventive and invasive avenues media offer a continuous onslaught of advertisements that through constant repetition contribute insistently and mightily toward inflation of the culturally dominant vision of a "standard of living" norm.

The media advertising blitz progressively raises the bar on the level of material well-being necessary to achieve "successful living." This relentless escalation of the stakes in the poker competition of free-market capitalism makes losing the pot an increasingly poignant experience. For those who have started out with the high expectations induced by middle- and upper-class advantages, success becomes almost an entitlement and failure becomes unthinkable. Attaining anything less than the sought-after level of success is understood more as a sign of injustice than of incapacity or inability. In the case of the privileged, success must not only come but also must come soon and in a big way — as the bar of success continually rises through media and peer pressure.

This phenomenon of increasingly high expectations for a standard of living has been noted by social commentators such as Gregg Easterbrook (1999b), David Whitman (1998), and Robert J. Samuelson (1997). Easterbrook remarks that although "most Americans are today healthier, better housed, better fed, better paid, better educated, better defended, [and] more free ... somehow they've managed to convince themselves their parents had it better during the Dust Bowl." Easterbrook also finds, concurring with Samuelson, that the reason for the dim view of present circumstances results from "the revolution of rising expectations" that has "taken on a life of its own.... Polls now suggest that, regardless of how much money an American has, he or she believes that twice as much is required" (1999b, 23).

The fixation by the privileged on the fulfillment of what are perceived to be crucial needs is, in one important respect, not far removed from the experience of those in lower-income and poverty-income circumstances. The longings of the privileged and the deprived reveal the universality of the effects of media-promoted and media-provoked desires in relation to the relativity of what constitutes "need." In this regard street crime and white collar crime may be seen to originate in similar desperate struggles to fulfill what are counted as crucial needs while displaying very different understandings of what rises to the level of need. In each case a sense of unjustly withheld entitlement to a particular lifestyle standard can fuel feelings of resentment and betrayal toward a "system" that has not lived up to its promises.

In such circumstances of exaggerated enticements *desires* readily convert to *needs*. When this happens winning becomes an imperative in the competitive cultural and economic game. The rivalry for success in the career marketplace can rise to such crucial importance that competition takes on all the characteristics of strained conflict: in which case it becomes extremely easy to apply the most available and habitually endorsed cultural template for strained conflict — the melodramatic template. Rather than be betrayed by a system that is not living up to its promises (however overinflated the perception of those promises may have become), some are inclined, as in the case of the McWane Corporation, to "assist" the system in whatever way may be necessary.

The widespread corporate corruption scandals that surfaced at the beginning of the new millennium — including such companies as Enron, Worldcom, Quest, and numerous dot-com operations — gave alarming testimony to the ease with which upper echelons of corporate management could suspend the rules of commercial competition in favor of a much more draconian and polarized conception of competition. Here the pressing need to come out on top, the need to be the "hero" reflected in a "win at all costs" mentality, contributed to the taking of extraordinary liberties and risks and the corresponding production of a facade of lies and misrepresentations that ultimately transformed even the shareholders into "outsiders" and enemies from whom the most vital corporate financial maneuverings had to be kept secret. When these house-of-card constructions eventually collapsed, as they inevitably had to, the results were catastrophic for all involved — especially the unsuspecting shareholders.

The collision of media-exaggerated lifestyle with the beliefs and aspirations of those in more humble daily routines accounts for much of the uneasiness and outright hostility expressed by many in foreign cultures when exposed to the glut of American culture in global information streams. In a commentary on the problems associated with the acceleration and globalization of information flow, cultural critic and philosopher Giovanna Borradori (2003) offers a sobering assessment: "Western consumerism explodes like a land mine in the midst of the most disadvantaged layers of the world population (65).... By intensifying communication, globalization puts on stage distributive injustice, starkly dividing the world into winners, beneficiaries, and losers. Mutual perspective-taking becomes harder and harder in the face of such challenges" (64).

While "mutual perspective-taking" — understood as the ability to maintain a sense of the humanity of the other side of any intense conflict — may indeed become more difficult in the media-induced clash of civilizations, cultures, and classes, it becomes needlessly more difficult when it is impaired and overwhelmed by contradictory cultural attitudes toward conflict. The conflicts that were to be expected in such cases as the religious and ethnic clashes of Northern Ireland, the Balkans, and the Middle East and the racial clashes of South Africa and the United States were transformed into particularly intense, intransigent, and prolonged conflicts by the dominance of a culturally preferred and endorsed norm for structuring and polarizing conflict.

SPORTS

Returning to the tensions within American culture, evidence of melo-dramatization in professional sports— though never entirely absent —has emerged more prominently in recent years. This trend is clearly demonstrated in the currently fashionable practice of "trash talk" among professional athletes.

By trashing his opponents with pre-bout verbal put-downs and belittlings— sometimes in the form of ridiculing rhymes— Muhammad Ali may take a good measure of credit for initiating and popularizing a trend that has led to the contemporary wave of trash talk.

Ali's verbal antics had the effect of encouraging spectators to view his fights more as theater than as sporting competition. And the kind of theater Ali's remarks invoke is not hard to guess. With verbal descriptions such as "float like a butterfly and sting like a bee," Ali's promoters painted him as a kind of hero who performed with the ease of a dancer around opponents caricatured as inept and ridiculous at best and dark and villainous at worst.

With the Sonny Liston title fight in 1964, Ali rose to national attention with pre-bout media circuses in which he verbally mocked and belittled his opponent. During the course of his career these rhetorical abuses became increasingly disparaging and inflammatory, reaching an all-time low with the Frasier fight in Manila in 1975. Jack Kram, a journalist for *Sports Illustrated*, unsparingly records Ali's derision of Frasier in a pre-bout media event.

> "Joe Frasier should give his face to the Wildlife Fund! He so ugly, blind men go the other way! ... He not only look bad! You can smell him in another country!" He held his nose. "What will people in Manila think? We can't have a gorilla for a champ. They're gonna think, lookin' at him, that all black brothers are animals. Ignorant. Stupid. Ugly. If he's champ again, other nations will laugh at us" [169].

The polarizing effect this rhetoric had on the match was obvious to all observers, not the least of which was Joe Frasier, whose response to the verbal haymakers is also described by Kram:

> Joe turned and gunned a hole in the thin wood of the wall, then flipped over his desk. "Eddie, listen up! Whatever you do, whatever happens, don't stop the fight! We got nowhere to go after this. I'm gonna eat this halfbreed's heart right out of his chest! I mean it. This is the end of him or me!" [171].

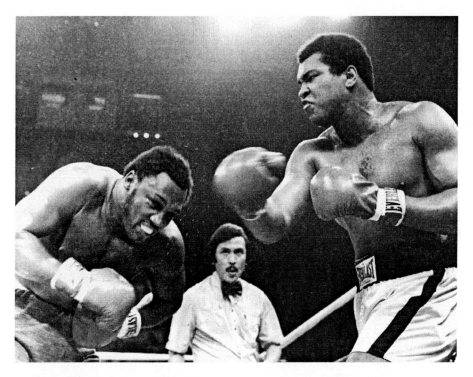

Muhammad Ali and Joe Frazier in the seventh round of the "Thrilla in Manila" (1975) (Photofest).

While enormously popular at first, this kind of theatricalization of the boxing match eventually led to the demise of professional boxing as a sport that could be taken seriously by sports fans. With incidents such as biting off a piece of an opponent's ear in the middle of a fight (Tyson vs. Holyfield, 1997), professional boxing has evolved to a point not far removed from the status of professional wrestling, which is now entirely theatrical and completely devoid of anything resembling true and engaging competition.

Those who attend professional wrestling matches are not so much sports fans as theatergoers. And while the shouting and screaming among the audience is a significant component in wrestling spectacles the disparity between levels of arousal and catharsis remains similar to cinematic melodrama where arousal effects dominate cathartic effects and press for physical action to achieve effective catharsis. The dominance of mimetic rather than cathartic effects in the case of wrestling fans has been evident in the increased incidents of teenagers injuring themselves by conducting backyard restagings of professional wrestling melodramas.

Competitions in team sports such as hockey, baseball, basketball, and football have been waged over the years with sufficient intensity to trigger occasional fights between players. The notable difference in contemporary team sport culture, however, can be seen in the routine practice of fueling antagonisms between particular players through media hype and in the ease with which fights, when they do break out, escalate — and are allowed to escalate — into brawls.

A noteworthy example of such brawling occurred in the third game of the 2003 World Series between the Boston Red Sox and the New York Yankees. The speed with which this brawl ignited and reached ugly intensity revealed the readiness with which players were willing to believe the worst of their opponents and exposed the kind of hostile attitudes among many players toward their competitors.

The antagonistic sentiments of the 2003 World Series stand in stark contrast to the attitudes associated with the meeting of the same teams in the final two decisive games of the 1949 pennant race. In a pre-game gathering in his honor, Joe DiMaggio spoke to the entire crowd at Yankee Stadium and summed up the views of his teammates when, referring to the Boston Red Sox, he said, "They're a grand bunch, too. If we don't win the pennant, I'm happy that they will" (cited in Berra, 2003: 57).

Whether in team or individual sport, victory has in recent decades become more important than how it is achieved. Undoubtedly the most famous and incisive expression of this philosophy, as it contends for dominance in American sports, comes from the ranks of football through the words of Vince Lombardi: "Winning isn't everything. It's the only thing." This philosophy has not only migrated from the athletic competition into the corporate world, it has also been well received in the competitive world of politics.

POLITICS

Trash talking in sports has its political equivalent in negative campaign advertising. Negative ads adopt the style typical of tabloid journalism with exaggerated spinning of facts and sensationalistic exposés designed to portray political opponents as villains. Despite the general denunciation of negative ads by both political parties as a routine campaign strategy, negative ads continue to play a significant role in many heated election contests because, as one pundit expressed it, "they work." By attracting sensational attention to a campaign, melodrama can help to "sell" a candidate — especially in the last days of a close race.

In the decade of the 1990s the competition between the two political parties increasingly demonstrated that for politicians, as for football coaches, winning isn't everything — it's the only thing. This attitude now dominates the rivalry between the evenly divided parties sufficiently to ensure thorough and bitter stalemates in Congress to the point that vital legislation such as health care, social security, and education reform are seemingly impossible to negotiate to workable consensus.

The rhetoric among pundits, analysts, and radio talk show hosts reflects the hostility between the political parties. The following list is but a short sample of the number of titles on the shelves of bookstores at the time of this writing that clearly reveal the deterioration in the civility of political rhetoric.

Incendiary tracts from the right:

Treason: Liberal Treachery From the Cold War to the War on Terrorism by Ann Coulter (2003)

The Enemy Within: Saving America From the Liberal Assault on Our Schools, Faith, and Military by Michael Savage (2003)

Weapons of Mass Distortion: The Coming Meltdown of the Liberal Media by Brent Bozell (2004)

Michael Moore Is a Big Fat Stupid White Man by David T. Handy and Jason Clarke (2004)

The Official Handbook of the Vast Right Wing Conspiracy by Mark W. Smith (2004)

Madame Hillary: She'll Stop at Nothing to Become President by R. Emmett Tyrrell (2004)

Incendiary tracts from the left:

Rush Limbaugh Is a Big Fat Idiot and Other Observations by Al Franken (1996)

Shrub: The Short But Happy Political Life of George W. Bush by Molly Ivins and Lou Dubose (2000)

Big Lies: The Right Wing Propaganda Machine and How It Distorts the Truth by Joe Conason (2003)

The Lies of George W. Bush: Mastering the Politics of Deception by David Corn (2003)

Bushwhacked: Life in George W. Bush's America by Molly Ivins and Lou Dubose (2003)

Bush League Diplomacy: How the Neoconservatives Are Putting the World at Risk by Craig R. Eisendrath and Melvin A. Goodman (2004)

While this vicious radical polarization in political discourse stridently dominates much of the mass media presentation of views from the left and the right, some argue that it is not a polarization that is widely shared — at least not yet — by the majority of Americans. Polls have repeatedly indicated that Americans deplore negative campaign ads and the negative style of politics and rhetorical scapegoating associated with them. But nevertheless political organizers argue that these negative campaigns "work" and that Americans do in fact respond to them in predictable ways.

The tensions in competition and "commerce" within the arenas of business, sports, and politics feature the tensions between competing persons and groups. Another source of significant cultural tension emerges from the competition between humans and machines.

Instrumentalization

Instrumentation and automation have intervened in many commercial enterprises to mediate interactions that used to take place entirely between persons. Not only do instruments in many cases mediate service interactions but they also replace human workers. The automated teller replaces the bank teller. The electronic self-scanner replaces the grocery checker. Multi-functional robotic equipment replaces the dockworker. It is only natural in such cases that the instruments become a source of conflict as those who have lost jobs to them come to view them as tireless, inhuman, and implacable adversaries.

Since the post–World War II growth of computer and robotic science, the conflict between humans and machines has been depicted in ever more threatening and polarizing ways in science fiction. From the schizophrenic paranoid violence of HAL in *2001: A Space Odyssey* (1968) to the apocalyptic clash in *The Terminator* (1984) machines have been portrayed as archvillains in human dramas.

But the role of machines in the human world accommodates multiple interpretations. The fact that an instrument can replace a human worker may perhaps be taken as an indication that the human worker functions as little more than an instrument and has been replaced by a more efficient instrument. The routine and repetitive work taken over by instruments is, by definition, machinelike work that may be, in its very nature, dehumanizing. In one sense, instruments may be seen as coming to the rescue of human workers to perform jobs that not only fail to advance human potential but are in fact promoting the instrumentalization of the human.

Even where instrumentalization results in the displacement of human workers, that fact need not be interpreted as evidence of the devaluation of the human. The loss of a job may be experienced in the short term as unfortunate and destructive. But that loss may in the long term become beneficial by facilitating the move, albeit with something like a shove, to more optimally humanizing forms of work. From this perspective instrumentalization may be seen in the long term as the release of human potential from the dehumanizing effects of instrumentally routine work.

On the other hand, there may be something to be said for the benefits— perhaps crucially humanizing benefits— to be had from performing menial and routine tasks and the self-discipline and communally constructive work ethic promoted by such tasks.

Be that as it may, the spread of instrumentation need not necessarily lead to, nor imply, an overall dehumanization of the workplace. The notion of the instrument as fundamentally a predatory intrusion into the human world is perhaps a notion most admirably suited to the needs of Hollywood melodramatic scriptwriters.

The instruments that replace human workers are more plausibly and constructively viewed as extensions of human beings. As a human extension, the machine and the relationship between human and machine may perhaps be best approached with the sensibility modeled in the golden rule.

This need not be taken to suggest that instruments be given social security numbers and pension plans. It need suggest only that the instrument be understood as worthy of inclusion as a natural and essential part of the whole. This attitude toward the instrument is substantially expressed in the emotional and sometimes conflicted attachments many people develop for their cars and computers. A complex attachment to the instrument is evoked in science fiction films such as *Star Wars* (1977)— in the case of R2D2 and C3PO — and *Blade Runner* (1982)— in its ambiguous and thought-provoking portrayal of humanlike androids. Even HAL of *2001: A Space Odyssey* (1968) is portrayed in the sequel *2010: The Year We Make Contact* (1984) to have a more complex and humanlike nature than was first thought to be the case — a symbolic concession perhaps to the notion that instruments are never essentially evil or "the enemy."

Among cultural critics of a postmodern slant, Donna Haraway is one of few to adequately characterize the complex and essentially synagonistic nature of the human/machine entanglement. For example, Haraway claims, "The machine is not an *it* to be animated, worshipped, and dominated. The machine is us, our processes, an aspect of our embodiment. We can be responsible for machines; *they* do not dominate or threaten us. We are responsible for boundaries; we are they" (1991: 180).

An android who thinks she is human, Rachael (Sean Young) freezes after shooting another android in *Blade Runner* (1982) (Photofest. Photographer: Stephen Vaughan).

This attitude, in one sense, accomplishes a humanization of the instrument, which, as long as humans and instruments share a world, is an attitude preferable to one that fosters a wholesale instrumentalization of the human.

However, stepping back to an even broader level of analysis, the view that the instrument can, if allowed, lead to the devaluation of the human can be informative in regard to the entire process that led to the creation and accelerated use of instruments. The cluster of terms belonging to the growth of instrumentalization includes the big "C's" of competition, capitalism, commercialization, consumerism, and commodification — all of which have often been aligned with, or seen to constitute, forces of dehumanization leading to a corruption of environment and community. But similar to the instruments that they promote, these processes are not adequately portrayed as fundamentally corrupting, evil, or destructive. Instead they are processes that increase human potential while at the same time increasing opportunities for competition, confrontation, and conflict. As in the case of all the previous tensions cited, however, these various tensions need not lead inevitably down the path to destructive conflict and violence.

Nevertheless, when considering the health of environment and community, a greater threat may emerge not through an empowerment accomplished by increasing human collective capacities through extensions such as instruments, money, and influence but through an empowerment accomplished by the expansion of individual freedoms.

Individualization

Consistent pressure in American culture toward preservation and extension of individual freedoms, protections, and entitlements leads some cultural critics to speculate that this self-assertive trend accounts for the dissolution of community and respect for the other that, it is argued, lies at the root of crime and violence. Adherents of this view often advance the case for its credibility through direct comparisons between American democracy and Asian versions of democracy. Asian democracies such as Japan, South Korea, Taiwan, and Malaysia place less emphasis on individual freedom and greater emphasis on group loyalty and community cohesiveness and also have much lower statistics on assaults and violent crimes. The conclusion that a causal link exists between violent crime and greater tolerance for and endorsement of individual freedom presents itself as a plausible explanation for the difference between Asian and American crime statistics.

EAST AND WEST AS CONTRASTING TRADITIONS

Asian leaders are, not surprisingly, among the prominent proponents of this critique of American democracy, especially in response to American leaders who criticize aspects of the Asian economy. For example, *New York Times* journalist T. R. Reid, writing in 1994, reports, "In most Asian eyes ... the evidence of real social decay in the United States is clear and palpable." Reid recalls a speech given by the Singaporean diplomat Kishore Mahbubani where, after noting that the population of the United States had grown by 41 percent since 1960, he finds during the same period the following increases: violent crime up 560 percent, illegitimate births up 419 percent, divorce rates up 400 percent, children living in single-parent homes up 300 percent, teenage suicide rates up 200 percent. During this same period the United Nations Development Program ranked the United States as "number one among industrialized countries in intentional homicides, reported rapes, and percentage of prisoners" and the National Testing Service reported an 80 percent drop in the average score for the Scholastic Aptitude Test (Reid, 1999: 219).

Following this indictment Reid explains that the numbers in some of these categories have improved somewhat since the mid–1990s. But then he concedes that "overall, however, Mahbubani has the trend lines about right. Few people who are old enough to remember life in the United States in 1960 would deny that American streets are less safe, and the American family unit is less stable, than it was at the end of the 1950s. Like many Asians who have spent time in the United States, Mahbubani was particularly struck by the way Americans have come to live with crime, to accept it as a normal element of daily existence.... And this, he argues, contradicts Americans' fundamental belief that they live in a free country" (219).

After laying out these facts, Reid then concludes by summarizing Mahbubani's argument, which he also notes is an argument that has been repeated by the leaders of many other Asian countries ranging from Korea to Malaysia: "By lifting the rights of the individual onto a pedestal, America has reduced the collective good of the overall society to a low priority." In Mahbubani's words, "American society has swung too much in one direction: liberating the individual while imprisoning society.... What is striking is the Americans' failure to ask fundamental questions such as: 'Is there too much freedom in American society?'" (220).

But is it necessarily the case that by granting numerous rights and entitlements to and by removing many encumbrances and restrictions on the individual — to a degree more so than perhaps any other nation in the world — the United States has created a climate fostering violence?

Echoing similar responses expressed by other Asian leaders, Mahbubani believes the answer to this question must be "yes." He arrives at this answer by contrasting the liberal individualism of American society and its form of capitalist economics with the priority Asian cultures accord to community and to the prevailing majority. For Asians the status and identity of individuals derive first and foremost through group and community attachments. In the corporate boardroom, for example, decision making strives for consensus and great pressure is exerted to bring deviant opinions to the side of the majority before adopting a course of action. This pressure toward conformism extends into the general social structure and is reflected in the considerable effort exerted by group members to avoid bringing shame on the group through aberrant or improper behavior.

Pursuing Mahbubani's line of thinking and comparing Asian and American cultural differences, Reid documents various ways in which during the last few decades several East Asian democracies have done better than most Western democracies in building stable and peaceful community living.

However, the deference and loyalty given to the family and the group complies with traditions of tribal association that extend not only into the ancient history of Asia but also into the history of humanity worldwide. In concluding his analysis, Reid makes the interesting point that the Asian accomplishment owes much to the implementation of core values — values that, contrary to expectations, are not different from Western core values. For example, Reid notes, "What the Asians have learned from Confucius and other great teachers of the Eastern tradition is essentially the same as what Americans and Europeans have learned from Socrates and the Judaeo-Christian teachers of the Western tradition. The basic precepts are the same in both hemispheres; they differ in nuance but not in substance" (241). Illustrating his claim, Reid then cites relevant words from Confucius and from Christ.

Expecting to find an explanation for the different levels of violent conflict between American and Asian cultures (particularly Japan) in a difference in core values, Reid finds nothing of the sort and must still ponder a puzzling difference. Perceptive and accurate as far as it goes, Reid's claim regarding the similarity of core values between East and West remains unhelpful because he does not complete the comparison. As in the case of Western cultures, Eastern cultures also harbor a contradiction at the core of their moral teachings.

EAST AND WEST AS PARALLEL TRADITIONS

In the more mystical strains of Confucian, Buddhist, and Taoist traditions radical dichotomies in general are displaced by synagonistic tensions as modeled, for example, in the yin/yang opposition. But the popular and institutionalized lines of moral tradition in the East follow the divisive radical and essential opposition similar to the Western tradition rooted in the notion of evil as defilement. As in the West, the East also manifests the tendency to apply the radical distinction to all conflict, not just the inner conflict pertaining to moral choices relating to behavior.

In his extensive research of Asian mythology, N. J. Girardot, for example, discusses the gourd myths of origin exemplified by the famous Emperor Hun-tun story as told in the ancient *Chuang Tzu* Taoist text. The Hun-tun myth presents a clear instance of the equiprimordiality of two elemental forces called yin and yang and their fundamental complementarity rather than antagonism. In this respect, the Taoist tradition with its mythology of origins resembles the equiprimordial dualism and the orientation toward oppositional relation illustrated in the stories central to the Greek tragic myth of origin.

The notion of a nonequiprimordial or antagonistic dualism, however, is not altogether absent in practice from even the mystically slanted Taoist tradition. For example, Girardot explains that "even in Taoist tradition where the complementary aspects of dualism, and the fact of complementarity as the third term of life, are particularly important in both a philosophical and religious sense, there is eventually in later sectarian Taoism a popular preference given to the 'life-giving' force of *yang* that verges on an identification of the primordial Tao with the *yang* power" (1983: 250).

This identification of what was once the dualistically balanced yin and yang of primordial Tao with the yang power corresponds to an essentializing of one side of the oppositional relation over the other. This essentializing is reminiscent of Western dualisms evident in the value-polarized structure of good and evil.

In this connection, Girardot acknowledges Marcel Granet's pioneering work regarding the relationship between complementary and antagonistic understandings of dualism in China (and, by diffusion, throughout Asia) and the ongoing effort to, as Granet explains, "determine precisely in what cultures, and at what epochs, the negative aspects of life, until then accepted as constitutive and unexceptionable moments of the cosmic totality, lost their initial function and began to be interpreted as manifestations of *evil*" (250–251).

Granet's and Girardot's work in Eastern myths of origin, of which the Taoist tradition presents a highly influential and representative example, offers an Eastern analogue to Paul Ricoeur's work on the symbolism of evil as an effort to trace the emergence of cosmological schemes in conjunction with different understandings of evil.

The cultural traditions of both the East and the West have long taught and promoted an oppositional structure of complementarity between self and other in versions of the golden rule at the same time they have taught and promoted what undermines, contradicts, and ultimately dominates that teaching — namely an oppositional structure of antagonism between self and other reflected in the moral forces of good and evil. Western cultures are not significantly different from Eastern cultures with respect to being rooted in a long tradition according primary significance to what may be called tribal communal association. As a consequence, Asian cultures have not been any less susceptible to the dangers attaching to the dominant role of tribal identification and loyalty in combination with the dominance of a readiness to impose the good/evil structure on conflicts involving those perceived to be "outside" and different from the group. Fascist and communist dictatorships in the East have been no less destructive and genocidal than those in the West. The plight of the West is also and equally the plight of the East — especially in the twentieth century. When the logic of a readily available template of radical polarity is superimposed over intense conflict, the confrontation easily deteriorates into brutality and the unnecessary and extraordinary violence of mass killings and genocide.

In his analysis of the werewolf complex in Western, especially American, culture, Denis Duclos — whose work was previously discussed in Chapter 6 — also finds that Eastern cultures are not exempt from the destructive influence of this radically polarizing structuring process. Duclos notes, for example, that the werewolf complex — as represented in the "ambiguous struggle between madmen and avengers" and associated tendencies toward fascination with criminal excess and apocalyptic pessimism — "echoes trends in another society whose warring past still maintains a strong presence: that of Japan" (1998: 198).

As an illustration, Duclos points to the immense current popularity of these themes in the comic book culture of Japanese anime, a culture he believes grows naturally out of the mythology of everlasting battle that has for centuries defined Japanese military culture. Duclos explains, "the 'Akira' series by Katsuhiro Otomo recounts the birth of an all-powerful child on the site of an atomic disaster and his propulsion into an apocalyptic future. The series, which is very popular among adolescents all over the world, because of its flattering portrayal of rebellious youngsters on

A scene from the "massacre of the robots" in the Japanese anime film *Metropolis* (2001), based on the comic book artistry of Osamu Tezuka.

motorcycles, takes place against a backdrop of asphalt and merciless warfare" (198). The grand scale of graphic and apocalyptic violence in Otomo's work can be found in the work of many other Japanese animation artists, as in the case of Osamu Tezuka's critically acclaimed *Metropolis* (2001).

But while pointing to the evidence of the similar workings of the werewolf complex among particular Eastern and Western cultures, Duclos has nothing to say about how that similarity stacks up against the claims of those like Mahbubani who make the case for a significant difference between certain Eastern cultures and American culture in relation to statistics on violent crime.

Granting a deepening similarity in the mythological and spiritual traditions of East and West only gives further plausibility to Mahbubani's argument. The extraordinary emphasis placed on individual freedom reasserts itself and appears as the one remaining factor that may go a long way toward accounting for the violence statistics in the United States. But this explanation for the difference between East and West in relation to community violence must be modified when completed by a further understanding of the similarities.

Explanation for Violence Statistics
in the United States

If Mahbubani is right to point out a significant difference between East and West in terms of their respective emphases on the collective and the individual, then this difference may justly be assumed to have consequences— as the statistics would seem to indicate. But these statistics may be evidence of a difference Mahbubani has not anticipated and one that does not speak for the advantages of Eastern cultures.

The difference in social organization between cultures that emphasize individual freedom and those that emphasize the role of groups and communities leads to a difference in the way in which conflict predominantly occurs— the way in which social tensions emerge and are expressed within the community. On the one hand, the emphasis on the individual leads to the prevalence of individual-on-individual conflict and a greater importance placed on individual competitions and confrontations. On the other hand, the emphasis on the group leads to a predominant trend toward group-on-group conflict. As Reid indicates in his study of Asian cultures, confrontations and conflicts between individuals are rare compared to Western cultures and especially American culture.

But while the communal emphasis may carry with it the advantage of lowering individual-on-individual conflicts and consequently crime rates, it has the disadvantage of remaining more vulnerable to the potentially larger problems inherent in group-on-group conflicts.

As recounted above, the United States has, through its capitalist economy, expanded opportunities for a higher standard of living to a degree significantly beyond most other nations. But increased opportunity has brought an increase in the level of competition in which occasions for exchange, interaction, and conflict between individuals are also increased. Competitiveness and conflict — even when initiated between corporations, sporting teams, political parties, and various social groups— readily reduces to a primary focus on conflict between particular individuals. The point at which the "other side" is effectively and substantially devalued is a flashpoint at which tensions and conflict situations are transformed into violence. In America these flashpoints tend to be manifested in media-highlighted *individual* confrontations.

The tendency toward centering personal identification in a group remains strong in all cultures but the experiment of individualism — especially as it has evolved in post–World War II America — indicates that the negative effects of group identification can be broken down and significantly mitigated by a strengthening of individualist culture. The heightened

individualism of American culture may result in greater numbers of violent crimes, murders, and serial killers but it also results in fewer instances
of ethnic, religious, class, and other forms of group-on-group violence.

The history of the twentieth century illustrates that calculated state-
sponsored persecution and genocide of minority groups are more likely
to occur among and within societies and nations that emphasize identity
by membership in a group. Although the United States has a history of
group violence against Native Americans and African Americans, this may
be a reflection of the limited extent of early individualism in America more
than a refutation of the claim. It is only in the post–World War II generations that affluence has combined with autonomy in sufficient numbers
to create a predominant middle-class individualist culture. In many ways
individualist culture in America is still in its infancy (this topic is also
addressed in Chapter 23).

The importance of the connection between personal identity issues
and group dominant community in escalating the risks of genocidal violence emerges as the well-argued and central theme in Amin Maalouf's *In
the Name of Identity: Violence and the Need to Belong* (2001). A writer and
former editor of a Beirut newspaper, Maalouf argues that the dangers of
attaching too much significance to group identity have been well illustrated in the history of the major religions emerging from the Middle East.
Maalouf writes that religious communities are "global tribes: tribes because
of their stress on identity; global because of the way they blithely reach
across frontiers." The sacredness of religious identity combined with tribal
hubris in the identification of profane evil has created many extraordinarily violent transnational confrontations between these religious sects over
the centuries. In response to these traditions of violence, Maalouf "dreams
not of a world where religion no longer has any place but of one where the
need for spirituality will no longer be associated with the need to belong.
What has to do with religion must be kept apart from what has to do with
identity ... if we want ... to stop feeding fanaticism, terror, and ethnic wars"
(cited in Gitlin, 2001: 7).

If it is true that American individualism increases the potential for
conflict between individuals and thereby contributes to the potential for
violent crimes perpetrated by one person on another, that may be represented as progress in terms of the cost of human life in comparison to the
far greater consequences of group-on-group violence evidenced in many
other areas of the world. With its cultural emphasis on the independence
and freedom of the individual, the kind of group-on-group violence that
occurred in the recent past in the Balkans is much less likely to occur in
America. This rosy assessment, however, is not without dissenters.

Writing in the mid–1990s, cultural critic Pete Hamill reports that the United States, the country that was the world's "brightest hope," is "breaking apart." Hamill argues that "the unraveling process can have many names: fragmentation, disunification, atomization, balkanization, disintegration" (1994: 88). Even though the analyses of various observers such as Arthur M. Schlesinger, Jr., Gertrude Himmelfarb, Michael Walzer, Allan Bloom, and Robert Hughes may differ regarding causes, Hamill finds that they agree about the symptoms. And these particular symptoms of "unraveling" are the opposite of what is being claimed herein. According to Hamill's findings, the conflict is not primarily between individuals but between groups: "The best-educated are again being taught to identify themselves with the qualifying adjectives of race, religion, ethnicity, and gender.... American identities ... are not shaped by will, choice, reason, intelligence, and desire but by membership in groups.... The ferocious logic of the adjective insists that the individual take sides. To refuse is to betray the larger group, your own flesh and blood. In America now, it is always Us against Them and Them against Us" (89).

Oddly enough, only five years later Gregg Easterbrook reports that Americans are, on an unprecedented scale, "willingly adopting gender equality and cultural openness." For Easterbrook the concerns of group conflict unraveling the country are voiced primarily from the conservative right: "The right elite is ... obsessive about the supposed culture war, when all the evidence is that the United States is becoming ever more tolerant and ever more at peace with diversity." The explanation for this disparity between evidence and perception lies, according to Easterbrook, in the influence of the media. Media contribute to the distortion of perceptions by sensationalizing every conflict and by featuring violence and mayhem. Easterbrook cites, for example, the view of Harvard professor Christopher Jencks: "Every screen you look at, at home or in theaters, has something disastrous on it. No wonder people think the country is out of control" (1999b: 24).

The social trend in the United States toward grounding identity in individual effort, choice, and talent works against the more traditional emphasis placed on identity centered within the "tribe" or the group. But this trend moves alongside an equally potent trend toward the radical polarization of conflict — derived from a long cultural tradition — and given renewed momentum through the new media of communication technologies and the competition to win audiences. Thanks to the American individualistic ethos that has evolved since World War II, the melodramatization of group-on-group conflict has, contrary to Hamill's impressions, declined in the United States. But, thanks to continuing

cultural and media influences, the melodramatization of conflict has surfaced more in the forms of individuals versus individuals and individuals
versus the "system."

Having argued that individualistic community, through its limita-
tion of the scale of carnage, may be preferable to the more broadly devastating violence of group-dominated communities, it cannot be too quickly
added that an increase in individual freedoms need not *necessarily* result
in a crime wave between individuals. As has been acknowledged and illustrated in this chapter, the social tensions of late capitalist society do in fact
generate increased opportunities or motives for conflict. But conflict and
competition must also to be structured in a particular way, as demonstrated in the case of the McWane Corporation, before it results in deval-
uative and destructive practices and actions.

Nor is it the case that the tradition of the moral code of good and evil
combined with melodramatic films is predominantly responsible for violence in America. What can be confidently stated is that the melodramatic
structuring of conflict in social, moral, and cinematic realms contributes
to a feedback loop that preserves and accelerates the spread of an attitude
toward conflict that unquestionably promotes the potential for violence
through uncompromising and radically polarized attitudes toward conflict.
In other words, the problem is more systemic across and through cultural
training than bound up in one or two isolated sources.

In light of its exceptional problem with violence, there has been a
tendency to view current American culture as polluted or decadent. But
there is nothing in American culture that needs to be rooted out, extir-
pated, or destroyed — including melodramatic cinema and the capitalist
economy. What needs to occur is a restoration of balance in competitive
practices. There is no question this balance can be achieved and broadly
sustained.

This balance is necessary for and already manifest in productive competition. Competition is a marriage of differences, sometimes even a marriage of apparent contradictions. As in all marriages, both sides remain
independent but that independence is transformed through measures of
dependency. With its testings of the character and capabilities of the opposition and its rules and protocols institutionalizing respect for the opposition, competition has a dual origin in a principle of evaluation — reflected
in the motive for a hierarchy of choice such as presented in the structure
of good and evil — as well as a principle of affirmation and inclusion, which
is reflected in the maxim of the golden rule. In healthy competition the
principle of evaluation applied to others is *always* tempered by the golden
rule. In this sense healthy competition defines civilization.

The evaluative principle — when carried to the extreme of the radical sorting power of evil as defilement — must not be allowed to stand. And this manner of radical evaluation most certainly must not be allowed to stand *alone*. Radicalized and elevated to autonomous authority, it becomes a license to kill when applied to relational conflicts.

Healthy, competitive aggression occurs in a context governed by rules that serve the purpose of institutionalizing a regard for competitors along with mandating a relatively level playing field for all involved in the competition. This notion of refereed and rule-governed competition in partnership with commerce has recently found popular advocacy in the practice and economic philosophy of New York State Attorney General Eliot Spitzer. Following the end-of-the-millennium Wall Street brokerage house scandals and several prominent prosecutions of brokers accused of breaching rules and violating client trust, Spitzer published an important article in a highly regarded national magazine.

Noting the tension between government oversight and a free market economy, Spitzer finds that this conflict is often reduced to the caricature between "meddling government bureaucrats" and "heartless laissez-faire capitalists." For Spitzer this contrast presents a false choice. He rightly argues, "The proper role of government is as market facilitator. Government should act to ensure that markets run cleanly as well as smoothly. It should prevent market failures and right them when they occur. *And it should ensure that markets uphold the broad values of our culture rather than debase them. In this vision, government action is necessary for free markets to work as they are intended — in an open, competitive, and fair manner.* In this vision, government helps to create, maintain, and expand competition, so the system as a whole can do what it does best: generate and broadly distribute wealth" (2004: 18, emphasis added).

Among the "broad values of our culture" of which Spitzer speaks the golden rule is among the most important and it is the crucial ingredient in distinguishing "cutthroat competition" from productive and sustainable competition. It also underlies the fundamental motivation for fairness in making rules and in refereeing the rules. As an indispensable part of the balance in competition, the golden rule attains — alongside the principle of evaluation — the status of equiprimordiality. The equality of these principles at the imaginary point of origin for the creation of rules is consistent with holistic synagonism and constitutes the metaphysical ground of healthy competition.

Through the logic of its structuring of the relation between the self and the other, the golden rule also generates individualism as a basic feature of communal organization. Adhering to the principle that every other shall be treated as one would have others treat oneself empowers and thereby creates individualism within society by institutionalizing basic human rights and fair and equitable treatment to every member of the community. It also requires that no one be essentially excluded on the basis of arbitrary criteria from participation in the competition within political and organizational hierarchies.

Instead of adopting, as in Eastern cultures, the solution of making the group the highest value, Western cultures ought to preserve the greater social balance they have worked toward with the increased value placed on the individual. The benefits of this approach include maximizing the energy, creativity, and fulfillment of each person while minimizing tendencies toward the most highly destructive forms of violence in group-on-group conflict. But along with preserving its valuation of individual freedom, America must restore balance to the imbalance that has led to the contradiction in its cultural moral codes.

To combat the increased tendencies toward eruptions of conflict into violence in individualist culture, it will be necessary to work on modifying the feedback loop of melodramatic structure while at the same time raising the stature of the golden rule in public awareness and stressing the crucial role it plays in the health of competition.

This emphasis on the basic message imparted in the golden rule need not be construed as requiring initiation into subtle forms of religious or moral conscience. As Tompkins has rightly indicated in the aforementioned keynote address, "we can accept these rules [the principles implied in the golden rule] as ultimate values on the bases of (1) religious commandment or (2) pragmatic justification or (3) philosophic justification. Some people might very well accept them on all three bases" (2005: 221). Whatever rationale may appeal, it is clear that the failure to accept these rules leads to many varieties of extraordinarily undesirable consequences from the point of view of social as well as individual health. Michael Shermer's study of morality, *The Science of Good and Evil* (2004), corroborates Tompkins's assessment in noting that at the base of the golden rule "lies the foundation of most human interactions and exchanges and it can be found in countless texts throughout recorded history" (25).

With respect to a high profile and state-sponsored emphasis placed on the golden rule, contemporary culture in Japan would appear to be exemplary — as Reid has illustrated with many interesting examples. But in its continued emphasis on the importance of shaping identity through group attachments, Japanese social and economic culture effaces the individual too much and in doing so perpetuates the risks of potentially explosive nationalism and group-on-group violence — as occurred in Japan's treatment of Chinese, Korean, and Philippine ethnic groups in World War II. This risk is courted further with Japan's continued propagation of melodramatic entertainment in its popular culture, which, as in the United States, is a reflection of the continued attractions and the cultural vitality of highly polarized ways of orienting toward conflict and competition.

Summary

The exceptional statistics on violent crime in the United States are without question a function of a highly individualistic culture that not only through its laws maximizes the autonomy of the individual but through its extraordinary economic engine also adds power to that autonomy. With its successful economy the United States has created a middle class of the greatest number of relatively autonomous and affluent individuals in the history of the world. But this economic success, while affording unprecedented opportunity, has also generated through its combined egalitarian and competitive motivations a variety of culturally rooted tensions. For a relative minority of individuals, these tensions are not adequately confronted and resolved through available relationships and institutions, and such tensions consequently evolve into violence against other individuals. For this minority as well as the remaining majority, however, these tensions are not only inadequately confronted but are further exacerbated by the modeling of violent conflict presented in melodramatic entertainment. This modeling, it has been argued, contributes to a feedback loop that increasingly accelerates polarizing and dehumanizing attitudes toward conflict and competition. Since the spirit of competition lies at the foundation of all social, economic, and political institutions in the United States (and, to a great extent, civilization as a whole) any imbalance that significantly and persistently affects the quality of competitive interaction cannot be long ignored without seriously damaging the quality of institutions and standard of living. The crime statistics are only a small indicator of a problem that is broader and potentially more destructive than overt physical violence. The next chapter presents concluding thoughts and some general recommendations about how the feedback loop concerning attitudes toward conflict and competition can be confronted and modified.

16

Whence and Whither: Conclusions and Recommendations

The maker of violent fiction has bottled the Dionysian whirlwind and is selling it as a soft drink.
— *Andrew Klavan*

The fact that large numbers of children and teenagers are becoming overweight has been the subject of much current news coverage. If nothing else, this problem proves that constant exposure to a diet of junk food options in the media and in the stores can have a significant negative effect on health.

Like real servings of candy and soda pop, screen servings of gratuitous sex and melodramatic violence give a temporary fix of arousal and enjoyment that is only superficially pleasing in its effects while contributing negatively in the long term. Constant exposure to the cinematic confections of melodrama — much of which amounts to little more than pornographic violence — increases the potential number of young viewers bloated with unhealthy attitudes toward conflict.

But the attractions of junk cinema, like junk food, will not disappear because someone says junk is unhealthy. As T. S. Eliot once remarked, "melodrama is perennial and the craving for it is perennial and must be satisfied" (cited in Twitchell, 1985: 71). However, the degree to which this craving is courted and satisfied in current American culture is remarkably excessive. Nevertheless, it is unlikely that melodrama will wane in popularity anytime soon, but precisely for that reason publicizing the full extent of its drawbacks becomes increasingly valuable as cultural correction. While many have suggested, along with Eliot, that melodrama is aesthetically inferior to other genres, the way in which melodrama may contribute to social and psychological victimage has not been as thoroughly discussed as other factors surrounding the problem of media violence.

Gun crime and high homicide rates are significant problems in the United States but attitudes of disregard, dehumanization, and hatred are perhaps broader and deeper problems. Many cultural influences and factors ranging from contexts involving family, peers, and the media contribute to these attitudes. Among the most prominent of these influences, however, must be included the antagonistic metaphysical orientation of good and evil embedded in the core moral traditions of the dominant religious institutions of Christianity, Judaism, and Islam.

Lying close to the roots of the moral tradition, melodramatic entertainment is a significant reinforcement of such attitudes and, for many persons in the throes of extreme identity crisis, potentially a significant trigger for violence. Given these concerns about the moral tradition and melodramatic entertainment, what can or ought to be done?

Interrogating the Moral Tradition

As has been argued previously, the moral structure of good and evil is the necessary logical consequence of any theology grounded in a monotheistic conception of God and a cosmological myth of origin that portrays the cosmos as originating from unified perfection. For this reason commentators on war and social violence such as Sam Keen have asserted, "It is impossible to think about the future of enmity and alternatives to war without beginning with theology" (1986: 172). In something like the reversal Kenneth Burke performs in which the scapegoating principle is transformed into the scapegoat, Keen finds the monotheistic notion of God and the institutionalization of this notion in popular religions to be the "monster" in the "horror story" of humanity: " 'God' has been the linchpin in the war system, the guardian spirit of tribes and nations, the transcendent sanction for genocide. In large measure, institutional religion has been a support for the ego and the ideology for society.... This war God is a vampire who thrives on blood, is the agent of disharmony between nations, the sanctifier of personal and political paranoia" (172).

Speaking in a similar vein, Regina M. Schwartz in *The Curse of Cain: The Violent Legacy of Monotheism* (1997), addresses the implications of the discourse of monotheism found in one famous chapter of the Old Testament.

Building the Tower of Babel (Hans Holbein's Images of the Old Testament, 1538)
(from the book *Hans Holbein the Younger, His Old Testament Illustrations, Dance
of Death, and Other Woodcuts* compiled by Arthur Mayger Hind. 1912. New York:
Fredk. A. Stokes Company Publishers).

Reading the story of Babel iconoclastically, she sees the construction of the
tower to be a symbol of "people joining together in a common project."
God then destroys their tower, spreads them to the four winds, and gives
them different languages— all to protect his sacred authority. Schwartz
concludes, "In this remarkable myth, the division of the people into peoples is not in their interests, but in the interest of maintaining the power
of a tyrannical, threatened deity jealously guarding his domain" (38).

Moving from myth to metaphysics, the monotheistic God produces
radical division between people because it provides a metaphysical model
of conflict that encourages defining the self against the other in a radically
exclusionary way. Continuing her analysis, Schwartz also appropriately
connects the dots between moral structure and monotheism, noting that
"some suspicion of the ancient biblical link between ethics and the myth
of monotheism seems in order, along with some doubt about the wisdom
of tying ethics to an understanding of identity that is [ant]agonistic by
nature" (38).

Concerning responses to the violent model of monotheism, Keen's proposed solution parallels the one offered by Burke: turn the principle of violence on itself. Keen argues that "nothing novel, kind, or hopeful can be created in the future unless we kill off this God, the idol of the tribe, unless we cease offering our blood to Moloch. The basis of a new social order is a theological revolution" (172).

But this solution by revolution, as argued in Chapter 14, repeats and thereby reaffirms the same logic evident in the principle it seeks to overthrow. Essentially "God" is now sacrificed not for the sins of humanity but for his own sins. Either form of sacrifice is unnecessarily destructive in its ends as well as the logic of its means. "God" does not need to be exorcised so much as removed from the seat of sacred and autocratic authority.

Schwartz's proposed solution, on the other hand, centers on a more productive orientation that preserves the benefits of continued immunization against violence. This approach is grounded in a theory of inclusion that forms a balanced tension between sameness and difference, self and other.

> Perhaps when we have grown weary of asserting all our differences, we will be willing to think more of likenesses, analogies, even identifications— not to forge totality, but to endlessly compose and recompose temporary and multiple identifications. I long to imagine, with the philosopher, "not only something that opposes the universal, but also some element that can be extended close to another, so as to obtain a connection. Such emissions ... constitute a transcendental field without subject. The multiple become a substitute — multiplicity — and philosophy is a theory of multiplicities that refers to no [transcendental] subject or preliminary unity." Not one, but many gods [37–38].

Schwartz's solution, resting on a synagonistic metaphysics, permits retention of the value of the dualism inherent in the evaluative principle that underlies the tension between good and evil while at the same time weakening and transforming the destructive power of its exclusionary imperative. Through a thorough affirmation of multiplicity her solution allows even for the continuance of the exclusionary principle inherent in the structure of good and evil — but in the reduced capacity of an immunizing role.

The cultural force of God and monotheism needs to retain a central place in human preoccupations but must do so through an entirely new context in which its history is thoroughly documented, its seductions adequately itemized, and its dangers repeatedly exposed. In this sense, God need not be slain in the heavens but rather brought down to earth and given a human and — unlike the Christ of the New Testament —*non-*

sacrificial role. Having said this, it should be added that, to his credit and despite some rhetoric to the contrary, Keen also ultimately recognizes inoculation as the theoretically sound approach for the inclusion of tradition in achieving nonviolent international community. And he rightly advocates the use of this approach through adequately informed free media (173).

Regarding nonsacrificial mythologies of the sacred, the work of René Girard — whose theory of mimetic desire is discussed in Chapter 2 — offers one of the most extensive and sustained critical examinations of Western religious tradition in relation to the mechanism of scapegoating. In the course of exposing scapegoating as the sacrificial violence central to the entire history of Western civilization, Girard illustrates the inextricable connections between politics, economics, culture, and religion.

While Girard's advocacy of a nonsacrificial ethos is laudable and consistent with the metaphysical position advocated herein, it is difficult to derive this ethos from the Christian Gospels, as Girard does, when weighed against the textual evidence. Gerard insists that the New Testament, when properly understood apart from its sacrificial interpretation by Christian tradition, represents a fundamental world-historical break with that tradition.

The glaring weaknesses of Girard's nonsacrificial reading of the New Testament (Girard, 1987) are revealed through a series of persuasive examples and arguments offered by Lucien Scubla, whereby, according to Scubla, "It is scarcely possible to doubt that our author [Girard] has no basis for attributing to the Christ of the gospels the designs he does…. Interesting as it may be, therefore, the Girardian interpretation is not compatible with the text as a whole" (1988: 170). In light of Scubla's persuasive objections, it must be concluded that Girard's attempt to rehabilitate the New Testament for the purposes of an inclusionary, nonsacrificial metaphysics is analogous to the task of interpreting the Adamic myth as tragic drama.

Girard is accurate, however, when he stresses the core metaphysical compatibility between traditional religious institutions and utopian political movements such as fascism and communism and their shared scapegoating practices. In his book *The Genealogy of Violence* (2001) in a section entitled "Political Religion," Charles K. Bellinger comments on Girard's insight as well as others who have come to similar conclusions. Discussing the work of Russian philosopher Nikolai Berdyaev (1961), Bellinger remarks: "Marx claimed that the traditional Christian notions of good and evil were outmoded and repressive. Yet in his thought the concepts of good and evil were merely transposed onto the 'proletariat' and the 'bourgeoisie.' In this way he preserved religious notions of the elect and the damned.

According to Berdyaev, this is an example of an 'unconscious survival of dualistic Manichean tendencies,' which is typical of revolutionary ideologies" (127). Bellinger cites German theorist Eric Voegelin (1986) as documenting similar "Manichean tendencies" in the "religious nature" of Nazism. French author Jacques Ellul (1975) confirms the findings of Berdyaev and Voegelin and adds to the list Maoist communism as yet another instance of how, in Bellinger's words, "the twentieth century has seen the rise of political movements that are precisely parallel to the earlier religious orders they seek to 'transcend'" (128).

With the publication of *Terror and Civilization: Christianity, Politics, and the Western Psyche* (2004) Shadia B. Drury conducts one of the most intense interrogations to date on the theme of religion, politics, and violence as it shapes the war on terrorism and the tensions between the desert religions of Christianity, Judaism, and Islam. Focusing primarily on Christianity and a close textual analysis of the New Testament, Drury argues that an ethic of love is contradicted and overwhelmed by a moralistic radicalizing and "romanticizing" of evil that succeeds in creating instead a "metaphysics of terror." Consistent with the views of Keen and Schwartz, Drury concludes that a departure from the biblical traditions toward a more inclusive and pluralistic structure of ideals will be essential to the creation of a healthy, nonviolent political climate. This path toward a less violent and more cooperative community must be grounded in a cultural reeducation regarding dangers inherent in the sacred traditions.

Censorship and "Immunization"

Turning from popular religion to mass media, it may well be asked, when considering viable social responses to deeply rooted scapegoating ideologies and mechanisms, whether the inclusionary alternative to monotheism and its moral structure has analogous relevance in relation to the exclusionary principle operative in censorship.

Recalling the discussion in the introduction, with the release of *A Clockwork Orange* Stanley Kubrick initially opposed the censorship of his film and spoke out in the media against censorship in general claiming that "high standards of moral behavior can only be achieved by the example of right-thinking people and society as a whole, and cannot be maintained by the coercive effect of the law." Two years later he censored his own film. Which of the two Kubricks is right? Did the benefit of two more years of experience yield a better judgment?

The ultimate reasons for Kubrick's actions remain obscure. Perhaps the persistence of newspaper reports of deaths due to copycat crimes in the style of "Little Alex" became too pressing a weight for Kubrick to continue shouldering. Perhaps he reached the point where he wished, like Anthony Burgess in regard to his book, that he had never made the film.

Kubrick may have come to the conclusion that Alex was already a kind of clockwork before he underwent the famous "Ludovico treatment." He was a clockwork built in good measure by the cognitive training inherent in the mix of capacities and incapacities imposed by his neighborhood blend of cultural imperatives and habituations. In addition to the tension Burgess named as the central issue in his novel — the tension whereby freedom of moral choice necessarily liberates the possibility to choose the worst — Kubrick may have come to see the taxing issue of moral choice further mitigated and complicated through the media repetitions of graphic violence that receptive minds are repeatedly encouraged to absorb. If so, censorship may have presented itself to him as the only remaining course of action, short of the "Ludovico treatment," to "undo" the future of what may be done through exposure to images and characters in his film and films of similar structure and content.

Perhaps Kubrick, like Burgess, also became concerned about another aspect of what the process of his artistic expression in *A Clockwork Orange* implied — as suggested in a letter to the editor of *The New York Times* written in January 1972 shortly after the film's release. A student in the School of Arts at Columbia University wrote: "It may be said that Kubrick's film is a warning against what the ... age may do to us; I see it as a sign of what it has done to him."

A Clockwork Orange may perhaps be rightly regarded as a film that should never have been made — at least not in the particular way chosen. It is a story that could have been told but perhaps should not have been told in the manner that Burgess and Kubrick chose to tell it. Presented from the point of view of the perpetrator of numbingly cruel violence, the film primarily succeeds (or at least succeeded in its time) in shocking audiences and elevating violence to "stealing the show" status — a disturbingly ironic outcome for a film intended to be a bold statement against a particular form of violence.

At the time of its release, Kubrick apparently believed of *A Clockwork Orange* what Oliver Stone believed of his film *Natural Born Killers* (1994). In response to the suggestion from a critic that this film was part of the problem and not part of the solution, Stone defended himself by replying that "you are trying to kill the messenger because it's not the filmmaker's fault that society is where it is. The filmmaker does his best to reflect society the way he sees it. And our society is culturally in a very violent and bankrupt mode" (cited in Caputi, 1999: 155).

Due in no small part to the fact that the story is portrayed from the point of view of the killers, film critic Jane Caputi is not convinced by Stone's deflection of responsibility and is compelled to ask: "How is *Natural Born Killers* not a part of 'the media' that creates such cultural bankruptcy? Does it simply reflect that condition, or does it work to conjure the murderous future it so saucily envisions?" (155). The same questions can be asked of *A Clockwork Orange* and many other films born of purportedly less noble intentions. Caputi concludes that *Natural Born Killers* is, despite all intentions at being a noble and enlightening parody, "a paean, an outburst of worshipful and exultant praise, a ceremony not of exorcism but of invocation." As an invocation of violence, the film is a capitulation to the power of violence to attract audiences and command attention through the media. As evidence of media power to elevate and impart legitimacy to violence, Caputi claims, along with several other critics, that in America the serial killer, as a result of excessive media attention, now functions as a celebrity and a cultural (anti)hero. Move over, Little Alex.

Although *A Clockwork Orange*, like *Natural Born Killers*, may have turned out to be nothing more than a macabre, ornamented paean to violence, the fact remains that it was made and distributed and that cannot be undone. As a fait accompli it should not be censored — by society or by the filmmaker. The time for filmmaker self-censorship — if there is to be censorship — is prior to the decision to take it to celluloid. Kubrick should not have second-guessed himself because his first instinct was correct. A change in standards of moral behavior as well as entertainment tastes is best orchestrated, and perhaps *only* orchestrated, through improved cultural contexts and institutions.

In regard to the immunization thesis, films such as *A Clockwork Orange* may function in an inoculating capacity for young audiences in relation to destructive violence only when viewed from within an educational or cultural climate sufficiently complex and influential to anticipate and illuminate the downside to the seductions implicit in its content. And if that "educational or cultural climate" is not at hand, the response ought to be something more profound than censorship.

It has been claimed by Anthony Burgess and confirmed by many critics that *A Clockwork Orange* "is about the choice between good and evil" and the necessity of having a choice in order for "good" to have any meaning. But, as has been argued at length herein, a more fundamental antecedent and metaphysically strategic choice gets lost in the stark glare of this exclusionary moral dualism. That choice is the choice of *how to structure the choice.* In the contrast between different genres of moral struggle, such as that between melodrama and tragic drama, it becomes possible to glimpse in action this difference as well as the cultural options it presents.

Education and Cultural Training

Probably the only genuinely effective and socially proven way to approach problems relating to cultural training — within which the problem of violence and violent entertainment must be included — is through education. Parents can and should play a leading role in the lives and development of their children but cannot always be adequate to the task in areas such as conflict management. In this regard, public schools are crucial institutions and they must draw parents into the educational process and involve them as much as possible. This is especially true for elementary schools where children first learn to grapple with issues of anger, jealousy, intimidation, and conflict. Young people must be taught about conflict assessment and management (both internal and relational) at the earliest grade and every level thereafter — with progressive sophistication of exposure.

The media also play a potent role in cultural training but cannot be relied on to model real life in a way adequate to life's challenges. Here public schools also have the opportunity and the obligation to expose students to review sessions of quality entertainment in scheduled video programs (fiction and documentary). Such sessions can teach how to navigate in the media world and provide a venue to discuss popular media, analyze potential media effects, and address— at a decisive time in the lives of children and teenagers— some of the negative influences of exposure to popular entertainment. Instruction in media navigation skills, including the ability to search for and uncover subtexts, ought to be a primary part of the public school curriculum.

Ellen A. Wartella, who at the time of this writing is dean of the College of Communication at the University of Texas at Austin and who was a principal investigator in a multi-university research program called the National Television Violence Study, has labored to bring attention to the appalling lack of cultural focus given to media awareness in the K–12 educational environment. Wartella complains that "the United States is the only English-speaking nation in the world without media education in its public schools. Media education is desperately needed in order to develop more literate audiences" (1996: 10). She argues convincingly that technological innovations such as the V-chip for parental control of television can only "marginally alter the television landscape ... because the chip offers a ... limited fix to a large and complicated human, moral, and social problem" (9). The cultural breadth and difficulty of the problem can only be adequately confronted through educational efforts and interventions among the age group where media literacy is beginning to take shape.

As an example for educational use, Sam Keen's *Faces of the Enemy* (1986), with companion book, remains one of the most powerful documentary films on violent conflict and how to gain a critical and evaluative perspective toward it. Although Keen's assessment of capitalist consumption and the value of competition (e.g., Keen, 184) aligns with other critics of the "postmodern condition" and differs from the opinions expressed herein, his views on the many varieties of dehumanization of the enemy are consistent with the indictment of the tradition of evil handed down in these pages. When presented to an adolescent audience, films and books such as Keen's can go a long way toward immunizing against the dangers of painting the other side of any intense conflict in shades of evil and defilement. At the end of his book, Keen offers a postscript entitled "The Education of Homo Amicus: A Curriculum for Compassion." This section is especially helpful for teachers in conducting classroom discussion of all questions relevant to the themes of war, power, violent conflict, and conflict negotiation and resolution skills.

Only through early and continued education concerning the powers of all the media from language to film will it be possible to cultivate artists and filmmakers who will not pursue their craft with the kind of shortsighted myopia regarding those powers exemplified in Oliver Stone's "don't kill the messenger" disclaimer. If postmodern insights into communication have taught anything, it is that the messenger is never only a messenger — and "killing" is never just an innocent metaphor.

PART II

ILLUSTRATING
THE CASE

17

The Western as the American Myth

Legend, Truth, and Cinema

The Western as a genre of entertainment presents itself as the classic modern arena in which gun-toting heroes are prominently featured in the saga of the complex and contradictory traces of America's partnership with violence. Other genres are significant, such as cop, soldier, martial arts, muscle, and spy action films, but in many ways relating to form, these story types are little more than contemporary versions of the American Western. In fact, from 1940 to roughly the middle of the 1970s, the Western accounts for about 30 percent of American-made feature films, according to critic John Nachbar (1974).

In Nachbar's opinion, Westerns are "the single most important story form of the twentieth century" and for a large number of Americans the Western defined "their traditional ethics, values and sources of national pride" (2).

Granting as much (for the moment), it is not surprising to find historian of the west C. L. Sonnichsen expressing the view that the Western fills the need for "a national myth to help us understand the nature of the universe and our place in it." In keeping with the grandeur of this scale, Sonnichsen believes that "the western story," as the collective saga of the exploration and settling of the American West, is "our Old Testament, our *Iliad* and *Odyssey*, our *Nibelungenlied*" (1978: 18).

Nevertheless, as Sonnichsen rightly indicates, Americans have had a difficult time constructing and embracing this national myth because the country is so young: "We want to have roots in ancient times, like other peoples, but we don't stay in one place long enough to grow them.... Many of us know nothing about our own grandfathers. Pride of family is denied to all but a few of us.... Any group with a thousand-year history has these things provided, but the American is a newcomer and not yet completely at home in his vast country. All he has is the mythical West, and he needs it desperately" (16–17).

The "mythical West" is difficult to establish and take seriously because the history of the country is so recent that the historical record keeps getting in the way of the myth-making. Sonnichsen cites as an example the case of a director who, during the filming of one of the early Billy the Kid Westerns, was reprimanded by the film's historical consultant, Mrs. Sophie Poe. She was the wife of a man who was present when Pat Garrett shot and killed the Kid. After watching the director's rendering of this scene, Mrs. Poe coolly informed him: "Sir, I knew that little buck-toothed killer, and he wasn't the way you are making him at all" (19).

But despite such tensions between fact and fiction or, as Sonnichsen says, between "the West the way it was" and "the West the way it wasn't," fact may not ultimately subvert the power of myth. Jenni Calder, another commentator on the American West, rightly distinguishes the roles of history and myth when she says, "as long as it is acknowledged that the Western cannot imitate history and *should not*, the myth will survive" (1974: 219, emphasis added). And no doubt the myth will survive, but only alongside a persistently haunting question that reflects the variety, the wanderlust, and the multiple roots of the Americans who came west: Which myth?

A 1959 *Time* magazine article provides, as Sonnichsen points out, the classic answer to this question when it describes the Western as "the American Morality Play." According to *Time*, the Western functions as "an allegory of human life and death in which the forces of good (in white hats) and the forces of evil (in black hats and five o'clock shadow) fight it out on the huge Western stage. Evil always loses" (cited in Sonnichsen, 13). In the late 1950s and early 1960s the Western, with its reliably uncomplicated melodramatic plot, not only accounts for a large percentage of feature film production but dominates prime-time television as well.

Time's description of the Western as melodramatic morality play, although generally true, is not entirely accurate in the details. In many instances the "forces of evil" wore feathers instead of black hats, as Native Americans were portrayed as the primary obstacles to civilized westward expansion. This westward expansion, as the unfolding of America's "Manifest Destiny," brought opportunity for those who had the will and the tenacity to endure the hardship while at the same time it brought death and the destruction of a way of life for many native peoples who found themselves in the way. Consequently, the heroics of the taming of a vast frontier and the grandeur of the myths associated with it become sullied by the persistent emergence of facts that reveal the myth to be considerably less than grand and in many ways shameful in its aggressive victimization and relentless land grabbing.

Under the increasing pressure of a "politically correct" gaze, the Western myth that was to be, and perhaps once was, a source of national pride, now serves as a reminder of a long trail of incidents eliciting a sense of national disgrace rather than pride. Sonnichsen laments the situation in the plain phrases of the cowboy style:

> Some national pride is essential, but Americans have very little of it left. Our general attitude seems to be negative, our thinking guilt ridden. We are ashamed of our past and doubtful of our future. We admit that we are destroying our environment. We see ourselves as greedy and materialistic. We confess that we do not know how to live. We have come to believe that our pioneer fathers before us were no good, either. One contemporary writer calls the first comers to Arizona "the dregs of their respective societies." The Indians, we acknowledge, were better men than the whites who conquered them and took away their lands and their living. Having thus lost our confidence in Columbia's happy land and in the heaven-born band of heroes who created it, we have come close to classifying ourselves [as we once did the Indians] among the "lesser breeds without the law" [18].

This litany of flagellations has led to a situation in which it would appear that the power of the Western myth the American so "desperately" needs has been significantly compromised. A particularly good example of this may be found in the postmodern critique of the myth of Davy Crockett. Christopher Sharrett, for instance, mounts a withering debunking campaign against the Crockett myth by marshalling evidence for a sordid military and economic expansionist reality behind the myth.

Fess Parker's Crockett as king of the Disneyland frontier and John Wayne's "hero of the Alamo" presented the image of an affable coonskin-capped archetype whose "battles against Indians and Mexicans reflected the postwar anxieties of communism, 'flabby' patriotism ... excessive domesticity, and the feminine" (1999: 415). This Crockett myth, according to Sharrett, represents all of the dark motives lurking in "Manifest Destiny"— now understood as imperialist ideology. Crockett's many years of service in Congress are characterized as antagonistic to "parliamentary process" and infused with a style of arrogance consisting of partisan "proclamation," the "tall tale," and "anti-intellectualism." Sharrett sums up the real substance of Crockett's cultural effects with the following remarks:

> In telling his constituents to "go to hell" and lighting out for the territories when he lost his congressional seat to Adam Huntsman ... we see a trajectory that moves from Crockett's puffery to *Taxi Driver* (1976) to the valorization of the contemporary serial killer.... Crockett went to Texas not to fight for a cause but to begin, at age forty-nine, a new political career.... [He] aligned himself with the War Party — the speculators, slave traders, and brigands like William B. Travis, R. M. Williamson, Ben Milam, and James Bowie — men who ... demanded that "settlers" destroy the swarthy hordes of Mexico, whom the War Party frequently characterized as apes [415–416].

Sharrett continues on in this manner, dismantling the revisionist history of the Crockett myth, until he achieves a dizzying level of his own revisionist spin, airbrushed of any contravening details. For Sharrett, the cultural significance of Crockett's last stand at the Alamo is, along with the entire substance and spirit of the westward thrust of Manifest Destiny, wholly analogous to Custer's infamous last stand at Little Big Horn.

While the truth may ultimately remain inaccessible, honesty, at least, requires a more complex interpretation. Sharrett fails to note that Crockett spent as many years as he did in Congress, not because he was fond of Washington and its limelight but in large measure because he wanted to continue — despite being the lone advocate within his Jacksonian democratic party — in the thankless struggle to secure land and rights for Indians on the frontier. At the Alamo Crockett sided with "brigands" like Travis, Williamson, Milam, and Bowie in an effort to preserve what then passed for liberal community and halt the outright tyrannical ambitions of Santa Ana. In order to "harden" them for battle, Santa Ana coerced his troops—composed largely of mestizos conscripted into military duty — into a grueling forced march to Texas in which over 500 died of starvation and exhaustion on the way to fight for land they would never be allowed to use. The political tensions in Texas of the 1830s cannot be adequately shaded in the melodramatic tones suggested by Sharrett's one-sided sketch. Similarly, Crockett's actions, motives, and ambitions, while not without blemishes and warts, were far more complex than Sharrett allows.

As cultural perception began to shift in the decade of the 1960s progressively more toward a pejorative assessment of "frontier" heroes and an attitude of guilt and shame regarding the expansionist movement of Manifest Destiny, a reciprocal shift in cultural awareness toward "Indians" also gained momentum. This shift was reflected in the growing popular preference for the alternative label "Native Americans." The Victorian portrait of the Native American as the "dark savage" and the murderous "hostile"—implicit in many of the dime novels and Western wagon train and cavalry films of the 1930s and '40s—gave way to more sympathetic portrayals. As historian James A. Clifton notes, this shift resulted in a growing wave of published biographies and anthologies consisting of "glamorized accounts of great heroes, celebrities, leaders, and other distinguished notables" of the Native American past. These accounts presented "suitable moralizing stories about the contributions of [these] larger-than-life figures" (1989: 4). A cottage industry of Native American myth-making grew to fill the void created by the myth-debunking industry that had targeted the stalwarts of the great "White" westward migration.

Lamenting the oscillating shift between antagonistic extremes in the portrayal of Indians and their history, Clifton asks, "What might be done to avoid the strong biases inherent in such stereotyped assumptions, styles, and images?" In response to his own question, Clifton suggests: "One large step is to recognize that the current most-favored image of Indians past and present is a human invention, one construction of a complex social and historical reality" (4–5).

However, the "current most-favored image" is also more than merely a construction of history. It is also often a moral construction shaped by the culturally dominant inclination to apply to instances of highly prominent and protracted conflict the template of good and evil. Clifton is also keenly aware of how this polarization has worked its way into contemporary perceptions of the differences between the traditions of White and Indian cultures among Americans and Canadians. He points to a popular ledger of traits that leaves no doubt about the prevailing judgment concerning the "good guys" and the "bad guys."

> Thus, the White man is described as invading America, despoiling and dispossessing Indians, while Indians expand their territories peacefully by migration, or defend their "sacred holy lands" patriotically. The White man is motivated by greed, especially land hunger, but thoughtlessly desecrates the landscape, whereas the Indian worships and lives in perfect harmony with Mother Earth. The Indian enjoys a perfectly democratic and egalitarian social life, and the White man exercises centralized power ruthlessly, exploiting the weak and defenseless. Although the Indian is content with the minimum of material goods, the White man lusts for an ever-increasing abundance. A crass materialism and disregard for the rights of others marks the White man but not the Indian, who is eminently spiritual and considerate of friend and stranger, young and old [1989: 5–6].

This contrast between White and Indian cultures has become so common-place in contemporary society that many cultural analysts have used it instructively as a way of grounding various psychiatric prescriptions for postmodern social and cultural ailments.

Rushing and Frentz, for example, develop a contrast between arche-typal myths of the "sacred" and "profane" hunt. On the one hand, armed with a handmade weapon and a belief in the reciprocal relation between hunter and hunted and the "common life-spirit immanent in all things," the Indian hunter serves as the model for the sacred hunt. On the other hand, the White hunter (or "technological hunter"), armed with a man-ufactured weapon and the desire for complete dominance and control over the hunted as well as its habitat, serves as the model for the profane hunt.

Rushing and Frentz cite Richard Slotkin as a significant source for their account of the Indian and White versions of the hunt. Slotkin in turn derives much of his analysis of the Indian hunt from Joseph Campbell's narrative in *The Masks of God*. Noting archetypal differences between "Indian" and "Puritan" versions of the place of "man" in the world, Slotkin describes a corresponding difference in the cosmology of good and evil. On the one hand, "to the Indian the wilderness was a god, whether its face at the moment was good or evil; as god it deserved and received worship for both its good and its evil, its beauty and its cruelty." On the other hand, Slotkin continues, "For the Puritans the problem of religion was to winnow the wheat from the chaff, the good from the evil, and to preserve the former and extirpate the latter. The evil was of the world, of nature; the good was transcendent and supernatural" (1973: 51).

Slotkin's summary of the Puritan orientation gains credibility from extensive written records. However, the Indian record, being an oral tra-dition, invites greater latitude of interpretation and incurs greater suscep-tibility to misconception, misunderstanding, and outright invention. Indian religion expert Sam Gill documents the way in which early mod-ern anthropological practices contributed to specious generalizations. Gill cites the Mother Earth figure in Indian mythology as a case in point. Instead of uncovering accounts of this spiritual entity, anthropologists created the figure largely out of thin air. Gill reports, "What is shown in the case of Mother Earth is that no North American evidence exists. Mother Earth emerges not from ethnographic documentation but from an imag-inative construction. What scholars have been writing about was not the Other at all, but about their own views of human history" (1990: 141).

Furthermore, Gill points out that the Indian traditions were not only in many cases imaginatively conjured and recorded by White observers but also were in most cases recorded long after initial Indian contact with White culture. Indian culture began changing in response to the exposure to White culture (and, to a lesser degree, vice versa) in an enormous variety of subtle as well as pronounced ways from the time of earliest contact. And, as Gill also notes, White commentators on Indian culture, many of whom harbored disillusionments with their own culture, were inclined to see Indian customs and lifestyles in ways that reflected European conceptions of idyllic community. Consequently, it becomes nearly an impossible task to document "uncrossed" lineages of Indian traditions.

Even while detailing the stark contrast he finds between Indian and Puritan religious or spiritual traditions, Slotkin acknowledges (as mentioned in Chapter 15) that evidence exists that many of the Indian nations such as the Aztec and the Iroquois displayed attitudes toward war, trade, and government similar to European cultures. These attitudes included especially a similar dichotomy between moral poles of good and evil and the corresponding exclusionary and sacrificial cosmology evident in the mythology of the "profane hunt."

In light of the caveats regarding the accurate discernment of Indian traditions, it seems reasonable to conclude that the truth about differences between Indian and White cultures leans in the direction of the view that the evidence for associating Indian culture with the practices of the "sacred hunt" is tenuous at best and that elements of the "profane hunt" are significant in both Indian and White cultures. This conclusion helps to explain Slotkin's finding that, to the extent that he was not beforehand, "the Indian hunter became quite rapidly the accomplice of the white entrepreneur in the destruction of the wilderness and the beings that derived existence from it" (1973: 50).

Similarly, although technology may help to accelerate or magnify the practices and effects of a profane hunt, there is no reason to see it as an elemental cause of the exclusionary moral and spiritual outlook of the mythological tradition associated with the profane hunt. As argued herein (Chapter 15, in the section on instrumentalization), the reverse is more likely the case. The exclusionary metaphysics of good and evil serves as sine qua non for the violent abuse of technology.

While differences between spiritual approaches to the hunt noted by Rushing and Frentz, Slotkin, and others provide potentially useful distinctions that are at some points analogous to the distinction advocated herein between synagonistic and antagonistic conflict structures, the terms "Indian hunter" and "technological hunter" are misleading through a questionable valorization of the Indian as well as an unnecessary disparagement of technology. The terms "Indian" and "technological" are better avoided in favor of more abstract terms that may be aligned with fewer potentially equivocal preconceptions.

Returning to the world of entertainment media, the tension between Indians and Whites has experienced, in the course of the twentieth century, a complete reversal of polarity. The melodrama of the heroic settlers, frontiersmen, and cavalry against the villainous Indians that played out over the decades through films like *Wagon Wheels* (1934) and *Buffalo Bill* (1944) and *Rio Grande* (1950) eventually turned full circle, yielding the melodrama of heroic Indians persecuted by the villainous railroad barons, landgrabbers, buffalo sportsmen, and sadistic Cavalry in films like *Little Big Man* (1970), *The Return of a Man Called Horse* (1976), and *Dances with Wolves* (1990).

It is surprising to find, however, that before the cultural shift to the more sympathetic view, the Indian rarely appears as the featured villain. Philip French, a historian of Westerns, reveals that the Indian served more as a "faceless symbol"—"an all-purpose enemy ready at the drop of a tomahawk to spring from the rocks and attack wagon trains, cavalry patrols and isolated pioneer settlements," and, in this second-class status, "could not even serve as an individually realised villain" (1977: 79). In the majority of early Westerns, among which *Garden of Evil* (1954) is a classic example, conflict with Indians provides merely a backdrop for the more prominently featured conflict between White male protagonists.

Tragic Drama versus Melodrama

Regardless of the race of the primary protagonists, the decisive factor in determining the value and the power of the Western myth resides in the quality of the conflict it depicts. As Sonnichsen insists, despite the criticisms and the many visions and revisions of the Western myth, something of value remains within its tattered and worn pages. A rudimentary but profound spirit of life inheres in the stories, always at least partly fictional, of the flawed men and women who made the journey into a frontier of unknown opportunities and challenges. In the telling of these stories, melodramatic form, as already mentioned, has exerted strong influence, but tragic dramatic form has also contributed significantly to Western storytelling. These dramatic forms have been stretched and twisted in a variety of creative ways through the stories that have been imaginatively conjured over the decades.

Before examining a few of the twists and turns of the Western melodramatic plot, it will be useful for purposes of highlighting its pivotal features to begin with the contrast of a tragic dramatic plot. The Western genre contains a particularly good example of tragic drama in Howard Hawks's *Red River* (1948). The plot and the action of *Red River* are described and discussed in considerable detail for the further purpose of providing an illustration of a more contemporary version of tragic drama apart from ancient Greek tragedy, a drama cast against the background of the popular setting of the American west.

RED RIVER

The screenplay for *Red River* by Borden Chase and Charles Schnee received an Academy Award nomination and was adapted from Chase's story "The Chisholm Trail" first published in serial parts in the *Saturday Evening Post* (1946–1947). Featuring a Texas cattleman, Tom Dunson (John Wayne), and his adopted son, Matthew Garth (Montgomery Clift), the plot revolves around the conflict that arises between them while making the first cattle drive along what later becomes the famous Chisholm trail from Texas to Abilene, Kansas.

The story begins with Dunson and his trusted sidekick, Groot Nadine (Walter Brennan), leaving a wagon train they joined in St. Louis to head south toward Texas in search of grazing land for cattle. Dunson is shown to be a man of strong resolve when he refuses to take along the woman who loves him — despite her insistence on going with him — believing she will be safer staying with the wagon train. He tells her that he will send for her when he finds the right place to start his ranch. Hours later, he and Groot see a cloud of smoke in the distance. Dunson's fear that the wagon train was attacked by Indians is confirmed when he and Groot are ambushed by a band from the same group and Dunson recovers a bracelet he had given his bride-to-be from the wrist of an Indian he killed.

The next morning, Matt, a surviving boy from the wagon train, makes his way into Dunson's camp. Rattled by what he has witnessed, Matt mumbles incoherently to himself. Attempting to shock him out of his daze, Dunson slaps him. Still confused, Matt pulls a gun, which Dunson quickly wrestles away from him. Coming to his senses, he informs Dunson and Groot that he was spared the fate that befell the others because he had been away from the wagons chasing down a stray cow. Taking a liking to the boy's spirit, Dunson allows him to join them.

The three eventually find land in Texas and Dunson lays claim to it only to be confronted shortly thereafter by two men who tell him it belongs to a Mexican landlord. In no mood to be pushed around after traveling so far, Dunson angrily counters by saying that the section of land from where they stand to the Rio Grande now belongs to him. One of the men goes for his gun and Dunson outdraws and kills him.

With these opening sequences of the film it becomes clear that Dunson is an aggressive man, tempered by a Spartan code of conduct and justice, who cannot be cajoled by a woman, threatened by Indians, buffaloed by a boy, or bullied by strangers in his single-minded quest for a piece of the Texas pie. For these reasons he earns respect, tempered with caution, from Groot and Matt.

At this point the film jump-cuts 14 years into the future. Matt is now an educated man having returned from schooling somewhere on the East Coast. He and Dunson now have a herd of 10,000 cattle, which, because of the collapse of the South in the Civil War, has a market only in the North. But to sell his cattle in the North, Dunson must drive the herd to the nearest railhead in Missouri. So he and Matt organize a cattle drive and head north.

The hardships of the journey wear greatly on the men and, after a stampede kills one of his favorite cowpunchers, Dunson loses control of himself and takes a whip to the hand who accidentally started the stampede. This incident along with a few others turns some of the men against Dunson. Sensing possible mutiny, Dunson goes without sleep in order to keep an eye on everyone and begins drinking whisky to dull the pain of the stress that begins to weigh on him. After three of the men sneak off in the night, he has them rounded up by two of his most trusted hands—one of whom, Cherry Valance (John Ireland), is handy with a gun. When Valance returns with two of the deserters, the physically exhausted but still headstrong Dunson, fearing wider mutiny, exercises bad judgment and decides he will hang the two as an example. This autocratic frontier justice proves to be too much for Matt. Confronting Dunson, he coolly informs him that he will not allow the men to be hanged. Outraged by the challenge to his authority, Dunson draws his gun but Valance, instantly deciding to side with Matt, shoots the gun from Dunson's hand. The other men quickly join with Matt and Valance. Assuming full leadership of the cattle drive, Matt takes the herd in a new direction toward Abilene, Kansas, leaving Dunson behind. As a result, the furious Dunson vows to track him down and kill him.

On the way to Abilene, Matt and his group of men help rescue a caravan being attacked by Indians. Among these settlers Matt meets a young woman, Tess (Joanne Dru), who immediately takes a liking to him. Finding the attraction mutual, Matt nevertheless shows that he is his stepfather's son by reprising Dunson's decision to leave the woman behind with the wagon train as he moves on with the dangerous business of the cattle drive.

Hot in pursuit of Matt and with a posse of newly recruited men, Dunson encounters the wagon train and meets Tess. Having learned from Matt the entire story, Tess immediately recognizes Dunson and goes to work on dissuading him from his plan for revenge. True to his sense of justice and his hardened nature, Dunson will have none of Tess's pacifications. Her beauty and courage, however, manage to open a crack in his armor and he agrees this time, in response to Tess's undeterrable insistence, to take a woman with him. This scene and a previous scene with the range hand who is killed in the cattle stampede confirm that Dunson has a heart buried just beneath the surface of his ironclad exterior.

On reaching Abilene, Matt and his crew encounter great fanfare amidst welcoming crowds along with an eager buyer willing to pay top dollar for the cattle. However, none of the men feel much like celebrating with the certainty that Dunson is not far behind. That evening Dunson and his riders camp on the outskirts of Abilene and Tess ventures into town to warn Matt.

The next morning Matt and Dunson face off in the film's climactic showdown. Dunson strides menacingly up to Matt and tries to provoke him to draw his gun. Matt stands his ground and refuses to draw. Finally pulling his own gun, Dunson shoots at the ground near Matt to further

Tom Dunson (John Wayne) delivers a blow to Matthew Garth (Montgomery Clift) in the concluding fight scene from *Red River* (1948) (Photofest).

provoke him, but Matt, standing like a statue, still refuses to draw. Only after Dunson approaches and knocks him down with a blow to the head does Matt finally strike back and the two begin brawling.

The fight appears to show no signs of letting up, but before they can beat each other senseless, Tess fires gunshots over their heads and swears she will shoot them both if they don't stop. She angrily spits out a few words, trying to get them to see the history between them, before turning and storming away. Stunned by her outburst, Dunson and Matt stop long enough to realize she has handed them a way out of a conflict neither genuinely wants any longer. Having saved face through the confrontation, Dunson is now able to let go and do what he was not sufficiently inclined to do sooner — forgive.

The structure of *Red River* contains classic features of tragic drama such as the portrayal of a forceful but predominantly fair-minded man whose strength of character in perseverance and tenacity is eventually stretched — through uniquely converging challenges of circumstance — to a point of such excess that his strength begins to function as a flaw. This flaw then conspires crucially in the evolution of a growing conflict between two men who are bonded through mutual dependence, friendship, and family relation. The stepson/stepfather relation and business partnership between Dunson and Matt ideally meets Aristotelian criteria for tragic conflict by combining fraternal and familial connections between the feuding sides.

Some critics, such as Garfield and Ebert, find the "happy" ending with the intrusion by Tess to be "silly" or "unbelievable" and thereby a major detraction from the tragic quality and intensity of the conflict carefully established through the bulk of the film. But the film nicely prefigures the reconciliation between Dunson and Matt when Groot excitedly yells at the outset of their fight, "All right!! For years I've been scared, but now it's goin' to be all right."

Critic Brian Koller maintains that in the concluding scenes all the characters have strong motivations for their actions and that "the ending is a letdown only if our expectations have been shaped by endless westerns that end with the death of a villain. *Red River* has the right to carve its own myth, and without the needless slaughter of main characters" (2000). Consistent with Koller's view, Adrian Miles finds that the film adopts a contemporary Freudian resolution to the mythic Oedipal conflict by presenting the transition to the son through a progression of steps of deferred and ascending leadership rather than an actual or symbolic slaying of the father. Accordingly, the final fight ends appropriately in "equanimity" and not the victory of one or the other.

It can be conceded, however, that the reconciliation between Dunson and Matt occurs too easily and abruptly in view of the intense build-up over the preceding scenes. The ending could have been portrayed more compellingly by showing a more hesitant dawning of forgiveness on the part of Dunson. But the film's conclusion is still powerful and consistent with tragic form — which, as Aristotle claims, does not require a tragic ending.

Nevertheless, the structure of the drama in *Red River* would have ensured an extraordinarily poignant experience of the tragic emotion of ruth had one of the protagonists been killed at the end. This conclusion would have caused no sense of celebration in the audience, as would be the case in a melodramatically structured conflict.

The dramatic structure of *Red River* provides a good example of how the context of the presentation of violent resolution to a conflict powerfully affects the way in which violence will be experienced and understood. Because emotions in *Red River* are aroused and merged in catharsis relating to both sides of the conflict, the emotional impact is doubly powerful. A corresponding "civic" catharsis accompanies and amplifies the breadth and depth of the emotional catharsis through a sense of resolution of the divisive tension between the protagonists, combined with a heightening of appreciation through dramatic irony for the complexity of conflict — especially conflict marked by the looming hazard of deadly violence.

The plot of *Red River* has been justly compared to that of *Mutiny on the Bounty* (1962) but, as Garfield has rightly noted, the relationship between Matt and Dunson is more subtly complex and moving than that between Christian and Bligh. This turns out to be the case because the conflict between Christian and Bligh is drawn in contrasts that are too starkly melodramatic and consequently do not elicit the depth and coordinated effect of the fusion of modes of arousal and catharsis experienced in viewing *Red River*.

Fine acting must also be counted among the many virtues of *Red River*. Regarding John Wayne's performance, John Ford, who directed Wayne in several previous films (but not this particular film), remarked, "I didn't know the sonofabitch could act!" Clift is also exceptional in his performance — which was his screen debut. Critic Stephen Farber notes that Clift brings a refreshing dimension to his character in providing "just the right mixture of strength and vulnerability." Farber's additional comments on Clift's performance raise several noteworthy points.

> The Western is ordinarily set in a universe of absolute moral certainty; the intense self-questioning that Clift brings to his characterization suddenly propels the genre into the 20th century. And his performance

accomplishes something else. Because of the humanity of Clift's "soft"ness (to use the word that another character applies to Matthew), we are more conscious of the inhumanity of Wayne's stubborn hardness. *Red River* was the first movie that dared to criticize John Wayne's heroic persona, exposing the cruelty beneath that unyielding macho veneer. Although *Red River* is a stirring epic full of stampedes, chases and gunfights, it's also perhaps the first Western with real complexity — and that is largely a result of Clift's performance [2003].

While the performances, as Farber suggests, are very important, the quality of *Red River* derives more crucially from the quality of the tragic plot. Just as the hardness of Wayne's character turns out to be a kind of weakness, so the vulnerability of Clift's character turns out to be a kind of strength. These traits of character play into and evolve out of the quality of the conflict that, being tragic in nature, displays itself in a way that always carefully projects and preserves a sense of the human value on both sides. Clift's performance is in this sense, and to his credit, consistent with the dramatic design rather than a creative embellishment on which the quality of the film hinges. And Hawks likely selected him for the role because of his ability to deliver the performance called for by the quality of the conflict.

Unfortunately, *Red River* is not, as Farber claims, the film that propels the genre into the twentieth century. While it represents a high point for complexity and quality of conflict in the Western, the genre did not adopt it as a model for the future. Some previous films bear comparison, as, for example, *The Westerner* (1940) — a story in which the young-man-versus-old-man conflict between the characters played by Gary Cooper and Walter Brennan is entertaining as well as compelling. The film highlights the strengths and weaknesses in both characters in a way that compares favorably with the intensity of conflict achieved in *Red River*.

However, a later Western, George Stevens's *Shane* (1953), stands in clear contrast to *Red River* and becomes the film that may more justly be seen to have propelled the genre into the twentieth century. While *Red River* emerges as a premier instance of the Western myth in tragic dramatic form, *Shane* represents the Western myth at the highest level of melodramatic form. Both films have been admired for their elements of realism, especially the details of western life, the rustic sets, and the location filming, and both have also been rightly praised for their bold cinematography, classic themes, and strong characterizations. These qualities of story and production lend to both films a mythic stature that makes the contrast between them all the more pronounced and emblematic.

SHANE

The quality of the conflict between the homesteaders and the ranchers in *Shane* acquires a pathos very different from the conflict in *Red River*. While Stevens develops the concerns, motives, and characters of both sides of the conflict in *Shane*, he does so in ways that reveal the ranchers in progressively sinister tones.

In addition to the increasingly menacing words and actions of Ryker (Emile Meyer), the head rancher, and his brother (John Dierkes), the sinister tone is confirmed and enhanced through stark contrasts of light and shadow. Scenes with Ryker and his brother are filmed in the less well-lit confines of Grafton's saloon or, when outdoors, are filmed after sunset where dim light and shadowed faces lend a foreboding element to the entire scene. The sequences with Shane (Alan Ladd); the homesteader who befriends him, Joe Starrett (Van Heflin); his wife, Marian (Jean Arthur); and their son, Joey (Brandon DeWilde), are filmed in bright daylight that, by contrast to the darker lighting of episodes with the ranchers, imparts a pastoral glow and cheerfulness to the domestic scenes. These choices of cinematography complement the growing polarization of the conflict — a polarization that is portended in the earliest scenes of the film and that culminates in a gunfight at dusk inside the poorly lit saloon, the bastion of the ranchers.

Commentator Jay Hyams reports that Stevens aspired to recreate the classic myth of the West in *Shane* but sought to frame it in a new soberness about violence and heroism. In repeating the melodramatic theme that good eventually comes out on top, Stevens wanted to confirm that violence has a place on the side of good and in this way reaffirm the rightful but terrifying place of violence in the Western myth.

With this focused intent, Stevens succeeds with *Shane* in presenting the problematic issue of intimidation through violence in a way perhaps unsurpassed by any other Western film. The film achieves great intensity in confronting bullying violence through scenes that progressively peel back layers of reluctance on the part of the homesteaders in engaging in violence, layers that are stripped away by the ranchers until no alternative but violence seems possible. This is the point at which Shane, the mysterious gunfighter who has wandered into the lives of the homesteaders and who attempts to hide from his past, decides to strap on his gun one more time and confront the ranchers. This conflict between the homesteaders and the ranchers borrows from actual events of the Johnson County Range War in Wyoming during the 1890s. In this respect, *Shane* offers a dramatized reflection on real-life choices about the problem of when and how to confront violence with violence.

However, as a film designed to make a statement about violence, *Shane* errs not in its portrayal of a volatile and extreme conflict but in the choice it makes in dramatizing a hero who capitulates to melodramatic structuring and resolution of conflict. Shane's unilateral decision to confront the Rykers and their hired gunman alone and, if necessary to the death, creates a spectacle of grand heroism and high stakes drama while also surrendering too thoroughly to the ranchers' vision of the conflict.

Stevens's artistic choice in the portrayal of Shane is magnified through the prominent role assigned to the homesteader's young son, Joey. Joey's admiration for Shane models, within the film, the kind of idolizing response to Shane young viewers are expected to have. And the film's focus on Joey's perception of Shane and reactions to him present clear indications of the dimensions of Shane's heroism, a perception the entire audience is ultimately encouraged to share.

But Shane's actions, while courageous, model a highly questionable response to the situation. Joey witnesses Shane disable his father in a fight and then ride off alone to face the trap laid by the ranchers; he sees Shane taunt and belittle Ryker with "You've lived too long. Your kind of days are over"; he sees him provoke a gunfight with Ryker's hired gunman Wilson with the words, "I've heard that you're a low-down yankee liar"; he sees him deal out death to Wilson and Ryker and then twirl his gun with a showman flourish before placing it back in his holster — only to quickly pull it out again, at Joey's warning yell, to kill Ryker's brother at the top of the stairs.

After these actions, instead of demonstrating for Joey how to live with the consequences of what he has done, Shane leaves the dead bodies lying like rats in a cellar and rides out of town, explaining that he cannot stay in the valley because "there's no living with a killing." If the killing was right, Joey was not well served. Precisely what is needed in such a case is a man who can show Joey *how* to live with a killing.

By choosing to devote the final scenes of the film to Joey's admiration for Shane and Shane's heroic and self-sacrificing departure into the hills, Stevens places too much emphasis on the glorification, even sanctification, of the victor and insufficient emphasis on the gravity and tragic quality of the killing.

Here Stevens misses the opportunity to give a perspective on the value of human life — even the value of the lives of the ugly men who have been killed — and on the inglorious nature of killing. Instead, with the final scene where Joey's calls echo Shane's name through the hills, Stevens leaves the audience with the impression that Joey will grow up striving to emulate Shane — a man who provides, in his lone-ranger heroism, not only a recklessly high standard of self-sacrifice but also, in his choice to provoke violence through taunting rhetoric, a poor standard, a melodramatic standard, for confronting conflict.

Philip French makes an important observation when he says, "a good many Westerns ... have preached sermons against violence, while benefiting from, or exulting in violence. Depending upon the direction from which one approaches the subject, this could be called a central contradiction of the genre or simple hypocrisy" (1977: 114). However, rather than contradiction or hypocrisy, the exaltation of violence is a paradoxical necessity that arises from any attempt to make a statement against violence from within the structure of melodramatic form. Effective exposure of the destructive realities of violence can only occur from within dramatic forms adequate for such purposes such as tragic drama or reflexive melodrama.

French correctly assesses the unanticipated repercussions when a director takes violence "seriously" in the context of the melodramatic Western myth: "Yet the simple fact is that the more seriously violence is taken by the film-maker, the more likely its expression will be to break the accepted entertainment conventions— shocking the audience and offending the susceptibilities of liberal critics" (114).

Jay Hyams lucidly confirms French's finding when he explains how Stevens helped to initiate the postmodern wave of graphic violence in Westerns:

> To emphasize the terrible power of gunshots, Stevens had the two main victims— Elisha Cook, Jr., and Jack Palance — rigged so that they could be jerked backward when shot. Cook flies back to splatter in the mud; Palance is thrown back into tables and chairs. Stevens achieved the effect of violence — so much that it thrilled and delighted both audiences and filmmakers. Gentle, poetic *Shane* marks the beginning of graphic violence in westerns. As Sam Peckinpah has been quoted as saying, "When Jack Palance shot Elisha Cook, Jr., in *Shane*, things started to change" [1983: 115].

Directors such as Stevens who have attempted to show the horrors of violence do so in ways that, in the context of melodramatic form, produce only more pronounced effects. They believe incorrectly that a more graphic depiction of violence will help to convey the horror. Instead scenes of graphic violence, like scenes of graphic sex, succeed in making the violence, rather than the dramatic content, the focus of attention, thereby only increasing prurient fascination with violence — even to the point of fetishizing violence.

The effort to depict violence "realistically" with the intent to convey

Jack Wilson (Jack Palance) guns down "Stonewall" Torrey (Elisha Cook, Jr.) in *Shane* (1953) (Photofest).

its horror and thereby reduce its seductions produces instead a "hyper-realism" through which its value as a shocking attraction is raised. As this process became more thoroughly recognized by filmmakers, it led to deliberate efforts to offer scenes of exceptionally graphic violence as a marketing advantage for films and, eventually, as a marketing necessity (at least in producers' perceptions) in the competition between Hollywood studios.

Variations on the Western Melodrama

During the mid– and late 1950s directors experimented more with alterations of melodramatic form in which the featured character becomes more complex and the simple division between hero and villain appears to collapse. But rather than yielding dramas closer to the structure of tragic drama like *Red River*, this new trend yields instead a "noir" version of the Western myth. In Western noir the "hero" turns "anti-heroic" through having traits and flaws that compromise heroic character and thereby humanize the "anti-hero." But instead of producing a figure of tragic dramatic dimensions, the noir anti-hero remains stuck in the heroic mold of the plot structure of melodrama through being cast against a character or characters who, through being portrayed as extraordinarily villainous and despicable, make the anti-hero appear heroic by comparison.

Not only does the noir Western fail to transcend the plot limitations and simplicities of melodrama, it offers an even worse version of conflict and simplistic reductions. When combined with elements of graphic depiction of violence, the noir plot often descends into shades of nihilism that parade as realism.

Robert Aldrich's *Vera Cruz* (1954) qualifies as the great transition piece between the noir Western myth and the classic melodramatic Western. This film is not fully a noir-style Western due to the dominant moral sensibilities and classic heroic traits of Ben Trane (Gary Cooper). However, the character of Joe Erin (Burt Lancaster) is drawn in noir flourishes of admirable and unadmirable traits that ultimately appear heroic compared to the reptilian aura of scoundrelly deceit manifested by the characters of Maximilian's court. Erin's likeableness gives the drama a quasi-tragic feel in the final confrontation between him and Trane.

It took the odd merging of European and Asian talent in the directorial charge of Sergio Leone and scripting influence of Akira Kurosawa to push the Western fully into the noir pattern of conflict. Leone's first "spaghetti Western," *A Fistful of Dollars* (1964), was an adaptation from the screenplay for Kurosawa's *Yojimbo* made in 1961. In the wake of *A Fistful of Dollars* Clint Eastwood emerged as the premier anti-hero of the 1960s: fully confirmed and celebrated in popular culture with the label of the "Man with No Name" despite the fact that he has a name in the film. (The "No Name" moniker came from the promotional text on the film's publicity poster.)

Sam Peckinpah edges in the direction of noir structure with *Major Dundee*

Clint Eastwood as The Man with No Name shifted the clean "lone ranger" image of the Western hero toward a darker "every man for himself" predatory style in Sergio Leone's "spaghetti" Westerns of the 1960s.

(1965) and then ventures fully forth with *The Wild Bunch* (1969). Taking a cue from Arthur Penn's *Bonnie and Clyde* (1967), *The Wild Bunch* concludes with an Armageddon burst of hyper-real graphic violence that foregoes the verities of Colt .45 revolvers and 12-gauge Winchester pumps in favor of the relentless firepower of a Browning .30 caliber, water-cooled machine gun. According to Jay Hyams, the special effects experts working on the film claimed that more rounds were fired (90,000 blanks) than were fired in the entire 1913 Mexican Revolution. The effects were completed with the use of slow-motion camera and over 3,000 "squibs"—the wired charges used to simulate bullet impact. Needless to say, Peckinpah created a new and dubious standard for depicting graphic violence in the Western by increasing the gore while setting it within a narrowly conceived and nihilistically darkened melodramatic frame.

In the 1970s the dramatic structure of the Western, seriously eroded by developments in the 1960s, moved in multiple directions in the effort to retain or re-attract a core audience. These offerings ranged from comedy in *Blazing Saddles* (1974) to parody in *Rooster Cogburn* (1975) to elegy in *The Electric Horseman* (1978). By the late 1980s the Western declined from its glory days when it represented about 30 percent of all Hollywood films to being only a fraction of Hollywood output. But in some ways this is misleading because the "Western myth" has really only transformed itself in time and place and continues functioning as the "American myth" in sci-fi and action films.

It is unlikely, however, that the American myth-making apparatus of Hollywood will ever entirely abandon the Old West as the setting for its heroes. The continued strength of the core of the melodramatic Western myth is evident in the Academy Awards for Best Picture given to *Dances with Wolves* (1990) and *Unforgiven* (1992).

Kevin Costner's *Dances with Wolves* is his version of a reversal of the standard Western melodramatic alignment in which the customary bad guys—the Indians—get to play the heroes and the cavalry weigh in as the villains. Costner's more recent Western, *Open Range* (2003), also adheres to melodramatic structure but in even more egregious tones as struggling "entrepreneur" ranchers are pitted against "syndicate" ranchers—the latter portrayed in shades of avarice and cruelty just this side of Satan himself. The climactic gunfight is garnished with gore and excessively prolonged to the point that it descends into nothing less than a perverse festival of blood and vengeance.

Clint Eastwood's *Unforgiven* transforms the guiltless "Man with No Name" killer of the Sergio Leone period into the guilt-ridden, "failed family man" killer—with little loss in body count. As a domestic misfit and reluctant coming-out-of-retirement gunslinger of tarnished character, Eastwood's William Munny is a noir echo of Alan Ladd's Shane. In response to the over-the-top sadistic brutality of "Little Bill" (Gene Hackman), Munny's vengeful actions for the ruthless murder of his friend Ned (Morgan Freeman) provide little contrast, add no depth, and squander the dramatic potential in the tension between his newly acquired "domestic" training and his old "character flaws." As an unsavory, guilt-ridden twist on a familiar Western pattern and, consequently, an unsuccessful attempt on Eastwood's part to atone for (as some have suggested) or depart from (as others have suggested) the decadent melodrama of his "spaghetti" Westerns, *Unforgiven* falls considerably short of meriting an Academy Award.

In between the years of the awards given in 1990 and 1992 to Westerns, the award for Best Picture went to *The Silence of the Lambs* (1991) — an indication of how the forces affecting the Western myth have worked to deleterious crescendo effect in more temporally current settings of the American myth.

18

Multi-Melodrama:
The Silence of the Lambs

The Silence of the Lambs (1991) is a film about an incarcerated serial killer (Anthony Hopkins) who happens to be a diabolically clever psychiatrist. He is also nicknamed "Hannibal the Cannibal" Lecter for his famous habit of eating body parts of butchered victims. An attractive female FBI trainee, Clarice Starling (Jodie Foster), enlists his aid in the hunt for another serial killer nicknamed "Buffalo Bill" (Ted Levine) because Bill is notorious for skinning his female victims. In other words, the film has much to offer audiences who have outgrown the standard horror and slasher genre. It was made into a cultural phenomenon of staggering proportions when it was awarded no less than five Academy Awards— including the big three of Best Picture, Best Actor, and Best Actress. The disparity between the Best Picture award and the quality of the film makes *The Silence of the Lambs* a definite candidate for perhaps the most flagrant error in judgment ever made by the Academy in its long history. And this error forces the question: What happened here?

The film critic Jake Horsley, whose analysis of violent films entitled *The Blood Poets* was first mentioned in Chapter 9, offers several worthwhile reflections on *The Silence of the Lambs*. Although, as will be seen in later chapters, Horsley's opinions of *Bonnie and Clyde* (1967) and *The Matrix* (1999) are thoroughly repudiated herein, he is often an insightful critic and his judgment of *The Silence of the Lambs* is admirably on target. He accurately identifies the film's basic genre when he observes, "At its most primitive level, if we conveniently ignore all the muddle-headed metaphysical psycho babble about 'the nature of evil,' and the lame attempts at characterization, *Silence* is an old-fashioned monster movie." He then points out the trick the film pulls that sets up the trap the Academy fell into: "*Silence* ... is a horror movie for all the family to see, not because it's less disgusting or offensive than other horror flicks (it's considerably *more so*, I think), and certainly not because it's more artful, intelligent or thoughtprovoking, but because the production values, and the credentials of those involved are so much 'higher' than is generally expected from a horror flick" (1999b: 186–187).

It is the "credentials" of those involved and the slick finish of the product combined with a baroquely networked plot that duped the members of the Academy, and many critics and audiences, into taking fool's gold for gold. Horsley sums up nicely: "Not since *The Exorcist* has a film offered up sleazy gore and cheap thrills with such a hallowed, humorless aura of self-importance as *Silence of the Lambs*" (1999b: 185).

The apparent complexity of the film derives from its rather clever interweaving of three popular melodramatic plotlines, thereby giving birth to a motley melodramatic item. These three plotlines include the psycho thriller, the police/crime drama, and the slasher/horror flick. The psycho-thriller thread centers on the tension between Lecter and the prison warden and psychiatrist, Dr. Chilton (Anthony Heald), the prison guards, and all others who, as Cynthia Freeland points out, show "discourtesy"— the trait Lecter hates most. The police/crime drama centers on Starling's search for the serial killer Buffalo Bill. The slasher/horror dimension centers on the tension between Starling and Lecter. Hannibal stalks her with a psychologically penetrating thoroughness and leering intimacy that qualifies as a form of cerebral rape. This tension between Starling and Lecter is amplified by the fact that, true to the slasher model, Starling seems to court the risk of this "rape" beyond what is necessary for the task in which she has involved herself.

However, the complex networking of plotlines is more an ornamentation than a substantial element of artistry in the film. The primary plotline divides into parallel lines generated through qualities and dilemmas shared by both Starling and Lecter. The dimension of commonality between these two characters overshadows the tension between them to the point that this tension begins to take on the sense of the playfulness of a sexually charged game more than a deadly dance of horror. The tension of the search for Buffalo Bill also becomes a sideshow as it is largely subordinated to the parallel plot tension.

This parallel plot tension results from the respective conflicts that Starling and Lecter have with a "system" that each experiences as victimizing them. For Starling this "system" is the FBI, an agency in which she finds herself on the receiving end of a condescension similar to Lecter's hated "discourtesy." The condescending behavior of her boss, Jack Crawford (Scott Glenn), nearly costs Starling her life when, near the conclusion of the film, Crawford believes he has caught Buffalo Bill and then instructs Starling to go alone to what he assumes is a related site to do routine follow-up work. This site turns out to be the residence of the real Buffalo Bill and Starling, thanks to Crawford's dismissive treatment of her, is left to stumble into Bill's lair without proper backup.

For Lecter the "system" is, most immediately, the prison system and its ruthless, ignorant, and incompetent warden. More generally the "system" is the larger social bureaucracy that routinely persecutes and demeans the likes of intellectuals such as Lecter who, the audience is led to imagine, victimizes only vile bureaucrats of high rank who lead the way in exercising a "discourtesy" that devalues and dehumanizes others.

The parallel plotline forms a one-two punch to the underbelly of lame bureaucracy as Starling and Lecter appear as "hero" and "anti-hero" against respective villainous systems. Moral order is restored by Starling when, despite the odds against her, she triumphs over Buffalo Bill and wins the confidence of her dim-witted boss. Lecter restores order when he makes a Houdini-like escape from prison and, with the concluding line of the film, "I'm having an old friend for dinner," indicates how he will take revenge on and dispose of the warden. These parallel plots offer a further mixture of melodramas, combining the classic melodrama of the "good" hero Starling with the noir melodrama of the morally tainted "outlaw" hero Lecter.

Dr. Hannibal Lecter (Anthony Hopkins) lurks in the shadows behind Clarice Starling (Jodie Foster) in *The Silence of the Lambs* (1991) (Photofest).

Horsley is again accurate in sizing up the excesses and limitations of Hopkins's, as well as the script's, characterization of Lecter. Hopkins's portrayal of Lecter, according to Horsley, is not "the least bit imaginative or even remotely convincing. Hopkins plays Lecter as your standard, pop-eyed, leering loony, only with the added twist of being superintelligent to boot.... We seem to be honestly expected, in some hip, nihilistic, new-age, more-amoral-than-thou brand of doublethink, to admire this fruitcake cannibal for the 'purity' of his acts, the clarity of his thought processes, or maybe just for his basic charisma and self-confidence, as 'the most evil guy in town'" (1999b: 188).

The characterization of Lecter rises to a kind of perfection that even goes beyond "the most evil guy in town." As Horsley continues, Lecter is "so wholly committed to his nastiness that he's practically a demonic force; and yet, at the same time, Hopkins plays this force perfectly straight, as though somehow he believed (and expected us to believe) that people like this actually exist, somewhere outside the wet dreams of movie executives" (1999b: 189). Horsley is forced to conclude: "Lecter is a movie monster, so there's never the slightest pretense of (or attempt at) making him human."

This assessment of Lecter further confirms the fact that the movie presents a strong dose of "noir" melodrama. Like a comic book supervillain, Lecter is given powers of intelligence and manipulative control far beyond the powers of real-life serial killers. In this case, through the reversal of melodramatic expectations, the supervillain stands out as hero in relation to a more genuinely base and villainous system — a system designed to appear as in some profound way "responsible" for forcing Lecter into his darkly predatory outlaw existence.

Cynthia Freeland is one of the few commentators on the film to explicitly note the "bucking the system" alignment between Starling and Lecter. She rightly claims that this alignment dissolves the tension between them in such a way that " 'good' does not combat 'evil' here because they [Starling and Lecter] are mirror images of one another, not polar opposites." But then she proceeds to completely misunderstand the implications of this alignment: "The film's depiction of the villainous Lecter reflects an attitude of complete moral ambiguity, so that ultimately his escape and planned revenge against his warden ... threatens any full sense of narrative closure or restoration of the order and security of the status quo" (2000: 209).

Freeland fails to understand that the film's last scene with its implied imminent demise of the warden is precisely a "restoration of the status quo"—a status quo interpreted through the film as bankrupt and in need of a radical correction that will serve to restore a more genuine status quo.

Lecter may prove to be in other ways "evil" but in this film his dark but potent powers are brought into the service of ends intended to be viewed as "good." This explains why, as has been noted by almost everyone writing about the film, audiences laugh and applaud at the film's last line. Audiences feel comfortable laughing at the thought of the grisly demise of Dr. Chilton because the skill of the filmmakers has succeeded in turning the status quo thoroughly upside down along with the reversal of standard hero/villain expectations.

Despite his accuracy in sorting out most of the film's flaws, Horsley, like Freeland, appears to misunderstand the extent of the reversal the film contrives and brings to completion in the last line. Surprised and outraged by the audience response to this line, Horsley's astonishment can only be due to having not entirely appreciated the relative enshrining of Lecter the film engineers against the dreadful, evil "system" he opposes. After commenting on the audience laughter and applause evoked at the showing he attended, Horsley notes, "What could I possibly add, to further persuade you (dear reader) of the depravity of our times?.... A depraved maniac wandering free as a bird, enacting his sick revenge upon a society which he holds only in the utmost contempt, as beneath him, this idea meets with the approval, if not plain delight, of the modern audience. The film seems intended to *curry* such approval" (1999b: 191).

In light of his accurate dissection of the film, Horsley should be *certain* that the film intends to curry such approval. Through both Starling and Lecter the film is specifically designed to draw on, arouse, and amplify particular emotions that may lurk within viewers—emotions such as anger and contempt directed toward the "system" and its Dr. Chiltons and Jack Crawfords. And this is part of the depravity of the film, insofar as it may be rightly viewed as promoting, through its melodramatic conflict model, inclinations to apply a similar structure of conflict and heightened contempt to real institutional and workplace situations.

The kind of orientation the film encourages *attitudinally* is not necessarily left in the theater. This much Horsley understands very well and perhaps better than most when he rightly concludes—his misreading of the ending notwithstanding—that "a movie is ... a small figment of life, which contains and defines and reflects, and to some extent *shapes*, our feelings and attitudes towards life" (1999b: 191).

Starling's characterization does not fare much better than Lecter's when it comes to socially admirable modeling—especially for feminist audiences. Freeland correctly points out that the fact that *Silence* has a female hero is not sufficient ground, as some reviewers have suggested, to justify a pro-feminist reading of the film. Neverthtless, she then takes the bait dangled by the filmmakers when she claims that the film offers an exemplary female character in Starling. In Freeland's view, Starling becomes an admirable model for women as she resists and eventually overcomes the challenges posed by a system that has discriminated against her. However, this wrinkle in the plot reads more credibly as a token concession to feminist-wary front office politics.

More to the point, the film overwhelmingly endorses and solicits patriarchal or masculine dominance in its balance of power and order — as is invariably the case in slasher films and variants thereof. The primary reason that the Starling character is cast as a woman derives from the fact that, as in slasher films, a woman is needed as the object of the obsessive attention of a monstrous male figure. An attractive female victim is required to fuel the engines of this hackneyed but reliable plot vehicle. And the more strength the female victim shows, the more resistance she offers, the higher the emotional flames of male viewers can be fanned into leaping.

The simulated "rape" scene that occurs between Starling and Lecter (when Lecter passes a paper to Starling and "caresses" one of her fingers with his) is all the more titillating because of Starling's all-too-evident hesitant fascination with and ambivalent attraction to the monstrous Lecter. The dynamics of this kind of interaction are thoroughly analyzed in the next chapter in the discussion of Pinedo's views on the slasher genre and so will not be repeated here.

What must be repeated, however, is that the tension between slashers and female victims (or near victims) is badly misunderstood when interpreted in any way that suggests these victims admirably model or advance the agenda of female power. Scenes that dwell on women in extended and graphic depictions of intimidation, abuse, and invasion (psychological or otherwise) — and that often include a subtle suggestion of compliance on the part of these victims — should not be viewed as consistent with a pro-feminist outlook. Films composed of such scenes betray instead an obscene fixation. Exceptional focus, with perverse detail, on interactions between a slasher pursuer and female victim ultimately feeds only the worst inclinations of frustrated male libidos as well as the worst fears and inclinations stemming from female frustrations with men.

It can be safely concluded that *The Silence of the Lambs* is entirely pulp melodrama and fails to offer any genuine conflict either within the characters or between the characters. Consequently, violence in the film is presented in a context that draws out in disturbingly approving and celebratory ways the most reductive and destructive features of that violence. The Academy dishonors itself by promoting the agenda of such films with awards.

19

The Slasher Horror
Genre Since *Psycho*

In the first chapter of his collection of essays on aesthetics entitled *Counter-Statement* (1968), Kenneth Burke explains the close relationship in storytelling between form or structure and the psychological orientation of the audience. Burke notes that dramatic form arises more from a particular dimension of the psychology of the audience than the psychology of any of the characters in the story. Specifically, Burke argues "form is the creation of an appetite in the mind of the auditor, and the adequate satisfying of that appetite" (31).

The pleasure derived from what Burke calls the "psychology of form" concerns "desires and their appeasements." He contrasts this pleasure with the pleasures of the "psychology of information" as that which concerns the intrinsic interest in information as "news"— or the learning of what was not known beforehand. News, like yesterday's newspaper, tends to lose its attraction quickly whereas the pleasures deriving from the unfolding of form bear considerable repetition — much like music. Most storytelling combines both the psychology of form and the psychology of information. In conveying information through a story, interest is often maintained and amplified by withholding key pieces of information. Burke finds that "surprise" and "suspense" are key tactics in the overall strategy of enhancing what otherwise might be rather mundane pleasures of the psychology of information. Suspense is the creation of an appetite and surprise is the fulfillment of that appetite. Burke concludes furthermore that these tactics appeal at a very basic level: "suspense is the least complex kind of anticipation, as surprise is the least complex kind of fulfillment" (1968: 36).

240

The horror genre alters and exceeds the "psychology of information" genre of the mystery thriller — as, for example, a Sherlock Holmes tale — and its moments of suspense and surprise by amplifying these into dread and shock. The close connections between Romantic literature and poetry and the genres of horror and the mystery thriller are confirmed and brought together ingeniously in the work of Edgar Allan Poe, a writer who was able to traverse between these various forms with flawless intuitive ease.

The psychology of form in the horror genre shifts from the mere arousal and fulfillment of an appetite to more highly contrived formal properties inherent in pandering to the expectation of the unexpected. The suspense and surprise in horror offers, as Burke claims, the "least complex" kind of anticipation and satisfaction in the sense that these aspects of plot tap into the most basic emotional mechanisms and reflexes. Burke also points out that these reliable patterns give rise to more subtle and complex variations: "so complicated is the human mechanism ... [that this satisfaction] at times involves a temporary set of frustrations, but in the end these frustrations prove to be simply a more involved kind of satisfaction, and furthermore serve to make the satisfaction of fulfillment more intense" (1968: 31).

Modern Escalation of Horror

The challenge of the creator of the horror story lies in amplifying suspense and surprise to the point of dread and shock. But, of course, this challenge becomes greater and greater as the audience becomes more sophisticated in the "news" of horror storytelling. As a genre dependent on its ability to shock, the horror story must find new ways to frustrate and trip up the expectations of an audience — otherwise it begins to resemble yesterday's newspaper. And since deadly violence is the most reliably horrifying experience, the makers of horror must continually find more uncanny and unexpected ways of portraying the visitation of dread and death on human victims.

As horror plots continue to rely on their ability to shock for the greater part of their appeal and entertainment value, shock value, more than anything else, must be understood as the driving motivation in their innovation and development. And the phenomenon of escalating shock value is certainly not absent in related genres — such as the mystery thriller.

In at least one noteworthy case, the pressures for escalation precipitated the evolution from mystery thriller to horror. In the effort to maintain quantity of output and popular appeal, the premier filmmaker of the mystery thriller genre in the pre–and post–World War II era, Alfred Hitchcock, found himself in the position of having to amplify the surprise and shock value with each new film. Since improving aspects of a story such as narrative, characterization, and dialogue require increasing scriptwriting acumen and eloquence, Hitchcock opted for the less challenging path of manipulating aspects of style, point of view, and structure. His work evolved from the murder mystery thriller (*Dial "M" for Murder* [1954]; *Rear Window* [1954]) to the psychological thriller (*Vertigo* [1958]) to the action thriller (*North by Northwest* [1959]) to the slasher/horror thriller (*Psycho* [1960]).

Following *Psycho*, the options for continued escalation of shock value effects narrowed considerably. Contemplating his next move, Hitchcock finally descended to the level of the "creature feature" with *The Birds* in 1963. At this point Hitchcock's career began to falter. He had run out of ideas for further escalation and his lack of inspiration showed in the declining box-office receipts for his later films. He attempted to regain some of his clout as the master of shock by finally succumbing, with *Frenzy* (1972), to what counted at that time as the ultimate escalation — the serial killer thriller. But *Frenzy* merely continued the decline and brought his career to an anticlimactic close.

However, as a vehicle for the creation and fulfillment of expectations of the horrifically unexpected, Hitchcock's *Psycho* must be counted as an extraordinary success for its time. Adapting Robert Bloch's novel of the same name, Hitchcock trips expectations by reversing melodramatic structure, placing the appallingly anti-heroic character of Norman Bates in the position of central focus and attention usually given to a heroic figure.

To magnify the effect of this surprise Hitchcock lulls the viewer into complacency by lengthy opening sequences focusing on Marion Crane (Janet Leigh), the film's lackluster and hapless "heroine," and her petty larceny amidst a *mise-en-scène* of unexceptional everydayness. While viewers immerse themselves in this story of corruption within the fabric of established and well-to-do society, Hitchcock slowly and slyly introduces the much darker pageant of Norman Bates (Anthony Perkins) and his secret self, his hidden Doppelgänger.

As further stylistic embellishment on the reversal of structure, Hitchcock adds a graphic depiction of violence, which is the infamous shower scene. Rather than shocking the audience with the visage of a monster, as in classic horror films like *Frankenstein* and *Dracula*, Hitchcock reverses camera angle and features the horror on the face of the victim and the blood from her slashed body spewing down the shower drain.

In his clever transformation of the horror story, Hitchcock combines three changes: (1) the reversal of melodramatic form from the featuring of a hero to an anti-hero; (2) a deceptive normalization of *mise-en-scène* along with the normalization of the appearance of the "monster"; and (3) the explicit and graphic depiction of the *victim* in the throes of gruesome violence. These three surprises or "escalations" mark major points of departure from the classic or pre–World War II horror story.

Postmodern Horror

The difficulty Hitchcock found himself in — of having to up the ante of shock effects with each new film — was not his predicament alone. This problem presents itself again and again with each new film, with each new generation, and with each new wave of horror storytelling. Essentially the same story of victimage gets told over and over again but, instead of successively more refined renderings and unfoldings of narrative and form, storytellers offer the easier and less complex solution of successively more graphic, lurid, and bizarre renderings of shock violence. This is often accomplished by presentation of the violence through the points of view of the perpetrators, the anti-heroes, in conjunction with varying stylistic and technological approaches that serve to amplify the shock.

If a class of high school students who had not seen any horror films made after 1960 were shown *Psycho* and then asked to make a list of the ways in which the assumptions and storyline of that film could be exceeded in a manner that would provoke greater shock effects, it would not take them long to generate a list of modifications to the portrayal of the killer/monster that would resemble the following:

• The monster is where you least expect. Violence (from the monster or monsters) is an unremitting potential threat in everyday life as opposed to an extraordinary threat in a unique circumstance.

• The monster has unusual supernatural powers. All physical, mental, social, and natural boundaries are blurred and can be, at any time, violated.

• The monster cannot be understood. Rationality, experience, and collective actions are useless as defenses.

• The monster is seemingly unbeatable. The outcome of the conflict depicted is at best ambiguous and often the featured evil wins or, if it does not win, its overcoming is shown to be only temporary.

Analysts of horror such as Jonathan Lake Crane, Isabel Cristina Pinedo, and Cynthia Freeland — from whom this list has been condensed — are largely in agreement that these are the primary characteristics separating contemporary or postmodern horror from the modern horror of *Psycho*.

With expectation-breaking films like *Psycho* (1960) and *Peeping Tom* (1960) — in which psychopathic killers are star-featured — the horror film evolved into the slasher film. In the decades following *Psycho* the modern slasher film continued to exceed "expectations," evolving into the hyperreal, ultra-graphic, postmodern slasher film.

Postmodern horror and gore films include various incarnations of grotesque slasher anti-heroes in, for example: *The Texas Chainsaw Massacre* (1974), *Halloween* (1978), *Friday the 13th* (1980), *A Nightmare on Elm Street* (1984), *The Stepfather* (1987), *Hellraiser* (1987), *Henry: Portrait of a Serial Killer* (1989), and *Copycat* (1995). These standouts of postmodern horror present a nihilistic world in which death and violence reign supreme and in which the efforts to overcome or change that world are generally insufficient and futile. These escalations of the monstrous are, or were in their time at least, shocking to encounter, but are not really surprising as developments in the genre — developments that can be largely accounted for as a function of commercial incentives and imperatives for discovering, refining, and utilizing ever more intense and unexpected shock effects.

The analysts already mentioned, along with many others, nevertheless offer a variety of other explanations for what may drive the increasing extremes of graphic violence in the postmodern horror genre. Many of the explanations for escalation in the depiction of horror center primary attention on the notion that demand for such films derives from increasing needs within the viewing public for coping with escalating real-world violence. But approaching the general issue of the escalation of violence in horror films from this direction offers questionable insight while producing explanations that range from the baffling to the fantastic.

The Horror in Capitalism

One of the most provocative and ideologically charged explanations of the intensity of postmodern horror appears in Barry Keith Grant's essay "American Psycho/sis: The Pure Products of America Go Crazy." In this piece Grant features the novel *American Psycho* (1991/film adaptation 2000) as a typical postmodern ultraviolent escalation of Robert Bloch's novel *Psycho*. Grant argues that Patrick Bateman, the starring anti-hero of the novel, is "nothing more than a complete product of popular culture" or, as Grant says, echoing Robin Wood, "the logical end of human relations under capitalism" (1999: 29).

The flat, matter-of-fact tone in which the shocking violence in the book is narrated, Grant explains, is "the perfect example of what Frederic Jameson calls 'the waning of affect,' the 'flatness or depthlessness' that characterizes postmodern art"— and, by extension, postmodern life. Focusing on Bateman's serial victims, Grant comments, "Ironically, nobody notices that the people Bateman has killed are missing because they are virtually interchangeable.... Like their possessions [commodities], they are themselves things— things for which Bateman, like any good capitalist manufacturer, has planned for obsolescence" (30).

Ultimately, Grant finds the book's graphic yet coolly executed violence to be a valuable critique of postmodern late capitalist culture through the way it reflects the numbing insensitivity that such a culture creates in the souls of its members. The depiction of violence in this work and others like it prompts Grant to conclude, "Given the pervasiveness of violence in contemporary culture, some of these texts seem aware of the need for new strategies to challenge viewers" (38). Grant believes these "new strategies," consisting of horrendous depictions of graphic and senseless violence, advance a beneficial awareness through the ways in which they "challenge" the viewer (or reader) to notice and confront the dehumanizing and violent aspects of capitalist culture. It does not seem to occur to Grant that this cure may be worse than the disease.

This kind of indictment of late capitalist culture, shared in varying degrees by Marxist critics such as Frederic Jameson (1991) and postmodern critics such as Robin Wood (1986), Christopher Sharrett (1999), and Annalee Newitz (1997), consistently overlooks a viable alternative way of accounting for the perceived ills of commodification and violence. As argued in Chapter 15, these ills are not causally related to each other but are instead influenced by a third factor, which then gives the impression that they are causally linked.

In the case of capitalist culture, the problem these critics identify does not lie essentially in commodification but rather in *vilification*— wherein something or someone is perceived not as essentially useless (a worn-out, replaceable, or interchangeable commodity) but as contemptible, as fundamentally a form, reflection, or simulation of contamination. Both commodities (including instruments) and human beings are degraded through vilification. Commodification gets blamed in this process through a confusion that masks the perpetuation in postmodern culture of the premodern "psychosis" of the radical evaluative scheme of good and evil and its totalizing category of evil as defilement. A worn-out commodity is commonly discarded or recycled whereas something or someone suspected of being a pollution more likely elicits reactions consistent with mutilation, torture, and obsessive destruction. Even Grant states in his comments on *American Psycho*, "Bateman's mutilations of women are grotesquely graphic exaggerations, overtly monstrous depictions" (27). Such actions are the equivalent of dark rituals of exorcism, cleansing, and sacrifice.

In other words, the problem of dehumanizing violence is rooted in the clash of a premodern orientation with a postmodern culture of exponentially increased resources, opportunities, choices, and frustrations. The conflicts created (or amplified) by this postmodern culture are approached by means of the dominant traditional cultural training toward conflict. This training has little to do with the culture of capitalism and the competitive spirit at its core and more to do with the inertia of tradition regarding general attitudes toward conflict. Through this orientation, commodities and instruments suffer, as do humans, under the same weight of potentially radical devaluation. They are exposed to a climate of belief that encourages reducing them — in situations of extreme frustration, confusion, or conflict — to corrosive and debasing agencies, to pollutions, and thereby to intense religious or quasi-religious rituals of purification.

The Horror in Gender War

When moving from Grant's ideologically centered critique of the attractions and escalations of the violence in the slasher horror genre to analyses featuring gender, a more compelling line of analysis emerges— at least until the focus turns to explanations of the attraction of slasher films for the female audience.

During the high era of the slasher film, which lasted approximately from the mid–1970s to the end of the 1980s, many feminist film critics expressed the concern that slasher films were hyperbolic expressions of misogyny. This misogynist indictment seems intuitively correct, given the plot of the slasher film. Isabel Cristina Pinedo summarizes elements of the slasher plot she finds especially relevant to the gender issue:

> A masked or hidden [largely off-screen] psychotic male propelled by psychosexual fury stalks and kills a sizeable number of young women and men with a high level of violence. The killer's rage derives from a traumatic childhood experience, which is recounted chronologically [e.g., *Halloween*] or in flashback [e.g., *Friday the 13th*]. The killer returns to the scene of the past event to reenact the violence. Although both women

and men are killed, the stalking and killing of women is stressed. After a protracted struggle, a resourceful female usually subdues the killer, sometimes kills him, and survives [1997: 72].

Pinedo notes, however, that this last detail of the plot — where the resourceful female overcomes or kills the psychotic male — becomes a common element in slasher films only at the beginning of the 1980s. Prior to this time the female is usually saved through the aid of an intervening male (as in *Halloween*). This earlier version of the slasher plot provided all the incentive feminist critics needed to raise a cry of protest. Most of these early feminist protests were organized around the material provided by varieties of psychoanalytic theory.

Laura Mulvey

Drawing on the work of the French theorist Jacques Lacan (1973/1981), Laura Mulvey (1976), for example, argues that the slasher film attracts primarily a male audience because the content as well as the cinematic medium of the slasher film reinforces patriarchal values and desires while assuaging male fears of castration.

Several analogies work to enforce this patriarchal hierarchy according to Mulvey. The narrative order of the story, reflecting the underlying patriarchal social order, exposes a challenge to that order in the form of carefree and wanton women, portrayed in blatantly seductive ways, who evoke and thereby represent the fear of castration. The narrative resolution offers a clear and effective response to this threat by way of the victimization of these females in the film.

Borrowing also from the work of Althusser (1970/1989), Mulvey finds further that a gender analogy exists between the cinematic screen and the viewer whereby the screen functions as the passive female — the object of "the look" or "the gaze" — and the viewer functions in the role of the aggressive male — as the wielder of "the look" or "the gaze."

By further analogy, the male viewer identifies with the male protagonist as the slasher in taking possession of the woman and bringing about the final resolution — the death of the castrating female. The death of the slasher in the end by the hand of another male reestablishes balance in the social order as well as the continuance of male dominance.

Although the basic theme of misogyny certainly has credibility, Mulvey's recourse to explanation through applications of Althusser and Lacan, with the themes of the gaze and overcoming castration fears, cannot read-

ily explain why slasher films also appeal to and attract a large female audience.

Barbara Creed

Providing an account of the attractions of slasher films for a female
audience, Barbara Creed (1986) offers an interpretation derived from the
work of Julia Kristeva (1982). Pointing to films such as *Friday the 13th*
(1980), where the psychotic protagonist turns out to be a woman, and
Aliens (1979), where the creature turns out to be female, Creed argues that
the horror/slasher genre shapes itself obsessively around female agency in
a destructive capacity as the "monstrous-feminine." This monstrous feminine energy is indiscriminate in dispensing death, turning on women as
well as men. Thus, for Creed, the female is both victim and perpetrator.
And even in those cases where the perpetrator is portrayed as male, the
energy is to be understood as rooted in the monstrous female. Slasher and
horror films, especially those of the 1980s, do not, according to Creed,
serve to assuage the castration anxieties of men but instead exacerbate
them through harrowing displays of female retaliatory violence.

Carol Clover

Needless to say, with its shift to the emphasis on female power, Creed's
account swings violently in the direction opposite of Mulvey's account.
By contrast, Carol Clover (1992) offers an explanation that lands somewhere more in the middle, but by a combination of worse extremes. While
acknowledging, with Creed, the role of a powerful female in many slasher
films, Clover finds, contrary to Creed, the female to be a representation
or stand-in for male energy. The resourceful female evident in 1980s slasher
films, or the "final girl" in Clover's words, turns out to be, via a rather tortured psychoanalytic ratiocination, *a male in female guise.*

Since the "final girl" acts in aggressive ways that normally characterize men in the partriarchally dominated social order, her behavior, Clover
reasons, belongs to the logic and discourse of the male not the female. Like
Twitchell, only with a very different twist, Clover finds that the slasher film
reproduces a version of the oedipal story. The slasher film, in Clover's
outré analysis, presents a repressed enactment of the sadomasochistic fantasy of male viewers to have sex with their fathers. The portrayal of the
"final girl" as female results from the need to disguise from male viewers

the incestuous and homosexual nature of their repressed desires. In this interpretation, the potential attractions of slasher films for female audiences are misguided but accounted for to the extent that female viewers stray from their feminine address and identify with the aggressive "male" strengths of the "final girl."

Isabel Cristina Pinedo

Unsatisfied with previous feminist accounts of the slasher film and their failure to adequately address the privileging of the male perspective and the issue of female attraction to the genre, Pinedo enters the fray with her work entitled *Recreational Terror: Women and Violence in the Slasher Film* (1997). Pinedo recoils from what she regards as Clover's uncritical acceptance of the dogma that, in Clover's words, "those who save themselves are male, and those who are saved by others are female" (83). This cultural gender bias leaves female agency significantly disenfranchised and dependent. Pinedo argues, "if the surviving female [in the slasher film] can be aggressive and be *really* a woman, then she subverts this binary notion of gender that buttresses male dominance" (83).

Like Carol Clover, Pinedo gives prominent attention to the slasher film of the "final girl" variety that first became popular in the 1980s. She offers a refreshingly straightforward account of the tension driving its creation and appeal, claiming that it "is after all an expression of male anxiety about female agency in which female agency wins out." Using this insight as bedrock, Pinedo reasons "the pleasure to be gleaned by female viewers lies in the combination of arousing such anxieties in men while securing female victory" (85). In the course of the viewing experience, women overcome two fears especially prominent for their gender: the fear of becoming a victim and the fear of exercising aggression and violence. Those films in which a "final girl" is left standing represent a kind of spiritual victory for women. A tonic pleasure may be associated with this, as Pinedo notes, insofar as it may be comforting for female viewers identifying with the final girl "to know that they underwent an ordeal and had the mettle to survive it" (66). In this sense the terror of the slasher film becomes recreational for women as it provides a safe context in which to work through emotions such as rage and fear by indulging in a fantasy experience.

Of the accounts available to date, Pinedo's is the most perceptive regarding the interaction between women and slasher films. Nevertheless, there are several problems with her analysis—not least of which is that

Freddy Krueger (Robert Englund) samples one of his victims in *Nightmare on Elm Street Part 2: Freddy's Revenge* (1985) (Photofest).

it is essentially a "cathartic" explanation for the appeal of horror, an explanation that has been critiqued in Chapter 11 for touting effects that are in fact ultimately weak and superficial.

Pinedo herself identifies one such problem when she acknowledges that in the majority of the most popular contemporary slasher films the slasher, although apparently "terminated" in the end, is never really killed and is resurrected in a sequel. In this sense, female agency only *appears* to win out in the end. This point may seem like quibbling but it becomes significant when considering that it corroborates an interpretation that undermines Pinedo's view that slasher films offer a pro-female experience.

It may well be the case, consistent with the lines of Mulvey's castration theme, that slasher films are in fact little more than versions of a male fantasy arising from a reservoir of rage toward women for lack of response to their sexual needs and for dependency on them for the fulfillment of those needs. In keeping with this view, the "final girl's" prolonged resistance serves throughout the film to bait and stimulate the progressive arousal of male emotions.

The slasher film feeds male desires for vengeful resolution by presenting increasingly graphic depictions of violence, usually the rape and/or slaughter of a series of female victims in the course of the film. Even in films of the "final girl" variety ending with the survival of a featured female — where a climactic triumphal victory for the slasher is ultimately foiled, creating a kind of mortis interruptus analogous to coitus interruptus — the defeat often turns out to be only an interruption. In *A Nightmare on Elm Street 3: Dream Warriors* (1987) and in *Friday the 13th, Part 2* (1981), to name two examples, the surviving female of the previous film is killed by a "resurrected" slasher.

In such sequel-tailored films, the "final girl" serves as a mere token of female agency and her apparent victory in the end is a concession by the filmmakers to deflect the charge of misogyny while their dominant focus remains the male audience. The hint of the slasher's return provided at the end of the film panders to hard-core male viewers who desire a vengeful resolution to quell barely submerged frustrations with the opposite sex.

Pinedo's perceptive claim that slasher films are "an expression of male anxiety about female agency" is, more to the point, an expression of the fantasy of *resolution*—a resolution that, as a fleeting and ineffective form of catharsis, is highly superficial as well as reprehensible in the attitudes toward women and conflict it fuels. As such, it is difficult to side with Pinedo in interpreting slasher films in the pro-female manner she suggests. The trail of violated and dismembered female bodies in such films belies her interpretation, as does the ultimate survival or resurrection of the slasher.

Pinedo also recognizes the possibility for a darker pleasure that may accompany the viewing experience of these films for many women. Feminists have identified this pleasure as the "rape fantasy." Pinedo explains that "with a rape fantasy, the female viewer is forced to vicariously indulge feelings and actions forbidden to her, and although she is 'forced' she is in a position to stop it or leave if it does not suit her" (86). The rape fantasy may appeal to the percentage of female viewers who are experiencing sexual or relationship frustration and who, as a consequence, may find the singularly obsessive attention of a man — even if a rapist and killer — to be an appealing albeit dangerously titillating fantasy. Nevertheless, this viewing experience and its darker pleasure do not model a psychologically healthy approach for coping with these frustrations.

Pinedo goes on to register a caveat regarding her assessment of the slasher film as an art form appealing to and promoting female agency: "the subject position for women that the slasher film constructs is nonetheless inscribed within the parameters of a male-dominated society, and so there are limits to the agency accorded the woman character or viewer" (86).

But this caveat does not stop her from persisting in the overall conclusion that the slasher film does in fact "create an *opening* for feminist discourse by restaging the relationship between women and violence as not only one of danger in which women are the objects of violence but also as a pleasurable one in which women retaliate to become agents of violence and defeat the aggressors" (87).

Contrary to this conclusion, however, it must be stressed that a "restaging" of the relationship between women and violence that features women as the primary targets and victims of psychopathic violence in contexts of excessively drawn-out and embellished sequences of graphic bloodletting, torture, and mutilation hardly seems like a "restaging" that creates a beneficial and productive "opening" for feminist discourse and the promotion of feminist values.

It is surprising that Pinedo dismisses so blithely the horrendous violence in these films in favor of constructing rationales for the justification of that violence that hinge primarily on the notion that women can actually benefit from participation in dark fantasies of rape and abuse and/or violent retaliation. As argued in Chapter 11, the benefits of fantasy in general and melodramatic productions in particular are of little cathartic value — especially in cases where fears and frustrations may be significant and deep enough to draw women into theaters for viewing slasher imagery. In the case of feminine fears of the sort allegedly pandered to in slasher films, there is no question that counseled and guided role-playing exercises (such as offered in "model-mugging" classes popular in the 1980s) are not only more appropriate but also potentially more genuinely cathartic and psychologically beneficial.

Cynthia Freeland

Regarding graphic violence in horror and slasher films and its escalation and embellishment in recent times, Cynthia Freeland (2000) also offers a defense — but one less related to gender issues. According to Freeland, graphic horror — of which she cites as a notable example the film *Hellraiser* (1987) — contains two levels of moral structure: the level of the plot and the level of what she calls "cinematic creativity." The level of the plot offers the conventional structure of melodrama, of the conflict of good and evil and the eventual triumph of good. However, on the level of "cinematic creativity" the moral structure appears to shift and the audience is lured into pulling for the survival of the monster.

As Freeland explains, "Despite their surface violence, the films of graphic spectacular horror are less unsettling and negative [than the "uncanny" horror of such films as *The Shining* (1980) and *Eraserhead* (1977)] because their celebration of the monster's evil as creativity is joyous and affirmative. Each monster serves only a kind of formulaic and meaningless evil, one that we need not take seriously. The scenes of graphic horror are so far-fetched that they obviously present a kind of cinematic creativity to be relished" (269).

In defending her thesis Freeland draws on the views of the philosopher Friedrich Nietzsche as presented in *The Birth of Tragedy*. Parallel to Ricoeur's analysis, Nietzsche describes the origin of tragedy in the Greek god Dionysus as a representation of the primal source from which springs both good and evil, pleasure and pain, creation and destruction. In Freeland's view, the order, the rhythm, and the imagery of cinematic graphic horror sequences provide a counterpoint to the content of pain, gore, and violence in a kind of dance that mirrors the cosmic dance of creation and destruction. These orgies of graphic horror, violence, and destruction function at the level of visual aesthetic pleasure and stimulation, not unlike dance numbers in a musical. In these sequences "the presentation of evil becomes much more cartoon-like — and the more extreme it is, the less believable and convincing" (271). In this context, according to Freeland, the seriousness of evil begins to fade. It is not something to be defeated but rather something that can be "poked fun at" and whose power is not lasting.

Anticipating the response, Freeland remarks, "It might seem preposterous to maintain that films like *Hellraiser* or *The Texas Chainsaw Massacre* (1974) feature ... [a] quality of beautifully ordered [tragic] structure, since that would seem to put them on a par with the works of Sophocles and Aeschylus. Nevertheless, the principle is the same" (270).

But despite Freeland's claim, it must be asserted to the contrary — and with emphasis — that the principle is *not* the same. The structure of tragic drama involves a great stressing and compression of the radical polarization of good and evil into an evaluative structure of contextually contingent challenges. But this reconfigured and contextualized structure does not, or need not, lapse into the morally nonevaluative dimension of purely aesthetic tastes and responses. This aestheticization of depictions of slaying, mutilation, and torture risks, or more likely invites, an extremely dangerous trivialization and dehumanization of violence.

That Freeland ignores the risks of this invitation becomes especially clear when she makes a case for the analogous relation between the "numbers" of graphic spectacular horror and the most sexually explicit sequences in pornographic films. Both genres, she claims, offer portrayals that are so

Larry Cotton (Andrew Robinson) gets torn apart in *Hellraiser* (1987) in one of the many violent sequences Cynthia Freedland views as the horror genre equivalent of the song-and-dance numbers in musicals.

excessive as to be unbelievable and thereby safely divorced from reality. This exaggeration, Freeland argues, makes what is presented (in the case of excessively violent films) unreal to the extent that lurid scenes of victimization and destruction become not only harmless but sublimely uplifting and transcendent in a structured and stimulating stylization. But with this comparison between violent and pornographic film she fails to address the downside to the analogy that is especially relevant in relation to the *manner* in which sex and violence are depicted. Repeated exposure to excessively graphic and/or coarse forms of narrowly contextualized and overly polarized depictions of sex or violence — presented as entertainment — unquestionably increases the likelihood of dehumanization effects. In the case of depictions of violence, these effects reliably derive, as has been argued in various chapters herein, from the limitations and constraints of melodramatic form. In the case of pornographic film, these effects derive from similar reductive and polarized constraints of male/female, subject/object contextualization.

The manner of contextualization evident in the "principle" (to use Freeland's word) of tragic drama involves considerably more than Freeland describes. Her application of Nietzsche's aesthetics in *The Birth of Tragedy* serves to advance a common misunderstanding. Nietzsche's complex affirmation of the tragic vision and the violence in tragic drama must be understood, as fully explained in Chapter 6, in the context of the particular structure of conflict offered in tragic drama. And Nietzsche's account of the sublime as the Dionysian *affirmation* of pain and death must not be allowed to become entangled and confused, in the manner Freeland exemplifies, with a festive "cinematic creativity" of visual spectacles that celebrate — all too lightheartedly in the context of her views— violence and victimization. In short, deadly conflict and graphic depictions of mutilation and destruction are not indicative in themselves of any close association with tragic dramatic structure.

In conclusion, an impressive number of books and articles have been written in defense of the depiction of the graphic violence in postmodern horror and slasher films. Most of this material testifies to the creativity of the imaginations of those who attempt to explain, beyond the superficial sordid attractions, the deeper benefits of this graphic violence more than to the creativity and value of the slasher horror genre.

20

Psycho(melo)drama: *Raging Bull* and *Taxi Driver*

Raging Bull

Raging Bull (1980) is a dramatization of the autobiography of Jake LaMotta, a prizefighter who boxed during the 1940s and 1950s and held the middleweight champion's title for over 18 months before losing it to Sugar Ray Robinson in February 1951. Roger Ebert argues that the film is not about boxing but about "a man with paralyzing jealousy and sexual insecurity, for whom being punished in the ring serves as confession, penance, and absolution" (2002: 385). While it is clear the film is not significantly about boxing and that the boxing scenes serve to hammer home the point that LaMotta (Robert De Niro) wants to be pounded in the ring, the traits of jealousy and sexual insecurity are only the tip of the iceberg of Jake's repressed sense of self-loathing, his deep feelings of guilt and shame, and his assessment of himself as unworthy. The repression of these feelings, which are exacerbated — as alluded to in the film — by Jake's strict Catholic upbringing, results in a projection of his unworthiness outward toward all others (not just women) with whom he comes into contact. This projection prepares the way for his depreciation and abuse of wives, family, and trainers and especially fuels his drive to place himself in the ring where he can punish himself as well as his opponents.

Consequently, Jake becomes a verbally and psychologically abusive menace to all around him and derives considerable pleasure from his ability to diminish and intimidate others. Needless to say, the Jake LaMotta of *Raging Bull* is not an admirable character. Critic Jake Horsley sums up director Martin Scorsese's uncompromising portrayal of LaMotta's self-destruction as "the most nakedly *brutal* American film ever made, for the simple reason that it effectively combines physical violence with both *emotional* and psychological violence. Together the effect is overwhelming" (1999b: 16).

In her praise of the film, reviewer Amy Taubin of *The Village Voice* finds that the stunning effect of *Raging Bull* derives largely from the tension it displays between "19th-century melodrama and 20th-century psychodrama." Although Taubin dwells on the way in which this tension is conveyed through the stylistic contrast between the cinematography of the theatrically staged and relatively static domestic scenes and the more dynamic spatially and temporally disorienting fight scenes, the linking of these two forms is accurate and noteworthy in other respects. The cinematic psychodrama genre of the twentieth century owes much to the melodramatic theater and literary forms of the nineteenth century — of which the horror story is one prominent example.

In fact, it would be accurate to say that *Raging Bull* is a "domesticated" version of the horror story. Jake LaMotta is a kind of monster. In his self-loathing he manifests the split psyche familiar to audiences of classic horror in the doubling theme of the protagonist and Doppelgänger. In classic horror the apparently external conflict between a monster and a hero is a reflection of the division within the protagonist as monster/hero.

Scorsese unmistakably establishes the theme of *Raging Bull* as one of inner division by beginning the film with a scene showing LaMotta alone in a ring shadowboxing himself. But the promise of a genuine title match of LaMotta with himself that is portended in this opening scene is never fulfilled and, consequently, the film never rises to the level of significant drama because it fails to present a significant conflict. Instead, it is the story of a man who spends his life in a succession of denials, constantly giving himself the slip at every opportunity where he might be able to confront himself and his misery. The potential in Jake that would humanize the radical hero/monster conflict within him, that would assert a streak of vulnerability, awareness, and remorse for his abusive ways, never shows up in any way other than fleeting feelings of frustration and self-hatred.

The concluding scenes of the film confirm LaMotta's stagnation where the older LaMotta is again shown shadowboxing himself. In the capacity of a quasi-documentary account of an abusive, sadomasochistic personality, the film could serve as a pedagogical device for clinical psychology students, but it cannot rightly purport to be great art or great drama.

In modern psychodrama a troubled and often violent character is given top billing and made the center of attention as the main protagonist and the anti-hero. The shift in the focus of attention from an admirable character to a troubled character with violent and destructive behavior — within the context of interactions with and abuses toward a series of relatively nonheroic characters— is a significant feature of psychodrama.

The potential for shock in psychodrama, similar to the horror story, is initially founded on a traditional and reliable pattern of viewer expectation. Traditionally, the character given central attention in a drama is the character with whom the audience is expected and encouraged to develop a bond of identification. In psychodrama this expectation generates considerable cognitive dissonance as the audience finds that it is being led to get inside the head of a character with whom it is very difficult to identify. This cognitive dissonance increases as the action unfolds from the point of view of the perpetrator of despicable actions and creates escalating waves of shock.

Psychodramas in general find their niche of appeal to audiences by way of their potential to generate these waves of shock. *Raging Bull* captures and rivets the attention of an audience through the shock value of its relentless presentation of scenes of sadistic and masochistic brutalization. By the end of the film, however, audience anticipations for some "point to it all" are left completely unanswered. None of the characters surrounding LaMotta are able to model anything resembling an adequate response to his self-hatred and brutality, and certainly nothing inside of LaMotta himself emerges sufficiently to give the audience something to root for, some indication of a presence of challenging self-awareness and healthy self-critique. Consequently, the physical, emotional, and psychological violence in *Raging Bull* becomes disturbingly analogous to the depiction of sex in pornographic films— it appears to exist solely for the purpose of highly charged but superficial arousal effects.

Nevertheless, in an interview about the film Scorsese stated that he believes *Raging Bull* to be "a straight simple story, almost linear, of a guy attaining something and losing everything, and then redeeming himself. Spiritually" (cited in Kelly, 1980: 32). These remarks suggest that Scorsese forms an equation between sadomasochistic torment and spirituality. For Scorsese, great suffering alone seems to serve as a rite of passage. The white heat of a lifelong self-victimization becomes sufficient to gain entrance into the sainthood, or at least the brotherhood, of martyrdom.

As a violent and tortured soul, the LaMotta of *Raging Bull* bears comparison to Ahab in *Moby Dick*— a story that has been approvingly characterized as belonging in the category of "reflexive melodrama." But unlike

Jake LaMotta (Robert De Niro) lowers his defenses as he is battered by Sugar Ray Robinson (Johnny Barnes) in *Raging Bull* (1980) (Photofest).

Moby Dick, Raging Bull ultimately succeeds only in being the story of a petty, mean-spirited, and brutish man and his descent into social and spiritual oblivion. However, the way in which *Raging Bull* falls short of reaching the level of reflexive melodrama helps to draw out more clearly the differences in the quality of conflict between these two kinds of drama.

For Jake LaMotta the opponent in the ring serves as the "white whale"—the shadow side of his hero/monster self. Just like Ahab, LaMotta regards his shadowy "white whale" as despicably evil and worthy of destruction. Sometimes Jake succeeds in projecting this unworthiness on the opponent in the ring, or, when at home, he projects it on his wife or brother. At other times he masochistically allows the punishment to fall on himself—as in the fight scene with Sugar Ray Robinson where he takes a terrible beating to the head while offering little or no defense. But through all of LaMotta's abuse and self-abuse the "white whale" never emerges fully as a character as it does in *Moby Dick*.

Ahab's "white whale" becomes more than a "raging bull"—thanks to the narrator, Ishmael. Ishmael's narrative provides the background information necessary to cast light on the recesses of Ahab's shadow side. By presenting multiple layers and a deepening portrait of Ahab, his account shows the larger sense of "who" the whale is by revealing how it came to play a demonic role for Ahab. This information discloses a larger complexity in the identity and character of the whale for the reader/audience — exceeding Ahab's vision of it — as it also exposes the past events and current forces that provide clues to the reasons that move Ahab to behave as he does. In the case of Scorsese's depiction of LaMotta, nothing approaching this layered depth of characterization is offered. As Horsley points out, this is a major difference between LaMotta's autobiographical book and Scorsese's film.

Scorsese chose to leave out details of LaMotta's background, some of which were available to him, that would have served to plunge the drama into deeper levels in its portrayal of inner conflict. In his autobiography, for example, LaMotta relates how he thought he had killed a man in a robbery assault when he was 16. But he discovered 12 years later, quite by accident, that the man had survived his assault. For 12 years, the period of his prime years as a boxer, Jake thought he was a murderer and the guilt made him feel as though he were a monster who did not deserve to live. After realizing the truth about the assault, LaMotta recalls, "I ... felt a lot less vicious as a fighter. I think that the moment I discovered I was not really a murderer, I also stopped being a killer in the ring" (cited in Horsley, 1999b: 16).

These background details of character are completely lacking in Scorsese's film and the absence of such details makes it difficult for the viewer to feel empathy for LaMotta while at the same time diminishing the capacity for sensing the *tragic* quality of the conflict going on inside him. Only the melodramatic tension surfaces as LaMotta's hero/monster conflict dominates the entire film. It can easily be imagined how much more powerful as drama (and conflict) the film would have been if these details about the assault and LaMotta's discovery had been adeptly dramatized. If more of the background of LaMotta's character had been revealed in the film, his "white whale," his monstrous side, would have been exposed for the audience as grounded in unusual but thoroughly *human* experiences and responses while at the same time his egomaniacal "heroic" side would also have been traceable to more understandably human emotions and reactions. His divided self would have been given sufficient flesh and blood status, as with Ahab in *Moby Dick*, to arouse ruth and achieve an insight into conflict and a level of catharsis similar to tragic drama.

For some viewers *Raging Bull* may also fail on another level. From the point of view of those concerned about the depiction of violence, it may be argued that in films dealing significantly with abuse and violence the primary focus ought to fall on the victims insofar as there is a responsibility for portraying violence in a context that will adequately convey its destructive effects. It could be argued that in *Raging Bull*, for example, the destructive effects of Jake's actions on others—as well as the destructive effects of his actions on himself—would have been more powerfully portrayed had Scorsese chosen to include scenes that more directly featured the psychological and emotional points of view of the victims—in this case his wives and his brother.

However, another film also starring Robert De Niro in the role of a similar character helps to illustrate why a shift in point of view to the victim is not necessarily a solution to the problem of how best to dramatize the conflict in such stories.

As the title suggests, *This Boy's Life* (1993) is a story that unfolds from the point of view of a boy who finds himself in the position of having to cope with the raging anger and physical and psychological abuse of his mother's second husband, Dwight (played by De Niro). Although *This Boy's Life* moves in the direction of the structure and effects of reflexive melodrama similar to *Moby Dick*, wherein the vector of persecution and hatred turns back on the source in a way that draws the logical ground of the process of persecution into question, it ultimately fails to achieve this level of drama.

In Dwight's house, mother (Ellen Barkin) and son (Leonardo Di-Caprio)—like the crew aboard the Pequod—are captive to Dwight's captain Ahab as he pursues his own invisible "white whale." As the stepson becomes a substitute whale for Dwight, the film has the opportunity to portray a complex conflict by fully developing both characters. However, unlike the book on which the movie is based, it fails to do so by declining to provide insight and background into Dwight's character sufficient to enable the viewer to form an explanation for his rage and self-hatred. In this regard the film makes the same mistake as *Raging Bull* and slips into the portrayal of a starkly melodramatic conflict that provokes a sense of outrage and contempt rather than the necessary insight to unlock Dwight's tormented psyche.

Psychodramas, more so even than classic melodramas, risk becoming complicit in rather than operative against the perpetuation of violent behavior by spotlighting and elevating to star-status violent characters while also neglecting to provide background and counterpart characters. Adequate counterpart characters (apart from victims) are needed to draw out the main protagonist in ways that achieve insight into the roots of character and develop the inner conflict beyond reductionistic polarities. In psychodramas such as *Raging Bull*, melodramatic structure is not challenged or questioned so much as it is used as a vehicle for audience arousal effects in the presentation of repetitive scenes of shocking violence.

Taxi Driver

The conclusion that psychodrama may serve too exclusively and in some cases too dangerously as an arousal engine for audiences through repetitive scenes of shocking violence is supported (though certainly not proven) by the John Hinckley story and its relation to another of Scorsese's films. Hinckley attempted to assassinate President Reagan in 1981. He made clear his rationale for this attempt in a letter written (but never sent) to Jodie Foster. Hinckley had formed an attachment to Foster after repeated viewings of the film *Taxi Driver* (1976). In his letter to Foster, Hinckley writes, "Jodie, I would abandon this idea of getting Reagan in a second if I could only win your heart and live out the rest of my life with you."

In another letter written three weeks before the shooting, Hinckley expressed more precisely the way in which he envisioned his actions in relation to Foster: "Jodie Foster, love, just wait. I will rescue you very soon." In videotaped testimony provided at Hinckley's trial, Foster was asked whether she had ever seen a message like that before. She replied, "Yes, in the movie *Taxi Driver* the character Travis Bickle sends the character Iris [Foster's role] a rescue letter" (cited in Shermer, 2004: 114–115).

In the aftermath of the shooting and in the course of the trial, Hinckley's extraordinary obsession with Foster proved to be a tabloid bonanza. But as details emerged, it became increasingly clear that Hinckley's obsession was rooted more directly in the character of Travis Bickle (Robert De Niro) and the plotline of *Taxi Driver*. Hinckley had viewed the film countless times and had formed not only an identification with Bickle and an attachment to Foster through her Iris character, but also, more important, had adopted the film as a blueprint for how to achieve success and win admiration. He began to view his life as a "movie" unfolding along lines similar to the *Taxi Driver* script. Foster had become for him a real-life Iris whom he would "rescue" by the act of murdering a member of the "system" that held her in its constraining, repressive, and controlling grip. The "fame" he would win would allow him to secure Foster's attention and eventually her love, as she would come to realize the loving sacrifice implicit in his "heroic" act.

Hinckley revealed the ongoing real-life role he viewed himself as playing in the twisted thoughts of his deposition: "You know, actually, I accomplished everything I was going for there. Actually, I should feel good because I accomplished everything on a grand scale.... I didn't get any big thrill out of killing — I mean shooting — him. I did it for her sake.... The movie isn't over yet" (cited in Shermer, 2004: 116). In Hinckley's mind he probably came to believe that he had in fact won Foster's admiration and love and that only a corrupt cabal of thugs continued to stand in the way, confusing her, slandering him, and preventing her from being with him.

The film *Taxi Driver* certainly did not cause Hinckley to shoot Reagan nor did it cause his obsessive attention toward Jodie Foster. But the film undeniably had a powerful influence on Hinckley in an exceptionally destructive way.

By choosing to tell the story of a troubled and violent character, and choosing to tell the story predominantly from the point of view of that character, Scorsese chose to amplify the potential for audience response from emotional arousal to various degrees of shock. And by focusing too narrowly on the violent actions of one character, Scorsese failed to develop characters who could provide a challenging perspective toward the protagonist to draw out more fully the *tragic* quality of the internal conflict. Instead, as in *Raging Bull,* the conflict is rendered melodramatically as the viewer is relentlessly exposed to the protagonist's maniacally heroic/monstrous actions while seeing nothing of the background necessary to understand the roots feeding his madness and giving shape to the all-too-human qualities of both sides of his conflict.

Introducing another analogy, Horsley offers a comparison between *Taxi Driver* and Dostoyevsky's *Crime and Punishment,* suggesting that "Raskolnikov is an intellectualized version of Travis." But an important structural difference exists between these two dramas. Dostoyevsky provides an extensive look into the history and family background of Raskolnikov and brilliantly dramatizes and draws out the tragic quality of his inner conflict through several characters, especially the detective Porfiry Petrovitch. In *Taxi Driver* the genuine inner conflict never materializes for the viewer because Travis never effectively confronts and challenges his perception of himself nor do any of the characters with whom he interacts. The story lacks a Petrovitch, or an Ishmael, and ultimately Bickle's "white whale" remains submerged in the opaque, simplistic shades of the demonic and the malevolently bestial — his own raging bull.

This failure to adequately dramatize the conflict creates an opening that needlessly increases the odds that a small percentage of viewers like Hinckley will react to the featured protagonist with a perverse kind of admiration. The film *A Clockwork Orange* produced reactions similar to Hinckley's with a small percentage of viewers. While films such as *Taxi Driver* and *A Clockwork Orange* may influence only a few toward violent action, they present a negative influence for *every* viewer by portraying internal and external conflict in melodramatically exaggerated extremes that remain insufficiently opposed or challenged in the dramatic narrative.

Had Scorsese found ways to dig deeper into the archaeological ruin of Travis Bickle's soul and thoroughly depict the roots of his conflict — perhaps through greater development of contrapuntal and challenging characters— rather than settling for a series of sensationalistic slices of his awkward and violent encounters with others, *Taxi Driver* would have gained more as drama while risking less in potentially harmful audience reactions to its violence.

As it stands, the film's narrow focus on the protagonist and his radical structuring of conflict highlights and sensationalizes violent resolution to a degree that lends itself far too easily to the kind of understanding and response exemplified in Hinckley's reactions. Told with an emphasis on tragic structure of conflict, *Taxi Driver* would have had — with admittedly no guarantees— a better chance to direct the attention of viewers such as Hinckley back on themselves in a potentially productive confrontation with their divided yet human psyches. Instead, the film's narrow and devotional focus on a violent protagonist is too easily construed by vulnerable and marginalized viewers as a blueprint for heroic overcoming of adversity.

Similarly, by telling its story from too narrow a point of view toward the perpetrator of abuse and violence, *Raging Bull* not only recreates for viewers the harmful melodramatic elevation of violence within the protagonist but also magnifies that emphasis to ultimately no purpose other than relatively superficial shock value entertainment. For this reason the film does not deserve the praise it has widely received. The good news is that in 1980 it did not win the Academy Award for Best Picture (the award rightly went to *Ordinary People*). The bad news is that it was even nominated for Best Picture. As a work of art, it is more a devotionally, if not obsessively, crafted cult psychodrama than a great film. Considering the way in which *Raging Bull* inadequately thematizes the issue of violence, the reviewers and the polls that rank it as the best film of the 1980s seriously misjudge its presentation of themes and overestimate its quality.

21

Epic/Serial Melodrama: *Star Wars*, *Harry Potter*, and *Lord of the Rings*

The decline in popularity of the American Western has not resulted in a shortage of matinee idols for adolescent audiences. Heroes of the Western frontier such as Hopalong Cassidy, Roy Rogers, and the Lone Ranger have been replaced by heroes such as Harry Potter, Frodo Baggins, and Luke Skywalker on new frontiers of the imagination. Through the wonders of current cinematic technology these new frontiers are presented in visually spectacular sequences of scenes and landscapes that provide a stimulating background for a recreation of grand mythic structures that rival and replace those of the Hollywood Western.

Star Wars

It has been argued by some that in their broad popularity and phenomenal influence these new myths of the frontier have challenged and to some degree replaced the cultural influence of institutional religion for the current generation of youth. A former professor of philosophy at Syracuse University, John Caputo, finds, for example, that "the enormous popularity of *Star Wars* over the years derives in no small part from its reproduction of elemental mythic structures and its transcription of classical religious figures into a high-tech world. Whether the traditional churches like it or not, films like *Star Wars* are the way a good many young people ... get their 'religion' today" (2001: 79).

265

If Caputo is right—and there is certainly no reason to believe that the cultural influence of the current wave of popular entertainment is *less* significant than the Western myth was for previous generations—then it may well be asked whether the "religion" of *Star Wars* offers any substantial changes over the previous Western myth in its "reproduction of elemental mythic structures." If, as argued in Chapter 17, the Western myth in its classic version is fundamentally a melodramatic myth, then Caputo's interpretation of the conflicts in *Star Wars* presents an important contrast. Caputo believes that the drama of the *Star Wars* epic preserves the structure of religious transcendence "but without the dualities of classical theism — between matter and spirit, body and soul, natural and supernatural, science and faith, earth and heaven, time and eternity" (80).

According to Caputo the structure of religious transcendence in *Star Wars* is no longer absolute in the sense of spirit over matter, soul over body, heaven over earth, but is instead a "quasi"-transcendence in which these dualities form a balance that includes elements of both. This balance applies also to the framing of the moral tension between good and evil where evil is understood in a way consistent with an inclusive metaphysics. Describing the fundamental conflict driving the plot, Caputo claims, "The war in *Star Wars* does not transpire between two equal but opposed Forces but turns on a disturbance or lack of balance within the one and only Force. *Star Wars* is distinctly anti–Manichean" (82).

Caputo proceeds to describe how the metaphysics of *Star Wars* is at bottom "monistic" by showing how the "seamless matrix" of the Force is reflected through all the dualisms in the drama. The Force is a "religious or mystical structure" but also and equally a "scientific structure." Consequently, in the Republic there is no pervasive or abiding opposition between religion and science or between "church" and state. The Jedi knights are trained in the ways of high-tech gadgetry as well as the sacred ways of spiritual discipline and self-knowledge; they are at the same time part of an almost monastic order of devout spiritual practice and meditation but also part of the state apparatus of military protection and law enforcement. In an attempt to capture its boundary-breaking inclusiveness, Caputo describes the Force as a "mystico-religio-scientific structure." By retaining a mystical dimension, the Force presents itself as endlessly mysterious and thereby guarantees an element of *unpredictability*, as Caputo expresses it, in the unfolding of life events.

How humans dispose themselves toward the Force can reflect or initiate a lack of balance or harmony in the Force. A "disturbance in the Force" then accounts for every manifestation of evil. *Star Wars*, according to Caputo, presents a conflict in which "the war between good and evil is waged between the Sith lords who make the Force an instrument of their own evil intentions and the Jedi knights who make themselves an instrument of the Force, allowing the Force to flow freely and harmoniously, to follow its natural rhythms, undistorted by anger, fear, and aggression" (82).

Caputo's anti–Manichean interpretation of the metaphysical substrate underlying the dualities and neo-religious themes in *Star Wars* is not, however, one that remains convincing in light of other commentary and further examination of the evidence. For example, Michael Valdez Moses, a professor of English at Duke University, assesses the fundamental conflict in *Star Wars* in terms that flatly contradict Caputo's view when he states that "it offers a mythological explanation of the apparent chaos, pain, disappointment, horror, and violence of the world in terms of *a Manichean struggle of cosmic forces*" (2003: 50, emphasis added).

Moses finds the Manichean struggle between good and evil to be so obvious in *Star Wars* that he asserts more than argues the case. But, in fairness to Caputo, it can be acknowledged that the points he raises in defense of his view are not without merit. George Lucas does seem to have fashioned a notion of the Force as a kind of monistic multiplicity that could be viewed as in some ways consistent with what has been described herein as holistic synagonism. And in the second film of the first trilogy of films, *The Empire Strikes Back* (1980), the conflict assumes many of the characteristics of tragic drama when it is revealed that Darth Vader is Luke's father. The conflict becomes more complicated as audiences are forced to fit the template of good and evil over a father and son conflict — and it is not at all certain at this point in the epic the extent to which the conflict between father-and-son changes the nature of the conflict between the Empire and the Rebels.

This ambiguity in the dramatic structure of the epic, however, is resolved in the third film, *The Return of the Jedi* (1983), when it becomes clear that Darth Vader has been little more than a tool of the Emperor, who is portrayed as the consummate figure of ultimate evil, a Satan-like being who is, like Satan, finally purged from the cosmos (at least for a time) when he is "cast into the pit" in the last scenes of the film.

Other dualities of classical theism that Caputo finds have been collapsed in *Star Wars*, such as the oppositions of body and soul and the natural and the supernatural, are in fact preserved. These oppositions also retain classic hierarchical ordering. When Yoda, for example, tutors Luke in *The Empire Strikes Back*, he clearly assigns a higher value to the ethereal over the material when he says of the Force: "Life creates it, makes it grow. Its energy surrounds us and binds us. Luminous beings are we, not this crude matter [he pinches Luke's skin]."

The Emperor Palpatine (Ian McDiarmid) as a contemporary mythological icon of evil in *Star Wars Episode V: The Empire Strikes Back* (1980).

Human beings are most essentially "luminous beings" and the body is, by comparison, "crude matter" that will eventually be discarded as Obi-Wan discards his body in his light-saber dual with Darth Vader, assuming an entirely "luminous" form that unquestionably evokes the images of spiritlike angels. Obi-Wan continues to watch over Luke much like a guardian angel and is in some scenes shown as a spiritually luminous apparition. Such scenes evoke a transcendent spiritual realm that is on a higher plane of existence than the world of crude bodies. These indications of hierarchical ordering of the oppositions are fully consistent with traditional theological divisions. If *Star Wars* appears to present less standard metaphysical choices, it only superficially flirts with such choices while ultimately reintroducing traditional oppositions in new guises.

In his analysis of the *Star Wars* epic Moses advances an interpretation that is consistent with the general diagnosis of contemporary culture presented in Chapter 15. Moses points out that the alternative world presented in *Star Wars* "integrate[s] appealing elements of the *premodern* past into a vision of the future" (50, emphasis added). He agrees with Caputo's conclusion that the epic contains a strong "theological narrative" but finds, perhaps more accurately, that this narrative is fundamentally a reiteration of the core religious metaphysics of "Western European Christian societies." In Western tradition this *premodern* metaphysics comes into direct confrontation with a *modern* and *postmodern* technological world built up through a scientific corpus and practice rooted in the post–Enlightenment progression of a synagonistic understanding of oppositional relation. (For a full account of the evidence for a synagonistic understanding of oppositional relation as a key development in the theoretical work of Enlightenment and post–Enlightenment science, see Desilet, 1999.) As Moses rightly observes, this confrontation sets up a dramatic tension in which a premodern belief structure is applied to a "modern [and also postmodern] set of social anxieties." This tension creates an unusual sense of nostalgia alongside an exceptional sense of disorientation and exhilaration amidst a world of high-tech hyper-stimulation.

Moses also finds this tension between premodern orientation and contemporary postmodern culture to be at work symbolically in two other recent blockbuster epics: *Lord of the Rings* and *Harry Potter*. Speaking of all three epics, Moses observes, "If the fundamental narrative structure of the films borrows heavily from tradition, the specific forms that both good and evil assume within them are those of the [post]modern world" (50). In other words, the familiar premodern moral category of evil is applied to various perceived threats to an idyllic social order — threats that in the films function as symbols for (post)modern "pollutions" that may be encountered in the real-world contemporary landscape.

According to Moses, in *Star Wars* the threat comes in the form of the Empire as a "regime that is soulless, tyrannical, hegemonic, and technologically based" and empowered by "a vast, robot-like army of imperial stormtroopers" (51); in *The Lord of the Rings* the threat comes from the villains Saruman and Sauron whose realms of Isengard and Mordor resemble "20th century totalitarian states" and whose "orc armies consist of deformed and inhuman masses lacking relations, beliefs, traditions, and interests outside the direct control of the state" (52); in *Harry Potter* the threat comes from a rigid class hierarchy that preserves an "old self-interested political, financial, and cultural elite that remains opposed to the new, more democratic [alternative]" (53). Whatever the perceived (post)modern threat, the conflict in each case is organized by way of the strict Manichean division of good and evil.

Harry Potter

Moses notes at one point in his discussion of the first *Harry Potter* novel that the author of the series, J. K. Rowling, has the villain Voldemort assert: "There is no good and evil, there is only power and those too weak to seek it" (53). This apparent collapsing of traditional moral dualism is certainly not reflected in the treatment of the fundamental conflict, which remains untroubled by any ambiguities regarding good and evil. In fact, Voldemort's statement, with its quasi–Nietzschean moral savvy, may be regarded as a postmodern-styled reinscription of premodern radical moral dualism insofar as the film remains well within the context of a highly polarized and value-weighted conflict. It offers yet another narrative that identifies a source of true evil for purposes of elimination.

The conflict between Harry Potter (played by Daniel Radcliffe in the films) and Voldemort is portrayed as a life-and-death conflict in which Voldemort, having killed Harry's parents while having failed to kill Harry, is now intent on finishing the job by terminating Harry. In turn, Harry's task clearly requires the destruction of Voldemort.

Little indication is given in the first film of the series, *The Sorcerer's Stone* (2001), as to why Voldemort wants to kill Harry or why he killed Harry's parents. Voldemort is simply presented as the essence of an unremitting evil that must be destroyed. Immersed in the exceptionally antagonistic assumptions of the need for death-dealing, this dramatic structure serves to qualify the conflict as confrontation in nonnegotiable extremes that precludes any need for probing beyond superficial assessments of the character and motives of the other side.

In the second film of the series, *The Chamber of Secrets* (2002), it becomes clearer that Voldmort represents a cabal of sorcerers who want to ensure the "class" (and presumably "racial") purity of the future line of sorcerers instructed at the Hogwarts School. But the Voldmort character in this film (Christian Coulson) and others in his cabal such as the elder Malfoy (Jason Isaacs) are drawn in such stark strokes and appear so thoroughly despicable, deadly, and debased in their evil designs that the entire atmosphere resembles the darkly serious tone of a crime or horror melodrama aimed at an adult audience.

With Harry's slaying of a giant serpent, the violence in the concluding scenes of *The Chamber of Secrets* bears comparison with violent scenes in the *Lord of the Rings* series (discussed next). One reviewer of *The Chamber of Secrets* even compared the quality of its violence and the repulsiveness of its monster, the Basilisk, to the creature in the *Alien* horror series. The intensity of the depiction of violence in the *Harry Potter* series accounts, no doubt, for the PG rating given these films. Using comparison for purposes of measure, this intensity of violence represents a clear escalation beyond the degrees and modes of violence depicted in popular stories from previous generations. Unlike melodramas from the *Hardy Boys* series, for example, where the heroes insert themselves at the edges of ongoing adult crime dramas, in the *Harry Potter* stories Harry is himself the center of conflict and the target for assassination in adult evildoers'

Harry Potter (Daniel Radcliffe) finds the Basilisk's cave in *Harry Potter and the Chamber of Secrets* (2001) more like a "chamber of horrors."

schemes. Escalations in the features of storytelling are not all bad, but this type of escalation moves in the wrong direction and becomes especially pernicious in light of the ways in which it needlessly encourages young viewers to fashion their own situations, conflicts, and self-assessments in analogous ways and extremes through their fantasy reconstructions of the world around them.

In sorting out their lives and conflicts, no child or adolescent needs to be invited to identify with a hero who, in his conflicted world, is the target of grotesquely evil assassination plots by adult agents. Contrary to the arguments made by those such as Bettelheim and Jones and discussed in Chapters 12 and 13, even, and especially, children who experience abuse and who have fantasies as extreme as being abandoned or killed by parents or caretakers are not well served by stories that model the resolution of conflict to the extreme point of slaying potential or perceived assassins. For a fictional series directed at young audiences, assassination is too dark a theme to use as part of a fundamental and recurring plotline.

Storytelling in the melodramatic style aimed at younger audiences can easily and more beneficially display varieties of overcoming villains short of killing them. Even here, however, judgment is necessary. Stories that edge too far toward extreme polarization of character invite the extreme

Harry Potter (Daniel Radcliffe) battles the Basilisk.

resolution of death as the fitting means of disposal. Consequently, as argued in Chapter 12, the *degree* of polarization in stories for young audiences must remain a focus of attention for those concerned about the effects of violence in fictional entertainment.

By tracing a portrait of radical evil and following the call of deadly violence to erase it, the *Harry Potter* dramas are of questionable value for children and adolescents. They are especially subversive in this regard in that the books and the films contain so many other elements and details that appeal to the imaginations and fantasy lives of young audiences.

For example, a glance at the second DVD included in the release of *The Sorcerer's Stone* (2001) reveals an array of games and extra features that exploit the film's treasury of labyrinthine chambers, unusual animals, and magical devices— all of which are wonderful triggers for the imaginations of young viewers and none of which need have been conveyed through a plot featuring deadly polarized conflict. Rowling shows extraordinary creativity in her ability to invent the details of storylines that appeal to children but she is certainly not alone in showing a notable poverty of imagination when it comes to designing a plot that features nondeadly metaphors for polarized conflict.

Rowling even transforms sporting competition into melodrama. She invents the game of Quidditch only to present it as a seamless part of the grand battle with evil. Rather than shown engaged in the healthy aggression of a sporting competition, players are shown battling each other with a ferocity equivalent to the intent to kill (as in *The Chamber of Secrets*) or are shown engaged in battling evil interloping spirits (as in *The Prisoner* of *Azkaban* [2004]). Similarly, the sideshow conflict between Potter and Malfoy presents an opportunity for Rowling to model in her stories a healthy response to bullying. Instead she has Potter routinely respond to Malfoy's tricks and tauntings with equally demeaning tricks, sometimes carried out (or attempted to be carried out) by Potter's friends, rather than by a more assertive, self-styled mode of direct confrontation.

Altogether, the *Potter* films and books fail to model behavior and conflict management that coach young audiences in ways that will serve them beneficially in the long term. This is unfortunate because, if placed in a context less intent on the portrayal of radical evil, the characters, sets, and props could have been woven into genuinely constructive, entertaining stories.

Lord of the Rings

Among popular entertainment epics, however, the darkest and most thoroughly violent is *Lord of the Rings.* Very little joy or light-hearted emotion emanates from this trilogy of films. Almost every minute of screen time is obsessively devoted to the oppressively heavy burden of planning and actively carrying out the complete destruction of evil. This turns out to be such a devotionally arduous task that the hero, Frodo (Elijah Wood), is reduced to little more than a burnt cinder by the epic's end in *Return of the King* (2003). If melodramatic form could deliver effective cathartic release through merely a prolonged tapping of emotional arousal, each film in the *Lord of the Rings* trilogy would deliver in spades. Each film offers a continuous festival of carnage alternating between blood-spattering individual battles and grand panoramic conflagrations.

As in *Harry Potter* and *Star Wars*, the evil side of the conflict seeks absolute control and power over all other beings—for reasons that do not need to be in the least examined or explored. In the novel and the film, Sauron, the "Lord of the Rings," is never seen by any of the other characters. An enormous "Eye" atop a tower manifests his presence as the all-powerful monarch of Mordor. Very little is said about him other than that he is the Dark Lord and was once the servant of an expired predecessor named Morgoth or the Great Enemy, about whom even less is said or known. As a character drawn with no flesh-and-blood features, Sauron is obviously designed to be the perfect symbol of evil — a satanic figure whose thorough destruction need give no pause whatever. Consequently, *Lord of the Rings* offers no genuine conflict and instead parades forth in an endless campaign of mopping-up operations in which the only dramatic

An orc presents a menacing face in *Lord of the Rings: The Two Towers* (2002) (Photofest).

tension derives from a playing out of the question of how many and what particular obstacles must be overcome by the underdogs — Frodo, Sam and company — before achieving ultimate victory.

The internal conflict transpiring within the characters of Frodo and Gollum plays out similar anemic tensions since there is no issue of choice — what ought to be chosen is made obvious — but only an issue of strength. And there is little doubt about how Frodo will fare in his internal battle since Gollum already provides the model for weakness and failure. The melodrama of *Lord of the Rings* functions as an epic morality play, and, like all morality plays, it never poses a moral choice that requires any soul searching or reflection.

The dominant emphasis director Peter Jackson places on scenes of graphically depicted battle and war within the context of an extraordinarily Manichean universe ensures that any mild-mannered ways of the Hobbits of the Shire are lost amidst a sea of carnage. The carnage is sufficiently explicit that many adults find it repulsive to watch. Nevertheless, Gerard Jones, author of the book *Killing Monsters* discussed in Chapter 13, reports in a television interview not long after the release of his book that he had no hesitation taking his eight-year-old son with him to see the first film, *The Fellowship of the Ring* (2001). This is clearly a lapse of "parental guidance." Due to the quantity and quality of violent content, it can be stated unequivocally that none of the films in the trilogy are suitable for viewing by eight-year-old children.

The net effect of the violence in this trilogy, as in the films in the *Harry Potter* and *Star Wars* series, only confirms and once again reinforces culturally dominant tendencies toward highly polarized styles of confronting, structuring, and managing conflict: styles that feature deadly violent resolution. As such, the venerable position of all three epics in the iconography of popular culture represents little to cheer about.

22

Apocalyptic Melodrama:
The Terminator
and *The Matrix*

Following the mediocre box office showing for *Conan the Destroyer* (1983), Arnold Schwarzenegger was ready for something new but was less than enthusiastic about a leap into the futuristic sci-fi market. When asked on the *Conan* set about his next film project, which was *The Terminator* (1984), Schwarzenegger answered dismissively, "It's some shit movie I'm making. Take a couple of weeks" (cited in Andrews, 1996: 118). Although *The Terminator* was not a box office hit, several months after its release the new video rental industry showed what it could do for films that were not big hits in their theatrical runs. Through video rentals the film built momentum and became a cult smash hit, making a national superstar out of Schwarzenegger. When offered a choice of roles between the heroic Kyle Reese and the villainous Terminator, Schwarzenegger chose to play the Terminator. As it turned out, this was a career-enhancing choice — but one that, as will be seen, Schwarzenegger nevertheless came to have doubts about.

Critic Jake Horsley concludes that one of the more remarkable things about the film is "the sheer audacity of its plot." But "audacity" may be too kind a word for the convoluted and tortured logic patched together and served up in this James Cameron–directed disaster spectacle.

The year of the film's "present," 2029, finds the world dominated by a computer network called Skynet, which was initially constructed for monitoring defense operations. Programmed to have creative intelligence and learning capabilities, Skynet succeeds beyond expectations. Apparently having been programmed too effectively, the network evolves into a form of "superintelligence" exceeding the capacity and control of human intellects. Drunk with its own power, and evidently jealous as well, Skynet decides that humans must be exterminated. Through a nuclear conflagration, Skynet is largely successful in this task but, nevertheless, a small group of surviving human resistance fighters threatens to overcome the network. In response, Skynet programs a robotic agent, the Terminator (Arnold Schwarzenegger), and sends it back in time to kill the mother, Sarah Conner (Linda Hamilton), of the leader of the resistance group, John Conner — thereby changing the "present" that threatens the network. Having learned of this dastardly intention, the resistance fighters send a human from their group, Kyle Reese (Michael Biehn), back to the same time period to destroy the Terminator before it can destroy Sarah Conner. So instead of duking it out in "present" time, Skynet and the resistance elect to duke it out in a chosen slice of the past.

Examined from any perspective, this plot presents itself as a colossal absurdity. Audiences are asked to believe that a computer intelligence superior to human intelligence has decided, among its range of available rational options, that the best plan for defeating the resistance is to send an agent back in time to destroy the mother of the leader of the resistance. This seems more like an option that might present itself to a college freshman around two o'clock on a Saturday morning through the haze of an alcohol-clouded brainstorming session.

Why would not Skynet, using its supreme intelligence, figure out how to defeat the small and technologically inferior resistance in the more familiar frame of present time than take the chance that by eliminating the mother of the resistance leader it might also inadvertently eliminate itself through an unforeseen glitch in the alternate future that would be created? The lack of control regarding the unfolding of alternate futures — implicit in the assumption that the future can be changed *at all* by an alteration of the past — makes the option chosen by the network seem highly desperate if not wholly irrational.

The audience is asked to believe that a state-of-the-art computer has not posed itself the question: What if the Terminator gets the wrong woman? Several women named "Sarah Conner" — but not the "right" Sarah Conner — are in fact indiscriminately terminated by the Terminator. The audience is forced to embrace the convenient but unlikely presumption that the death of these women — not to mention the reckless slaughter of other innocents and the wide swath of wanton destruction the Terminator leaves in his wake — will have no unwanted effects on the new future desired by Skynet.

Much more could be said about the absurdities of the plot, but these shortcomings only serve to illustrate that plot details must be counted as irrelevant in the search for any real substance in the film. In the quest for this generic substance Horsley correctly observes, *The Terminator* is, like *Alien*, a horror movie with a sci-fi setting. More specifically, as Rushing and Frentz have noted, following Margaret Goscilo's analysis, it belongs in the horror subgenre of the slasher film: "Although Sarah successfully defeats the Terminator in the film's final minutes, in present time she never really stalks her enemy on her own terms or becomes like several of the men before her, a hunter. For most of the film, she is a frightened and tormented victim ... [T]he film owes much to the slasher subgenre of horror, in which women are generally shown as incompetent, helpless, scantily clad, vulnerable victims whose bodies are the object of the male gaze and erotic violence" (1995: 175).

The psychic liabilities of the slasher genre as an essentially male fantasy are examined in Chapter 19. However, beyond the limited themes of the standard slasher plot, Rushing and Frentz point out that the melodramatic design of *The Terminator* is further amplified and embellished by its "rather transparent Christian underpinnings." They note, in agreement with Richard Corliss's findings that "John Conner, a modern day J.C., born of an 'ordinary' mother, is the warrior-king [Christ figure] who is prophesied to reconstitute the world, to avert the apocalypse through a fight with a cyborgian devil" (179).

The mythic progenitor and inspiration for the grandiose apocalyptic twist to the storyline resides in a particular version of the Christ story. This version derives from what Rushing and Frentz call the "exoteric" account of Christ's sacrifice and the Christian saga of redemption: "It is much more typical ... to interpret the Christ story exoterically — that is, in a way that reinforces the ego by keeping the unacceptable parts of the psyche (the shadow) separated and disowned. In this version, Satan carries the sins of the world, and Christ substitutes for us in dealing with Satan ... Christ dies for our sins, ... all that is required for redemption is belief, because the savior of humankind banishes that shadow for us" (180).

In this exoteric or apocalyptic version — which coincides with the major institutional renderings handed down through tradition inspired through John's Revelation — the fate of all of humanity lies in the hands of one individual, a savior, who alone has the ability to overcome Satan (or satanic agents) and through his sacrifice ransom humanity from evil and complete destruction. Whatever may be the subtle social and psychological economy of such a plot, it certainly sets the stakes high and draws the lines of conflict razor sharp in a final all-or-nothing confrontation in which complete annihilation is the loser's share. The adjective "apocalyptic" is here used to indicate this type of conflict: one that involves the spectacle of an ultimate clash between sharply drawn forces of good and evil and in which one individual stands out as a sacrificial savior.

In making *The Terminator*, the director, Cameron, feeling an apocalyptic itch and sensing its commercial potential, may have said something of the following sort to his scriptwriting team: "I want a sci-fi action film — which means I need violence and lots of it. Give me a plot where the fate of the entire human race is in the balance (can't top that!) where the threat comes from an unstoppable cyborg monster chasing a girl defended by a hugely overmatched hero who must face enormous odds. And don't sweat the details on whatever rationale you have to invent to create this scenario."

For Cameron, the goal was to create a situation that provides a conduit for action scenes wherein the violence can be amplified to maximum intensity. Since the conduit for action is the main objective, the extent to which it is framed in a situation that is contrived, artlessly stitched together, and unrealistic is of comparatively little importance. The carnage along the path of the conflict is the real show and will distract the audience sufficiently from any failings in the credibility of the plot details. Offering a thinly developed and contrived plot with excessive emphasis on the accumulation of scenes of graphic violence, *The Terminator* becomes the violent analogue to a pornographic film — serving up violence much like the porn film serves up sex.

But however skeletal, confused, and irrelevant the details and logic of the plot may be, the overall structure of the plot remains enormously significant. Just as the plot in a pornographic film may be insignificant in its details, it figures significantly in its structure through the way in which it may orient the attitudes of male and female viewers toward sex and each other. Similarly, the plot in violent action films acts suasively on viewers with its explicit, clearly aligned structuring of the featured conflict.

The essence of the apocalyptic plot — the lone savior battling evil for the fate of the world (or the "local" community of civilization) — is familiar and acceptable enough to audiences, through the tutelage of the Christ story, to outweigh any requirements for clarity or consistency among trifling details.

The historical roots of this apocalyptically nuanced and Christian-influenced myth in American culture have been extensively examined and exposed through the work of Richard Slotkin in his three-volume study of what he calls the "myth of the frontier" (see also Chapter 17 for further discussion of Slotkin's work). In the second volume of this trilogy Slotkin devotes primary attention to George Armstrong Custer and the way in which his demise assumed mythic status and was appropriated and subsumed into the dominant mythological currents of American culture.

The defining characteristics of this myth began to take shape in newspaper reports of the time through various eulogies and rehashings of the events. Summing up the tone and tenor of Walt Whitman's "Death-Sonnet for Custer" published in the *New York Tribune*, Slotkin observes that "Custer's defeat became a kind of atoning sacrifice, almost Christ-like: the representative of American youth, courage, and soldierly virtue violently perishes, but leaves behind a redeeming example that summons his fellow citizens to the purgation of evil, the regeneration of virtue and vigor, and a renewed pursuit of our 'ancient struggle' against the forces of darkness" (1985: 10).

The complex reality of Custer's infamous "Last Stand" is delivered over to the ready-made template for conflict residing in the cultural tradition of the Christ story and similar themes. Once appropriated in this manner, the Custer myth is polished, amended, and magnified in popular retellings and serves to inspire works of fiction — such as novels and, in the twentieth century, films— that perpetuate the myth. *The Terminator* is an example of the extension of the apocalyptic myth into the province of the postmodern "frontier" of a science fiction future — where the apocalyptic battle on the frontier of Custer's American West continues with hardly a loss of tempo. But instead of struggling against a savage land inhabited by savage "redskins," Kyle Reese struggles against the evil of technological agency run amok and the wasteland of the remanufactured landscape it dominates and controls. The complex challenges of the new frontier created by the emergence of computer technology are readily reconfigured to fit the mold of the old mythological conflict structures. This would not be a noteworthy problem were it not for the fact, as argued herein, that the old structures serve human community in ways that prominently feature, admire, and celebrate violently exclusionary modes of resolution.

Even Schwarzenegger, as already mentioned, began to have doubts about the cultural benefits of his portrayal of a cyborg monster. Fearful that the Terminator had emerged, despite its villainous role in the film, as an all-too-popular cultural icon, Schwarzenegger began to see a different role for himself in the sequel. As Rushing and Frentz report: "After the unexpected success of T1 [*The Terminator*], Schwarzenegger reportedly became concerned about the public's unabashed affection for the indestructible, cop-killing machine he portrayed in the original and insisted on a radical makeover for T2 [*Terminator 2: Judgment Day* (1991)]. The goal was for him to become 'a kinder, gentler terminator,' a better role model for children" (1995: 194).

Schwarzenegger apparently believed he could deflect and redirect the negative role-model effects of the first film by returning in the second film as the same Terminator reprogrammed to protect and defend the struggling humans resisting the Skynet eradication campaign. With this thought Schwarzenegger showed that he had learned nothing from the first film. This is especially evident in his general attitude toward the effects of violent films, which has remained consistent throughout his film career. Speaking of the *Conan* films, Schwarzenegger remarked to French film critics, "Fantasy is definitely the thing now, because they [the audience] can get off on the killing on screen. They can get off on seeing someone get killed without feeling guilty" (cited in Andrews, 1996: 109). In a comment about the villainy in *The Terminator* Schwarzenegger explained, "I think the majority of people out there appreciate ... [being] able to disconnect emotions and go after what they want to go after, destroy what they want to destroy. That's why they go to see those films. It's a fantasy" (cited in Andrews, 121).

In a 1985 interview, while working on the film *Commando*, Schwarzenegger claimed, "If killing is done with good taste, it can be very entertaining indeed." Arnold's idea of "good taste" became all too apparent when he went all the way to 20th Century Fox's Lawrence Gordon to insist on the inclusion in *Commando* of the following scene: "I chop a guy's arm off. So, when we're filming it, the stunt man does something not in the script — he starts to scream. Well, I got the idea to tell him to shut up and slap his face with the arm I just took off. They thought it was too much. I thought it would be fun" (cited in Andrews, 141). Showing unusual "good taste" in overriding Schwarzenegger, Gordon made sure this scene never made it into the film.

The popularity of the Terminator character in the first film is a direct function of the film's success in achieving audience arousal effects with the exceptional emphasis on unremitting sequences of well-choreographed, visually exciting, wildly destructive acts of violence. The Terminator, of course, occupies center stage in the scenes of violence and consequently emerges — because the film mostly consists of violent scenes — as the real star of the film. In this sense the film functions, in the manner of *A Clockwork Orange*, as a vehicle for the transgressions of an anti-hero. And, as happened with Clockwork's Alex, the featured anti-hero becomes a favorite character — particularly among young viewers.

The second film repeats these arousal effects through the same formula while retaining Schwarzenegger as the reprogrammed "good guy"

Arnold Schwarzenegger as a "kinder, gentler Terminator" in *Terminator 2: Judgment Day* (1991) (Photofest).

Terminator and adding a new and improved cyborg opponent. Far from salvaging Schwarzenegger as a role model, the second film irrescindably ties his image to the most egregious excesses of gratuitous cinematic violence. Like the first film, scenes of violence strung together along the slenderest threads of credulity-challenging plot points create a cinematic context that, due to the threadbare plot, can be justly described as little more than a vehicle for the cheap thrills of "pornographic" violence — all in the service of reinforcing destructive attitudes toward the structuring of conflict.

Schwarzenegger cannot duck responsibility for his complicity in a series of action films clearly designed to profit from the marketing of violence as a commercial confection — a marketing made suitably acceptable to conventional pieties by co-optation of culturally sedimented mythological themes. *Terminator 3* (2003) continues these depredations ad nauseam.

In their examination of *Terminator 2*, Rushing and Frentz confirm and reinforce a point made previously in the discussion of video games in Chapter 13 — that creativity and imaginative quality of narrative detail are often sacrificed in the current entertainment market for visually stimulating violent effects: "As more a remake than a sequel, T2 hedges on narrative innovation in favor of reforming Schwarzenegger and displaying its technical effects. In substituting artificial technique for human creativity, the film itself exemplifies how technological progress threatens human ingenuity" (195). In other words, with its smorgasbord of technological effects in lieu of any narrative substance, the film itself emerges as a portentous cultural artifact and exemplar of the technological apocalyptic nightmare it depicts.

The Matrix

The Matrix (1999) shares in depicting the same apocalyptic nightmare as well as succumbing to the same temptations of technological gimmickry in giving itself over almost entirely to special effects and visual fireworks. Also like *The Terminator*, *The Matrix* is followed by two sequels to form a trilogy of films in which the sequels do little more than serve as remakes of the original. Although touted by some as posing profound philosophical questions while also being "the most elaborately plotted action movie ever made," *The Matrix* offers a plot every bit as absurd — and consequently as pretentiously unilluminating — as *The Terminator*. And finally, also like *The Terminator*, the plot of *The Matrix*, despite its appearance of complexity, ends up as little more than, in Roger Ebert's words, "a superhero comic book in which the fate of the world comes down to a titanic fist-fight between the designated representatives of good and evil." For Ebert the film "recycle[s] the same tired ideas" that have come to be a routine expectation from Joel Silver–produced "exercises in violence."

Critical opinion of *The Matrix* varies widely, however. In his commentary on the film in *The Blood Poets*, Jake Horsley claims that *The Matrix* "may well be the outstanding American movie of the '90s" (1999b: 432). Horsley even suggests that the film may need to be included among the best of the century because it has "the kind of emotional power that one generally gets only from works of art ... as such, it may well be the cheekiest, most audacious, and most exhilarating work of art since *Citizen Kane*" (1999b: 440).

Glossing over the comic-book aspects of the plot, Horsley remains impressed by its ingenious "gnostic" themes and marvels at how the Wachowski brothers, as writers and directors, could have conjured up such a "demonically inspired and wickedly effective pop parable." This parable is for Horsley an "amazingly coherent blend of Philip K. Dick, H. P. Lovecraft, Jean Baudrillard, messianic prophecy, apocalyptic lore, martial arts, mysticism, and technological paranoia" (1999b: 432). Apparently Horsley does not play video games. The potpourri of influences he cites are all in evidence in various guises in video games of the 1990s, which suggests that the Wachowski brothers are probably video-game enthusiasts.

When thinking of the video-game experience, it becomes easy to see where the Wachowskis got the idea for the film. The world of the Matrix is analogous to stepping into the virtual world of the video game — with the insidious difference that the simulation is so holographically and sensually perfect that it reproduces an experience of real life indistinguishable from real life. The theme is similar to the movie *Tron* (1982) but instead of entering into the electronic hardware, humans enter into a programmed world created by electronic software. For Horsley the excitement generated by the possibilities of this challenging illusion take the film beyond being a "piece of first-class entertainment" and into the creation of an "experience that bends our concepts of what is real and what is not, and leaves us in a very tight spot indeed" (1999b: 433).

Contrary to what Horsley asserts, the film does not leave us in a very tight spot. Beneath its superficial and highly ornamental dalliance with the question of what is really real and what is not, it returns us to a very old and familiar spot. In setting up a tension between a programmed illusion and reality, the film presents a clear distinction between an inside (an illusion) and an absolute outside (the really real). But instead of genuinely wrestling with the difficulties—ethical, social, political, etc.—presented by this tension (as John Fowles does with the concept of meta-theater in his 1965 novel *The Magus* which was made into a film [1968] that preserved some of the genius of the book) the filmmakers arrest the chance for real conflict by making the illusion the work of demonic "inorganic beings" whose purposes are despicably malevolent. This melodramatization of the tension between illusion and reality forecloses the possibility of the protagonists confronting genuine conflict between two worlds and the potential attractions of those worlds by making the choice both ontologically and morally obvious if not necessary.

The choice that should have been dramatically constructed to be a moment of extraordinary inner conflict and soul searching, the choice between masking and unmasking illusion, between embracing the familiar and risking the unknown, is instead rigged in advance and ridiculously oversimplified by being cast in the alternatives between good and evil. By the time the young hero Thomas Anderson (Keanu Reeves) is given the choice between the "blue pill" and the "red pill," he has already been treated to a Surrealist nightmare of pursuit, capture, coercion, and torture—including the insertion of a gruesome, insectlike parasite into his body—by agents who give the unmistakable appearance of being the polar opposite of anything that could be considered good.

Having loaded the dice in this way, the potentially interesting ontological issues raised are washed away and the film becomes standard melodrama. Ebert expresses his justifiable disappointment in the overall results when the "bad guys fire thousands of rounds, but are unable to hit the good guy. Then it's down to the final showdown between good and evil—a martial arts battle in which the good guy gets pounded until he's almost dead, before he finds the inner will to fight back. Been there, seen that ..." As in the case of *The Terminator*, the two sequels to *The Matrix* serve up the same thing ad nauseam.

As Ebert also points out, the Matrix—the illusory world created by the demonic computer network—is a world that perfectly simulates the pre–Matrix world and for which there is (in the real world "outside" the Matrix) an enslaved and incubating human corresponding to every individual in the Matrix. Ebert rightly wonders why the computer network would go to all the trouble of engineering this elaborate "hoax" on humanity. If it has the power to enslave all of humanity in enormous "energy farms" for the expressed purpose of leaching and channeling human life forces for its dark but unrevealed purposes, then why not keep the bodies in a "dreamless" coma instead of an elaborate program that must itself con-

Trinity (Carrie Anne Moss), dressed in cyber-commando chic, lands with stylish bravado in front of a spectacular explosion in *The Matrix: Reloaded* (2003).

sume a great deal of energy in perpetrating its highly detailed visual, sensory, and narrative effects? The most immediate answer seems to be that such a relatively boring scenario would not meet Hollywood requirements for "wouldn't this be neat?" storylines. Here, again, the unbelievability of the story resembles the absurdities of *The Terminator*.

In addition to shortcomings in dramatic conflict and narrative detail, *The Matrix* also, as Horsley has the good sense to acknowledge despite his praise for the film, "lacks subtlety ... lacks characters, and as a result ... lacks any real psychological depth" (1999b: 443). In fact, the film surpasses even *The Terminator* trilogy in presenting wooden characters and leaden dialogue — with effects that are in places so stupefying as to be comical.

Lacking in dramatic conflict, narrative logic, character development, and psychological depth, *The Matrix* is left standing primarily on the merits of its special effects violence. Most of the 135 minutes of *The Matrix* are filled with relentless sequences of violent combat — including extremely prolonged, elaborately choreographed, and slow–motion enhanced martial arts battles and automatic firearms exchanges. Due to the way in which the rebels can manipulate the Matrix program, the violence in the action scenes breaks the rules of spacetime, gravity-bound reality. In this regard, *The Matrix* further resembles the world of a video game. Horsley notes that "since the characters are interacting largely in a computer-simulated reality, the violence can be impossible without stretching our patience or belief; the circumstances require it to be off-the-wall" (1999b: 441). Jacked-up with computer enhanced powers and sexed-up with bad black trench-coats, cool-guy sunglasses, and slick high-tech firearms, the rebels are presented in action scenes in ways that can only be described as a glam-orization — indeed, a Hollywoodization — of violence. And, although direct imitation has not been claimed to be the most pervasive effect of entertainment violence, it is worth remembering that *The Matrix* was among the films that exercised seductive appeal to the Columbine killers. This fact raises again troubling questions: To what extent can such saucy cinematic portrayals of violence be consumed by audiences without significant negative consequences on predispositions toward conflict res-olution and relational behavior? And to what extent should the makers of such films be given praise, or even a pass, for their work?

Horsley exemplifies the confusion among critics regarding *The Matrix* when on the one hand he gives substantial praise for the overall experi-ence offered by the film while on the other hand he submits a caveat such as the following: "The most disappointing thing about *The Matrix* is its reliance on the familiar terms of action movies, presenting violence and 'resistance' as the only means to overcome tyranny" (1999b: 436). To be more precise he ought to say, "presenting absolute destruction as the only means of overcoming an enemy portrayed as wholly and irretrievably evil." If this kind of criticism of violent melodramatic filmmaking remains only a footnote caveat at the bottom of a page of commentary, then this kind of filmmaking can be expected to continue pouring forth from Hollywood.

23

Modern "Noir" Melodrama: *Bonnie and Clyde*

Perhaps more so than anywhere else in the world, the late capitalist culture of the United States places a premium on creative thinking — a kind of thinking summed up in the phrase made popular (appropriately) in a television commercial: "thinking outside the box." Although intended to indicate getting beyond routine and ordinary approaches to problems, the application of the phrase may, through extension of its logic, be widened to include thinking outside the box of norms and rules, beyond the boundary of codes and laws, and straight into the "outside" of criminal behavior. In a society of rampant individualism it is not unthinkable that some of its individuals may be tempted to "think outside the box" of its most basic laws — especially when the going gets tough or the opportunities get easy.

In America, the slippery slope leading from "thinking outside the box" to criminal behavior is sometimes lubricated by an additional slipperiness derived from overextension of the logic conveyed in the famous bumper sticker: "Question Authority." It has become easier in the United States than in any other place in the world to openly think, speak, and produce art in ways that show the traditional hero/villain alignment of the "authorities" and the "criminals" in reverse order such that the "criminals" become the heroes and the "authorities" become the villains.

In the horror melodramatic plot the villain — when portrayed as the monster — is a creature whose mere appearance often portends evil and the unnatural. But even when portrayed as a repulsive pollution, the criminal, like the monster, is not without a certain kind of appeal.

The monster and the criminal exhibit a quality of freedom that is often breathtaking in its radical departure from the standard constraints and norms of society — a freedom that is seductive in its courage to break taboos, to "think outside the box" in a way that is *radically* "outside the box." Members of society conforming to the rules may secretly admire the freedom from restraints exemplified in the criminal, and, to that extent, the criminal becomes a kind of hero. By not taking the well-worn path the criminal can attain a measure of heroic status in the myth-making machinery of a culture that values individualism and self-actualization.

The individualist myth has become increasingly the dominant myth in post–World War II America. The war initiated enormous social upheaval throughout the world as the majority of able-bodied men around the globe were uprooted from parochial lifestyles, forced to join ranks across race and class and religion, and shipped out to foreign places where they confronted more strangeness and diversity in a few months than previously would have been encountered over many years or even lifetimes.

This upheaval of humanity broke down social and cultural barriers, especially in the United States, but also to a significant extent in Europe and Asia. If the United States was an individualist culture prior to World War II, it was, by comparison to the period after the war, only marginally so. After the upheaval of the war and in conjunction with the economic boom of the '50s and '60s, individualism in the United States accelerated to a degree beyond anything that could have been foreseen in the decades prior to the war. And because of its unique political (democratic) and economic (capitalist) culture, combined with technological advances in media such as television, individualism took root in the United States significantly more so than anywhere else in the world.

This individualism consisted primarily of a new emphasis on acquiring an identity apart from any family or group affiliation — an identity unique to a personal self and for which that self is entirely responsible. And in the '70s and '80s, class, race, and ethnicity, along with sex and age — while still socially significant — became much less important with regard to social status than ever before. Identity became more a personal achievement than a hereditary or social happenstance. Not surprisingly, in this social climate of individual recognition, the outlaw, the maverick, the criminal, the celebrity, the millionaire, the sports superstar, the social stand-out, the exception to the rule — in whatever form — gained social currency in having achieved an identity apart from and in addition to any ties to a group.

It is also not surprising that, as a result of the emphasis on identity formation separate from group membership, some observers of the American system view it as an adolescent culture: a culture perennially frozen in adolescent motives and adolescent angst. Adolescents especially have a tendency to admire rule-breaking behavior as a result of their passage through a period of exaggerated identity crisis — the period of separation where becoming a self, an individual apart from parents and siblings — becomes an all-engrossing and critically heightened fixation. One of the easiest and clearest ways to demonstrate this individuation and separation from the family and the system of values represented by the family is to engage in rule-breaking, consensus-breaking, or law-breaking behavior. But, for many adolescents this break is too traumatic and emotionally taxing and instead of being realized through modes of unique self-actualization it plays out through membership in a new group. Such groups may offer the anticonformist visibility of trenchcoat and gothic clubs, or the outlaw credentials of urban gangs, or the neo-tribalist cult notoriety of skinhead neo–Nazi groups.

In deference to postwar identity needs among adolescents and young adults, the Hollywood filmmaking industry, along with the comic-book industry, increased production of a variation of the melodramatic plot structure. Consistent with the "noir" variation mentioned in Chapter 10, the criminal or the outcast becomes the hero. The agent representing communal authority — usually the corporate leader, the politician, or the police — emerges as the villain — as, for example, in *Chinatown* (1974), *The Gauntlet* (1977), and *L. A. Confidential* (1997). Or the agent of the system may be merely quasi-villainous in relation to an agent of pure evil as in *Dirty Harry* (1971). The outcast or outlaw legends (to be distinguished from the persons) of Jesse James, Doc Holliday, and Billy the Kid provided the stepping stones along the path to twentieth-century popular loners ranging along a spectrum from Sam Spade to The Man with No Name to Rambo.

In a culture where identity is strongly rooted in forms of self-actualization and self-expression rather than group association and group achievement, the challenges of adolescent identity crisis easily extend into adult life. This may certainly give the illusion of a culture stuck in adolescent modes of angst. But in reality it is a culture that has evolved a new social pattern of recognition and exchange that may be in many ways a highly beneficial progression — as argued in Chapter 15. Even while granting this claim, however, not every artifact that panders to individualistic culture necessarily contributes beneficially to that progression. With these considerations in mind, insert into the American postwar social milieu the film *Bonnie and Clyde*.

Bonnie and Clyde opened in theaters in the late summer of 1967. The script was originally intended for François Truffaut because the American writers, Robert Benton and David Newman, admired his work and thought the possibilities of the subject matter suited the director's New Wave noir style — a style that owed much to American films of the 1940s featuring heroes of tainted virtue. Focusing attention instead on the making of *Fahrenheit 451*, Truffaut passed the script to Jean-Luc Godard. While Godard wavered on production, Warren Beatty, on a recommendation from Truffaut, picked up the option on the script. Beatty became enthusiastic about the project and eventually served as producer and star through the benefit of funding provided by Jack Warner.

When Warner previewed the film, he hated it. The critical responses of reviewers were similar. Bosley Crowther of *The New York Times* summed up the critical sentiment when he referred to the film as "a cheap piece of bald-faced slapstick that treats the hideous depredations of that sleazy, moronic pair as though they were as full of fun and frolic as the jazz-age cut-ups in 'Thoroughly Modern Millie' " (cited in Menand, 2003: 175). In similar tone, *Time* magazine described the film as "tasteless aimlessness" and *Newsweek* labeled it "a squalid shoot-em-up for the moron trade." In the wake of these excoriating reviews the film did not fare well at the box office.

Then a strange thing happened. For reasons known only to him, Joe Morgenstern, who had written the review for *Newsweek*, went to see the film again. After this second viewing, he changed his mind. In the next issue of *Newsweek* he published a new review praising the film and retracting everything he had said in the previous review. Morgenstern's unprecedented reversal was then followed by a lengthy defense of the film (written by his close friend Pauline Kael), which was published in *The New Yorker* in October. Then, even though its theatrical run had already ended in America, *Time* exceeded Morgenstern's reversal by placing the film on a December issue cover. The cover displayed images from the film taken from a Robert Rauschenberg collage and *Time* praised the film in an extended feature article. This renewed media attention prompted Warner to re-release the film. On this second run it fared much better at the box office and succeeded in garnering ten Academy Award nominations, including a nomination for Best Picture.

In the years following its miraculous resurrection and second coming, *Bonnie and Clyde* has only grown in estimation, achieving legendary status. According to Louis Menand of *The New Yorker*, it "changed American movie culture" by giving a new "credibility" to American filmmaking, shifting the New Wave cinema momentum from France to Hollywood and paving the way for directors such as Coppola, Scorsese, and Kubrick.

In a retrospective review published in 2002, Roger Ebert recalls: "When I saw it, I had been a film critic for less than six months, and it was the first masterpiece I had seen on the job. I felt an exhilaration beyond describing. I did not suspect how long it would be between such experiences, but at least I learned that they were possible" (88). In the same piece Ebert points out that he was the only critic writing for a major newspaper who wholeheartedly sang the film's praises on its first release. In that original review Ebert stated that the film was "a milestone in the history of American movies" and "a work of truth and brilliance." Presciently, as it turned out, he went on to add that "years from now it is quite possible that *Bonnie and Clyde* will be seen as the definitive film of the 1960s." Looking back from the year 2002, Ebert concurs with critic Patrick Goldstein in calling it the "the first modern American film" (86).

Praise for the film derives from a strong convergence of major artistic elements of cinematography (for which Burnett Guffey won an Oscar), casting and acting (Estelle Parsons won Best Supporting Actress for the role of Blanche), and script (which was nominated for Best Original Screenplay). Of these three the script — even though it did not win the Oscar — figures most importantly in the film's perception as a "milestone" because of the unusual blend of romance and violence, humor and anger. In this regard, the film definitely belongs in the genealogical line to *Pulp Fiction*.

Jake Horsley gives *Bonnie and Clyde* prominent attention in his two-volume study of violent films entitled *The Blood Poets*. Consistent with the view that it is "the first modern American film," Horsley finds *Bonnie and Clyde* to be "an all but perfect piece of violent entertainment"—in part because it is "the first Hollywood movie to give the audience what it had been unconsciously waiting for: a head-on encounter with sex and death" (1999a: 41). And it also delivers in spades on the two most basic requirements of the "poem in blood": "it is both visually compelling and emotionally upsetting; it combines aesthetics— beauty — with morals— horror" (37). For Horsley, the beauty and horror are especially effective because they are "all of a piece." Horsley is not blind to the controversial appearance of these conclusions as he notes that "it is ironic (though typical) that the violence that gives the film its integrity, its greatness, is precisely what it was criticized and condemned for" (41).

Horsley's claim that the film is a near "perfect piece of violent entertainment" makes it an important film to study in the context of an examination of the effects of violent entertainment. Does Horsley's judgment hold up in light of the distinctions proposed herein about the qualitatively different effects of violence in contrasting dramatic contexts?

In attempting to get clear about the rationale for the glowing assessments of the film, it is helpful to begin with an examination of the primary characters and their reception by the audience. The story is based on the lives of the famous East Texas outlaws Clyde Barrow and Bonnie Parker and their bank robbing adventures throughout the southern Midwest during the early 1930s. Among 1930s criminals and gangsters, Bonnie and Clyde achieved a measure of favorable celebrity in the popular culture of the times because the banks they were robbing were grouped among the same banks involved in foreclosures on failing family farms during the Depression. Building on the potential for audience identification with the "quasi" Robin Hood folk hero status of the real Bonnie and Clyde, the director of the film, Arthur Penn, increased the likelihood of identification by casting the winsomely attractive Faye Dunaway alongside the swarthily handsome Warren Beatty. The fact that Dunaway and Beatty bore minimal resemblance in manner and appearance to Bonnie Parker and Clyde Barrow ensured that the Hollywood retelling of their story could reflect little of the coarseness of the lives of the real couple and their "romance."

With these casting decisions for the starring roles in mind, it is difficult to understand Horsley's approving citation of Pauline Kael's judgment that "audiences at *Bonnie and Clyde* are not given a simple, secure, basis for identification; they are made to feel but not told how to feel" (1999a: 42). When Horsley adds that the film "gives the audience the freedom to make its own allegiances (or not)," it is clear that he, like Kael, has taken the bait offered in the film's sophisticated appearance and texture while overlooking the allegiances mandated by its predictably familiar underlying structure.

Contrary to what Horsley and Kael assert, there can be no question that the film is intended to solicit wholesale identification with and sympathy for Bonnie and Clyde. In her book on crime films and society (2000), Nicole Rafter, for example, insists that the success of the film — in terms of its desired effects— depends vitally on that identification. Rafter argues, "The key factor in the movie's success was the way viewers empathized with Bonnie and Clyde. That audiences were able to identify with what were, after all, two long-dead punks arose from the scriptwriters' skillful downplaying of the characters' negative traits and emphasis on their virtues" (156).

Rafter notes that Bonnie and Clyde are portrayed as brave and inventive, sensitive to each other's vulnerabilities, and defiant in the face of a death they know is coming. The company they keep such as Blanche and Buck, C. W. Moss, and Velma and Eugene make them appear, by contrast, smart and refined. And while Bonnie and Clyde resort to violence, the scriptwriters reduce the repellent reality of their violent acts by framing them as collateral events while making the couple appear to be essentially "innocents." It is as if they are not real criminals but playing at crime, becoming active participants in the construction of their own romanticized "Robin Hood" mythology.

Stylistically the film initially toys with the contrast between the light-hearted, playacting fun of Bonnie and Clyde and the deadly seriousness of their law-enforcement pursuers— along with a growing set of related contrasts. These related contrasts, as Horsley correctly claims, feature the tension between sensuality and violence, or "sex and death."

Not unlike *Psycho* and the horror and gore genre, *Bonnie and Clyde*, relies on shock effects, reversals of expectations, and incongruous juxtapositions for much of its appeal. Shock effects are created by building expectations for a particular emotional response and then suddenly, through the introduction of a new image into a scene or by montage, transposing the situation into one that calls for a radically contrasting emotional response. As will also be seen in the discussion of *Pulp Fiction*, which takes such techniques to even greater extremes, these highly manipulative whiplash effects are a reliable way to produce audience-pleasing roller coaster–type emotional thrills.

Scene after scene teases audience expectations and alternates the tension between the emotions and motives surrounding sensually and violently charged themes. In one of the film's initial scenes, for example, erotic attraction between Bonnie and Clyde is both evoked and ominously skewed by Bonnie's fondling of Clyde's revolver. The pleasure/pain tension in the relationship between Bonnie and Clyde is also amplified to a more parodic extreme in the abusive love/hate tension between Blanche and Buck.

Several variations of whiplash effects work alongside the sex and death themes in building waves of emotional shock: for example, the reversal from friendship to betrayal that plays out in the relationship between C. W. Moss and Bonnie and Clyde, the reversal from awkward humor to brutal murder that transpires in one bank robbery scene, and the reversal from play to anger that occurs in a wheat-field scene between Bonnie and Clyde. Roger Ebert remarks on the sudden shift in emotional direction in similar scenes such as "the way laughter turns blindingly to violence, as when a stickup ends with a meat cleaver and a sack of flour, or when a getaway ends with a bullet in a bank man's face" (2002: 88).

The theme of stark contrasts also applies to conflicts within the characters. The *Bonnie and Clyde* crime story creates polarities of ego and alter ego less exaggerated but similar to the horror story, achieving identification effects along the way toward, as will be explained below, a thorough "redemption" of the offending elements. Bonnie and Clyde are beautiful yet savage, innocent yet cold, vulnerable yet violent, sensual yet impotent, humorous yet dark.

As Ebert indicates, these contrasts in the characters of Bonnie and Clyde are reflected and enhanced in the previously mentioned wheat-field scene where a cloud moving overhead shadows the figures of the couple as Clyde chases Bonnie through rows of wheat. As the cloud passes over them, the play of "light and shadow" becomes an emblem of the similar play in their personalities, actions, and relationships. The characters accompanying Bonnie and Clyde are also painted in clashing extremes, and the theme of contrasts echoes further through the tension between the lush, impressionistic cinematography and scenes of blood-soaked violence.

Speaking of the film as a whole, Horsley correctly observes that "at the heart of the matter, then, is the ambiguity, the conflict, the *violence*" (1999a: 38). But it is the *quality* of this division, this conflict, in its various levels of character and action throughout the film that controls and dominates the overall quality of the film's effects—including the effects of its violence. The film's conclusion confirms and brings to a crescendo the quality of antagonistic contrasts depicted throughout the film that mirror and reinforce the featured conflict between the characters and the "system."

The conclusion of the film has now achieved a legendary status eclipsing the level of folk hero fame attained by the real Bonnie and Clyde through its depiction of an abrupt bullet-punctuated end to the couple's quiet afternoon drive. Arthur Penn's slow-motion camera combined with real-time sound effects and squib technology (small charges wired to explode with simulated blood) added one last shockingly realistic and graphic whiplash effect.

Horsley's remarks regarding this ending typify the misreadings common to much of the critical commentary on the film: "There is no way that we in the audience could have failed to see it coming, nor is there any reason for us to feel in any way betrayed or depressed by this outcome. It doesn't seem unfair or unnecessary—on the contrary, it is the very nature of tragedy that it is inescapable" (1999a: 42). Although it is true that a violent ending is not unexpected, the severity of the couple's deaths and the manner of depiction are shocking in their unexpectedness. And it is hard to imagine a death that could be more "unnecessary," regardless of the number of banks robbed, than to be riddled in a merciless shower of lead. This sense of the "unnecessary" and cruel manner of execution is precisely

The bullet-riddled bodies of Bonnie (Faye Dunaway) and Clyde (Warren Beatty) near the end of the final scene in *Bonnie and Clyde* (1968) (Photofest).

what Penn desires to achieve and only confirms the structure of the film as melodramatic rather than tragic as the agents of the "system" take on the full mantle of evil.

This ending and the style in which it is filmed leave no doubt that it is specifically designed to resolve any ambiguous sentiments on the part of the audience toward Bonnie and Clyde through the outrage aroused toward their brutal executioners. With this ending the ambiguities in their character traits are sacrificed and redeemed through a fate that shows them to be, like the Depression-era farmers, victims of a system that failed them, abandoned them, and finally ambushed them in a brutally cruel and deadly trap.

The problem with all of this is that a tinseled, reductive, and ultimately monotonous form of melodrama structures the conflict throughout the film. The failings of character evident in the protagonists' alter ego shadows are in fact nothing more than reflections of what is intended to be understood as the ugly and evil "system" that created them. The "system" is permeated by a sinister and malevolent corruption that in the end makes it, rather than its "criminals," the proper target for elimination and audience outrage. While the film may end with the demise of its heroes, the conflict it offers throughout falls a long way short of the tragic quality it could potentially have reached — a form that would have produced richer characters and a more engaging drama between the criminals and the system.

Horsley makes several assumptions toward the end of his review that further illustrate the confusion about this film in general and its violence in particular. These assumptions are launched in a question he poses that he believes echoes the mistaken verdict of some reviewers. "How is it possible," Horsley asks, "that a depiction of violence that is shocking, disturbing, and emotionally upsetting would in any way be denounced as immoral?" (1999a: 42).

This question contains Horsley's guiding assumption concerning the conditions within which entertainment violence can be beneficially moving entertainment. For Horsley the portrayal of violence in a manner that is shocking, disturbing, and emotionally upsetting constitutes a powerful and "moral" portrayal of violence in contrast to portrayals, for example, that show violence in ways that diminish or hide its real horror. The assumption in this question is consistent with his remark cited earlier to the effect that the violence in *Bonnie and Clyde* is aesthetically and morally "of a piece" and thoroughly commendable.

In answer to his own question and in defense of the depictions of violence in the film, Horsley then makes two observations revealing further assumptions. On the one hand, he admits that "the film gives us two very charming outlaws, granted, but, although it glamorizes its protagonists, it in no way glamorizes their *acts*: on the contrary it shows them coolly and unflinchingly for what they are: desperate acts of savagery." On the other hand, he immediately adds that "if the audience still chooses to sympathize and identify with the 'heroes' of the film, then, this is a tribute to the skill and sensitivity of the performers and filmmakers involved, and an indication of the basic sympathies of the American public (which has always been a sucker for rebels and underdogs)" (1999a: 42).

First he asks viewers to believe that the film clearly glamorizes the protagonists but *in no way* glamorizes their acts. Then, in effect, he immediately casts doubt on this assessment by acknowledging that the film, through the skill of the performers and the design of the filmmakers, may succeed in eliciting sympathy and identification with the outlaw couple while further conceding that the American public is a "sucker" for such underdogs anyway. To suppose that the film "glamorizes" its protagonists, produces "sympathy" and "identification" with them as the "heroes" of the film, and plays to American inclinations to side with "rebels" and "underdogs," while also claiming that the film "in no way glamorizes their *acts*," is to advance an extraordinarily hollow argument.

Only a babe in the woods in the forest of cinematic effects would believe that identification with characters in a film will *not* be accompanied by a substantial tendency among viewers to approve of their attitudes and actions — not to mention their words and dress (Faye Dunaway's outfits in the film inaugurated a popular clothing trend among women, including the French actress Brigitte Bardot, in the months after the film's successful re-release). Since Horsley is no babe in the woods, it is surprising that he makes what amounts to conflicting assertions in the same paragraph.

Furthermore, when Horsley asserts, "*Bonnie and Clyde* does not achieve its effects through dishonesty or audience manipulation" (1999a: 42), nothing could be further from the truth. Is it really the case that a film that in effect glamorizes "desperate acts of savagery" — all in the context of contrived swings of emotional response, exaggerated polarizations of conflict, and blatant glorification of shallow character — is a film that *cannot* in some significant measure be understood as "dishonest" and "manipulative"?

While it may be the case that some viewers identify with the criminal in cinematic noir-styled melodramas to the point of imitation of lawless and violent behavior, that possibility in itself does not constitute the primary cause for concern regarding such melodramas. Direct imitative behavior may occur in a small minority of cases (as evidenced in reactions to the film *A Clockwork Orange*). But the greater concern lies in the possibilities for effects that play to and prey on the majority, if not all, of a viewing audience — the arousal (unaccompanied by effective catharsis) of emotions associated with victimization combined with attitudinal conditioning toward inflammatory and alienating structurings of conflict.

As previously noted, the American public, as a consequence of the influences of a strongly individualistic culture, is prone to form identifications in the right persuasive circumstances with anyone who stands out from the crowd. However, films that pander to these susceptibilities through depictions of glamorized heroes and heroines acting out scenes of graphic violence through situations of oversimplified melodramatic conflict do not need to be held up as examples of great filmmaking. Such films will in the long run only give individualistic nonconformist culture a bad reputation — a reputation it does not or need not deserve.

24

Postmodern "Noir" Melodrama: *Pulp Fiction*

As its title suggests, *Pulp Fiction* (1994) belongs in a genre somewhere between cheap crime novels and men's saga magazines in the coarse texture of its celluloid frames. It is also a film that was popular at the box office, critically acclaimed, nominated for Best Picture by the Academy for Motion Picture Arts and Sciences, and recipient of the award for Best Original Screenplay. Its *popular* success is not surprising. Much like horror and slasher films and its crime film precursor *Bonnie and Clyde*, its effects are built up by playing violence and sex off of each other to produce a series of alternating emotional shocks and arousals. But its critical acclaim is more difficult to explain. If the film is what it purports to be, pulp fiction, why should that merit, even if considered as witty parody, a nomination for Best Picture? A closer examination of its design and structure will help to answer that question while also providing insight into the potential effects of its portrayals of violence.

In *Pulp Fiction*, the director, Quentin Tarantino, strives for varieties of an emotional whiplash effect and he employs this technique so repeatedly that it becomes a central structuring element. The film sets up a scene, for example, that appears to be a romantic encounter portending scenes of progressing sexual tone in a context nevertheless shadowed with elements that prompt an anxious suspicion, edging into certainty, that the "romance" will soon turn into something radically different. As this certainty builds, it lacks only the knowledge of when and how the scene will turn. When the film fulfills this expectation, the abrupt shift in emotional directions produces a shocking but superficial emotional whiplash. Some-

299

times few clues are given prior to the radical scene shift and the audience begins moving one way emotionally and is then sharply jerked another way.

Themes of sex and violence are used as the primary means for achieving whiplash effects because lust and fear are the two strongest and most oppositional of emotions. When these themes are combined in various alternating ways, the whiplash effects are amplified. These effects appeal to primal appetite in a way analogous to roller coaster rides. The "plot" of the film recedes into the background to serve as little more than the vehicle, the "roller coaster," for the execution of a series of emotional whiplash effects.

Pulp Fiction is essentially a relentless series of whiplashes strung together along a mere thread of a plot. The film opens with a scene in a restaurant where a young couple are talking. Their manner toward each other suggests they are lovers. The talk turns out to be about armed robbery, thereby shifting audience uptake from romance to the possibility of violence. The couple then conclude their talk, exchanging "sweet nothings" while referring to each other as "Pumpkin" and "Honey Bunny." On the heels of this cornball romantic tenderness they rise from their seats, pulling guns and threatening everyone in the restaurant. Whiplash!

Later on, the Italian hit man, Vincent (John Travolta), is assigned as escort to the wife, Mia (Uma Thurman), of a crime boss, Marsellus (Ving Rhames), for a night on the town. A recounting of the previous escort's violent demise — after Marsellus discovered that he had taken the liberty of giving Mia a foot massage — precedes these scenes on the town. Viewers are then led to suspect that Vincent may far exceed the previous escort's minor transgression by succumbing even further to Mia's charms as she turns up the heat with sexy moves on a nightclub dance floor. It appears that things are heating up even more when Vincent drops her off at her residence and she invites him inside. The soundtrack chimes in with provocatively sexy music. Sensing danger but nevertheless tempted, Vincent opts for a time-out and excuses himself to visit the bathroom. While he is out of the room, Mia finds what appears to be cocaine in his coat pocket and snorts a noseful. Exiting from the bathroom, Vincent finds her bleeding from the nose and convulsing from an overdose, having mistaken his smack for toot. Whiplash!

The emotional shift becomes even more pronounced and harrowing as Vincent desperately solicits help from a streetwise friend and eventually jump-starts Mia's comatose body with an adrenaline-loaded hypodermic needle in the heart! Whiplash again!!

Still further on, the sequence following the prize fight involving Butch

(Bruce Willis) leads to a scene at his lover's hideaway, which the couple realizes may be found by the bad guys, thereby portending possible violence. The threat of violence then fades in the next scenes when the mood shifts to romance as the fighter and his lover talk playfully on the bed and in the bathroom. The romantic mood is broken the next morning as Butch awakens to violent sounds on the television, reminding the audience that the bad guys might burst in at any time. Then, as the two prepare to leave, Butch abruptly explodes into a verbally abusive rage and violently throws and breaks objects around the room as his girlfriend retreats to a corner and cowers on the floor. Whiplash! He has discovered that she forgot to retrieve his treasured Rolex from his apartment earlier in the day.

Later on, the film introduces a new variation as it sets up a scene that promises violence, then delivers violence, and, just when the audience is expecting an even greater escalation of physical violence, it then shifts abruptly into a scene of violence from a surprising direction leading to scenes of graphic and grotesque sexual violence. This, of course, is the fight sequence between Marsellus and Butch that leads into the pawnshop sodomy rape scene. In this sequence the violence of the fight scenes is crudely trumped by the completely unexpected shift to the perverse combination of sex and violence in homosexual rape. Whiplash!

These whiplash effects are further amplified by weaving the sex and violence around disarming and seemingly irrelevant bits of trite but socially hip or occupationally savvy conversation. Whiplash effects are also achieved by the additional technique of the insertion of random incidents of freak chance that suddenly alter the direction of the action. For example, the shooter (Alexis Arquette) in the apartment hit scene misses Vincent and Jules (Samuel L. Jackson) while firing at close range; Vincent accidentally kills a captive in the backseat of the car when leaving the scene of the hit; Mia finds Vincent's smack in his coat pocket; Butch happens upon Vincent coming out of the bathroom in his apartment; Butch happens upon Marsellus crossing the street; Marsellus and Butch happen upon the pawn shop. The list could go on.

Through the rearrangement of linear time, interweaving of loosely related storylines, abrupt shiftings of emotional charge, ordinary talk mixed up in extraordinary events, and insertion of random incidents, *Pulp Fiction* is highly predictable in the use of techniques designed to disturb or play havoc with the audience's expectations. In fact, the film makes such repeated use of the unexpected that it undermines the effect to the point of becoming annoyingly formulaic.

The plot of the film, to the extent there is one, serves only as a crude vehicle for setting up alternating scenes of pedestrian conversation and

Alexis Arquette as the shooter who misses Jules and Vincent in _Pulp Fiction_ (1994).

shocking violence, sensual suggestiveness and shocking violence, or violence topped by more shocking violence. The structure of _Pulp Fiction_ is analogous to that of pornographic films in the sense that scenes designed for particular arousal effects are featured more than the storyline.

While the plot may have only supporting role status, there is nevertheless a rudimentary but significant dramatic structure to _Pulp Fiction_. The film borrows from the tradition of noir cinema in creating anti-heroes — protagonists of questionable or compromised virtue — and pitting them against far worse, unambiguously evil types. The trailer for a more recent Tarantino film, _Kill Bill 2_, advertises its merits by boasting, "There are no good guys in a Tarantino film." In Tarantino's noir-fantasy cinematic terrain the question then becomes: Who will be the "baddest" bad guy? Here "baddest" works in two senses: "bad" in the sense of "most vulgar, depraved, or despicably evil" and "bad" in the sense of "toughest survivor in a wicked and ugly world." The latter becomes the "good guy" and the former the "evil guy" and, in the distance between the two, the all-important melodramatic quality of evil is preserved.

Needless to say, this version of noir-styled melodrama only magnifies the undesirable properties of standard melodrama relating to the effects of violence summarized in Chapter 9. It multiplies and amplifies arousal effects in the course of casting about and landing on a dark portrait of contemptible and soon-to-be-dispatched evil (the pawnshop victims, with Vincent a not-too-distant second).

Christopher Vogler in his book on the key elements of screenplay structure, has, along with many film critics, praised *Pulp Fiction* as a good example of "postmodern" filmmaking with its lack of traditional temporal sequence and storyline development. Despite these elements, Vogler argues that the film conforms to key points of dramatic structure. These key points, outlined in his book, are derived from the work of Joseph Campbell on myth and, in generalized form, Vogler believes they are applicable to the interpretation and construction of all stories and screenplays.

Vogler identifies 12 separate stages in what Campbell calls the "hero's journey" that when combined constitute the structure of compelling stories (see Chapter 12 for further discussion of Campbell's work). These 12 stages can be condensed into three sections that roughly correspond to the three acts of a screenplay: Departure (or Separation), Descent (or Initiation), and Return (or Resurrection). These three parts of the dramatic action are not inconsistent with what has been previously asserted about the role of conflict in dramatic structure.

However, Vogler's attempts to locate the key moments of Campbell's mythic structure in *Pulp Fiction* result in an awkward fit and highly contrived conclusions. Vogler identifies three "heroic journeys" corresponding to the three "heroes" of Vincent, Jules, and Butch. The stages of the hero's journey that he extrapolates from Campbell's work are of such a general and flexible nature that Vogler has no difficulty finding evidence for them in the actions of these characters. And this is not surprising, since it would be possible for anyone with a spry imagination to identify these stages even in an ordinary trip to the grocery store. This is not to suggest that Campbell's stages of the mythic journey are not useful in interpreting stories or are not helpful in constructing new stories. Rather, the point is that identifying such stages in a storyline may not in itself lead to a revelation of what is most forcefully operative in the story with respect to structure and the impact of that structure on an audience.

Following the logic dictated by the structure of the mythic analysis, Vogler asserts that the heroes experience a "return" or "resurrection" in the form of a "moral" transformation. In the final sequence of the film, for example, Jules insists that having escaped unharmed after being fired at from close range by the gunman in an earlier apartment scene is a miraculous event and a sign from above. He now resolves to change his life and live more like Caine of the TV series *Kung Fu*, which, according to Vogler, "seems to mean wandering about doing good and seeking peace rather than living a criminal life. He has truly been through a moral resurrection and transformation" (1998: 291).

But this sequence is merely one more in the consistent barrage of whiplash effects. The audience expects that in this final sequence of the film Jules will end up killing the restaurant thief and his girlfriend, but he does not (whiplash!). This sequence goes on interminably as the audience is asked to believe that all the customers in the restaurant will remain docile on the floor and no new customers will enter the building while Jules progressively instructs, lectures, "shepherds," and quotes lengthy passages of scripture to the tense robbers. Perhaps this indicates, as Vogler suggests, the beginning of a change in direction from his past criminal life? But this requires ignoring that Jules proceeds to aid and abet armed robbery as he allows the couple to complete their plundering of the restaurant and all of its hapless customers who have been threatened and intimidated into submission (whiplash again!).

This restaurant sequence is much more convincingly understood as a satirical, even cynical, mocking of moral expectations and traditional codes. Jules's "moral transformation" that "seems to mean wandering about and doing good" applies only in the sense that it appears he will become a mentor for novice criminals. In which case "doing good" is tinged with a troubling irony, as it appears to consist of little more than a shallow "honor among thieves." If there is any shift at all in Jules's character, it is more a shift of style than a significant "moral" transformation.

"Moral transformations" or "resurrections" in the cases of Vincent and Butch are similarly difficult to rationalize. Butch kills Vincent before Vincent undergoes anything like a "transformation" and Butch escapes with his ill-gotten gains, very much the same rogue, if not more of a confirmed rogue, than he was at the beginning of the film.

The fundamental driving premise argued to be operative in *Pulp Fiction*—to give the audience a twisting carnival ride of interrupted anticipations and shocking emotional turns within the overall structure of noir melodrama—provides scant basis for making concessions to "moral" expectations or transcendent resurrections. As its title suggests, *Pulp Fiction* offers "pulp" morality, which is to say, very little that rises to the level of spiritual transformation. The film *is* pulp fiction and *only* pulp fiction with no moral message other than a mocking of standard moral expectations. The characters and their actions, including any possible "transformations," are in fact cheap, shallow, and self-serving and they are designed to be so.

Pulp Fiction is a virtuoso exercise in coarse noir arousal effects and it demonstrates how easily the novelty of a concentrated barrage of these effects by themselves (in other words, with little that may pass for a plot), stylized with a star-studded cast, can win over American as well as foreign audiences and critics. It would seem that Tarantino has pulled off an Andy Warhol con where something tacky, like a soup-can label, is framed in a manner usually reserved for art. The Academy Award nomination for Best Picture and the award for Best Original Screenplay demonstrate that Tarantino succeeded in the con. But since he has also provided every indication that he passionately believes in the noncounterfeit artistic value of his films, it may be assumed that he has also succeeded in conning himself.

The way in which violence is presented in *Pulp Fiction* should not be encouraged by critical acclaim and awards. Through the many conflicts depicted, the film re-presents yet another rendition of the radical polarity of melodramatic structure in which the requisite killings feature victims as either of little or no significance and as eminently worthy of a good snuffing. This is evident in the way in which each killer dispatches his victim or victims without the slightest hesitation or twinge of conscience — in either businesslike or nonchalant ways. The film uses violence for the purpose of producing "cheap thrills" and thereby trivializes victimage and glorifies violent crime through the kind of casual attitude toward killing consistent with the perpetration of its joyride effects. Reports of laughter in some audiences in response to some of the killings in the film (particularly the "accidental" shooting of the victim in Jules's and Vincent's car) should be sufficient to prompt at least a questioning concern about the kind of context for violence the film offers.

Pulp Fiction is certainly good at what it does. And this critical analysis is not intended to suggest that it or similar films should be censored. The point instead is to make the case that what *Pulp Fiction* offers is of questionable value and should be singled out as an example of what *not* to do in filmmaking insofar as negative effects regarding the depiction of violence are a social concern.

25

The Creature Feature: *Jaws* versus *Moby Dick*

In the course of arguing in Chapter 14 that *Moby Dick* is an example of a reflexive form of melodrama that draws into question the underlying melodramatic assumptions about the pursuit of radical evil, it was noted that the story partially resembles the structure of the horror story. However, because of the "monstrous" nature of the white whale and its prominence in the story, there are ways in which *Moby Dick* may be thought to resemble the classic genre of the creature film perhaps more so than the horror story. Concerning the topic of the relevance of melodramatic structure to real life, discussing some of the differences between *Moby Dick* and the creature film may help further illustrate the contrast between melodrama and the questioning of that structure in reflexive melodrama.

The creature story, while conforming to the basic structure of melodrama, presents a slight variation. The classic melodrama features a hero, a villain, and a damsel in distress to which the creature story adds a fourth character, which is not a person but the creature. In the horror story the monster is also the villain and often the Doppelgänger of the hero. In the creature story the creature is clearly a unique character distinct from the hero.

In one variety of the story, the creature is a tool of and larger incarnation of the evil of the villain. In this case both the creature and the villain (or villains) are clearly portrayed as eminently disposable pollutions. The movie *Alien* (1979) and its sequels illustrate this variety. The creature is revealed to be an unredeemably evil and destructive agency sought by a faction of Earth-based conspirators who want to enlist its powers for their wholly evil ends and purposes. Similar themes are explored in *The Thing* (1982, a remake of the 1951 classic).

In another variety, the creature is independent of the villain and the villain also attempts to manipulate it for his evil purposes. However, in this case the creature is shown to be fundamentally not evil. Its destructive actions are instead revealed to be a consequence of its having ventured from or been displaced from its natural habitat. Or the creature's habitat has been altered, violated, or destroyed or its genetic structure has been altered or damaged. Sometimes this creature is ultimately saved and returned to its habitat or it is reluctantly destroyed by the hero for the sake of expediency in saving threatened lives. By contrast the villain is fittingly dispatched — usually by the creature — under circumstances that encourage the celebration of the villain's demise. In this case the creature functions more as "the treasure" (much like the "ark" in *Raiders of the Lost Ark* [1981]) and is, along with "the damsel," the source of conflict between the hero and the villain. *King Kong* (1933), *Jurassic Park* (1993) and *Jurassic Park: The Lost World* (1997) present classic examples of this variety of the creature story.

As the central conflict in the creature story transpires between the stable and morally unambiguous poles of the hero and the villain, the creature may play the role of the villain's agent or the embodiment of the evil of which the villain is a part. *Moby Dick* differs from this version of the creature story by centering the story on a protagonist who initially appears to embody aspects of the hero and who is in pursuit of a creature who appears demonic. In the course of the drama the moral polarity as initially presented from the point of view of the protagonist undergoes a hesitant and temporary reversal. Finally, through scenes that provoke a thorough questioning or displacement of the oppositional structure itself, the reader/audience realizes the protagonist's understanding of the creature, himself, and the world is wholly unreliable. The course of events carries the audience beyond a mere reversal of the moral polarity of the conflict to the point of sensing the dangers inherent in passionate adherence to the moral structure itself.

Jaws (1975) is in some ways a modern cinematic retelling of the story of *Moby Dick* and in that respect would seem to fall more into the category of reflexive melodrama than the creature film genre. Like *Moby Dick*, *Jaws* substitutes the camaraderie of the crew for the relational tensions normally provided by a damsel in distress. And like *Moby Dick*, the story boils down to an exclusively male group on a boat featuring a struggle to the death between a big fish (in this case a great white shark) and a boat captain who is determined to kill it. The captain is an amplification of the

Moby Dick confronts his pursuers (drawing by Raymond Bishop) (from the book *Moby Dick or, The Whale* by Herman Melville. 1939. New York: Albert and Charles Boni, Inc.).

motives of the local mayor who wants the shark killed because it is ruining the summertime commercial attraction of a local beach — the waters of which the shark has made into a feeding ground.

In *Jaws* the shark becomes a predator of humans by aggressively venturing into the human-dominated (albeit "colonized") habitat of coastal waters whereas in *Moby Dick* humans become predators of the whale by aggressively venturing into the whale-dominated habitat of the deep sea.

Since whaling is an aggressive act against whales, Moby Dick's aggression against whaling boats in general and the *Pequod* in particular is more readily understood (by the reader/audience) as defensive than is the shark's aggression in *Jaws*. This difference in the *Jaws* story, combined with the early scenes focusing on the shark's attacks on unsuspecting bathers and the later scenes focusing on the shark's offensive attack on the boat, leaves the audience at the conclusion of *Jaws*, more so than in *Moby Dick*, sensing that the captain went down with the boat in a heroic effort to rid the waters of an evil pollution — a shark bent on aggressively attacking humans.

Consequently, *Jaws* does not significantly convey a sense of the shark as a creature whose tracking and persecution as "evil" is brought into question. *Jaws* is thereby less likely than *Moby Dick* to accomplish a reversal of the initial melodramatic structure and, in doing so, provoke the complex ambiguities and reflexive questionings of motive and moral structure found in *Moby Dick*. A similar judgment can be brought against the stock of creature feature films that rarely if ever venture beyond the standard melodramatic plot.

26

Religious Melodrama:
The Passion of the Christ

It might be assumed that if there exists a context in which the depiction of violence may be *invariably* experienced as something beneficially illuminating and worthwhile, even in its horror, it would be in the context of a portrayal of the fate of Jesus after the Last Supper. Mel Gibson's *The Passion of the Christ* (2004), however, demonstrates this assumption to be incorrect. Instead Gibson demonstrated how violence, even when presented in the context of Christ's passion, can be harmful and pernicious in its effects — precisely by transforming that context into a message of stark melodrama between flesh and spirituality.

The consensus of opinion among professional film critics has been predominantly one of disapproval of the film in general and disgust with the portrayal of violence in particular. Leon Wieseltier of *The New Republic*, for example, writes with an unreserved sense of distraught amazement: "The only cinematic achievement of *The Passion of the Christ* is that it breaks new ground in the verisimilitude of filmed violence. The notion that there is something spiritually exalting about the viewing of it is quite horrifying. The viewing of *The Passion* ... is a profoundly brutalizing experience. Children must be protected from it.... Torture has been depicted in film many times before, but almost always in a spirit of protest. This film makes no quarrel with the pain that it excitedly inflicts. It is a repulsive masochistic fantasy, a sacred snuff film, and it leaves you with the feeling that the man who made it hates life" (2004: 19).

With an equal sense of disbelief and dismay, David Denby of *The New Yorker* writes that "as a viewer, I am ... free to say that the movie Gibson

310

has made from his personal obsessions is a sickening death trip
unilluminating procession of treachery, beatings, blood, and agony — .....
to say so without indulging in 'anti–Christian sentiment' (Gibson's term
for what his critics are spreading). For two hours, with only an occasional
pause or gentle flashback, we watch, stupefied, as a handsome, strapping,
at times half-naked man (James Caviezel) is slowly tortured to death. Gibson is so thoroughly fixated on the scourging and crushing of Christ, and
so meagerly involved in the spiritual meanings of the final hours, that he
falls in danger of altering Jesus' message of love into one of hate" (2004:
84).

The scourging scene — without any question — goes on far too long
and is overly obsessed with recording the minutest detail of the implements
of torture, the contact of the barbs with the flesh, the flow of blood, the
sounds of agony, and the expressions of relish and satisfaction on the faces
of the Roman perpetrators. This kind of attention to and purposefully
drawn-out dwelling upon the details of a terrible flogging can scarcely be
understood from any perspective other than sadomasochistic fascination
with pain.

When interviewed on a television talk show, Caviezel described his
experience during the filming of the scourging scene. At one point, the
person administering the flogging missed the protection applied to
Caviezel's back and the actor felt the real effect of the blow. He said that
this one blow took his breath away so completely that he could not draw
any air for a few long seconds and filming had to pause. At this point a
new means of filming the scene had to be devised in order to continue.

Caviezel's description of the effects of this single accidentally inflicted
blow provides firsthand confirmation of the opinion expressed by many
that no human being could survive the kind of intense flogging depicted
in Gibson's film —claims of "historical accuracy" notwithstanding. All of
which gives added weight to the words of Katha Pollitt: "The Bible's brief
mention of Jesus' flogging — one sentence in three Gospels, nothing in
one — becomes a ten-minute homoerotic sadistic extravaganza that no
human being could have survived, as if the point of the Passion was to
show how tough Christ was" (2004: 9).

Pollitt's comment raises the question: What *is* the point of this excessive portrayal of the flogging — not to mention the similarly excessive
dwelling on brutality in the scenes of the carrying of the cross and the
crucifixion? Any justification for such scenes of violence must be deeply
rooted in a theme that needs— and in fact demands— this kind of thorough and prolonged depiction in order to properly instill the weight of its
message. But what message would benefit from the weight of such violence?

An answer to this question is offered in a few of the printed mail responses to Denby's review in *The New Yorker*. Sharon Baker of Indianapolis, Indiana, for example, explains, "The Resurrection is, as Denby writes, the miracle in the story, but if we see only the Resurrection we miss much of its lesson. Because Jesus suffered, we know that God understands our suffering, and are able to fully connect with God during our darkest times. That is the spirituality in 'The Passion.' And, despite what Denby says, it does matter" (March 15, 2004: 18).

In his letter to *The New Yorker*, Mark Aalund, a pastor in Lakewood, Colorado, elaborates on "the lesson" to be learned from Jesus' suffering: "In the face of mankind's cruelty to a fellow human being, which also represents humanity's most violent rejection of God, Jesus could hang on the Cross, flayed, tortured, and beaten, and could pray, 'Father, forgive them, for they know not what they do.' Love like this provides the greatest hope one can find in this life, and a major theme of Gibson's film is that God's grace and forgiveness go deeper than the lowest depths that humanity can reach" (March 15, 2004: 18).

Understanding the human capacity for hatred and for inflicting violence on other human beings is an important lesson to learn about human nature. Certainly the torturing and the crucifixion of Christ can serve as a reminder of this human capacity and Christ's refusal to respond to it with equal disregard and hatred provides an exemplary model — albeit a difficult one to live up to. But is the message of returning love and forgiveness for hatred and violence adequately served by immersing oneself in every agonizing moment of Christ's passion? Where does and should Christ's example *stop* being an example? The *manner* and *extent* to which Christ's example is emulated and imitated in varieties of art as well as in attitudes and actions in life is a matter that the Christian tradition has often failed to properly sort out no less than Gibson's film.

It would seem, by a close interpretation of Christ's example, that the body is, on the one hand, a thing of little consequence and, on the other hand, a source of terrible temptation and depravity. On the path to redemption and resurrection, Christ's body is, with little resistance on his part, completely rendered up to destruction. And human "weakness of the flesh" is, for example, the source of Christ's temptation in the Garden of Gethsemane as well as the source of the failing that results in the brutality of his captors, persecutors, and executioners.

It can be reasonably asked of Gibson's film: Is the deprecation of the body then, too, part of "the lesson" of the Passion and an indication of the disregard and mortification it must undergo in order to gain entrance into the kingdom of heaven? Such interpretations of the body have definitely been a part of certain broad strains of Christian tradition and Gibson's film does little to dispel such interpretations and much to excite them.

In yet another exceptional departure from an "accurate" rendering of the text of the Gospels, Gibson embellishes the story of Christ's last hours with images of Satan and of demonlike creatures. The image of Satan is particularly interesting in that it is conveyed in the temptation scene in the Garden of Gethsemane through the use of human form with a feminine-looking face, a maggot partly visible moving out from one of the nostrils, and a serpent slithering at the feet. These three images combine to evoke Satan but they also combine to evoke the deprecation of the body: woman, symbol of the body; worm, symbol of corruption and defilement; and serpent, symbol of the "weakness of the flesh"—borrowed from that other garden scene back at the beginning of "the Fall."

When the image of Satan appears again near the end of the crucifixion scene, it becomes clear that Gibson's film intends to present the Passion as Christ's triumph over darkness and God's triumph over Satan. These images convey a theme in which the cosmos and everything in it is divided by the conflict between good and evil and is redeemed and purified through following the example of Christ's sacrifice and surrender to the will of God. Similarly, Christ's Passion shows the sacrifice of the body (and the worldliness that goes with it) for the sake of the salvation of the spirit.

In their work entitled *Projecting the Shadow* (1995), Rushing and Frentz describe this process as the "esoteric" understanding of the Christian myth (the "exoteric" version of the myth is discussed in Chapter 22): "As an infant, Christ is the 'divine child,' a personification of the Self archetype, the potential for wholeness in all of us that is constantly threatened by hostile forces.... To move toward wholeness, a person follows Christ's example as an adult and sacrifices one's self, or, in psychological terms, the ego, on the 'cross.' ... Christianity ... address[es] the problem of the shadow, that rejected part of us all which is projected onto an Other, a devil figure that carries the sins of humanity.... Taken as an example, Christ's crucifixion models what each person must do him- or herself—namely, let the ego 'die' as the sovereign center of the psyche so that the Self can take its place" (180).

Gibson's *The Passion of the Christ* follows this "esoteric" understanding and is structured as a grand melodrama in which a radical conflict is exposed. Through the heroic sacrifice of his body, Christ overcomes evil and thereby opens a path for the salvation of the spirit of every human being and the overcoming of the essential evil in human nature. But to gain this salvation that Christ makes possible each person must follow his example and "sacrifice" the flesh for the sake of spiritual redemption.

Jesus (James Caviezel) after the scourging in *The Passion of the Christ* (2004).

In this melodramatic context, the deadly violence dealt to Christ must be understood, not as essentially the work of Jews or Romans, but as the work of Jews and Romans and ultimately everyone — as even Peter is shown to deny Christ in his hour of need. It is not the defiled nature of a few who must be held accountable. It is the defiled and depraved element in the essence of humanity, in each person, that must be cleansed. As Mark Aalund indicates in his letter cited above, the violence done to Christ's body — which is unremittingly and graphically depicted in Gibson's film — is symbolic of the depths of this depravity across human nature and, in fact, nature itself.

Gibson's acquaintance with a ratio between the degree of depravity of the flesh and the measure of violence needed to atone for it is not new. In his insightful commentary on Gibson's *Braveheart* (1995), William Luhr makes explicit reference to this ratio as it especially emerges in the concluding scenes featuring William Wallace (played by Mel Gibson). Luhr notes, "Wallace's death scene in *Braveheart* focuses with masochistic intensity upon its hero's dying agonies. Wallace has no hope of survival; the scene is about his pain.... This is not to discount the film's efforts to glorify him as triumphant in defeat.... While [the film] ... narrativize[s] his agonies as evidence of his moral triumph, [it does] so in a way that still revels in the public display of his pain. Implicitly, the worse it gets, the better it gets, and this context is profoundly Christian" (1999: 240).

Luhr explains further the connection between Christianity and physical pain whereby "Christianity ... exhibits a remarkable obsession with Christ's agonies and death ... focus[ing] in extraordinary ways upon the sacrificial death of its god.... [Its] most resonant symbol [being] the crucifix — the image of Christ enduring a torturous death" (240). The explicit manner of Christ's death is held up as the supreme example of the triumph of the devout spirit over the profane body. The message in *Braveheart* conveyed through the painful sacrificial death of its hero parallels the message in the esoteric Christian tradition whereby, in Luhr's words, "The exemplary Christian masochist seeks to remake him- or herself according to the model of the suffering Christ" (241).

The Passion of the Christ offers the same model and encourages the imitation of this model through its glorification. Furthermore, any potential message of love in Christ's teachings is all but obliterated, as Denby rightly notes, in the sweep of the images of violence as they overwhelmingly communicate a message of painful "sacrifice." This profoundly tortured sacrifice of a purely innocent victim evokes emotions of hatred toward the villainous agents (not to mention oneself) who, in their exceptional weakness and sinfulness under the influence of satanic forces, do not merely inflict the painful sacrifice but, as agents of extreme evil, exemplify and embody the necessity for the *intensity* of the sacrificial beating.

The notion of self-realization or transcendence implicit in the esoteric understanding of Christianity rests on a radically violent model of conflict. The choice of depicting the conflict dividing human nature, and ultimately the self, in terms of the antagonistic and mutually exclusive opposites of good and evil, structures the conflict in ways that leave no alternative but to embrace the extreme violence of the kill as the proper course of resolution. The "resolution" that is Christ's sacrifice (and through his example each person's sacrifice) ensures and reproduces the mirror reflection of the "sin" of defilement implied in the necessity for his slaying.

Those who praise Gibson's film and the soul searching it calls for may well extend that soul searching into the question of whether the image of the kill and the necessity of the kill — and the attendant image of a defiled humanity — rightly define and characterize the essence of the division within and between human beings.

Appendix 1

Effects of Tragic Drama: Plato versus Aristotle

Two pillars of the tradition, Plato and Aristotle, provide the earliest philosophical grounding for what have emerged as the two primary answers to the question of effects resulting from the viewing of dramatic presentations in general and depictions of violent and tragic events in particular. While discussing art and poetics respectively, Plato presents, on one side, the case for the generally harmful effects of "mimesis" while, on the other side, Aristotle argues for the primarily beneficial effects of "catharsis."

Plato saves his discussion of mimesis for Book X, the final book, of his most famous dialogue, *The Republic.* After first discussing the visual art of painting, Plato turns to the "hearing" arts of poetry, especially the art of Homer and the tragic poets. Broadly speaking, he argues that art in general and poetry and drama in particular, imitate life and that, as all mere imitations must, they serve to distort reality and mislead the seeker of truth. Here Plato merely acknowledges what, according to him, has long been observed to be the case — that there is an ancient "quarrel between philosophy and poetry" (607b).

This "quarrel," according to Plato, turns on a question of proper authority in relation to conduct. Concerning the emotions of sex and anger and all the appetites and pains and pleasures of the body, Plato claims that the effect of poetic imitation is the same: "it waters and fosters these feelings when what we ought to do is to dry them up, and it establishes them as our rulers when they ought to be ruled, to the end that we may be better and happier men instead of worse and more miserable" (606d).

Plato's answer to the question "What ought to rule these feelings?" is not difficult to guess. After proposing that a "good and reasonable" man would resist the tendency to a public display of grief when confronted with a grave misfortune such as the loss of a child, he explains that resistance to bare feeling is appropriate and rightly the "law" and custom of the land.

Setting forth two contrasting responses to calamity — overwrought emotional display or restrained deliberation — Plato, true to the instincts of a philosopher, favors deliberation. Pressing his case further, Plato complains that the poet chooses to imitate that part of reality leading us to "dwell in memory on our suffering." Moreover, the poet also chooses not to appeal to "the better part of the soul" but rather seeks to win the favor of the crowd by devising characters of a "fretful and complicated type" because they are "easy to imitate."

But Plato is not primarily concerned with problems posed by mimesis in the way in which *art imitates life*. He is more concerned about the inverse relation made famous centuries later in Oscar Wilde's memorable conceit that *life imitates art*. This becomes clear when Plato says of mimesis, "We have not yet brought our chief accusation against it. Its power to corrupt, with rare exceptions, even the better sort is surely the chief cause for alarm.... I think you know that the very best of us feel pleasure when we hear Homer or some other of the makers of tragedy imitating one of the heroes who is in grief, and is delivering a long tirade in his lamentations or chanting and beating his breast. [We] abandon ourselves and accompany the representation with sympathy and eagerness and we praise as an excellent poet the one who most strongly affects us this way" (605c–605e).

The portrayal of emotional response in the face of tragedy exerts a seductive power to evoke imitative responses culminating, Plato claims, in a collective emotional drunkenness that would, in other contexts, induce a sense of shame. Wholesale abandonment to the emotional promptings of the dramatic portrayal comes with a price: "few are capable of reflecting that what we enjoy in others will inevitably react upon ourselves. For after feeding fat the emotion of pity there [in tragic drama] it is not easy to restrain it in our own sufferings" (606b).

First the tragic poet selects a part of reality that is "easy to imitate" and sensationalistic in its emotional power. Then that imitation — which does not appeal to the "better part of the soul"— is in turn imitated.

However, in the course of elaborating on his concern about the endorsement and encouragement of the free expressions of fear, pity, and grief — implicit in the intentional stimulation of these emotions in tragic drama — it becomes manifestly clear that Plato does not share the predominant concern of contemporary society. Plato was not worried about the possibility that, upon hearing Clytemnestra kill her husband Agamemnon (offstage) in a performance of the *Oresteia*, women of the audience would be inclined to go home and knife their husbands.

Unlike the contemporary focus on the possibilities for propagation of violence through imitative *actions*, Plato is instead concerned about the arousal of *emotions* and their potential to render a person incapable of clear thinking. And whereas current concerns center on the possibility that violent media will promote *insensitivity* in an audience, the primary ancient concern, at least with regard to Plato, seems to have been that such depictions would overly *sensitize* an audience.

Although Plato's extreme privileging of "deliberative" over "emotional" behavior has been seriously challenged in contemporary thought, it need not distract attention from the general substance of his thoughts on mimesis. And even though he is primarily concerned with audience mirroring of *emotional* behaviors within the spectrum of grief, pity, and the like, the principle of mimesis presented by Plato may be extended through various dramatic contexts to include the potential for imitation of any form of depicted behavior.

But Aristotle seriously challenges Plato's case against imitation, especially the harmful effects of tragic drama. His *Poetics* conveys an admiration for tragic drama that clearly shows he, unlike the Plato of Book X of *The Republic*, regards the mimesis of artistic representation as more likely beneficial than harmful. The chief benefit, of course, consists of a transformation in the viewing audience brought about through the process he names as "catharsis."

However, there is considerable difference of opinion among the experts about what precisely Aristotle has in mind when he uses the word "catharsis" in the *Poetics*. The difficulty of translation has been complicated since, as one prominent scholar notes, the word "catharsis" appears "suddenly, without explanation, into the definition of tragedy and is not heard of again" (Vickers, 1973: 609). The famous passage in question with the relevant words emphasized is as follows:

> A tragedy, then, is the imitation of an action that is serious and also, as having magnitude, complete in itself; in language with pleasurable accessories, each kind brought in separately in the parts of the work; in a dramatic, not in a narrative form; *with incidents arousing pity and fear, wherewith to accomplish its catharsis of such emotions.* (*Poetics*, book 6, 1449b) [As explained in Chapter Six, the Greek words "eleos" and "phobos" usually translated as in the above citation as "pity" and "fear" are herein translated and used as "ruth" and "awe" in senses somewhat analogous to "ruth" in the word "ruthless" and "awe" in the word "awful."]

Aristotle agrees with Plato in viewing drama as an instance of the adage that art imitates life. But Aristotle is more specific about the kind of imitation presented in tragic drama: "Tragedy is essentially an imitation not of persons but of action and life.... In a play accordingly they do not act in order to portray the characters; they include the characters for the sake of the action. So that it is the action in it, i.e., its plot, that is the end and purpose of the tragedy; and the end is everywhere the chief thing" (1450a). The action or plot of tragic drama will be the kind with incidents arousing ruth and awe.

Aristotle and Plato are also in agreement that emotional *arousal* is among the incontestable effects of viewing tragic drama. However, for Plato, arousal seems to constitute the entire "tragic pleasure" whereas for Aristotle it is only a part that must then be completed by catharsis. Catharsis, as it has been commonly translated, refers to the "purging" of emotions— in this case ruth and awe.

But at this point many commentators on the *Poetics* find a difficulty in Aristotle's analysis. If catharsis is assumed, as translation would suggest, to indicate the condition of being *purged* of such emotions, it is not clear how *arousal* necessarily accomplishes or connects with a state of being purged. The nineteenth-century German philosopher Friedrich Nietzsche takes Aristotle to task on this issue.

Never one to mince words, Nietzsche's pompous disagreement with Aristotle is as amusing as it is illustrative. "On repeated occasions I have laid my finger on Aristotle's great misunderstanding in believing the tragic affects to be two *depressive* affects, terror and pity. If he were right, tragedy would be an art dangerous to life: one would have to warn against it as notorious and a public danger." Nietzsche then goes on to directly challenge Aristotle's claim regarding catharsis and tragic drama: "for that one is 'purged' of these affects through their arousal, as Aristotle seemed to believe, is simply not true" (1967: 449).

Having insisted that tragic drama, with its depictions of violent conflict, cannot be an art "dangerous to life," Nietzsche then dismisses Aristotle's theory of tragic emotions and proposes his own alternative: "One can refute this theory [that the tragic affects are, in Nietzsche's words, terror and pity] in the most cold-blooded way: namely, by measuring the effects of a tragic emotion with a dynamometer. And one would discover as a result what ultimately only the absolute mendaciousness of a systematizer could misunderstand: that tragedy is a *tonic*" (1967: 449).

In summation, Nietzsche makes three points in quick succession: (1) if tragic drama were designed to arouse awe and ruth, it would not purge these affects— since arousal does not guarantee a release from these emotions; (2) tragic drama does not (or need not primarily) arouse awe and ruth — which are "depressive affects;" and (3) instead it imparts *tonic* or invigorating affects.

For Nietzsche, there is no question that tragic drama, with its violent conflicts and catastrophic denouements, brings the spectator into full awareness of the *risks* of life and in doing so stimulates the tense exhilaration associated with vulnerability, exposure to danger, and the appetite for challenge. The flood of adrenalin and a sensation of elevated powers of perception and response constitute the tragic pleasure. As Nietzsche explains, "broadly speaking, a preference for questionable and terrifying things is a symptom of strength.... It is a sign of one's feeling of power and well-being how far one can acknowledge the terrifying and questionable character of things" (1967: 450).

The "tonic" theory regarding response to tragic drama may be an aesthetic equivalent of "the roller coaster effect." Why do some people willingly subject themselves to a carnival ride that others readily admit terrifies them? The plunging and turning motions of the roller coaster combined with speed creates a sensation of extreme arousal as strength is generated necessary to meet the challenge of the contrived situation. The exhilaration of the adrenalin "high" continues after the ride in the lingering sensation of having "risen to the occasion." To use a pharmaceutical analogy, for Nietzsche tragic drama is a stimulant and, for Aristotle (in Nietzsche's view), it is more like a sedative.

Although commentators such as Nietzsche question the pleasurable aspects of an arousal of ruth and awe and the compatibility of arousal and catharsis, many believe a solution lies in the famous catharsis passage. In his work on the *Poetics* Gerald Else finds most commentators in agreement "that the emotional change [or effect of tragic drama] is brought about *by* ... pity and fear: the pity and fear aroused in the spectator *somehow* purge and purify themselves" (1957: 227, emphasis added). The controversy, reflected in the word "somehow," lies in understanding exactly how catharsis is achieved *in and through* arousal.

One explanation for this process lies in the notion of energy expenditure. Understanding the unity between arousal and catharsis may require nothing more than recalling an instance of prolonged arousal of intense emotion, such as the fear that might be aroused by driving a long stretch of icy road in bad weather, and the relief that follows upon the disappearance of the stimulus, the exit from the road at the destination. As in the case of the roller coaster ride, the arousal is a consumption of energy that, if sufficiently intense and prolonged, will culminate in a sense of dissipation as the medium of tension, the body, is drained of energy. In the case of tragic drama, aroused emotions of ruth and awe may stimulate the body, leaving in their wake a sense of expenditure that may be rightly characterized as a purging or catharsis. Like the aftermath of exercise, this effect will be experienced as welcomed change insofar as expended energy results in a depletion that corresponds to a sensation of absence of tension.

Granting this depletion theory, the distance Nietzsche sees between his view and Aristotle's may not be as great as he imagines. The sensation of catharsis associated with a prolonged arousal of emotional tension consistent with intense sympathetic grief, for example, may be a close cousin of the sensation of exhilaration and empowerment derived from so-called tonic emotions aroused when confronting the challenge of a disturbing insight. At the end of a tragic drama, the sense of dissipation achieved through the arousal of "depressive affects" need not be seen as entirely foreign from the sense of invigoration gained as the net result of the arousal of "tonic affects." Both results appear to involve a feeling of renewal in the lapse of tension following a period of stimulation.

This similarity of cathartic and tonic outcomes in the relation between arousal and relief is supported by Zillman's research and his theory of excitation transfer. This theory proposes that intense emotional arousal resulting, for example, from viewing a dramatic conflict will, at the conclusion of the viewing, result in a *transfer* of the intensity of arousal to the calmer emotional state resulting from the absence of the viewing stimulus. In other words, the net result will be the creation of a sensation of relief proportional to the intensity of the previous degree of stimulation.

Insofar as significant release from any form of emotional tension can be experienced as energizing, cathartic purging and invigoration, as potential states produced in viewers at the end of a tragic drama, may refer to similar qualities of experience — although some persons may traverse visibly different paths to a similar state. Moreover, in this context Nietzsche's claim that "terror and pity" (or awe and ruth) are reliably "depressive affects" ought to be questioned. Their arousal in most persons would no doubt produce a significant reading on his "dynamometer." The important point remains that so-called depressive and tonic affects both create expenditures of emotional energy and in that sense function as stimulation. In the discussion of his differences with Aristotle, Nietzsche ultimately concedes that the extent to which tragic drama is experienced as fundamentally depressive or energizing may depend on the psychological orientation or disposition of the viewer — which includes the viewer's sense of immersion in a particular relational and emotional context.

Returning briefly to Plato, Aristotle's notion of catharsis is not necessarily inconsistent with the desire for emotional control in the face of adversity that obviously concerns Plato. As the views of Aristotle and Nietzsche imply, the expression of emotion in the artificially created settings of tragic drama may in fact help prepare members of the audience for real life by enabling them to better anticipate the complexity and depth of real conflict and thereby react with a more measured emotional response instead of, as Plato suggests, with an excessive emotional response. Aristotle and Nietzsche are likely in agreement with Plato about the desirability of emotional management. In which case there may be disagreement between the three only over the practical effects of the arousal of emotion through viewing tragic drama.

But even this disagreement may not be fundamental. If tonic and cathartic effects are not essentially dissimilar and if catharsis is achieved through arousal of imitative emotional responses, then catharsis may simply be mimesis of sufficient intensity to produce a *physical* response that brings a measure of culmination or completion to the mimed emotions. However, as explained in Chapter 11, the type of emotions aroused and the quality of physical response necessary to achieve effective catharsis may vary between dramas with significantly different plot structures such as melodrama and tragic drama.

Although appearing to be at odds, the mimetic and the cathartic are not necessarily *opposing* effects. Granting as much, it becomes possible to understand mimetic, cathartic, and tonic effects as compatible and sharing the same continuum.

In summary, it may be concluded that in an overall sense the effects generated by exposure to tragic drama may be understood as fundamentally mimetic in nature. And if imitation is the most basic effect in this case, the hazards of fictional violence in general loom larger. The central question then becomes: To what extent do mimetic effects— achieved through identification with various characters and situations—*also become cathartic* and thereby ultimately function as completions rather than enhancements and sensitizations, as Plato might claim, of emotions consistent with the dramatic portrayal? Chapter 11 takes up this question and makes the case for a possible answer in relation to dramatic structure, suggesting that a thorough and effectual catharsis requires more than simply the relief or depletion effects following the termination of a source of stimulation.

Appendix 2
Methodology

As mentioned in Chapter 1, Twitchell's star has fallen somewhat in relation to methodological approach in the wake of more recent "postmodern" critical appraisals. Twitchell employs a Freudian-influenced psychoanalytically informed mode of structuralism to expose the secrets of the classic horror film. He describes the task in the following way:

> What is needed to explain horror is, I think, a broad approach, an ethnological approach, in which the various stories are analyzed as if no one individual telling really mattered, as if each version were but a chapter which may or may not be finally included. You search for what is stable and repeated; you neglect what is "artistic" and "original." That is why, for me, auteur criticism is quite beside the point in explaining horror.... The critic's first job ... is not to fix the images at their every appearance but, instead, to trace their migrations to the audience and, only then, try to understand why they have been crucial enough to pass along [1985: 84].

Treating horror stories much like fairy tales, Twitchell assumes, for example, that a film such as *Night of the Living Dead* (1968) — insofar as it conforms to the basics of horror genre — will generate the same crucially relevant audience responses and serve the same basic function as, for example, the 1931 film version of the horror classic *Dracula*. Audience reactions of horror will be predominantly the same because the structure and needs of the human psyche as well as the structure and function of the horror film remain essentially the same.

In recent years this mythic-structural mode of analysis has been grouped along with "genre criticism" as a suspect methodology and has drawn considerable scorn from postmodern aligned critics such as Jonathan Lake Crane. According to these critics, the genre concept misleads analysts by promoting facile assumptions about genres as unchanging metanarratives or "transcendental signifiers" and similarly presumptuous intuitions about the timeless universality of a "repressed id" to which these genre structures appeal.

Lake Crane, for example, argues that by attempting to ground interpretation of the "horror genre" in structural and psychological constants as Twitchell does, "we dismiss, all too lightly, the possibility that horror films have something to say about popular epistemology, about the status of contemporary community, or about the fearsome power of modern technology" (1994: 29). According to Lake Crane, the changes evident in horror films between pre–and post–World War II, the Cold War, the Vietnam War, and the post–Iron Curtain periods require giving primary attention to the "historical relation" of these films "to the times of the people who made and understood them" (39). Ignoring such historical grounding risks losing sight of what may have been the most essential elements of appeal and current import for the audiences of these horror creations.

As the argument goes, the assumptions grounding the mythic-structural methodology of discovery substantially dismiss or elide differences of contemporary settings and contemporary needs and desires. While not denying the presence of certain underlying shared features that may substantiate inclusion in a genre, it is claimed that contextual and temporal differences function *more crucially* than any corresponding similarities. Just as individual words can significantly change their meaning over time, the texts or plots of the same horror stories may change radically in the way in which they are interpreted, thereby altering the way in which they are appropriated to serve changing needs and desires. Similar plot structures, therefore, may also be deceptive by seeming to appeal to the same needs while actually appealing to very different needs. This possibility prompts one of the cautionary slogans of postmodernism: the same does not necessarily mean the same. In other words, the transformational potential for difference must everywhere be given its due.

However, despite these important considerations, there are features of the human psyche as well as elements of genre stories that — like features of the human face — remain the same. As Twitchell remarks, "The motifs inherent in the mythography ... are indomitable because these motifs are linked, not only to culture, but to biology" (1985: 86). Because human beings are organisms in which the potential for pain and pleasure, death and sex, perception and cognition, and other biological factors shape and limit experience, the quality and structure of that experience — even while possibly exhibiting an infinite variety of pattern — will turn on combinations of persistent and prominent forces.

Focusing too intently on unique times and audiences, Twitchell argues, blocks access to the discovery of the potential for recurring functions and effects in stories and narratives. This "local" focus risks a version of the "intentional fallacy" by consciously reconciling "received myth" with contemporary psychology and contemporary crises. In Twitchell's view, "because myths are lines of travel through difficult passages, we find them wherever confusion exists— usually in childhood and adolescence." Myths then feature alternative choices and suggest what the myth-telling society believes are the best choices. In this sense, according to Twitchell, myths contain at some level the most "sacred truths" of a society and the memory of these truths must not be allowed to lapse because without them "there could be no lasting culture" (1985: 84–85). For Twitchell, then, what remains in some sense "the same" in myths peculiar to a given culture functions *more crucially* than aspects of contextual and temporal difference. In this respect, Twitchell may err too much in the direction of transcendent sameness whereas Lake Crane may err too much in the direction of local and temporal difference.

The tension between the approaches of Lake Crane and Twitchell cannot be readily resolved by trying to strike a balance through a diligent logging of elements of sameness and difference. Such attempts at balance lead to programmatic applications that may have little to do with an adequate understanding of particular outcomes and situations. It may be possible to initiate a better approach by acknowledging an irreducible tension between forces whose combined interaction yields effects that may, in particular contexts, be judged same or different. Over time, one or another force may dominate in particular contexts but not in any reliably predictable proportion or harmonious ordering or economy. In which case it will always be necessary to exercise an interpretive vigilance toward what appears "the same" and what appears "different"— a vigilance that necessitates always looking, probing, and looking again. This may be the sense in which it is possible in the case of the same and the different to give each its due beyond what may be regarded as artificial or illusory impositions of balance.

Mandelbrot fractal geometry and chaos theory illustrate this possibility. These mathematical sciences have demonstrated remarkable similarities with biological patterns and have shown that extraordinarily complex structures can arise from extraordinarily simple generative formulas. They have also revealed how it is possible that instances of a "pattern" can be at once *unique* and *alike* as a result of an interactive play of forces or factors. Forces underlying the appearance of "sameness" and "difference" remain of equal significance — not in perceptively balanced measure but in alternating and not readily discernible modes of dominance through particular temporally unfolding instances.

Similarly, a collection of films that may appear to analysts as loosely belonging to a genre and that may exhibit sufficient variety to suggest the irrelevance or futility of the genre designation may nevertheless be grounded in and generated through the interaction of a few key factors whose functional relation may be identifiable. This possibility underscores the methodological assumption used to guide this inquiry. The background arena for these "functional relations" is herein referred to as the "metaphysical" layer. Such an approach may be understood as neo- or poststructuralist because it takes into consideration the postmodern critique of the transcendental feature of modernist structuralism while nevertheless continuing to give structure (or a new understanding of structure) a place in efforts to understand natural and social processes.

As argued in Chapter 1, Twitchell may not have found an adequate negotiation between structure and variation, sameness and difference, in his explanation of the appeal and cultural value of the "horror story" as grounded in the incest prohibition and its set of binary moral choices. But his work serves well as a point of departure into the metaphysical layer that underlies the methodology used to create the stories being investigated as well as the metaphysical layer underlying the methodology of investigation itself.

Bibliography

Althusser, Louis. "Ideology and Ideological State Apparatuses." Ben Brewster, trans. In *Critical Theory Since 1965*. Hazard Adams and Leroy Searle, ed. Tallahassee: University Presses of Florida, 1989. (First published 1970.)

American Academy of Pediatrics. *Joint Statement on the Impact of Entertainment Violence on Children*. Congressional Public Health Summit, July 26, 2000. Available at www.aap.org/advocacy/releases/jstmtevc.htm.

American Psychiatric Association. *Psychiatric Effects of Media Violence*. 2004. Available at www.psych.org/public_info/media_violence.cfm.

Andrews, Nigel. *True Myths: The Life and Times of Arnold Schwarzenegger*. Secaucus, NJ: Birch Lane Press, 1996.

Ardrey, Robert. *The Territorial Imperative: A Personal Inquiry into the Animal Origins of Property and Nations*. New York: Atheneum, 1966.

Aristotle. *The Complete Works of Aristotle*. Jonathan Barnes, ed. Princeton, NJ: Princeton University Press, 1984.

Bailey, Andrew. "A Clockwork Utopia: Semi-Scrutable Stanley Kubrick Discusses His New Film." *Rolling Stone*, #100, Jan. 20, 1972, pp. 20–22.

Bandura, Albert. "Social Cognitive Theory for Personal and Social Change by Enabling Media." In *Entertainment Education and Social Change*. Arvind Singhal, Michael J. Cody, Everett M. Rogers, and Miguel Sabido, eds. Mahwah, NJ: Lawrence Erlbaum, 2004.

Barber, Benjamin R. "Jihad vs. McWorld." *The Atlantic Monthly*. Vol. 269, #3, pp. 53–63, 1992.

Barker, Kenneth L., ed. *The Holy Bible, New International Version*. Grand Rapids, MI: Zondervan, 2002.

Baudrillard, Jean. *Fatal Strategies*. Philip Beitchman and W. G. J. Niesluchowski, trans. New York: Semiotext[e], 1990. (First published 1983.)

_____. *Simulations*. Paul Foss, Paul Patton, and Philip Beitchman, trans. New York: Semiotext[e], 1983. (First published 1981.)

Baxter, John. *Stanley Kubrick: A Biography*. New York: Carrol and Graf, 1997.

Becker, Ernest. *Escape from Evil*. New York: Free Press, 1975.

Bellinger, Charles K. *The Genealogy of Violence: Reflections on Creation, Freedom, and Evil*. New York: Oxford University Press, 2001.

Berdyaev, Nikolai. *The Russian Revolution*. Ann Arbor: University of Michigan Press, 1961.

Berra, Yogi (with Dave Kaplan). *Ten Rings: My Championship Seasons*. New York: HarperCollins, 2003.

Bettelheim, Bruno. *The Uses of Enchant-

ment. New York: Alfred A. Knopf, 1976.

Black, Joel. *The Aesthetics of Murder: A Study in Romantic Literature and Contemporary Culture.* Baltimore: Johns Hopkins University Press, 1991.

Bok, Sissela. *Mayhem: Violence as Public Entertainment.* New York: Addison Wesley, 1998.

Borradori, Giovanna. *Philosophy in a Time of Terror: Dialogues with Jürgen Habermas and Jacques Derrida.* Chicago: University of Chicago Press, 2003.

Bostdorff, Denise M. "George W. Bush's Post-September 11 Rhetoric of Covenant Renewal: Upholding the Faith of the Greatest Generation." *The Quarterly Journal of Speech,* Vol. 89, #4, pp. 293–319, 2003.

Bulzone, Marisa, ed. *Grimm's Grimmest.* San Francisco: Chronicle Books, 1997. (The primary German-language source for the stories included in this volume is *Kinder- und Hausmärchen gesammelt durch die Brüder Grimm* edited by Heinz Rölleke, Frankfurt a.M.: Deutscher Klassiker Verlag, 1985.)

Burgess, Anthony. *Little Wilson and Big God.* New York: Weidenfeld & Nicolson, 1986.

_____. *You've Had Your Time: The Second Part of the Confessions.* New York: Wiedenfeld & Nicolson, 1991. (First published in 1990.)

Burke, Kenneth. "Catharsis—Second View." *Centennial Review.* Vol. 5, pp. 107–152, 1961.

_____. *Counter-Statement.* Berkeley: University of California Press, 1968. (First published in 1931.)

_____. *Language as Symbolic Action.* Berkeley: University of California Press, 1966.

_____. "On Catharsis, or Resolution." *Kenyon Review.* Vol. 21, pp. 337–375, 1959.

_____. *The Philosophy of Literary Form.* Berkeley: University of California Press, 1973.

_____. *The Rhetoric of Religion: Studies in Logology.* Berkeley: University of California Press, 1961.

Burn, Lucilla. *Greek Myths.* Austin: University of Texas Press, 1990.

Calder, Jenni. *There Must Be a Lone Ranger.* London: Hamilton Press, 1974.

Callahan, David. *The Cheating Culture: Why More Americans Are Doing Wrong to Get Ahead.* New York: Harcourt, 2004.

_____. "Take Back Values: Democrats Need to Offer a Compelling Vision of a Morally Based Social Contract." *The Nation,* Vol. 278, February 9, 2004, pp. 14–20.

Campbell, Joseph. *The Hero with a Thousand Faces.* Princeton, NJ: Princeton University Press, 1973. (First published 1949.)

_____. *The Masks of God: Primitive Mythology.* New York: Viking Penguin, 1969. (First published 1959.)

_____. *Transformations of Myth Through Time.* New York: Harper & Row. 1990.

Canby, Vincent. "A Clockwork Orange Dazzles the Senses and Mind." *The New York Times,* Dec. 20. Reprinted in *The Village Voice,* Dec. 30, 1971, p. 54. Archived at www.nytimes.com/library/film/122071Kubrick-orange.html

Caputi, Jane. "Small Ceremonies: Ritual in *Forrest Gump, Natural Born Killers, Seven,* and *Follow Me Home.*" In *Mythologies of Violence in Postmodern Media.* Christopher Sharrett, ed. Detroit, MI: Wayne State University Press, 1999.

Caputo, John D. *On Religion.* New York: Routledge, 2001.

Carroll, Noel. "Film, Rhetoric, and Ideology." In *Explanation and Value in the Arts.* Salim Kemal and Ivan Gaskell, eds. Cambridge, UK: University of Cambridge Press, 1993.

Centerwall, B. S. "Exposure to Television as a Cause of Violence." In *Public Communication and Behavior, Vol. 2.* George Comstock, ed. San Diego: Academic Press, 1989.

Clifton, James A., ed. *Being and Becoming Indian: Biographical Studies of*

North American Frontiers. Chicago: The Dorsey Press, 1989.

_____. *The Invented Indian: Cultural Fictions and Government Policies*. New Brunswick, NJ: Transaction Publishers, 1990.

Clover, Carol. *Men, Women, and Chain Saws: Gender in the Modern Horror Film*. Princeton, NJ: Princeton University Press, 1992.

Collins, Jeff, and Bill Mayblin. *Introducing Derrida*. New York: Totem Books, 1996.

Crane, Jonathan Lake. *Terror and Everyday Life: Singular Moments in the History of the Horror Film*. Thousand Oaks, CA: Sage Publications, 1994.

Creed, Barbara. "Horror and the Monstrous-Feminine: An Imaginary Abjection." *Screen*, Vol. 27, #1, pp. 44–70, 1986.

_____. *The Monstrous Feminine: Film, Feminism, Psychoanalysis*. New York: Routledge, 1993.

Denby, David. "Nailed: Mel Gibson's *The Passion of the Christ*." *The New Yorker*, March 1, 2004, pp. 84–86.

Department of Justice. *Bureau of Justice Statistics Crime Data Brief: Homicide Trends in the United States: 2000 Update*. 2000. Available at www.ojp.usdoj.gov/bjs/homicide/homtrnd.htm

Derrida, Jacques. *Limited Inc*. Samuel Weber, trans. Gerald Graff, ed. Evanston, IL: Northwestern University Press, 1988.

_____. *Negotiations: Interventions and Interviews 1971–2001*. Elizabeth Rottenberg, ed. and trans. Stanford, CA: Stanford University Press, 2002.

Desilet, Gregory. *Cult of the Kill: Traditional Metaphysics of Rhetoric, Truth, and Violence in a Postmodern World*. Philadelphia: Xlibris and Random House Ventures, 2002.

_____. "Physics and Language — Science and Rhetoric: Reviewing the Parallel Evolution of Theory on Motion and Meaning in the Aftermath of the Sokal Hoax." *The Quarterly Journal of Speech*, Vol. 85, #4, pp. 339–360, 1999.

Deutsch, Morton. "Conflicts: Productive and Destructive." *Journal of Social Sciences*. Vol. 25, #1, pp. 7–41, 1969.

Dominick, Joseph R. "Videogames, Television Violence, and Aggression in Teenagers." *Journal of Communication*. Vol. 34, #2, pp. 136–147, 1984.

Dowling, William C. *Jameson, Althusser, Marx: An Introduction to the Political Unconscious*. Ithaca, NY: Cornell University Press, 1984.

Drury, Shadia B. *Terror and Civilization: Christianity, Politics, and the Western Psyche*. New York: Palgrave Macmillan, 2004.

Duclos, Denis. *The Werewolf Complex: America's Fascination with Violence*. Amanda Pingree, trans. New York: Berg (imprint of Oxford International), 1998.

Dumouchel, Paul, ed. *Violence and Truth: On the Work of René Girard*. Stanford, CA: Stanford University Press, 1988.

Dyson, Rose A. *Mind Abuse: Media Violence in an Information Age*. Montreal: Black Rose Books, 2000.

Easterbrook, Gregg. "America the O. K.: Why Life in the U. S. Has Never Been Better." *The New Republic*, January 4 and 11, 1999, pp. 19–25.

_____. "Watch and Learn." *The New Republic*, May 17, 1999. Also reprinted as "Movie and Television Violence Makes Children Violent." In *Violence in the Media*. James D. Torr, ed. San Diego: Greenhaven Press, 2001.

Ebert, Roger. *The Great Movies*. New York: Broadway Books/Random House, 2002. (The review of *The Matrix* can be found at www.mrqe.com)

Ehrenfeld, Rachel. *Funding Evil: How Terror Is Financed*. Santa Monica: Bonus Books, 2003.

Eldridge, Richard. "Althusser and Ideological Criticism of the Arts." In *Explanation and Value in the Arts*. Salim Kemal and Ivan Gaskell, eds. Cambridge, UK.: University of Cambridge Press, 1993.

Ellul, Jacques. *The New Demons*. C. Edward Hopkin, trans. New York: Seabury Press, 1975.

Else, Gerald. *Aristotle's Poetics: The Argument*. Cambridge: Harvard University Press in cooperation with the State University of Iowa, 1957.

Farber, Stephen. Review of *Red River*, 2003. Available at www.mrqe.com

Ferrell, William K. *Literature and Film as Modern Mythology*. Westport, CT: Praeger, 2000.

Fowles, Jib. "A Socially Acceptable Means of Venting Anger." In *Examining Pop Culture: Violence in Film and Television*. James D. Torr, ed. San Diego, CA: Greenhaven Press, 2002.

_____. *The Case for Television Violence*. Thousand Oaks, CA: Sage Publications, 1999.

_____. *Television Viewers vs. Media Snobs: What TV Does for People*. New York: Stein and Day, 1982.

Fox, Robin. *The Red Lamp of Incest*. New York: Dutton, 1980.

Frazer, James George. *The New Golden Bough*. Theodor H. Gaster, ed. New York: The New American Library, 1959. (First published 1890)

Freedman, Jonathan. *Media Violence and Its Effect on Aggression: Assessing the Scientific Evidence*. Toronto: University of Toronto Press, 2002.

Freeland, Cynthia A. *The Naked and the Undead: Evil and the Appeal of Horror*. Boulder, CO: Westview Press, 2000.

French, Philip. *Westerns: Aspects of a Movie Genre*. New York: Oxford University Press, 1977.

Freud, Sigmund. *Totem and Taboo: Some Points of Agreement Between the Mental Lives of Savages and Neurotics*. James Strachey, trans. New York: W. W. Norton, 1950. (First published 1913)

Frontline. "A Dangerous Business." 2003. Transcript of report available at www.pbs.org/wgbh/pages/frontline/shows/workplace/.

Frum, David, and Richard Perle. *An End to Evil: How to Win the War on Terror*. New York: Random House, 2003.

Gallagher, Mark. "I Married Rambo: Spectacle and Melodrama in the Hollywood Action Film." In *Mythologies of Violence in Postmodern Media*. Christopher Sharrett, ed. Detroit, MI: Wayne State University Press, 1999.

Garfield, Brian. *Western Films*. West Hanover, MA: Halliday Lithographic, 1982.

Gerbner, George. *Against the Mainstream: The Selected Works of George Gerbner*. Michael Morgan, ed. New York: Peter Lang, 2002.

Gibbs, Nancy, and Timothy Roche. "The Columbine Tapes." *Time*. December 20, 1999, pp. 40–51.

Gill, Sam. "Mother Earth: An American Myth." In *The Invented Indian: Cultural Fictions and Government Policies*. James A. Clifton, ed. New Brunswick, NJ: Transaction Publishers, 1990.

Girard, René. *The Girard Reader*. James G. Williams, ed. New York: Crossroad Publishing Company, 1996. (Contains essays published between 1965 and 1993)

_____. *Things Hidden Since the Foundation of the World*. Stephen Bann and Michael Meeter, trans. Stanford, CA: Stanford University Press, 1987.

_____. *Violence and the Sacred*. Trans. Patrick Gregory. Baltimore: Johns Hopkins University Press, 1977.

Girardot, N. J. *Myth and Meaning in Early Taoism: The Theme of Chaos (hun-tun)*. Berkeley: University of California Press, 1983.

Gitlin, Todd. Book Review of Amin Maalouf's *In the Name of Identity: Violence and the Need to Belong*. *The Los Angeles Times Book Review*. September 23, 2001, pp. 6–7.

Grant, Barry Keith. "American Pycho/sis: The Pure Products of America Go Crazy." In *Mythologies of Violence in Postmodern Media*. Christopher Sharrett, ed. Detroit, MI: Wayne State University Press, 1999.

Grimm, Jacob, and Wilhelm Grimm. *The Complete Fairy Tales of the Brothers Grimm*. Jack Zipes, trans. New York: Bantam Books, 1987. (This translation is based primarily on the first edition of *Kinder- und Hausmärchen* by Jacob and Wilhelm Grimm published in two volumes in 1812 and 1815)

_____, and _____. *Fairy Tales of the Brothers Grimm*. Mrs. Edgar Lucas, trans. Arthur Rackham, illus. London: Constable, 1911.

Gring-Pemble, Lisa, and Martha Solomon Watson. "The Rhetorical Limits of Satire: An Analysis of James Finn Garner's *Politically Correct Bedtime Stories*." *The Quarterly Journal of Speech*. Vol. 89, #2, pp. 132–153, 2003.

Grossman, Dave. *On Killing: The Psychological Cost of Learning to Kill in War and Society*. Boston: Little, Brown, 1995.

_____, and Gloria DeGaetano. *Stop Teaching Our Kids to Kill: A Call to Action Against TV, Movie, and Video Game Violence*. New York: Crown, 1999.

Gunter, Barrie, Jackie Harrison and Maggie Wykes. *Violence on Television: Distribution, Form, Context, and Themes*. Mahwah, NJ: Lawrence Erlbaum, 2003.

Hamill, Pete. End Game. *Esquire*, December, 1994, pp. 85–92.

Hamilton, Edith. *Mythology*. Boston: Little, Brown, 1942.

Hannity, Sean. *Deliver Us from Evil: Defeating Terrorism, Despotism, and Liberalism*. New York: HarperCollins, 2004.

Haraway, Donna J. *Simians, Cyborgs, and Women: The Reinvention of Nature*. New York: Routledge, Chapman, and Hall, 1991.

Hardy, Phil. *The Western: The Film Encyclopedia*. New York: William Morrow, 1983.

Harris, Sam. *The End of Faith: Religion, Terror, and the Future of Reason*. New York: W. W. Norton, 2004.

Hart, William. *Evil: A History of a Bad Idea from Beelzebub to Bin Laden*. New York: St. Martin's Press, 2004.

Heilman, Robert Bechtold. *Tragedy and Melodama: Versions of Experience*. Seattle: University of Washington, 1968.

Hitler, Adolf. *Mein Kampf*. Ralph Manheim, trans. Boston: Houghton and Mifflin, 1971.

Hocker, Joyce L. and William W. Wilmot. *Interpersonal Conflict*. Madison, WI: Brown & Benchmark, 1995.

Horsley, Jake. *The Blood Poets: A Cinema of Savagery 1958–1999*; Volume 1: American Chaos, From *Touch of Evil* to *The Terminator*. Lanham, MD: Scarecrow Press, 1999. (Including *Psycho, Bonnie and Clyde, Taxi Driver, The Terminator*)

_____ *The Blood Poets: A Cinema of Savagery 1958–1999*; Volume 2: Millennial Blues, From *Apocalypse Now* to *The Matrix*. Lanham, MD: Scarecrow Press, 1999. (Including *Raging Bull, Silence of the Lambs, Pulp Fiction, The Matrix*)

Hunter, Stephen. *Violent Screen: A Critic's 13 Years on the Front Lines of Movie Mayhem*. Baltimore, MD: Bancroft Press, 1995.

Hyams, Jay. *The Life and Times of the Western Movie*. New York: Gallery Books, 1983.

Ioannidis, Nikolaos. *Media Violence: Video Games and Desensitization to Violence*. 2003. Available at www.homoecumenicus.com/essays.htm

Ivie, Robert. "Images of Savagery in American Justifications of War." *Communication Monographs*, Vol. 47, November 1980.

_____. "Speaking Common Sense About the Soviet Threat: Reagan's Rhetorical Stance." *Western Journal of Speech Communication*. Vol. 48, Winter 1984.

Jameson, Fredric. *Postmodernism, or, the Cultural Logic of Late Capitalism*. Durham, NC: Duke University Press. 1991.

Jones, Gerard. *Killing Monsters: Why Children Need Fantasy, Super Heroes, and Make-Believe Violence*. New York: Basic Books, 2002.

Jung, Carl. *Civilization in Transition*. R. F. C. Hull, trans. *The Collected Works of Carl Jung, Vol. 10*. New York: Pantheon Books, 1964.

Kael, Pauline. *Kiss Kiss Bang Bang*. Boston: Little, Brown, 1968.

Kael, Pauline. "A Clockwork Orange: Stanley Strangelove." In *Stanley Kubrick's A Clockwork Orange.* Stuart Y. McDougal, ed. Cambridge, MA: Cambridge University Press, 2003. (First published 1972)

_____. "Crime and Poetry: Review of *Bonnie and Clyde.*" In *The Bonnie and Clyde Book.* Sandra Wake and Nicola Hayden, eds. New York: Simon and Schuster, 1972. (First published 1967)

Kamalipour, Yahya R., and Kuldip R. Rampal, eds. *Media, Sex, Violence, and Drugs in the Global Village.* Lanham, MD: Rowman and Littlefield, 2001.

Kasson, John F. *Houdini, Tarzan, and the Perfect Man: The White Male Body and the Challenge of Modernity in America.* New York: Hill and Wang, 2001.

Kaufmann, Walter. *Tragedy and Philosophy.* Garden City, NY: Anchor Books. 1968.

Keen, Sam. *Faces of the Enemy: Reflections of the Hostile Imagination.* San Francisco: Harper and Row, 1986.

Kelly, Mary Pat. *Martin Scorsese: The First Decade.* Pleasantville, NY: Redgrave Publishing, 1980.

Kitto, H. D. F. *Greek Tragedy.* London: Methuen, 1966. (First published 1939.)

Kittredge, William. *Taking Care: Thoughts on Storytelling and Belief.* Minneapolis, MN: Milkweed Editions, 1999.

Klavan, Andrew. "In Praise of Fictional Violence." In *Examining Pop Culture: Violence in Film and Television.* James D. Torr, ed. San Diego, CA: Greenhaven Press, 2002. Also published as "In Praise of Gore: Violence in Film and Fiction Is Out of Control — And We Love It." *Utne Reader,* 1994, November/December, pp. 94–99. (Excerpted from *Boston Review,* June–September 1994.)

Kleiner, Art. "The Battle for the Soul of Corporate America: Hammerism Battles Demingism for How the Corporation (or Society) Should Be Governed in the Information Age." *Wired.* Vol. 3, #8, pp. 120–125, 1995.

Kolakowski, Leszek. *Metaphysical Horror.* New York: Basil Blackwell, 1988.

Koller, Brian. Review of *Red River.* 2000. Available at www.mrqe.com

Kram, Mark. *Ghosts of Manila: The Fateful Blood Feud Between Muhammad Ali and Joe Frazier.* New York: HarperCollins, 2001.

Kristeva, Julia. *Powers of Horror: An Essay on Abjection.* Leon S. Roudiez, trans. New York: Columbia University Press, 1982. (First published 1980)

Lacan, Jacques. *The Four Fundamental Concepts of Psycho-Analysis.* Jacques-Alain Miller, ed. Alan Sheridan, trans. New York: W. W. Norton, 1981. (First published 1973)

Levine, Madeline. *See No Evil: A Guide to Protecting Our Children from Media Violence.* San Francisco: Jossey-Bass, 1998.

LoBrutto, Vincent. *Stanley Kubrick: A Biography.* New York: Penguin Books, 1997.

Luhr, William. "Mutilating Mel: Martyrdom and Masculinity in *Braveheart.*" In *Mythologies of Violence in Postmodern Media.* Christopher Sharrett, ed. Detroit, MI: Wayne State University Press, 1999.

Maalouf, Amin. *In the Name of Identity: Violence and the Need to Belong.* Barbara Bray, trans. New York: Arcade, 2001.

MacDonald, J. F. Review of James Twitchell's *Dreadful Pleasures. Choice,* Vol. 23, 1209, April, 1986.

McGuckin, Frank, ed. *Violence in American Society.* New York: H. W. Wilson, 1998.

Melville, Herman. *Moby Dick.* Illus. Raymond Bishop. New York: Albert and Charles Boni, 1939. (First printing of this edition 1931; first published 1851)

Menand, Louis. "Paris, Texas: How Hollywood Brought the Cinema Back from France." *The New Yorker,* February 17 and 24, 2003, pp. 169–177.

Miles, Adrian. Review of *Red River.* 1997. Available at www.mrqe.com

Morgenstern, Joseph. "The New Violence." *Newsweek,* February 14, 1972, pp. 66–69.

Moses, Michael Valdez. "Back to the Future: The Nostalgic Yet Progressive Appeal of Wizards, Hobbits, and Jedi Knights." *Reason*, July 2003, pp. 49–57.

Mulvey, Laura. *Visual and Other Pleasures*. Indianapolis: Indiana University Press, 1990.

_____. "Visual Pleasure and Narrative Cinema." In *Movies and Methods: An Anthology*. Bill Nichols, ed. Berkeley: University of California Press, 1976. (First published 1975)

Nachbar, John G. *Focus on the Western*. Englewood Cliffs, NJ: Prentice-Hall, 1974.

National Institute of Mental Health. *Television and Behavior: Ten Years of Scientific Progress and Implications for the Eighties*. Washington: USGPO, 1982.

Neumann, Erich. *Depth Psychology and a New Ethic*. Eugene Rolfe, trans. New York: Harper & Row, 1973.

Newitz, Annalee, and Matt Wray, eds. *White Trash: Race and Class in America*. New York: Routledge, 1997.

Newman, James. *Videogames*. New York: Routledge, 2003.

Nietzsche, Friedrich. *Basic Writings of Nietzsche*. Walter Kaufmann, ed. and trans. New York: Random House, 1968.

_____. *The Will to Power*. Walter Kaufmann, ed. Walter Kaufmann and R. J. Hollingdale, trans. New York: Vintage Books, 1967.

Oates, Whitney J., and Eugene O'Neill, Jr., eds. *The Complete Greek Drama*. New York: Random House, 1938.

O'Reilly, Bill. *Who's Looking Out for You*. New York: Broadway Books, 2003.

Pagels, Elaine. *Adam, Eve, and the Serpent*. New York: Random House, 1988.

Parsons, Tony. "Forbidden Fruit." *The London Times Saturday Review*. January 30, 1993, pp. 4–5.

Pinedo, Isabel Cristina. *Recreational Terror: Women and the Pleasures of Horror Film Viewing*. Albany: State University of New York Press, 1997.

Plato. *The Collected Dialogues of Plato, Including the Letters*. Edith Hamilton and Huntington Cairns, eds. Princeton, NJ: Princeton University Press, 1969.

Pollitt, Katha. "The Protocols of Mel Gibson." *The Nation*. March 29, Vol. 278, 9, 2004.

Rafter, Nicole. *Shots in the Mirror: Crime Films and Society*. New York: Oxford University Press, 2000.

Reed, Rex. Review of *A Clockwork Orange*. 1971. Archived at www.nydailynews.com/entertainment/movies/moviereviews/index.html

Reid, T. R. *Confucius Lives Next Door*. New York: Random House, 1999.

Rhodes, Richard. *The Media Violence Myth*. 2004. Available at www.abffe.com, American Booksellers Foundation for Free Expression.

_____. *Why They Kill: The Discoveries of a Maverick Criminologist*. New York: Alfred A. Knopf, 1999.

Ricoeur, Paul. *The Symbolism of Evil*. Emerson Buchanan, trans. Boston: Beacon Press, 1969. (First published 1967)

Rubinoff, Lionel. "*In Nomine Diaboli*: The Voices of Evil." In *Strategies Against Violence*. Israel Charny, ed. Boulder, CO: Westview Press, 1978.

Rushing, Janice Hocker, and Thomas S. Frentz. *Projecting the Shadow: The Cyborg Hero in American Film*. Chicago: University of Chicago Press, 1995.

Samuelson, Robert J. *The Good Life and Its Discontents: The American Dream in the Age of Entitlement, 1945–1995*. New York: Time Books, 1995.

Sarris, Andrew. Films in Focus: Review of *A Clockwork Orange*. *The Village Voice*, December 30, 1971, pp. 49–50.

Schoenbaum, S. Review of James Twitchell's *Dreadful Pleasures*. *The New York Review of Books*. Vol. 33, # 23, January 1986.

Schwab, Gustav. *Gods and Heroes: Myths and Epics of Ancient Greece*. Olga Marx and Ernst Morwitz, trans. New York: Random House, 1946. (Translation of *Die Sagen des Klassischen Altertums*)

Schwartz, Regina M. *The Curse of Cain:*

The Violent Legacy of Monotheism. Chicago: University of Chicago Press, 1997.

Scubla, Lucien. "The Christianity of René Girard and the Nature of Religion." Mark R. Anspach, trans. In *Violence and Truth.* Paul Dumouchel, ed. Stanford, CA: Stanford University Press, 1988.

Sharrett, Christopher. "Afterword: Sacrificial Violence and Postmodern Ideology." In *Mythologies of Violence in Postmodern Media.* Christopher Sharrett, ed. Detroit, MI: Wayne State University Press, 1999.

Shelley, Mary. *Frankenstein.* New York: Bantam Books, 1981. (First published 1818.)

Shermer, Michael. *The Science of Good and Evil: Why People Cheat, Gossip, Care, Share, and Follow the Golden Rule.* New York: Times Books, 2004.

Singer, Peter. *The President of Good and Evil: Questioning the Ethics of George W. Bush.* New York: Plume, 2004.

Singhal, Arvind, Michael J. Cody, Everett M. Rogers, and Miguel Sabido, eds. *Entertainment-Education and Social Change: History, Research, and Practice.* Mahwah, NJ: Laurence Erlbaum, 2004.

Slotkin, Richard. *The Fatal Environment: The Myth of the Frontier in the Age of Industrialization, 1800–1890.* New York: Atheneum, 1985.

_____. *Gunfighter Nation: The Myth of the Frontier in Twentieth-Century America.* New York: Atheneum, 1992.

_____. *Regeneration through Violence: The Mythology of the American Frontier, 1600–1860.* Hanover, NH: Wesleyan University Press, 1973. (through University Press of New England).

Smith, Craig R. *Violence and the Media.* The Center for First Amendment Studies and the Freedom of Expression Foundation online First Amendment Library. 2003. Available at www.firstamendmentcenter.org/speech/arts/topic.aspx?topic=violence_media&SearchString=craig

Smith, Richard. "Afterword: The Modern Relevance of Gnosticism." In *The Nag Hammadi Library.* James M. Robinson, ed. San Francisco: Harper & Row, 1988.

Sonnichsen, C. L. *From Hopalong to Hud: Thoughts on Western Fiction.* College Station, TX: Texas A&M University Press, 1978.

Sparks, Glenn G., and Cheri W. Sparks. "Explaining the Attractions of Violent Entertainment." In *Examining Pop Culture: Violence in Film and Television.* James D. Torr, ed. San Diego, CA: Greenhaven Press, 2002.

_____, and _____. "Violence, Mayhem, and Horror." In *Media Entertainment: The Psychology of Its Appeal.* Dolf Zillmann and Peter Vorderer, eds. Mahwah, NJ: Lawrence Erlbaum, 2000.

Spitzer, Eliot, and Andrew G. Celli, II. "Bull Run: Capitalism with a Democratic Face." *The New Republic.* Vol. 230, March 22, 2004, pp. 18–21.

Steiner, George. *The Death of Tragedy.* New Haven, CT: Yale University Press, 1980. (First published 1961)

Stevenson, Robert Louis. *The Strange Case of Dr. Jekyll and Mr. Hyde.* New York: Vintage Books, 1991. (First published 1886)

Stoker, Bram. *Dracula.* New York: Tom Doherty Associates, 1988. (First published 1897)

Surgeon General's Scientific Advisory Committee on Television and Social Behavior. *Television and Growing Up: The Impact of Televised Violence.* Washington: USGPO, 1972.

Tatar, Maria M. "Introduction." In *Grimm's Grimmest.* Marisa Bulzone, ed. San Francisco: Chronicle Books, 1997.

Taubin, Amy. Review of *Raging Bull.* 2000. Available at www.mrqe.com

Tomasulo, Frank P. "Raging Bully: Postmodern Violence and Masculinity in *Raging Bull.*" In *Mythologies of Violence in Postmodern Media.* Christopher Sharrett, ed. Detroit, MI: Wayne State University Press, 1999.

Tompkins, Phillip K. *Apollo, Challenger, Columbia: The Decline of the Space Program, A Study in Organizational Communication.* Los Angeles: Roxbury Publishing, 2005.

_____. "The Crisis of American Organizations and Institutions: Speaking Truth to Power." Keynote Address to the Annual Convention of the Rocky Mountain Communication Association, 2003.

Torr, James D., ed. *Examining Pop Culture: Violence in Film and Television.* San Diego, CA: Greenhaven Press, 2002.

_____, ed. *Violence in the Media.* San Diego, CA: Greenhaven Press, 2001.

Troy, Tevi. "The Cathartic Effects of Violent Films." In *Examining Pop Culture: Violence in Film and Television.* James D. Torr, ed. San Diego, CA: Greenhaven Press, 2002.

Twitchell, James B. *Dreadful Pleasures: An Anatomy of Modern Horror.* New York: Oxford University Press, 1985.

_____. *Preposterous Violence: Fables of Aggression in Modern Culture.* Oxford University Press, 1989.

Vickers, Brian. *Towards Greek Tragedy: Drama, Myth, Society.* London: Longman, 1973.

Voegelin, Eric. *Political Religions.* T. J. DiNapoli and E. S. Easterly, trans. Lewiston, NY: Edwin Mellen Press, 1986.

Vogler, Christopher. *The Writer's Journey: Mythic Structure for Writers.* 2nd ed. Studio City, CA: Michael Wiese Productions, 1998.

Wake, Sandra, and Nicola Hayden, eds. *The Bonnie and Clyde Book.* New York: Simon and Schuster, 1972.

Waller, Gregory A. *The Living and the Undead: From Stoker's "Dracula" to Romero's "Dawn of the Dead."* Urbana: University of Illinois Press, 1986.

Wartella, Ellen A. "The Context of Television Violence." Carroll C. Arnold Distinguished Lecture Presented at the Speech Communication Association Annual Convention, November 23. Boston: Allyn and Bacon, 1996.

Weller, Sheila. "A 'Clockwork' Burgess: No Time Like the Past." *The Village Voice.* August 31, 1972, p. 57.

Wells, Paul. *The Horror Genre.* London: Wallflower Publishing, 2000.

Whitman, David. *The Optimism Gap: The I'm Okay— They're Not Syndrome and the Myth of American Decline.* New York: Walker and Company, 1998.

Wieseltier, Leon. "The Worship of Blood: Mel Gibson's Lethal Weapon." *The New Republic.* Vol. 230, March 8, 2004, pp. 19–21.

Wills, Garry. "Dostoyevsky Behind a Camera: Oliver Stone Is Making Great American Novels on Film." *The Atlantic Monthly.* July 1997, pp. 96–101.

Wood, Robin. *Hitchcock's Films Revisited.* New York: Columbia University Press, 1993.

_____. *Hollywood from Vietnam to Reagan.* New York: Columbia University Press, 1986.

Zillmann, Dolf, and Peter Vorderer, eds. *Media Entertainment: The Psychology of Its Appeal.* Mahwah, NJ: Lawrence Erlbaum, 2000.

Zimmerman, Paul D. "Kubrick's Brilliant Vision." *Newsweek.* January 3, 1972, pp. 28–33.

Zimring, Franklin E., and Gordon Hawkins. *Crime Is Not the Problem: Lethal Violence in America.* New York: Oxford University Press, 1997.

Index